Children's
Literature
Review

Guide to Gale Literary Criticism Series

For criticism on	Consult these Gale series
Authors now living or who died after December 31, 1999	*CONTEMPORARY LITERARY CRITICISM (CLC)*
Authors who died between 1900 and 1999	*TWENTIETH-CENTURY LITERARY CRITICISM (TCLC)*
Authors who died between 1800 and 1899	*NINETEENTH-CENTURY LITERATURE CRITICISM (NCLC)*
Authors who died between 1400 and 1799	*LITERATURE CRITICISM FROM 1400 TO 1800 (LC)* *SHAKESPEAREAN CRITICISM (SC)*
Authors who died before 1400	*CLASSICAL AND MEDIEVAL LITERATURE CRITICISM (CMLC)*
Authors of books for children and young adults	*CHILDREN'S LITERATURE REVIEW (CLR)*
Dramatists	*DRAMA CRITICISM (DC)*
Poets	*POETRY CRITICISM (PC)*
Short story writers	*SHORT STORY CRITICISM (SSC)*
Black writers of the past two hundred years	*BLACK LITERATURE CRITICISM (BLC)* *BLACK LITERATURE CRITICISM SUPPLEMENT (BLCS)*
Hispanic writers of the late nineteenth and twentieth centuries	*HISPANIC LITERATURE CRITICISM (HLC)* *HISPANIC LITERATURE CRITICISM SUPPLEMENT (HLCS)*
Native North American writers and orators of the eighteenth, nineteenth, and twentieth centuries	*NATIVE NORTH AMERICAN LITERATURE (NNAL)*
Major authors from the Renaissance to the present	*WORLD LITERATURE CRITICISM, 1500 TO THE PRESENT (WLC)* *WORLD LITERATURE CRITICISM SUPPLEMENT (WLCS)*

ISSN 0362-4145

volume 67

Children's Literature Review

Excerpts from Reviews,
Criticism, and Commentary
on Books for Children
and Young People

Jennifer Baise
Editor

Thomas Ligotti
Associate Editor

GALE GROUP

Detroit
New York
San Francisco
London
Boston
Woodbridge, CT

STAFF

Library of Congress Catalog Card Number 76-643301
ISBN 0-7876-4573-7
ISSN 0362-4145
Printed in the United States of America

10 9 8 7 6 5 4 3 2 1

Contents

Preface vii

Acknowledgments xi

Preface

Literature for children and young adults has evolved into both a respected branch of creative writing and a successful industry. Currently, books for young readers are considered among the most popular segments of publishing. Criticism of juvenile literature is instrumental in recording the literary or artistic development of the creators of children's books as well as the trends and controversies that result from changing values or attitudes about young people and their literature. Designed to provide a permanent, accessible record of this ongoing scholarship, *Children's Literature Review* (*CLR*) presents parents, teachers, and librarians—those responsible for bringing children and books together—with the opportunity to make informed choices when selecting reading materials for the young. In addition, *CLR* provides researchers of children's literature with easy access to a wide variety of critical information from English-language sources in the field. Users will find balanced overviews of the careers of the authors and illustrators of the books that children and young adults are reading; these entries, which contain excerpts from published criticism in books and periodicals, assist users by sparking ideas for papers and assignments and suggesting supplementary and classroom reading. Ann L. Kalkhoff, president and editor of *Children's Book Review Service Inc.,* writes that "*CLR* has filled a gap in the field of children's books, and it is one series that will never lose its validity or importance."

Scope of the Series

Each volume of *CLR* profiles the careers of a selection of authors and illustrators of books for children and young adults from preschool through high school. Author lists in each volume reflect:

- an international scope

- representation of authors of all eras

- the variety of genres covered by children's and/or YA literature: picture books, fiction, nonfiction, poetry, folklore, and drama

Although the focus of the series is on authors new to *CLR,* entries will be updated as the need arises.

Organization of the Book

A *CLR* entry consists of the following elements:

- The **Author Heading** consists of the author's name followed by birth and death dates. The portion of the name outside the parentheses denotes the form under which the author is most frequently published. If the author wrote consistently under a pseudonym, the pseudonym will be listed in the author heading and the author's actual name given in parentheses on the first line of the biographical and critical information. Also located here are any name variations under which an author wrote, including transliterated forms for authors whose native languages use non-roman alphabets. Uncertain birth or death dates are indicated by question marks.

- A **Portrait of the Author** is included when available.

- The **Author Introduction** contains information designed to introduce an author to *CLR* users by presenting an overview of the author's themes and styles, biographical facts that relate to the author's literary career or critical responses to the author's works, and information about major awards and prizes the author has received. The introduction begins by identifying the nationality of the author and by listing genres in which s/he has written for children and young adults. Introductions also list a group of representative titles for which the author or illustrator being profiled is best known; this section, which begins with the words "major works include," follows the genre line of the introduction. For seminal figures, a listing of major works about the author follows when appropriate, high-lighting important biographies about the author or illustrator that are not excerpted in the entry. The centered head-ing "Introduction" announces the body of the text.

■ **Criticism** is located in three sections: **Author Commentary** (when available) **General Commentary** (when avail-able), and **Title Commentary** (commentary on specific titles).

The **Author Commentary** presents background material written by the author or by an interviewer. This commentary may cover a specific work or several works. Author commentary on more than one work appears after the author intro-duction, while commentary on an individual book follows the title entry heading.

The **General Commentary** consists of critical excerpts that consider more than one work by the author or illustrator being profiled. General commentary is preceded by the critic's name in boldface type or, in the case of unsigned criti-cism, by the title of the journal. *CLR* also features entries that emphasize general criticism on the oeuvre of an author or illustrator. When appropriate, a selection of reviews is included to supplement the general commentary.

The **Title Commentary** begins with the title entry headings, which precede the criticism on a title and cite publication information on the work being reviewed. Title headings list the title of the work as it appeared in its first English-language edition. The first English-language publication date of each work (unless otherwise noted) is listed in paren-theses following the title. Differing U.S. and British titles follow the publication date within parentheses. When a work is written by an individual other than the one being profiled, as is the case when illustrators are featured, the parentheti-cal material following the title cites the author of the work before listing its publication date.

Entries in each title commentary section consist of critical excerpts on the author's individual works, arranged chronologi-cally by publication date. The entries generally contain two to seven reviews per title, depending on the stature of the book and the amount of criticism it has generated. The editors select titles that reflect the entire scope of the author's literary contribution, covering each genre and subject. An effort is made to reprint criticism that represents the full range of each title's reception, from the year of its initial publication to current assessments. Thus, the reader is provided with a record of the author's critical history. Publication information (such as publisher names and book prices) and parenthetical numerical references (such as footnotes or page and line references to specific editions of works) have been deleted at the discretion of the editors to provide smoother reading of the text.

■ A complete **Bibliographical Citation** of the original essay or book precedes each piece of criticism.

■ Selected excerpts are preceded by brief **Annotations,** which provide information on the critic or work of criticism to enhance the reader's understanding of the excerpt.

■ Numerous **Illustrations** are featured in *CLR*. For entries on illustrators, an effort has been made to include illustra-tions that reflect the characteristics discussed in the criticism. Entries on authors who do not illustrate their own works my include photographs and other illustrative material pertinent to their careers.

Special Features: Entries on Illustrators

Entries on authors who are also illustrators will occasionally feature commentary on selected works illustrated but not writ-ten by the author being profiled. These works are strongly associated with the illustrator and have received critical acclaim for their art. By including critical comment on works of this type, the editors wish to provide a more complete representa-tion of the artist's career. Criticism on these works has been chosen to stress artistic, rather than literary, contributions. Title entry headings for works illustrated by the author being profiled are arranged chronologically within the entry by date of publication and include notes identifying the author of the illustrated work. In order to provide easier access for users, all titles illustrated by the subject of the entry are boldfaced.

CLR also includes entries on prominent illustrators who have contributed to the field of children's literature. These entries are designed to represent the development of the illustrator as an artist rather than as a literary stylist. The illustrator's sec-tion is organized like that of an author, with two exceptions: the introduction presents an overview of the illustrator's styles and techniques rather than outlining his or her literary background, and the commentary written by the illustrator on his or her works is called "Illustrator's Commentary" rather than "Author's Commentary." All titles of books containing illustrations by the artist being profiled are highlighted in boldface type.

Indexes

A **Cumulative Author Index** lists all of the authors who have appeared in *CLR* with cross-references to the biographical, autobiographical, and literary criticism series published by the Gale Group. A complete list of these sources is found facing the first page of the Author Index. The index also includes birth and death dates and cross-references between pseudonyms and actual names.

A **Cumulative Nationality Index** lists all authors featured in *CLR* by nationality, followed by the number of the *CLR* volume in which their entry appears.

A **Cumulative Title Index** lists all author titles covered in *CLR*. Each title is followed by the author&apso;s name and corresponding volume and page numbers where commentary on the work is located.

Citing *Children's Literature Review*

When writing papers, students who quote directly from any volume in the Literary Criticism Series may use the following general format to footnote reprinted criticism. The first example pertains to material drawn from periodicals, the second to material reprinted from books.

Cynthia Zarin, "It's Easy Being Green," *The New York Times Book Review* (November 14, 1993): 48; excerpted and reprinted in *Children's Literature Review,* vol. 58, ed. Deborah J. Morad (Farmington Hills, Mich: The Gale Group, 2000), 57.

Paul Walker, *Speaking of Science Fiction: The Paul Walker Interviews,* (Luna Publications, 1978), 108-20; excerpted and reprinted in *Children's Literature Review,* vol. 58, ed. Deborah J. Morad (Farmington Hills, Mich: The Gale Group, 2000), 3-8.

Suggestions are Welcome

In response to various suggestions, several features have been added to *CLR* since the beginning of the series, including author entries on retellers of traditional literature as well as those who have been the first to record oral tales and other folklore; entries on prominent illustrators featuring commentary on their styles and techniques; entries on authors whose works are considered controversial; occasional entries devoted to criticism on a single work or a series of works; sections in author introductions that list major works by and about the author or illustrator being profiled; explanatory notes that provide information on the critic or work of criticism to enhance the usefulness of the excerpt; more extensive illustrative material, such as holographs of manuscript pages and photographs of people and places pertinent to the careers of the authors and artists; a cumulative nationality index for easy access to authors by nationality; and occasional guest essays written specifically for *CLR* by prominent critics on subjects of their choice.

Readers who wish to suggest new features, topics, or authors to appear in future volumes, or who have other suggestions or comments are cordially invited to call, write, or fax the Managing Editor:

Managing Editor, Literary Criticism Series
The Gale Group
27500 Drake Road
Farmington Hills, MI 48331-3535
1-800-347-4253 (GALE)
Fax: 248-699-8054

Acknowledgments

The editors wish to thank the copyright holders of the excerpted criticism included in this volume and the permissions managers of many book and magazine publishing companies for assisting us in securing reproduction rights. We are also grateful to the staffs of the Detroit Public Library, the Library of Congress, the University of Detroit Mercy Library, Wayne State University Purdy/Kresge Library Complex, and the University of Michigan Libraries for making their resources available to us. Following is a list of the copyright holders who have granted us permission to reproduce material in this volume of *CLR*. Every effort has been made to trace copyright, but if omissions have been made, please let us know.

COPYRIGHTED EXCERPTS IN *CLR*, VOLUME 67, WERE REPRODUCED FROM THE FOLLOWING PERIODICALS:

Susan Cooper
1935-

English author of fiction for children and young adults.

For further information on Cooper's life and career, see *CLR,* Volume 4.

INTRODUCTION

Known primarily as the author of the popular fantasy quintet for young adults, "The Dark Is Rising," Susan Cooper has been praised for her successful blending of Celtic folklore and history, her realistic dialogue, and her compelling evocation of time and place. In all her fantasy novels for young adults, Cooper skillfully blends ancient British mythology with the realities of our modern world, creating a fascinating blend of enchantment and adventure. "The Dark Is Rising," certainly her most loved work, comprises five books—*Over Sea, Under Stone* (1965), *The Dark is Rising* (1973), *Greenwitch* (1974), *The Grey King* (1975), and *Silver on the Tree* (1975). The ongoing story involves the three Drew children, their elderly uncle who is, in reality, the wizard Merlin, and young Will Stanton, the last of the Old Ones. In a compelling tale of the classic battle between good and evil, the children, their adult mentors, and various assistants are given the responsibility of saving the world from the creeping evil of The Dark, overcoming its force with the power of The Light to rouse King Arthur from his centuries long sleep. All of Cooper's work for young adults, some of it fantasy and some more reality based, utilize this theme of good fighting against the power of evil, usually in less epic proportions, and examine the nature of good and evil within the context of both the natural and the supernatural worlds. In her essay about Cooper in *Horn Book,* Margaret K. McElderry wrote, "[She] is one of the small and very select company of writers who—somehow, somewhere—have been touched by magic; the gift of creations is theirs, the power to bring to life for ordinary mortals the 'best of symbolic high fantasy.'"

BIOGRAPHICAL INFORMATION

Cooper was born in Burnham, Buckinghamshire, England, about twenty miles outside of London during the advent of Word War II. The war broke out when

she was four and continued until she was ten, and her childhood memories are of the devastation caused by the Blitz. These experiences color much of her writing, most notably *Dawn of Fear* (1972) which Cooper describes as "a thinly disguised autobiographical novel." She and her brother Roderick (who later became a popular mystery writer for adults) were raised by their intellectual parents in an atmosphere of poetry, music, and fine literature, and by their maternal grandparents who encouraged cultural activities, imaginative play, and a love of the literary classics. Cooper's grandmother was from Wales, and this heritage plays a large role in Cooper's writings. She knew she wanted to be a writer from the age of eight, writing puppet plays and collaborating on a weekly newspaper with a neighbor.

While attending Somerville College at Oxford University, she majored in English and became the first female editor of the Oxford newspaper, *Cherwell.*

Graduating in 1956, Cooper began her professional career writing for newspapers in London, first the *Sunday Express*, and then the *Sunday Times*, as a reporter and feature writer, producing her first novels in her spare time. It was when she was writing a short story to enter a competition that *Over Sea, Under Stone* began to take shape, and in her enthusiasm for the developing story, Cooper produced a book. It was rejected by twenty publishers before it was finally published in 1965. When she was 27, she married American scientist Nicholas Grant, a widower with three children, and moved to America, to a community near Boston. She continued to write for the *Sunday Times*, reporting on events in America, such as the trial of Jack Ruby, and wrote a weekly column for the national daily paper of Wales, the *Western Mail*, explaining American life to the Welsh. These columns led to a nonfiction book for adults, *Behind the Golden Curtain* (1965), in which Cooper attempted to explain the Americans to the British and the British to the Americans.

Cooper had two children with Grant, and while they were small she had less time to write, but she had the inspiration for the "Dark is Rising" series and was finally able to resume her career with *The Dark is Rising*. Since then, she has produced many books for young adults and won nearly every award available for children's fiction. Her eclectic career has also found her in collaboration with Hume Cronyn and Jessica Tandy on the play *Foxfire* and with John Langstaff on the *Christmas Revels* at Harvard University. The biography she wrote about her friend and mentor, *J. B. Priestley: Portrait of an Author* (1970), is authoritative.

MAJOR WORKS

Cooper's writings for children include fantasy novels and realistic fiction for young adults and retellings, stories, and picture books for younger children. Aside from "The Dark Is Rising" series, she has written many other award-winning works. *Dawn of Fear* is her young adult novel of Word War II. In it, the rivalry between two gangs of boys parallels the horror of the war going on around them. Experiences of childhood are mixed with experiences of the Blitz— air raids, taking shelter in the London Underground, and the death of a friend in a bomb attack.

In *Seaward* (1983), Cooper returns to the fantasy genre. This story is about two children who find themselves in a parallel universe with many of the elements of Celtic mythology. When they meet, there is a battle for their souls between two wizards, the Lady Taranis, the spirit of death, and her brother Lugan, who offers them eternal life. In the end, the children realize that only they can determine their fate, and they choose to return to their mortal world, there to live and grow and eventually die, for only in life subject to death are there possibilities for growth and change. A reviewer for *Horn Book* was impressed by Cooper's "endow[ing] the concept of human responsibility—of human choice—with the face of fantasy." *The Boggart* (1993) is a more recent fantasy for young adults, again drawing on folklore. The Boggart is a Scottish poltergeist who lives in a Scottish castle in a comfortable relationship with the elderly owner he harasses. When the castle is inherited by a Canadian family, the Boggart is accidentally shipped off to Canada, hidden in the desk where he has taken refuge to mourn the death of the castle owner. The children of the family discover the Boggart when he clashes with the unimaginative and serious modern world. They learn to communicate with him through the computer, and when they realize how homesick he is, they concoct a plan to send him home that involves the use of modern computer technology. Thus does Cooper blend Scottish folklore and the modern world. Praising this book in *The New York Times*, Rafael Yglesias wrote, "The inevitable failure of a spirit to coexist with our dreary practical world isn't a new theme, although in *The Boggart* it seems fresher than ever. The author's point of view would be utterly persuasive except for the obvious fact that as long as writers with Susan Cooper's skill continue to publish, magic is always available." Cooper wrote a sequel, *The Boggart and the Monster* (1997), in which the children visit their friend in Scotland and meet his cousin, the Loch Ness Monster.

The Silver Cow (1983), *The Selkie Girl* (1986), and *Tam Lin* (1991) are all retellings of old Celtic stories. *The Silver Cow* is the story of a young farm boy who is blessed by the water spirits with a herd of silver cattle because of his beautiful music. His father's greed causes the loss of the herd, and also of the son's loyalty when the magic people take back their gift and give the boy a golden harp so that he can leave his abusive parent and make his own future. *The Selkie Girl* is the well-known story of a seal turned into a human female, captured by a young fisherman who makes her his wife. Although she is a mother and loves her husband and family, she longs for her father and sisters and the children she has left behind. Eventually, with the help of her human children, she recovers her seal skin and returns to the sea. In *Tam Lin*, Margaret, a Scottish princess, saves the life and soul of a handsome young knight when he is bewitched by the Elfin Queen. With her much bemoaned tenacity, she clings to him while he transforms from one frightening shape to another until the spell on him is broken.

Cooper has also written two picture books for young children, *Matthew's Dragon* (1991), about a boy whose imaginary pet dragon may not be so imaginary, and *Danny and the Kings* (1993) about a little boy trying to get a Christmas tree for his little brother with the help of three Magi-like truck drivers.

AWARDS

Cooper has received both popular and critical acclaim for her writing, as evidenced by the numerous awards her work has received. *The Grey King* won the prestigious Newbery Medal in 1976 as well as a Carnegie Medal Commendation and the Tir Na N'og Award for a story using a Welsh theme. *The Dark is Rising* was a Newbery Award Honor Book in 1974 and winner of the *Boston Globe-Horn Book* award and a runner-up for the Carnegie Medal in 1973. Cooper also received *Horn Book* honor list citations for *Over Sea, Under Stone, Dawn of Fear* in 1970, *The Grey King* in 1976, and *The Selkie Girl* in 1987. Named as American Library Association Notable Books were *Dawn of Fear* in 1970, *The Dark is Rising* in 1973, *Greenwitch*, and *The Grey King* in 1976. She received a second Tir Na N'og Award in 1978 for *Silver on the Tree*, the Parents' Choice Award in 1983 for *The Silver Cow*, and, in 1984, for *Seaward*, both the Janusz Korczak Award from B'nai B'rith and runner-up for the Universe Award.

AUTHOR COMMENTARY

Bookbird

SOURCE: "Susan Cooper—A Famous Author from Wales Who Writes about Wales," in *Bookbird*, Vol. 4, 1979, pp. 19-21.

It's a strange chance that the Tir na n-Og awards for Anglo-Welsh books should have gone so far to Nancy Bond and myself: one of us American, the other—me—a British subject living in the U.S.A. But then, Wales has always reached out across the sea. When I first went to live in America fifteen years ago, I remember feeling very homesick, and very hostile towards this horrible brash new country—until I looked at a map one day and saw that there was a town in the state of Maine called Bangor, and another in Pennsylvania called Bala Cynwyd. Then I decided that the place couldn't be all bad. When I leave the real Bangor tomorrow I shall go home—and that means to Aberdyfi, on the southern edge of Gwynedd. My grandmother was born there (which does make me one-quarter Welsh), my parents have lived there for the last twenty years, and that whole area round Cader Idris was a very vivid part of my childhood.

It's the setting for *Silver on the Tree*, and for another book *The Grey King*, which was lucky enough to win this same award two years ago. No other place has as strong a hold on my imagination, except the hills and woodlands of Buckinghamshire, in which I grew up. But while my part of Bucks is dead and gone, buried under concrete now, my part of Wales is very little changed. In spite of rashes of boxy holiday homes, and caravans from Birmingham, the Dyfi valley endures; the magic is still there.

And it was that magic, reaching out through reality and memory, which produced these books. *Silver on the Tree* was the last of a sequence of five interlinked books called *The Dark Is Rising.* I wrote the first of them, *Over Sea, Under Stone*, while I was still living in Britain, working for *The Sunday Times* in London. I had no idea then that it would be the first of a series, though I did leave it sort of open-ended, because I'd fallen in love with the characters in it, and couldn't bear the thought of never seeing them again.

The magic came later. I married an American and moved to America, and I was, as I've said, terribly homesick. Everything I wrote was about Britain—it still is. Everything I read was about Britain: myth, folk-tale, history, Arthurian legend—all of them life-long preoccupations anyway. I'd been haunted by Arthur ever since I first began writing, at the age of about eight.

So here I was in this state of longing, and one day I had an idea for a book, about a small boy who would wake up one morning on his eleventh birthday and find that he could work magic. I sat down to sketch out the idea, and for some reason I picked up my first children's book, *Over Sea, Under Stone*, and began re-reading it for the first time in years. And out of that, and all the *hiraeth* and the haunting, something went click in my head, and to my great astonishment I found myself writing down the outline of a series of five books. All of them would be about the unending battle between those two timeless forces that I call the Light and the Dark. *Over Sea,* already published, would be the first; there would be four others, two of them set in England and two in Wales.

I wrote down, that strange day, the places of each; the times of the year, the characters (who would all wander in and out of the whole sequence), the themes, and the titles. Then, still in this bemused enchanted condition, I took a new sheet of paper and wrote the last page of what would be the very last book, *Silver on the Tree.* And when at last I came to write that book, I used, at the end, the words I had written then.

I still have those two pieces of paper: the outline, and the last page. They're very tattered now, but they remind me always of the marvellous unpredictability of the imagination. And of the magical power of place—which can keep hold of you always, no matter how far away you may go from home. . . . .

I feel great admiration, as well as gratitude, towards the Welsh branch of the Youth Libraries Group, the Welsh Arts Council and Welsh Joint Education Committee. It's marvellous that the two Tir na n-Og awards exist. They can't fail to encourage writing in Wales and about Wales, in Welsh or English—because what these awards are saying is: 'Look. Somebody cares'.

For writers of books published for children, that's important. Very often we meet the people who don't care. Like the man at a party who says when introduced, 'Oh, you're a writer! What sort of books d'you write?' Now if you said you wrote sexy novels, or large boring encyclopaedias, he would be very impressed—depending on what kind of man he was. He'd say: *'Oh!'* But of course you say, 'I write children's books'. And he says, 'Oh. How charming'. And you know he's thinking: 'Kids' books? They don't count'.

But it's possible that in fact they count more than anything. The books you read now, if you're young, will stay with you. If you really like one, it becomes part of you. That's why writers so often have more pleasure from the children who read their books than from the adults. Mind you, the things those readers say can be confusing sometimes. One little boy wrote to me after one of my books came out, and said, *'The Dark is Rising* was a very good book but I thought it was rather thick'. The one I wrote after that was thinner, and another little boy wrote a letter that said, 'I thought *Greenwitch* was wonderful but it was disappointingly short'. You can't win.

Most of the things children say, though, really show simply that they're *with* you. Like the one whose letter said: 'dear Miss Cooper, We have had lots of fun reading your books at school. Some of us wanted the Light to win and some wanted the Dark to win, but they were the ones who are usually in trouble'.

Tir na n-Og. The land of the ever young. That timeless golden fairy-tale land really does exist. But it isn't westward, somewhere lost in the mist; it isn't over the sea. It exists in the minds of children and, I think, in the minds of those who write for children. Maybe we're still partly children ourselves.

Perhaps part of my imagination is still ten years old, like my daughter. Or twelve years old, like my son. At any rate, like them, I'm overjoyed when somebody gives me a marvellous present. And that's happened today.

Magpies

SOURCE: "Preserving the Light," in *Magpies,* Vol. 3, No. 2, May, 1988, pp. 5-9.

[Transcribed from a talk delivered at the Magpies *Fantasy Seminar in September, 1987.]*

Once upon a time when I was a reporter on a newspaper, with an office instead of a gypsy author, I looked out of my office window one day and I saw a man climbing a flagpole on the top of a very tall building nearby. It was a very precarious looking position and I kept looking back at him from my work hoping that when he had finished what he was doing he would go away. It was really a very thin flagpole, but he was still there. I was in anguish about the chances of his falling off and I was about to call the fire brigade. Another reporter walked into the office and I said, "Look at that crazy man climbing that flagpole!" She looked out of the window and she said very compassionately, "Susan, that's not a man, that's a flag." So I put my glasses on and, of course, she was right . . . I'm very short sighted, as you may guess.

There was another writer who was short sighted: James Thurber, American writer and cartoonist. He was even worse than me and he was gradually losing his sight through the last part of his life. A friend of mine once said to me that he had said cheerfully, "Those of us who are half blind are luckier than you think. Where the rest of you see a paper bag blowing down the street we see an old lady turning somersaults."

Now those, the imaginative flights of short sighted people, are not unlike the perceptions of those of us who write what is classified as fantasy. We live in the same world as the rest of you. Its realities are the same but we perceive them differently; we don't see quite what you see. It's a bit like abstract painting or poetry and it's not at all like the realistic novel. The material of fantasy is myth, folk tale, legend, the mystery of dream and the greater mystery of time. With all that haunting our heads it really isn't surprising that we write stories about an ordinary world in which extraordinary things can happen.

From an historical point of view, fantasy is the oldest form of story that there is. It began with those things that I have just mentioned: myth, folk tale, legend. There's nothing new about Superman; he's just a simplistic recreation of the god Mercury, with a bit of Hercules thrown in.

Mankind has always needed heroes, just as it's always needed gods, as we've always needed them. The great focus figures of our greatest religions, Christ, Buddha, Muhammed, are all the heroes and the gods combined.

Once upon a time mankind was not ashamed of the fact that it also needed fantasy. Those stories were a normal part of everybody's life. Storytellers had their own names even. There was the Anglo-Saxon scop, the Anglo-French minstrel later on performing the same function. Those myths and folk tales, the legends that we read today only when we are children, weren't written for children. Folk tale is written for folk. *Beowulf* was not written for children. Nor was Spenser's *Faerie Queen*, neither was *Morte d'Arthur* nor was *Sir Gawain and the Green Knight.* Nor was *Gulliver's Travels,* for that matter. Between yesterday and today things have changed a lot and today written down fantasy is almost exclusively written for and published for children.

I'm not complaining; I'm just commenting. Publishers aren't idiots. They want to make money and if they felt they could do that by selling fantasy to grownups then they would. The only book that has ever crossed that boundary is *Watership Down* which was head of the children's best seller lists in Britain and of the adult best seller list in America. But, in general, you people out there who want to read fantasy, unless it is classified as science fiction, you have to go to the children's list. Now why? . . .

Children understand fantasy. They accept it on its own terms from the moment it starts. It's only in writing about adult fiction in the theatre or anywhere else that critics talk about the need for the willing suspension of disbelief. Kids don't have to suspend it; they start off just as we at their age started off, with the faith that anything can happen, that fantasy is as real as other inexplicable marvels like the blue sky or the waves in the sea, that it deals with truth. Disbelief is what we learn when we grow up. . . .

Professor Tolkien called fantasy, among other things, "the making and glimpsing of other worlds" and there's a wonderful Canadian librarian called Lillian Smith who wrote a book called *The Unreluctant Years* in which she says that "fantasy uses the metaphorical approach to the perception of universal truths. That it comes out of the creative imagination, making life out of abstraction," and then she says something that I find a great comfort in difficult moments. She says "it is more true perhaps with writers of fantasy than of any other writers except poets that they struggle with the inexpressible. According to their varying capacities they are able to evoke ideas and clothe them in symbols, allegory and dream." What she doesn't tell is that we don't know how we do it, at least I don't. I think writers of fantasy are like musicians or fast bowlers, they are born not made.

You can't, of course, teach any kind of writer how to write. You can teach someone grammar and prose construction and the techniques of verse or prose, for that matter, but if he or she hasn't been born creative no course in what we call in America "creative writing" is going to do them any good at all. By the same token if he is a writer by birth, by luck, then he is going to be able to do only those kinds of writing that he was born able to do, or at least that's what he will do best. His imagination is creative but only in its own quirky way and the writing of fantasy is a kind of genetic quirk. It's also a bit like an apple strudel, it's full of layers. The trouble is there's no recipe. In a story that deals with magic and enchantment only the top two layers or so are the result of conscious effort. The rest are provided by the unconscious, subconscious (I don't quite know where the divide comes-even when I'm reading Jung), that great welter of images and hopes and fears and dreams by which the minds of every one of us are inescapably linked with the minds of every other man and woman, past or present. We are so inescapably linked that it's possible for a writer to invent what appears to be a wholly new story shining with originality and then to find out that some tenth century bard dreamed up the whole thing nine hundred years ago. Most of us have had that happen; it's very disconcerting. There are no new stories. There are certainly no new fantasies. There is only what Tolkien called "the cauldron of stories" into which we all dip, and pull up something. We can't even see what we are pulling up half the time. Children are forever writing to authors and saying, "Where do you get your ideas?" and the only possible answer is, "Out of my head".

But we don't really know what's in our heads. The ideas come out of a dark place in the back somewhere, behind a door that's usually locked but sometimes swings open: the unconscious, I guess. All good fantasy, I think, is full of very deep, hidden echoes. As Ms Smith says, symbols, allegory and dream, but I think that they must be deep and hidden, hidden in particular from the writer. If you use the wrong purpose your magic doesn't work. The symbols have to be intuitive and the allegory has to be unconscious. Adult readers sometimes try to drag these hidden meanings up to the surface, and that's not very wise either. They are like a fisherman hoping to catch a fish and he comes up with an old boot. . . . .

If you're a professional writer you start out with all the basic equipment. You've got the talent for using words, for making people come alive, for creating suspense in a story but you aren't in complete rational control of it. In my own writing life, I suppose I've produced about equal amounts of non fiction as a journalist and realist fiction as a novelist and playwright and screenwriter, and fantasy. I find the subconscious, unconscious, whatever, taking over far more often when I am writing fantasy than when I am writing realist stories. Quite often I start a book or a chapter or even any one day's work knowing very vaguely that my story is going to go from point A to point B but without really very much idea of how it is going to get there. The answer appears once I have begun working; the imagination tells me. The images flicker in and out sometimes quite unexpectedly and you have to grab them before they evaporate. You don't sit there waiting for them to hit you on the head, of course, otherwise you would never finish. People who think it is possible only to write a book when you are in the right mood are the ones who never finish a book. You write if you are inspired, you write if you aren't inspired, just the same. You go on. If you can't hitch, then you walk. The one vital thing is to scribble away once the idea or the image presents itself. There's a lovely thing Dylan Thomas once said about the poem that he wrote called "The Ballad of the Long Legged Bait". He said that writing it had been like carrying a huge armful of words to a table that he thought was upstairs and wondering if he could get there in time before he dropped them or even if the table would still be there. That's where the conscious urgency comes

in, the struggle to catch what you have been offered by the subconscious. And sometimes it can come when you least expect it.

I think that's why I started writing the books that I have done. I was a very young reporter on the London *Sunday Times* a long while ago, spending my time interviewing politicians, film stars, business men, and you name it, and in my spare time I was writing novels, one of which was not published. It was a story about a woman having a wild affair with a pot-bellied Welshman, written, of course, because I had just been having a wild affair with a pot-bellied Welshman. Not very good. The other was a futuristic novel which was published, rather much to my surprise, as science fiction. Sometimes I was also writing articles on books for a half-page feature in the paper that we had called "Mainly for Children". One day the literary editor of the newspaper who knew I was doing all this stuff came into my office and dropped a press release on the desk. He said, "Look at this. You ought to try it." This turned out to be a competition organized by a British publishing house, Ernest Benn Ltd I think they were, offering what they called the "E. Nesbit Prize" for a family adventure story. There was a deadline which I liked for I was a journalist. There was a prize which I also liked for journalists didn't get paid very much. I'd already finished my adult novel, so I did try. I invented three rather stereotyped, middle class children called Simon, Jane and Barney and I put them in a train from London to Cornwall to begin a rather vague tale about a treasure hunt. It all lasted for about two chapters, both of which I cut later on. I don't quite know what changed things but change they did. Perhaps my childhood memories of holidays in Cornwall took over, maybe it was the ghostly influence of E. Nesbit who was also a journalist and turned to writing fantasy novels, but at any rate the adventure story got overtaken by magic. I found myself giving the children a very odd great uncle called Merriman Lyon. It became a fantasy with Arthurian overtones and with a kind of question mark ending to it. I had absolutely no intention of writing a sequel. I just liked my people too much, especially Merriman to be able to say goodbye to them. The book was accepted by an English publisher—not the one who had organized the competition. I was by then about twenty-six, twenty-seven years old and a rising feature writer on the *Sunday Times*. . . .

My reading became focused even more than before on Britain, on my roots. It covered an enormous muddled range from Margaret Murray to James Fraser's long version of *The Golden Bough,* to Robert Graves's *The White Goddess,* which is one of the books I would take to a desert island, and everything ever written about King Arthur thrown in. I remember two particular refuges in time of misery were Jacquetta Hawk's book *A Land* and Walter de la Mare's wonderful anthology called *Come Hither.* I wasn't doing research, I wasn't reading for anything, I was reading for myself and then one winter's day I was cross country skiing with my husband in the woods near where we live just outside Boston in Massachusetts. People moving in single file along a ski path don't engage in very much conversation, they're physically trying not to fall down as I was usually, so I was shuffling along, looking at the tips of branches sticking out of snow drifts, thinking idly that they looked like the tips of antlers from buried deer and I suddenly—you know that door opened and the idea popped out—thought one day I am going to write a book set in snow like this, but in my England, about a small boy who wakes up one morning and finds that he can work magic. That was the idea, that was all there was of it. So I went home to my desk and that night I wrote the idea down and when I tried to turn it into a story it turned into some terrible facetious thing that I didn't like at all so I just put it away in the file labelled "New Work" which gets fatter every year—not always followed up on.

Several years went by in the course of which my children got a bit older and I wrote several more books for adults, at least I thought they were all for adults. Margaret McElderry, who knows best, published one of them as a children's book, *Dawn of Fear.* One day I came across the idea about the snow again, thumbing through that file, and something sent me back to re-read *Over Sea, Under Stone,* the first children's book I had ever written. One does not re-read one's own work, at least I don't, and I don't know what the trigger was. Your mind, if you are an author, is a bit like a pot of soup, thick soup, Tolkien's cauldron I suppose, simmering on the back of the stove and once in a while a bubble comes up and goes "pop" all on its own. For no reason the idea comes and the ripples spread out. The ripples in my mind on that day as I sat there gazing at the stony wall went to and fro I suppose between the boy waking up on his birthday and the snow and the children of *Over Sea* and most of all probably the Merlin figure, Merriman. I did a very strange thing. I took a piece of paper and found myself writing down not just the name of one book but an outline of five books with *Over Sea* which was already published serving as the first one. I wrote down the titles, the time of the year, magical times of the year, the place and the characters in each book. The titles eventually changed

a little. I wrote very very sketchy things about what would be in each book, things like my part of Wales at Hallowe'en, the Welsh boy Bran and the Druids, nothing that could have meant a thing to anybody else and didn't mean too much to me at the time, but each sketch had this very rough picture of what would happen in each book all told in this long archetypal struggle between the Light and the Dark, the good and evil in men and then, feeling very bemused by now, I took another piece of paper and I wrote out the very last page of what would be the very last book and I looked at that and I thought "goodness" and I put that one away and I started work on what was going to be book two, *The Dark is Rising,* the story of Will Stanton the seventh son of a seventh son, the boy who wakes up on his eleventh birthday in part of Buckinghamshire where I grew up in England and finds to his dismay that he is no longer an ordinary member of his large bouncy family but also the last of the Old Ones, immortals of the Light, destined to help mankind save itself from domination by the Dark.

Where do those ideas come from? Nobody knows. I set that book *The Dark is Rising* very precisely in the countryside of Buckinghamshire in the part of England where I spent my early childhood and as I sat there writing in my American study all sorts of visual details came jumping out of my head that I hadn't remembered for thirty years: a certain manor house with a garden where a great wave of daffodils used to bloom in early spring, a certain little Saxon church called Saint James the Less, a certain noisy rookery close to it, a certain old lady who was in a local sweet shop and used to dye her hair with tea, and because memory and imagination each have their own two-way connection with that part of the unconscious mind some things came out without my even recognizing them until they were there.

There was one thing for instance, I decided that my Old Ones, the creatures of the Light, should have certain charted tracks of their own through the land of Britain, ancient routes like the Ridgeways of the Bronze Age that go along the tops of hills, but uncharted in this case, invisible. I called them the Old Ways. I guess they had something in common with the ancestral Aboriginal tracks in this country, the song lines, the way of the north, things I had never heard of then. I told you there were no new ideas. I set as one of my old ways a large tree-lined, unpaved, dirt track where Will Stanton my hero was going to be attacked by the Dark. Like every other setting in the book this was a real one from my own childhood. It was the rather sinister little dirt track that we had always called Tramps' Alley and I had

Will call it that too. There really were tramps in Britain in those days, shambling ancient old men before the welfare state saved them or ruined them. We could see them camping by the road, their newspaper tucked in their boots, their pants tied up with string. Anyway I wrote the scene and Will was saved from the Dark by the enchantment of the Old Way on which he stood. I had his master Merriman reprimand him a bit ponderously for using an ugly name like Tramps' Alley for so sacred a road. Then my pen stopped because into my head popped the name that was the real name for Tramps' Alley, that my parents always tried to make us use when we were kids. It was called Old Way Lane.

I have been working mostly since I started writing *The Dark is Rising* books and finished them, a process of about seven years after that big gap between the first book and the last one, mostly since then in film and the theatre, television film mostly, and the theatre is of course its own fantasy. It's the making of another world, the answering of a need for the audience. I always like to think that in that lovely hushed moment before the curtain goes up when the lights have gone down and the bright world on the stage is not visible yet that the audience is like a child curled up with a book, full of anticipation hoping for magic, reaching for questions that they didn't know how to ask. The human mind is like that I think, it always has been. The world around us has been changing so fast in this century that we forget that the people in it haven't changed a bit. Just as the deepest needs and responses of an adult really don't differ very much from what they were when he was a child, we all need stories, we all need wonder and amazement to teach us how to survive and understand and enjoy the lives we lead. I think maybe the greatest strengths of fantasy and the reason why it will always survive is the fact that we also need to be shown things that we never understand, we need that sense of mystery, writer or reader, first because we are getting further and further away from the sense of god in this century, in this civilization. I know I shall never properly understand T. S. Eliot's *Four Quartets* for instance, but I also know that I have to read them about once a year because of what they do to my head. And if some child somewhere gets that same sense of wonder from the fantasies that we write, then we have done the best that we can do. For any one of us who is still capable of noticing it there will always be a flash of delight waiting around the corner for something inexplicable.

There was one day some years ago I was driving in Britain from London to north Wales where my parents lived their last twenty years, and there are great unfamiliar roaring motorways out of London now. They had been put there since I had been living there. I took the wrong one. I am very good at doing that. About thirty miles west of London I realized the mistake and I pulled off at the nearest exit from the motorway and pulled over into a narrow little sideway to check the map. It took me quite a while to realize that the ground over which I had been driving was the exact countryside of my childhood based book *The Dark is Rising,* all of it buried now in concrete, roaring roads, and it took me longer still to recover from the sight of a very small street sign on the little paved suburban road beside the motorway that I had pulled off onto. The trees were gone and the tramps were gone and everything was different but the sign said, "Old Way Lane".

The Horn Book Magazine

SOURCE: "Fantasy in the Real World," in *The Horn Book Magazine,* Vol. LXVI, No. 3, May-June, 1990, pp. 304-15.

Fantasy, our subject and my preoccupation, comes from and appeals to the unconscious. It draws all its images from that dark wonderland, through the mysterious catalyst of the creative imagination. Nobody has ever described the process better than that great librarian, Lillian H. Smith, in her book *The Unreluctant Years.* "Creative imagination," she said, "is more than mere invention. It is that power which creates, out of abstractions, life. It goes to the heart of the unseen, and puts that which is so mysteriously hidden from ordinary mortals into the clear light of their understanding, or at least of their partial understanding. It is more true, perhaps, of writers of fantasy than of any other writers except poets that they struggle with the inexpressible. According to their varying capacities, they are able to evoke ideas and clothe them in symbols, allegory, and dream."

Symbols, allegory, and dream. Like ritual and myth, those other mighty ancestors of fantasy, they have in recent years been much more widely discussed than is usual in this country, thanks to the television journalist Bill Moyers. First, public television gave us "Moyers: Joseph Campbell and the Power of Myth," Moyers's six one-hour interviews with the mythologist Joseph Campbell, and then Doubleday published what I suppose should be called the book of the series, *The Power of Myth.* The interviews were watched by two-and-a-half million people, and the book was on the *New York Times* best-seller list for six months. Between them they made Campbell's ideas far more accessible than his own books had done over the last forty years; he was a good writer but a better teacher, and *The Power of Myth,* both on film and on the page, is captivating. . . .

He's saying that artists have inherited the mythmaking function of the shaman and the seer, and of course he's right. Where the art of writing is concerned, his point applies most of all to the poets and to the writers of fantasy. Both deal with images, and with their links to and within the unconscious mind. And the fantasist—not one of my favorite words—deals with the substance of myth: the deep archetypal patterns of emotion and behavior which haunt us all whether we know it or not.

All of us who write fantasy are creating, in one way or another, variations on a single theme: we have a hero—or heroine—who has to cross the threshold from his familiar world into the unknown. In search of some person or thing or ideal, he has a series of adventures, undergoes trials, survives dangers and disasters, until he achieves his goal, his quest. And having achieved it, he comes home again a wiser person, better prepared for the longer journey which is now ahead of him, the adventure of living his life. . . .

The children who write to authors of fantasy novels fumble to explain why they like such books, and come up with sentences like these from my own mail. From a thirteen-year-old in Texas: "Your books are my escape from the world I live in. I often wish I were one of the Old Ones, fighting the Dark and protecting Mankind from harm." A thirteen-year-old in Britain: "When I open your books I feel myself slipping out of this world and into another. I am one of those people who long for Adventure, and reading your books is the closest I have ever come to being in one." From a twenty-year-old in Illinois: "You give all of us the chance to leave the mundane struggles we face and enter a slightly grander struggle for a while." A sixteen-year-old in Sweden: "I get such a feeling when I read your books. It's like I want to climb up to the pages and walk straight into it and help Will and his friends." And from a twelve-year-old in Britain, the simplest and perhaps the most accurate: "Your books seem to fit me just right." . . .

It would be nice to be able to say: let's make all the children in the country read more, and let's introduce more of them to fantasy. Make sure curricula and reading lists are full of the myths of the founding civilizations—Greek, Roman, Norse, Celtic, native American, and so on. Make sure too that children have the chance to read new fantasy, in which—let

us hope—patterns for the future emerge from the mythic echoes of the past. Yes, we must do these things. But a great proportion of our children will never voluntarily open a book outside the doors of school, mostly because their parents don't. They may never even be able properly to read, but become part of the mind-boggling percentage of functional illiterates which our educational system lets slip through the cracks. You can be pretty sure that when these children were between the ages of two and eleven, they were at the very high end of the scale which in a recent report produced an *average* figure, for children in that age group, of twenty-eight hours of television watched every week. Twenty-eight hours a week! Four hours a day, including schooldays! That's my idea of hell, not pleasure—proof, if it were needed, that television is a drug.

The screen, small or large, is not intrinsically a bad thing. Like most other drugs, it can serve wonderful ends. The pressure of commerce keeps its standards low, but individuals of talent and determination can use the screen to re-create a mythological pattern as powerful as any story written down, or told aloud. And if one of them does it well, the results can be astounding. *Star Wars* and *E.T.* are both variants of the fantasy hero pattern that I was describing earlier; Luke Skywalker's quest runs through a "galaxy far, far away," and the little Extra-Terrestrial comes from his world to ours and back again. More people have seen those two films, throughout the world, than have seen any other film ever made; not because they are the best films ever made, but because they managed, for a couple of hours, to satisfy the longings of the collective unconscious. "Mum!" said my children, as we left the cinema after seeing *Star Wars* twelve years ago, "it's all about your books!" They sounded indignant, as if they felt George Lucas had been cribbing from **The Dark Is Rising,** but of course he hadn't; their indignation only served to point up the fact that where the archetypes of myth are concerned, there is no such thing as a new story. There is only, as Professor Tolkien observed, the cauldron of story, which is available to all of us through the unconscious, and from which we all draw. Nearly every fantasy author I've ever met has had the experience of having a glorious new idea for a story, only to find that some bard or minstrel had the same idea eight hundred years ago. . . .

So fantasy and its archetypal patterns are not going to reach a mass audience very often today. Even amongst that limited part of the population which reads books—books, not newspapers or magazines or escapist thrillers or romances—even amongst them, it isn't going to reach everyone. Every teacher or li-

brarian knows the sturdy child who is a dogged realist and thinks fantasy is for the birds. There are more
children like that than there are fantasy readers, and
from a practical point of view that's probably just as
well. Back in the mists of time, as everyone sat
around the campfire listening to the shaman telling
the sacred stories, there was always the realist in the
group. "I don't want to listen to those boring old
myths," he said, and he went off on his own and invented the wheel.

"Your books seem to fit me just right," said the little
girl. *Those* are the children we have to reach: to drop
into the shadowy pool of their unconscious minds a
few images that—perhaps, with luck—will echo
through their lives and help them understand and
even improve their world, our world. If America
doesn't have what Aristotle and Mr. Campbell call an
ethos, if instead there is a gap, we need to make sure
that our children are given an early awareness of the
timeless, placeless archetypes of myth. And since we
have no one single myth, that has to mean all the different—and yet similar—mythic patterns we inherit,
collectively, in this country from our very diverse be-
ginnings. I am speaking not only of ancient myth but
of the modern fantasy which is its descendant, its in-
heritor. Like poetry, these are the books which speak
most directly to the imagination. As Ursula Le Guin
once wrote, "It is by such statements as 'Once upon
a time there was a dragon,' or 'In a hole in the ground
there lived a hobbit'—it is by such beautiful non-
facts that we fantastic human beings may arrive, in
our peculiar fashion, at the truth."

Parents, teachers, librarians, authors, publishers; we
are the people with the responsibility for putting together the right child and the right book. Any child
and any book will do, but it helps if they match. The
biggest truism of our professional lives is that hugely
important fact too many civilians still forget: *every
child should be encouraged to read books, words on
a page, for his or her own pleasure, in his own time,
dreaming his own—and the author's—dream.* When
December comes, I shall be found whispering to
people I know (and wanting to shout to a great many
I don't): "For every toy you buy a child this Christmas, add to the package a paperback book." In a de-
mythologized world, where the sunlight of the imagination has to filter past the great looming skyscrapers
of the computer and television set, books need all the
help they can get.

Booklist

SOURCE: An interview in *Booklist,* Vol. 94, No. 2,
September 15, 1997, pp. 226-27.

*BKL: You have written a lot for adults and for TV as
well as for children. Is it different?*

COOPER: Oh goodness, yes, because writing for
children I write for myself. It's my own thing. It's
private. I go into my head and write what I've seen
in it. Then my editor, Margaret McElderry, tells me
which age group it's for. But for television you write
something for a film, and generally you have a committee of X number of people telling you how they
think it should be changed or you have to rewrite it
in a different shape because there are seven commercial breaks instead of six. And it is much less satisfying and not at all private. [I] really got into doing it
because I was divorced and needed the money.

I've never aimed at any age group. With my early
book, *Dawn of Fear,* about a child in London in
World War II, I thought I was writing an adult novel,
and all the publishers said they didn't know how to
market this book because it was about a child. Margaret McElderry was the only one to say, "It's a children's book." All we did was to take out a few reflective passages that were too adult.

BKL: And the child in that book was you?

COOPER: Yes, that was a case of sinking myself
back into my own childhood. Everything that happened in that book was in some way true. I was 4
when the war broke out in Britain and 10 when it
ended. If there was any formative thing in my early
years, I should think that was it. I mean, when you
go to bed at night, and you know you are going to be
woken up by people dropping a bomb on your head,
or trying to, I think it forms certain assumptions at
the back of your mind that never go away. There's a
threat of absolute evil as part of life; the sort of om-
nipresence of someone trying to do bad things. It
gives you this feeling of the dark and the light, the
good and the bad, Us and Them.

BKL: That sounds like **The Dark Is Rising** *series.*

COOPER: Well, *Dawn of Fear* is straight reporting.
Factual. *The Dark Is Rising* books came through a
sort of fantasy, a metaphor. There is a point somewhere in the series, I've forgotten in which book,
when somebody says to Will, "You are both alike in
the long run . . . the Light and the Dark . . . you are

extreme. You are sort of cold. And people, we ordinary people in the middle are a mixture, and we are battered around by both of you."

BKL: Why do you think you moved to fantasy?

COOPER: When I was writing **Over Sea, Under Stone,** it started as a realistic family adventure, and it turned into a fantasy. I don't know whether it's from an inability to cope with real life, whether it's some extreme sense of privacy. I mean everything turns into a metaphor. It's escapism, running away.

BKL: In your Newbery acceptance speech, you said that you found yourself writing a fantasy full of images that had haunted you since childhood.

COOPER: Fantasy is talking about deep, deep truths but not revealing them through realistic details. We're not escaping out, we're escaping in, into the unconscious. It's a way we discover ourselves. Fantasies are stories about journeys, perils, ordeals, and instead of being copies of what will happen to you in your real life, they take you into your imagination and the ordeal takes place there.

BKL: When kids write to you, do they ever talk about that?

COOPER: Every so often you get an amazing letter from a kid. There's one girl who always sticks with me. She said, "I love your books. They've taught me to see the good and evil in myself." And when I do book-signings invariably somebody in their twenties or thirties says, "You can't imagine what your books did for me when I was growing up." And, I think, for them, too, it is the same as it is for the writer, that they are escaping into themselves through this story; they are recognizing something within the fantasy that is a mirror of the sort of struggle that is going on inside their heads as they grow up.

BKL: In the 1995 Zena Sutherland Lecture in Chicago, you said that you don't do schools, that you don't know how to behave with children. Is this just American children?

COOPER: No, it's children in general. It's mostly shyness. I don't know what to say to them. Most authors who are very good with classes have their own shtick. Either they perform like my friend Ashley Bryan or, if they are illustrators, they can draw pictures. I don't draw pictures. Or they're very outgoing, which I am not, and can jolly the kids along. I never know what to say to them. If they ask me questions, I can answer them. But that's not enough, you know, if you sit down with a class of 30 kids, some of whom are as shy as you are, then you need a shtick or an act. I've never worked one out.

BKL: Can you as an adult actually see as a child? Do you believe you can recover the child's vision?

COOPER: The writer Penelope Lively says you can't connect; it's gone, that children live in another country. I don't agree. I think I can remember the inside of the head or the emotions of a very shy seven-year-old very clearly, and I think she is still there inside me at the age of 62. I mean, people talk about children as if they were just a different species, and they're not. What was it I said somewhere? They are us, not yet wearing our heavy jacket of time.

BKL: What can books say to children about war, about conflict?

COOPER: I think the best you can say is what Merriman says at the end of **Silver on the Tree,** that there is the power of good and the power of evil, and both of them are in you, and it is up to you to make of the world the best that you can. And I think what books can do for kids is to help them find the ability to see where we go wrong and how we can stop going wrong. And one hopes they will remember it when they get to crises in their own lives. So I guess it's much the same as raising kids, the same as it is for a parent. What can you really teach them?

BKL: Has being an immigrant here influenced how you write?

COOPER: I think I have resisted being an immigrant here. Even after 35 years, I still have a green card. The last four **Dark Is Rising** books I wrote after I'd lived in the U.S. for more than 10 years, and I wrote them out of homesickness. I was married, I had teenage stepchildren, and two babies of my own. But it was all the Englishness that wrote those books. I was going home in my head.

BKL: Maybe it's the homesickness that helped make them so good.

COOPER: That's what the English writer J. B. Priestley said to me. He was a friend of mine and in one of his letters to me he said, don't worry about it; you will find that you write better about a place when you are away from it. There's also a great quote from his autobiography that I keep up on my wall: "Perhaps it would be better not to be a writer, but if you must be one—then, I say, write. You feel dull, you have a headache, nobody loves you—write. It all seems hopeless, that famous "inspiration" will not come—write. If you are a great genius, you will make your own rules; but if you are not—and the odds are heavily against it—go to your desk, no matter how high or low your mood, face the icy challenge of the paper—write. Sooner or later, the goddess will recognize in this a devotional act, worthy of grace. But if what I am saying seems nonsense, do not attempt to write for a living. Try elsewhere, making sure the position carries a pension."

BKL: Have there been times when it's been hard for you to write?

COOPER: Oh, yes. I wrote those last four **Dark Is Rising** books over a period of six and one half years. Then there was this long gap when I didn't write much, and that may have been refueling. It was partly to do with getting divorced and writing for television and running around the country with Hume Cronyn and his late wife, Jessica Tandy, when we did the play **Foxfire** together. I wrote the YA fantasy **Seaward.** Then recently I wrote these two books about the boggart, an ancient trick-playing, shape-shifting, creature. The first one is set in Toronto.

BKL: Kids love the way you make the boggart so contemporary, bringing this Celtic mischief-maker into the world of computers and traffic lights and "cool." And in the second boggart story, you take them all back to Scotland. Do you think you were finally connecting America with back home?

COOPER: I don't know. I had always wanted to do this piece about this bird who gets across the Atlantic by accident. Maybe I was trying to ease myself into accepting the fact that I was actually never going to leave America. I had such fun doing it. It was a sort of romp. It hardly took any time or effort.

BKL: How do you handle sequels and series? Do you know from the start that there's going to be more than one book?

COOPER: With **Over Sea, Under Stone,** I didn't plan a series, but with the next four, it was like writing a symphony with four more movements. I knew the shape of the four, very roughly. And I wrote the last page of the very last book before I even started writing.

BKL: Are there any special problems with keeping to a series?

COOPER: If it's an open-ended series that just goes on and on, like the Babysitters Club, then of course you don't have a problem, but when you have a par-

ticular finite shape for a sequence, there's always a danger that you feel the last book should be the best and the most powerful and the most satisfying. I think that happened with **Silver on the Tree**; I tried too hard to make it carry everything.

*BKL: And with **The Boggart,** did you know when you wrote the first one that you were going to do another one?*

COOPER: No, I didn't. But he wouldn't go away. Then I remembered this little squib that I had read somewhere about the boggart's cousin being the Loch Ness monster, who was just rather lazy and laid at the bottom of his lake and slept. So that story grew and became a book.

BKL: Any chance of your finding a story in this country?

COOPER: I've never felt the same strong sense of place in this country. The only place it's happened is down in New Mexico, which is very odd, because it's so different there. I think it fascinates me, and I respond to it because that region is as soaked in human history as the British Isles are. And I think that's one reason why Americans like **The Dark Is Rising** books; it's because they haven't got that sense of omnipresent history themselves.

BKL: At college at Oxford you were taught by the great fantasy people C.S. Lewis and J. R. R. Tolkien.

COOPER: Yes, but Tolkien was lecturing on Anglo-Saxon literature and Lewis on Renaissance and medieval literature. I never met either of these gentlemen, I just went to their lectures. Tolkien wrote a marvelous essay "On Fairy Tales." He talks about "the cauldron of story," which is available to all of us through the unconscious.

BKL: That sounds like Joseph Campbell. Were you influenced by him at all?

COOPER: I never read Campbell. I tried to read *Hero with a Thousand Faces* many years ago and found it almost unreadable. He was a great teacher, but he wasn't a great writer. And I really only came across him when Bill Moyers did that wonderful television series *The Power of Myth.*

BKL: And then you realized you'd been doing what he said all along.

COOPER: Actually, I saw the connection when I took my children to see *Star Wars,* and they came out of the movie most indignant. They said, "Mum, it's like your books. He's been cribbing from *The Dark Is Rising*!" I thought about George Lucas and the shape of that story, and I realized that we all tell the same story in the end. There is no such thing as a new story. Then I read an article that said Lucas was strongly influenced by Joseph Campbell, and I thought, "Well, there you go, of course!" I think we're all in the same business.

GENERAL COMMENTARY

Linda K. Corbett

SOURCE: "'Not Wise the Thought—A Grave for Arthur'," in *The ALAN Review*, Vol. 21, No. 1, Fall, 1993, pp. 45-8.

There are five books in Susan Cooper's series: *Over Sea, Under Stone; Greenwitch; The Grey King; The Dark Is Rising;* and *Silver on the Tree.* With the exception of the first book, mysticism and the supernatural play a large part. The Celtic mythological figure of Arthur is addressed rather than the historical (however exaggerated) Romano-British Christian leader of Gildas and Geoffrey of Monmouth. While not all of the mysticism and supernatural inferences of the book appear in Celtic mythology, many do. . . .

In Cooper's first book, *Over Sea, Under Stone,* we meet the Drew children, Simon, Jane, and Barney, and their Great Uncle, Merriman Lyon. Barney, the youngest of the Drews, is enthralled by the legends of Arthur and equally enthralled to find himself in Cornwall, legendary land of Arthur. With the help of their great-uncle, the children recover a Grail, which they donate to a museum. "Merriman Lyon," Barney said softly to himself. "Merry Lyon . . . Merlion . . . *Merlin.* . . ." Except for some night action beside the standing stones, this book has no supernatural overtones, just the search for the mythical grail.

In Christian legend, the Holy Grail is the cup used not only by Christ at the last supper but also to catch His blood from the cross. In Arthurian legend the Grail was brought by Joseph of Arimethea to the west of England, supposedly Glastonbury, and hidden. The Grail kings traced their lineage to Joseph and seek to find the Grail. Seeking the Grail represents the highest quest that Arthur's Christian knights can undertake and to achieve the Grail, that is, to be granted the vision of it, their highest honor. In Cooper's book, the Grail is of Celtic workmanship, possibly sixth century A.D. It does not represent Christianity necessarily, but it does represent the Light; and finding it does involve danger and trial for the young Grail seekers.

The second book of the series, *The Dark Is Rising,* introduces young Will Stanton, the twelve-year-old seventh son of a seventh son and an Old One. Merriman Lyon is also an Old One and together they are able to secure the six signs of the Light to be used against the Dark. Herne the Hunter and his pack of hounds appear. Herne's hounds are the legendary white hounds of hell that appear in the *Mabinogion* as the pack of Arawn, one of the British gods of Hades. On the Yorkshire and Devon moors, there are those who say they still hear them ride at night.

Greenwitch is a traditional offering made to the sea in the spring. There are a number of similar traditions throughout England: the blessing of the waters, dressing the well. All predate Christianity in their substance, though not in form. In the third book, *Greenwitch,* the Drews and Will Stanton meet each other through Great-Uncle Merriman back in Trewisseck. Their goal is to find the Grail which has been stolen by the Dark and also a further clue that was lost in the first book without being read and found by the Greenwitch when she was given to the sea. They achieve this goal and discover their quest for the next twelve months.

The Grey King moves the story to Wales, another legendary home of Arthur. And here another character enters, the sixth member of the group needed to stop the Dark, Bran, Arthur's son, brought forward through time by Guenevere to escape the Dark. Bran and Will work together to retrieve the golden harp to waken the Sleepers as the last great battle between the light and dark approaches.

Just as Drake sleeps in his hammock waiting to be roused to fight for England, so Arthur waits in Avalon for the time when his country will have need of him again. In the "Verses of the Graves of the Warriors," found in the *Black Book of Caermarthen,* the final resting places of many of the gods are listed, but the author felt that "Not wise (was) the thought—a grave for Arthur." While *The Grey King* does not indicate that Arthur is one of the Sleepers, the implication of the old legend is strong.

In *Silver on the Tree,* the story comes full circle. The Drews come to Wales also, and the end of the frantic race towards the midsummer tree is in sight. Will and Bran face the Mari Llyd, visit the Lost Land, and regain the sword from the Castle of Glass. This last book includes more of the Celtic mythology in pure form. The legend of the lost land whose king Taliesen was served by the poet is presented here, as is Taliesen. The Castle of Glass was where Arthur kept the thirteen treasures, two of which were a horn and a sword, both appearing in these stories. And at the end, at the midsummer tree, comes Arthur, no longer to sleep beneath the hill, for he has joined with the other Old Ones to defeat the Dark. Now it is time for man to find his own way.

Cooper's five books deal with the mythological Arthur. There is no story here of holding back the Saxons. This is a tale that the old bards might have told—of monsters and magic, of kings, queens, gods, and goddesses, and above all, of the on-going battle between good and evil, the Light and the Dark, not necessarily interpreted as Christianity and Paganism.

The appeal of these books goes beyond the invitation to study further about Arthur and the Matter of Britain, but any student who reads these books should be encouraged to search through the literature, fiction and nonfiction, so that they may come to their own conclusions about Arthur and his importance, if any, in their lives. Perhaps the ultimate appeal of Arthur, whether mythological or historical, is that, while he always fights, even in his mythological guise, he sometimes loses. He is human. We see our frailties in him. And, we also see that we, too, have successes. . . .

While I believe that any reading is better than no reading, these are the kinds of books I would really like to see students read. Books that encourage them to find out the facts behind the legends from other books, from magazines, from articles by archaeologists and researchers. Very few will have the opportunity to read the original manuscripts, kept safely for the most part to preserve them from deterioration. Indeed, very few will ever walk the cliffs of Cornwall, stand in the Welsh mountains or beneath the Seat of Arthur in Edinburgh. But it is possible to travel vicariously to these places; to feel the strength of the time-honored legends. Young people, twelve to fifteen, may not be ready for books like *Firelord* or even *Sword at Sunset,* which are close to 500 pages long even in paperback. But the five books in **The Dark Is Rising** series, the longest of which is 270 pages, may be short enough to whet their appetite while being long enough not to insult their intelligence. And I believe that the key phrase is, "whet their appetite." Give them a taste of the excitement of the Arthurian cycle so that they ask for more.

Does this sound idealistic? Yes, but then Arthur was idealistic. To restate Graeme Fife, isn't Luke Sky-walker idealistic? Why should Arthur's supporters not be equally so? It may not be Arthur who catches the mind of a student and encourages that student to read. Whatever or whoever reaches out from the past or the future and encourages reading and research should be supported.

TITLE COMMENTARY

SEAWARD (1983)

Publishers Weekly

SOURCE: A review of *Seaward,* in *Publishers Weekly,* Vol. 224, No. 11, September 9, 1983, p. 65.

This is Cooper's most exhilarating novel since her honored five-book cycle, **The Dark Is Rising.** The writing reverberates with the emotions experienced by the story's two principals, a girl named Cally (Calliope) and a boy named West (Westerly).

Cally is alone after her moribund father and mother leave their home in the care of a white-haired woman who seems oddly familiar to the girl. The parents are on their way to a nursing home when Cally steps through a mirror and onto an alien landscape. At the same time, across the world from her, West is fleeing from a hooded figure like the person who has taken Cally's father and mother in charge. Unknown to each other, the young people make their way toward a central place where they meet and the battle for their souls is joined.

Drawing on Celtic myths, Cooper has created an entirely original story, a spellbinder even in its recondite allusions. The symbolism of the dominant woman—who entraps Cally and West repeatedly—becomes clear as they escape her with the help of the seducer's antagonist, a man who needs the young people for his own ends.

In the final clash, Cally and West realize that neither magician can control their wills; that they must make enormous choices about their existence themselves.

Anna Connor

SOURCE: A review of *Seaward,* in *School Library Journal,* Vol. 30, No. 2, October, 1983, p. 157.

West goes through a door into another world to escape his mother's murderers; Cally, with her selkie hands, is drawn through by a plaintive song. Once in this parallel world, the teenagers begin a seaward journey which both feel compelled to complete. But their travels are hampered by the Lady Taranis, the spirit of death, who uses her powers to ensnare them in dreams and memories and to terrorize them with their own fears. Fortunately they are protected by Lugan, Taranis's brother and opposing power, who sends his "folk" to rescue West and Cally and to re-affirm in them the life spirit. Reaching the sea, they are offered a choice between eternal youth on Lugan's island or return to their mortal world. Although it means they will be separated for a while, both decide to return home to grow up; to experience love and all of the changes possible only in a world subject to death. Shorter and faster paced than the **The Dark Is Rising** and its sequels, this metaphysical adventure has appeal for beginning fantasy readers. Cooper's fans, however, will find only hints of the rich mythic and folkloric detail they have come to expect of her. While the plot, with its abrupt rescues, tends to be episodic, there is a real development in characterization and in the relationship between Cally and West. Though not Cooper's best, it still leaves one wondering if there will be a sequel in which she will more fully realize her parallel world.

The Horn Book Magazine

SOURCE: A review of *Seaward,* in *The Horn Book Magazine,* Vol. LX, No. 1, February, 1984, pp. 59-60.

In a symbolic fantasy which brings together two adolescents—Westerly, a boy, and Cally, a girl—the author has devised a dreamlike narrative. By means of a hidden door revealed by his dying mother, Westerly had escaped from a land ruled by the military, and Cally had slipped through a mirror after her fatally ill parents had been taken away. Both boy and girl felt impelled to reach a far-off sea; and wandering together through countryside and forest, contending with desert land and stony escarpment, they were accosted at the crucial moments of their adventures by a gold-robed man, Lugan, and a bluerobed woman, Lady Taranis. Finally arriving at the shore, Westerly and Cally learned that Lugan and Lady Taranis were the spirits of life and of death, who at times were antagonistic and at times were complementary. The episodes of the uncanny, unconventional fantasy are convincingly concrete and embody the emotional and imaginative states of mind of the two protagonists; there are also occasional references to myths and legends: selkies, Rhiannon, Tir Na N'og. Neither idyllic nor nightmarish, the nonsequential movement of the events suggests the suddenness and vividness of dreams. In the manner of George Macdonald the story develops an allegory, and like Macdonald the author has endowed the concept of human responsibility—of human choice—with the face of fantasy.

Jean Kaufman

SOURCE: A review of *Seaward,* in *Voice of Youth Advocates,* Vol. 7, No. 1, April, 1984, p. 37.

Torn from the world by grief, plunged into a strange land with no direction except to find the sea, Cally and Westerly set off on their adventure. This world is ruled by two creatures, Lugan and Lady Taranis. Lugan and Lugan's Folk Peth, Snake and Ryan, help Cally and Westerly on their quest while Lady Taranis and her helpers, Nightmare, Stonecutter, and Zombies, try to keep Westerly and Cally from completing their journey. After many adventures and much maturing Cally and Westerly reach the sea where they must make the final choice between immortality on Tir Na N'og, the land of ever-young, where their parents are, or to return to their world and life with its joys, sorrows, and eventual death.

This novel can be read on many levels: as an adventure fantasy with the heroes battling many evils on their journey to the sea; as a creative outgrowth of many Celtic legends including the Selchies and the Celtic Otherworld, or as not even a fantasy at all but instead a tale of two young people learning to cope with the death of their loved ones. Best of all, Cooper has woven all these threads together superbly into a tale that will speak to all who read it. A must for all collections.

📖 *THE SILVER COW* (1983)

Publishers Weekly

SOURCE: A review of *The Silver Cow: A Welsh Tale,* in *Publishers Weekly,* Vol. 223, No. 14, April 8, 1983, p. 59.

This Welsh version of a fairy tale has a fairly standard storyline and moral: a greedy man favored by fate loses all when he shows his disrespect for that which caused his good fortune in the first place. Gwilym is a mean-spirited farmer who won't allow his son Huw to go to school and forbids Huw to play the harp while tending the cattle by the lake. Sometimes Huw sneaks the harp there anyway, and one day the Tylwyth Teg (magic lake people) send a gift in gratitude for Huw's music: a shimmering cow, "silver as a new coin, glinting in the sun." The cow gives three times the milk of Gwilym's other cows, plus it bears silver offspring, causing the farmer to become very rich. But he hoards his coins, and when he tries to sell the cow for its beef the Tylwyth Teg call their creatures back into the lake, and Gwilym's money disappears. Huw cannot bear to live with his father any longer, and setting forth, he plays a farewell on his harp to the silver cow. Hutton's lovely, delicate watercolors are dominated by soft blues and greens, evoking the lush countryside of Wales.

The Horn Book Magazine

SOURCE: A review of *The Silver Cow: A Welsh Tale,* in *The Horn Book Magazine,* Vol. LIX, No. 3, June, 1983, pp. 287-88.

A lilting text, complemented by luminous watercolor illustrations (by Warwick Hutton), captures the enchantment inherent in a traditional tale explaining the genesis of the water lilies fringing Llyn Barfog, "the bearded lake," set high in the Welsh hills. According to the book jacket, the author has slightly reshaped the legend known to her from childhood, by adding as a central character the young harpist Huw, whose music so enchanted the Tylwyth Teg—the magic people of Wales—that they sent a wonderful silver cow from the waters to join the herd he tended for his father. Although the cow and her silver offspring brought wealth and fame, the greedy parent, "a man with a heart as small and mean as his beady black eyes," forbade his son to play the harp or to attend school. And when the cow grew old, he exhibited the same callous disregard for the source of his good fortune by summoning the local butcher to slaughter her. Huw is a felicitous addition, for he heightens the tension of the story, develops the characterization of the farmer, and provides a sympathetic central figure. The illustrations incorporate details extending the text and contrast the crafty earthiness of the townsfolk with the otherworldliness of the time and place.

Margery Fisher

SOURCE: A review of *The Silver Cow,* in *Growing Point,* Vol. 22, No. 4, November, 1983, p. 4158.

The true piercing magic of landscape shines through Susan Cooper's extended version of a Welsh legend, *The Silver Cow,* in which a down-trodden farm boy sees the herd in his charge augmented by a mysterious silver beast from the lake who breeds true off-

spring. When Huw's mean master decides to sell the beautiful beast to fill his repleted money-chest, she vanishes into the water with her calves but rewards the boy who had tried to save her by bestowing on him a talent with the harp that opens a better future for him. Evocative words distinguish a retelling whose strong verbal flavour is accentuated by off-natural ink and wash pictures suggesting a generalised medieval period in details of costume and buildings and picking up the feel of Welsh hills and valleys into the bargain.

THE SELKIE GIRL (1986)

Kirkus Reviews

SOURCE: A review of *The Selkie Girl,* in *Kirkus Reviews,* Vol. LIV, No. 18, September 15, 1986, pp. 1443-44.

The familiar Scottish/Irish tale of a crofter who captures and marries a seal maiden whose beauty and magical singing have entraced him.

Old Thomas tells Donallan he will be able to catch the selkie only by stealing her sealskin when she's taken the form of a maiden, "but a wild creature will always go back to the wild, in the end." Donallan is too much in love to heed. The resulting union is tranquil; "Mairi" smiles when she bears her first child, and four more follow; yet she never laughs or sings. At last the youngest discovers the sealskin, carefully preserved. When Mairi tells her children that she has five more children in the sea, her younger daughter says, "You must go to them. It's their turn."

Cooper's economical, elegant retelling has such a lovely lilt that it begs to be read aloud. Hutton's serene watercolors perfectly evoke the lonely sea and shore, a primitive world where elemental events are given their true importance. His pictures are deceptively simple, as simple as the blue/green inside curve of the towering breaker on the book's penultimate double spread, but with as much power, inner tension, and beauty.

Diane Manuel

SOURCE: "Reading Aloud to Children Needn't End When School Begins," in *The Christian Science Monitor,* Vol. 78, No. 241, November 7, 1986, p. B2.

The Selkie Girl should help to introduce a new generation of readers to the lyric talents of Newbery Medalist Susan Cooper, one of the richest voices in children's literature today. In her latest work, she teams up with illustrator Warwick Hutton to retell a favorite folk legend from her native Great Britain. Versions of the "selkie" (seal) girl can be heard all along the coasts of Scotland and Ireland, where "the islands rise green out of the sea . . . and strange things may happen." Cooper has found poetic new fields to plow, and her rendition of the story of a young crofter, his seal bride, and their family is both poignant and imaginatively hopeful. In a comforting turnabout on the familiar theme of parents rescuing children, it's the children in this tale who come to the aid of their mother, and their intuitive caring is rewarded many times over. Hutton's dappled watercolor paintings lend an appealing wistfulness.

The Horn Book Magazine

SOURCE: A review of *The Selkie Girl*, in *The Horn Book Magazine*, Vol. LXII, No. 6, November-December, 1986, pp. 731-32.

The Celtic legend of a seal maiden, who is captured and wed by a mortal young man, is related again by an author who remains faithful to the spirit and magic of the story but gives it a fullness and inevitability that only a true storyteller can evoke. By the time the lad Donallan captures the Selkie—on the one day in the year when she sheds her seal skin and is, for twenty-four hours, a young woman—hints of the story's conclusion have already been given through the prophecy of Old Thomas, who tells Donallan how to capture the girl and warns him "'But a wild creature will always go back to the wild, in the end.'" The girl's ambivalence is clearly defined in the handsome illustrations which portray her affection for her island family and her longing to return to the sea. The watercolors, thinly washed in blues and greens, blend the homely reality of life on a small, seabound croft with a controlled but intense sense of drama through the use of lengthy shadows, varieties of perspective, and the slightly larger than life stature of the central characters. The smoothly told story, well paced to keep the interest high, and the lilting cadence of the language make the retelling an especially fine one, capturing both the beauty and the bittersweet quality of an ancient legend.

Margery Fisher

SOURCE: A review of *The Selkie Girl*, in *Growing Point*, Vol. 26, No. 6, March, 1998, p. 4940.

For *The Selkie Girl* two equal talents have re-created the vital components of the seal-woman legend, hu-

man feeling between opposites and the element of water. Susan Cooper imagines a family where two of the five children of the mixed marriage are sensitive to the mother's nature; when the boy James sees his father examining the hidden sealskin, which must be kept supple, a special dimension for a young reader or listener is added to the universal pathos of the tale. Meanwhile the artist's lucent paintings contrast a sturdy farmer and a wistful woman and set their figures against grassy banks and huge seascapes. Both writer and artist use the idea of an island setting to suggest the isolation of marriage and the private nature of human love while in serene prose and smooth paint the mystery of shape-changing is subtly conveyed.

TAM LIN (1991)

Kirkus Reviews

SOURCE: A review of *Tam Lin*, in *Kirkus Reviews*, Vol. LIX, No. 1, January 1, 1991, pp. 43-44.

Another excellent presentation of the Scottish legend, . . . Cooper makes . . . a feminist point of her heroine's independence, introducing "Margaret" as a rebel who remarks that she is "not a flower waiting to be picked. I would rather do my own picking"—a neat prediction of the act that will introduce her to her enchanted prince; she also omits religious references and makes Tam Lin's symbolic rebirth explicit. Her nicely honed telling is brisk and witty; . . . Hutton's . . . couple could be spotted in any high school, drawn poignantly together, intently plotting their escape from a higher power; misty and authentic, his moonlit Scottish landscapes feed the imgination.

Publishers Weekly

SOURCE: A review of *Tam Lin*, in *Publishers Weekly*, Vol. 238, No. 1, January 4, 1991, p. 71.

With this Scottish ballad, these collaborators present the third episode of their Celtic trilogy, following **The Selkie Girl** and **The Silver Cow.** In Cooper's able hands, the story of how Margaret, a fiery-spirited Scottish princess, saves Tam Lin, a handsome young knight, from the clutches of the Elfin Queen, is molded into captivating shape. Cooper paces the tale well, deftly building to the climactic, magical struggle between Margaret and the Elfin Queen in which Margaret's tenacity—much bemoaned by all the ladies in the castle—carries the day. Unfortunately, Hutton's watercolors are not on a par with Cooper's superb prose. His images here are less distinct than usual, the lines of the figures are awkward and their faces are nondescript. . . . [T]he stirring text makes this version a good choice for reading aloud.

The Horn Book Magazine

SOURCE: A review of *Tam Lin,* in *The Horn Book Magazine,* Vol. LXVII, No. 3, May-June, 1991, pp. 340-41.

Long after minstrels had ceased to wander the countryside, the tales they had sung remained in human memory and were passed along from generation to generation, differing in details from region to region. Thus, when literary antiquarians began to collect ballads, they were faced with a bewildering array of versions. But the ballads remained characteristically full of action, swift and economical in the telling. One of the finest of the supernatural Scottish ballads, "Tam Lin"—or "Tamlane"—incorporates much fairy lore. Susan Cooper's prose rendering, based on several versions, is a beautifully paced literary fairy tale, told and pictured with precision and restraint. Margaret, spirited and defiant daughter of the king, runs to the forbidden wood where dwells Tam Lin, the enchanted knight. There she learns that as a small child the young man was stolen by the elfin queen and that he has ever since been under her spell, which can be broken only by the steadfast love of a mortal maid. On Midsummer's Eve, a night of magic and witchery, Margaret holds fast to Tam Lin while the vengeful queen—her "face lovelier than spring and colder than a winter wind"—transforms him from one terrifying shape to another; but at last all the fairy folk "fly up into the air like a flock of silver birds and vanish into the night." Warwick Hutton is a masterful watercolorist, and his paintings literally and figuratively illuminate the story of faithfulness, heroism, and love. Close-ups lend immediacy to the dramatic action, and panoramic scenes, often with the use of chiaroscuro, convey emotion and establish atmosphere—idyllic, eerie, fearful, and ultimately triumphant.

📖 *MATTHEW'S DRAGON* (1991)

Publishers Weekly

SOURCE: A review of *Matthew's Dragon,* in *Publishers Weekly,* Vol. 238, No. 30, July 12, 1991, p. 65.

In another display of impressive story-telling, Newbery Medalist Cooper recounts Matthew's post-bedtime escapade. As he settles into his pillow, the boy watches the pages of his book open to reveal a dragon with golden scales and eyes like rubies. Matthew becomes as small as this personable creature, and the two slip under the window. After snacking on tomatoes and doing battle with the nasty neighborhood cat, Matthew and the dragon—who grows to be as large as a house—fly high into the sky, where they meet up with "all the dragons ever put into the world of story." Filled with imaginative creatures, incandescent colors and thrilling motion, Smith's paintings of the dragon-crowded sky are truly breathtaking. This is an inspired pairing of author and illustrator.

Kirkus Reviews

SOURCE: A review of *Matthew's Dragon,* in *Kirkus Reviews,* Vol. LIX, No. 14, July 15, 1991, p. 929.

A nifty variant on the theme of a bedtime adventure with a fabulous friend. The dragon comes out of Matthew's book as a miniature. First, Matthew also becomes tiny, and the two explore his own garden and have a terrifying encounter with a cat; then, suddenly growing enormous, the dragon effects a quick rescue and whirls Matthew off to meet a convocation of "every dragon ever imagined" before bringing him home to bed. Smith's paintings make it all seem real—the companionable feast on Dad's tomatoes, the voracious cat, and especially the endearing dragon. Thoroughly satisfying.

Anna De Wind

SOURCE: A review of *Matthew's Dragon,* in *School Library Journal,* Vol. 37, No. 10, October, 1991, pp. 86, 88.

Matthew's mother has just read him a bedtime story about dragons, and he is snuggled down, ready for sleep, when the book begins to glow. Matthew pushes up its cover, and the dragon on the last page sits up and smiles. The young boy arises from bed, becomes as small as the dragon, and the two embark on a nocturnal voyage fraught with danger and delight. The neighbor's cat, a razor-clawed monster who will leave ailurophobes trembling, stalks the pair and almost makes a meal out of Matthew before the dragon snatches him up to safety in the air. There they encounter every sort of dragon ever imagined. In a spectacular double-page spread, the winged creatures glide across the starry sky like exploding fireworks. Distinguished writing and dramatic illustrations make for an attractive package, but the length of the story and the terrifying aspect of the ferocious feline require a one-on-one sharing experience between a child and a trusted adult for optimal enjoyment.

Susan Fromberg Schaeffer

SOURCE: "There's No Escaping Them," in *The New York Times,* November 10, 1991.

[T]he dragon of *Matthew's Dragon* by Susan Cooper emerges from a book, and when he does he is a very tiny dragon, capable of reducing Matthew, the book's owner and hence his master and friend, to his own miniscule size. The two of them proceed from bedroom to garden, where they encounter a suddenly huge world and the neighbor's cat, who is, in comparison to them, immense, frightening and *really* threatening. Wonderfully illustrated by Jos. A. Smith, this book lets the dragon and the imagination soar.

The dragon, (who, for one reason or another, almost always appears in children's books as either an evil force or a protector) here comes to the rescue of his young friend. He grows huge, immense enough to blot out the world, and when, at the end of their adventures, he again shrinks down and returns to his book, we have the sense that the dragon goes back because that is where he *lives,* just as the little boy lives in a house, and that both the boy and the dragon are equally free to roam the world. I believed in this dragon and his penchant for eating cherry tomatoes, and I spent a great deal of time staring at the illustrations of dragon, child, and cat.

📖 *THE BOGGART* (1992)

Kirkus Reviews

SOURCE: A review of *The Boggart,* in *Kirkus Reviews,* Vol. LX, No. 24, December 15, 1992, p. 1570.

In Cooper's classic *The Dark is Rising* cycle, Will Stanton, an ordinary boy, is also one of the powerful "Old Ones" engaged in the age-old struggle against evil. Now, in a long-awaited return, Cooper turns to a different representative of the "Old Magic": a homely mischief-maker. From time immemorial, the invisible Boggart has lived in a Scottish castle, enjoying the sport of teasing and mystifying each new human occupant before settling down to his own peculiar brand of an affectionate relationship. The latest heir is a Canadian theater director, who brings his children (Jessup and Emily) for a brief visit before

the castle is sold. Between long naps in odd corners, the Boggart makes himself known with baffling pranks—inventive but never malicious; when he curls up to snooze in a desk, he's accidentally shipped to Toronto, where he makes some delightful discoveries (pizza, peanut butter) but also tangles with modern technology, which—though it can marvelously enhance his tricks (notably, when he invades the theater's computer-run lights) leads to some dangerously unpredictable results. Cleverly getting into Jessup's computer, he manages to deliver a time-honored message: he wants to go home. A comfortably old-fashioned story, told with Cooper's usual imagination and grace: the Boggart is entrancing—a magically witty mix of fey spirit, comfort-loving cat, old man set in his ways, and child taking gleeful delight in his own mischief—of which there is plenty, all splendidly comical.

Ellen Fader

SOURCE: A review of *The Boggart,* in *School Library Journal,* Vol. 39, No. 1, January, 1993, p. 96.

The Volnik family inherits a rundown old castle on an island off Scotland and visits their new property. After returning home, 12-year-old Emily and 10-year-old Jessup notice strange things happening. Their detective work eventually discloses the cause—a mischievous boggart has accidentally become trapped in a piece of furniture the family shipped home to Canada. Unfortunately, no adults believe them. The children claim innocence on Halloween night as pieces of furniture fly through the air and a bucket of water soaks their mother. Eventually, the boggart's pranks begin to cause serious problems; he becomes intrigued with the power of electricity, and causes a traffic accident that lands Emily in the hospital. Finally, he learns to communicate with the children by computer, causing the message—"I want to go to my own country"—to appear in Gaelic on Jessup's screen. When he gets trapped in a black hole in a computer space-adventure game, the youngsters devise a daring, risky, and ultimately successful plan to help the boggart return home. The novel is fleshed out with numerous, vividly realized secondary characters, including various actors at the Chervil Playhouse, where Mr. Volnik is artistic director, as well as the novel's true villain, Dr. Stigmore, a psychiatrist and a parapsychology scholar who insists that Emily is a troubled adolescent in need of hospitalization. The intelligently thought-out clash between the ancient folkloric creature and modern science guarantees a wide audience. A lively story, compelling from first page to last; and a good bet for a read-aloud.

Rafael Yglesias

SOURCE: "The Gremlin and the Floppy Disk," in *The New York Times,* May 16, 1993.

In *The Boggart,* Susan Cooper plays a tried and true trick. She invents a magical creature that lives by special rules and then humanizes its feelings and circumstances. Her gift for rubbing fantasy and reality together to make storytelling fire has been proved in the much-loved series *The Dark Is Rising.* Here she uses a peripheral part of that imagined world to create her mischievous main character, an Old Thing from the Wild Magic, and brings him into hilarious, tragic contact with our unimaginative civilization.

The Boggart, an immortal, invisible Scottish spirit, has lived in Castle Keep as a companion of the Mac Devon clan for longer than even he can remember, playing the same role with its last resident member as Dennis the Menace does with Mr. Wilson. The Boggart ties shoelaces together while this MacDevon sleeps, finishes off pints of vanilla ice cream, puts spiders on the dog's nose and doesn't like people who have no sense of humor or fun. Unfortunately for the Boggart, people are mortal, and his usually lighthearted state of mind is overwhelmed by sorrow whenever a favorite member of the clan dies. His mourning at the death of the last MacDevon is beautifully realized by Ms. Cooper, rendered without condescension for young readers, who no doubt share the Boggart's baffled pain at the rude cruelty of permanent loss.

At first, it seems lucky for the Boggart when a distant relative of the MacDevons, who lives in Toronto, brings his family to inspect their rundown inheritance. Emily and her younger brother, Jessup, a computer prodigy, explore the castle while their parents fret over whether to sell or rent the white elephant. The Boggart wakes from his grief-stricken sleep, happy at the noise of new children with MacDevon blood. It is inevitable, and delightful, when the Boggart is unintentionally transported in a roll-top desk back to their home in Canada.

Jessup and Emily's world has many new pleasures for the impish spirit. There's peanut butter, hundreds of flavors of ice cream and, most amazing of all, electricity to play tricks on the earthbound. But in a world that depends for safety on the absence of magic, the Boggart's practical jokes are dangerous. He fools with television sets and blenders and only causes confusion. He plays with traffic lights and causes accidents. To the Boggart, there's no difference. Worst of all, he is now living with people who don't believe in spirits, and blame Jessup and Emily for his practical jokes. Even the children take a long time before comprehending that they have the equivalent of an invisible toddler on their hands.

The plot of a mysterious and possibly ancient being befriending modern kids and making trouble in their world will be familiar to any young reader who has seen "Gremlins" or "E.T.," but that doesn't make its working out in *The Boggart* any less suspenseful or, in one lovely scene at a theater in Toronto, surprising and moving. Ms. Cooper's grasp of reality is as firm as her hold on the surreal. Jessup and Emily are convicing, neither sentimental nor unsympathetic to the Boggart once they, and they alone, understand what's going on.

The author does falter briefly by resorting to an implausible and quickly abandoned threat that Emily will be institutionalized by a psychiatrist who has taken Stephen King's *Carrie* too literally. He believes Emily's repressed rage at her mother is causing objects to fly through the air. Ms. Cooper recovers gracefully from that misstep, using the only magic the modern world has to offer: the Boggart inhabits a computer game designed by Jessup, pleads in Gaelic to go home and is shipped back to his castle on a floppy disk.

The inevitable failure of a spirit to coexist with our dreary practical world isn't new theme, although in *The Boggart* it seems fresher than ever. The author's point of view would be utterly persuasive except for the obvious fact that as long as writers with Susan Cooper's skill continue to publish, magic is always available.

Gary D. Schmidt

SOURCE: A review of *The Boggart,* in *The Five Owls,* Vol. VII, No. 5, May-June, 1993, p. 117.

More than fifteen years have passed since the final volume of *The Dark Is Rising* sequence was published, and a full decade since Susan Cooper's last fantasy, *Seaward.* Those eagerly awaiting Cooper's return to this genre will not be disappointed with *The Boggart.* Like her earlier novels, this one fuses the experience of contemporary children with ancient mythic creatures—here the invisible and spirited Boggart, who loves to sleep and make mischief on the inhabitants of Castle Keep.

In despair over the death of the last Scottish owner of the castle, the Boggart has gone to sleep, only to be awakened by the noise and bustle of the castle's new owners, a family from Toronto. They, however, cannot keep the castle and have come only to arrange for its sale. When they ship some of the castle's furniture back to Toronto, the Boggart is accidentally shipped along. Once in Toronto, he finds an entirely new world, and he stays close to the children. Though Jessup and Emily come to recognize his presence, their parents, having grown up in a world where the Old Magic has been discounted, grope for other explanations of the strange tricks being played on the family. It is left to the children to find a way to return the Boggart to his Scottish home, for which he yearns.

The distinction between the scientific realism of the modern world and the imaginative possibilities of the Old Magic dominate the novel, and the successful resolution of the Boggart's dilemma in fact rests upon the successful union of the new technology with the Old Magic. But this is a fragile and tenuous union; those familiar with Cooper's abilities to generate suspense will anticipate the power of her final scenes, where the Boggart must take a chance with what he perceives to be modern magic in order to return home.

Unlike *The Dark Is Rising* or *Silver on the Tree,* *The Boggart* is not dominated by the high seriousness of the quest, or the battle between good and evil. The tone is much lighter and even at times comic. Yet at the same time Cooper is able to make rich distinctions between the bustle of Toronto and the quiet of Scotland, between the new technology and the Old Magic, between imagination and pseudo-scientific pretension. Cooper is able to achieve these different effects by working from the perspective of not only the children, but also the Boggart. The result is a delightful and quick read, with a conclusion perhaps not as high and noble and cosmic as that of *Silver on the Tree* but in its own way just as satisfying and just as complete.

The Horn Book Magazine

SOURCE: A review of *The Boggart,* in *The Horn Book Magazine,* Vol. LXIX, No. 3, May-June, 1993, pp. 330-32.

The Volnik family are overwhelmed by surprise when they inherit a Scottish castle from a hitherto unknown and distant relative. The parents and their two children, Emily and Jessup, fly from their home in Toronto to take a look at Castle Keep. Big and square and very old and very, very inconvenient—no heat, no electricity, no telephone—it sits on a minute island. Although the Volniks are charmed with its long history and picturesque setting, they cannot afford its upkeep. So they send some of the antique furniture home to Canada and put Castle Keep up for sale. However, one of the castle's more notable inconveniences, the boggart—an ancient, mischievous spirit—is inadvertently packed into a desk and arrives at the Volnik's home in Canada upset and annoyed. The boggart is still mourning the death of the previous owner of Castle Keep, who understood the proper relationship between humans and boggarts—humans exist to enjoy boggarts' trickery. But he is hoping that Emily and Jessup will turn out to be suitable partners in his fun. As Emily and Jessup begin to notice the boggart's tricks—teasing the cat, moving small articles, stealing food—they are baffled. The boggart escalates his tricks, thrilled with the possibilities of electricity and other modern conveniences. Some of the tricks are comic in the extreme, but others are so damaging and dangerous that Emily is suspected of causing psychic disturbances. Emily and Jessup finally understand what has happened, and, although now attached to the boggart, realize that he is better off at Castle Keep. In a deeply satisfactory ending, they help him to return to Scotland by using Jessup's remarkable computer skills. The boggart is a fascinating character, sly, ingenious, and endearing—as long as he belongs to someone else. Emily and Jessup and their parents, as well as a host of minor characters, are roundly and believably depicted. But what is most admirable is Susan Cooper's seamless fusion of the newest technology and one of the oldest forms of wild magic.

DANNY AND THE KINGS (1993)

School Library Journal

SOURCE: A review of *Danny and the Kings,* in *School Library Journal,* Vol. 39, No. 10, October, 1993, p. 42.

An improbable story about a boy's single-minded efforts to get a Christmas tree for his younger brother. The main premise—that three truck drivers heading east become the proverbial kings and provide it—is clever. But the execution is shabby, with a static, flat text; forced, hollow dialogue; and a series of unlikely coincidences. First, a classmate who punched Danny at school does an abrupt turnaround and offers to let him dig up a tree in his yard. So, he takes the bus home with this boy, walks home in the dark by himself, and even crosses the highway, where his tree is squashed by one of the trucks. It's very convenient that the truck driver is so concerned, and that Danny goes to a truck-stop cafe with him so willingly. This diner happens to be the very place where Danny's neighbor works. Lovely watercolor illustrations range from impressionistic scenes of falling snow to realistically detailed paintings, but they cannot fill in where the narrative falls short.

Booklist

SOURCE: A review of *Danny and the Kings,* in *Booklist,* Vol. 90, No. 4, October 15, 1993, p. 451.

After Steve punches Danny in the nose over whether the kings were more important than the shepherds in the Christmas play, their teacher settles the issue calmly, saying, "My old granny even used to say that those Three Kings are still traveling the world, carrying presents." Feeling guilty for the punch, Steve gives Danny, whose mother can't afford a Christmas tree, a little tree from Steve's yard. Unfortunately, the tree is smashed by a truck while Danny is dragging it across the highway. Though they give Danny a ride home and take his family to school for the play, the truck driver and his two friends can't stay for the performance. When Danny, his mother, and brother return home, a lovely tree awaits them. In spite of the predictability of the plot, the genuine warmth of the season glows through the smooth text. Snowy winter scenes and indoor views in lovely watercolor paintings enhance the story's emotional feeling. Although Cooper's prose does not equal her compelling novels for middle and older readers, such as *The Boggart* this gentle holiday story wears well.

The Horn Book Magazine

SOURCE: A review of *Danny and the Kings,* in *The Horn Book Magazine,* Vol. LXIX, No. 6, November-December, 1993, p. 722.

Young Danny lives with his widowed mother and little brother Joe in a trailer. Christmas is coming, and Danny is proud to be one of the Three Kings in the school play. But he so much wants to get a Christmas tree for his little brother, although his mother says she cannot afford one. His friend Steve gives

him a little one from his yard, but Danny, walking home through the snow, loses it—and nearly his life—under the wheels of a big truck on the highway. The truck driver, alarmed, takes him to a diner and hears his story, along with two other drivers, all of whom call themselves King of the Road. Danny is a hit in his play, and when he gets home, there is a little tree, bedecked with lights that had been used to decorate the three trucks. This modern version of the celebrated story cleverly carries out the Three Kings theme: the drivers are of three different races and say they are traveling east. A warm-hearted story with warm and glowing Christmas illustrations.

Betsy Hearne

SOURCE: A review of *Danny and the Kings,* in *The Bulletin of the Center for Children's Books,* Vol. 47, No. 6, February, 1994, p. 184.

Okay, so it's February and you should have had this book before Christmas, but some holiday books deserve year-around attention and not many of them feature the elements that make this one so appealing. Danny lives in a trailer near the highway that takes him to school and his mother to work as a truck-stop waitress. They can't afford a Christmas tree this year, and the one Danny's schoolmate donates from a garden gets smashed by a truck. In an old roadside tradition, the truck driver saves the situation, and kids will find here a comforting sense that the value of gifts is all in the giving. It's a down-to-earth story, simply told, that projects feeling without getting too sentimental. The pictures, also, are unpretentious—literal enough to extend the action in closeup interior scenes, but skillfully varied with mysterious landscapes that leave room for magic of human or mythical proportions. At the risk of sounding both sexist and classist, it's hard to find working-class boy-books, so put this one on your Christmas list for next year.

THE BOGGART AND THE MONSTER (1997)

Publishers Weekly

SOURCE: A review of *The Boggart and the Monster,* in *Publishers Weekly,* Vol. 244, No. 7, February 17, 1997, p. 219-20.

The invisible sprite featured in *The Boggart* has all but forgotten his Canadian friends, Emily Volnik and her younger brother Jessup, until the two children revisit their Scottish ancestral estate, Castle Keep, and its present occupant, "Mr. Mac." When Mr. Mac takes them on a camping trip, Boggart, accidentally packed in their gear, finds himself on the shore of Loch Ness, where his cousin, the infamous Loch Ness Monster, broods at the bottom of murky waters, unable to return to his proper boggart shape. While the campers and other spectators (including a news reporter and a scientist) try to track the beast, Boggart is busy trying to raise Nessie's spirits and convince him to leave the loch for his own safety. Wrought with a slightly more somber tone than its predecessor, this sequel brings such human characteristics as compassion, empathy, determination and even speech to trickster Boggart. His and his cousin's conflicts take center stage once the children and Mr. Mac discover the monster's true identity, and readers will have fun with the book's outlandish and suspenseful plot. Again, Cooper adroitly incorporates ancient lore into a contemporary setting while producing an imaginative and compelling tale.

Amy E. Brandt

SOURCE: A review of *The Boggart and the Monster,* in *The Bulletin of the Center for Children's Books,* Vol. 50, No. 9, May, 1997, p. 317.

The Loch Ness Monster is kin to the Boggart. But Nessie had forgotten the shape-changing shenanigans peculiar to boggarts and lies asleep and depressed, in the shape of an immense monster, at the bottom of Loch Ness. Little do Emily and Jessup realize when they befriend a scientist trailing the Loch Ness Monster that they will soon be rescuing the Boggart's more famous cousin from the very same scientist and his computerized gadgetry. Sequels can be tricky propositions, and unfortunately this sequel is more of a proposal than it is a thoroughly developed story. Whereas the Boggart's mischief and the misdiagnosis of Emily's extrasensory abilities were skillfully woven together in the earlier title, this book tends to be disjointed and unconvincing. Many characters (such as friend Tommy's reporter father) and relationships (especially Tommy and Emily's "romance") seem merely stereotypes and plot-fillers, and few are fully realized. While the prose is characteristically Cooper—graceful, vivid, playful—plot contrivances interrupt the flow, including a letter "explaining" the Boggart to the new owner of Castle Keep, the Boggart's sudden propensity toward speech and family ties, and the thrice-squeezed cockleshell aiding Nessie's escape. Nonetheless, the high-speed chase across Loch Ness, suggestive of cops-and-robbers television, deftly illustrates the tension between modern technology and the Boggart's Old Magic. There is also an easy camaraderie between the children, the lawyer Mr. Maconochie, and the Boggart that may satisfy readers enamored of boggartry.

Caroline Ward

SOURCE: A review of *The Boggart and the Monster,* in *School Library Journal,* Vol. 43, No. 5, May, 1997, p. 131.

The mystery of the Loch Ness monster has finally been solved—at least according to Susan Cooper— he's a boggart. In this engaging sequel to the tremendously popular **The Boggart,** Emily and Jessup Volnik are visiting Mr. Maconochie, a retired Edinburgh lawyer who has purchased the Volniks' ancestral home, Castle Keep. At the same time, a group of scientists are about to mount an exhaustive search for the illusive Nessie, utilizing the latest in robot submersibles. When Mr. Mac and his young charges plan a camping trip to Loch Ness, the Boggart, inadvertently trapped in the camping gear, comes too. Nessie, "mattressed on mud and blanketed with slime," has long since forgotten his boggart origins, but the Boggart, feeling a strong connection with his long-lost cousin, is determined to rescue him from the scientists. The explanations of how this all plays out are not as seamless as in the earlier book, and the delightful mischievousness of the Boggart is not maintained when he sentimentally steps out of character to lead his cousin to safety. Nevertheless, these plotting contrivances are balanced by Cooper's exquisite use of language and complex character development. A climactic tour de force, in which the Boggart creates havoc by inhabiting the computer of the remotely operated vehicle, will have young readers cheering. Maintaining suspense until the final pages, Cooper successfully blends technology and ancient beliefs to give readers a fresh spin on Nessie's origins. This entertaining romp can be appreciated as a gratifying fantasy and a thought-provoking story on the nature of freedom and the transforming power of love.

Jim Gladstone

SOURCE: "Magical Mysteries," in *The New York Times,* May 18, 1997.

Susan Cooper's novel **The Boggart and the Monster** occupies an ideal next level of complexity. Full of humor and excitement, this adventure by the author of the classic **Dark Is Rising** sequence of novels, may not offer mirror writing, but it provides plenty of opportunity for reflection. With remote-control submarines, invisible sprites, modern-day dinosaurs and even a pinch of adolescent romance (worry not, cootie-fearing youngsters won't even notice!), Ms. Cooper sets up a provocative elision of technological, natural, emotional and spiritual forces. Not that children will necessarily notice. The story is swiftly plotted and densely populated, zipping along with the speed of a video game.

In a previous volume, the Boggart, the titular Gaelic phantom, traveled with Jessup and Emily Volnik to Canada, where he got caught up in computer mischief. Now, back in the bonny Highlands, the Boggart again becomes a ghost in the machine. In one of this book's most imaginative scenes, the shape-shifting creature infuses himself into a high-tech exploratory device being used to track the Loch Ness monster. From deep in the loch, he transmits images of tulips through the vessel's underwater camera. It's a funny, surreal fusion of the scientific and the supernatural, and it shimmers in the reader's mind.

When your young friends laughingly report to you about the Boggart's mischief making, you might take the opportunity to point out Ms. Cooper's masterly weaving of disparate realms. You might note that the book is unillustrated and that, in fact, the ephemeral Boggart can only be conjured in the mind. You might offhandedly wonder aloud if being spurred to imagine such wonders isn't highly, um, interactive experience.

Additional coverage of Cooper's life and career is contained in the following sources published by the Gale Group: *Authors and Artists for Young Adults*, **Vol. 13;** *Contemporary Authors New Revision Series*, **Vols. 15, 37, 63;** *Dictionary of Literary Biography*, **Vol. 161;** *Junior DISCovering Authors; Major Authors and Illustrators for Children and Young Adults; Major 20th-Century Writers*, **first edition;** *Something about the Author Autobiography Series*, **Vol. 6;** and *Something about the Author*, **Vols. 4, 64, 104.**

Robert Frost
1874-1963

American poet.

Major works about the poet include *Swinger of Birches: A Portrait of Robert Frost* (Sidney Cox, 1957), *The Dimensions of Robert Frost* (Reginald L. Cook, 1958), *Robert Frost* (Lawrence Thompson, 1959), *Introduction to Robert Frost* (Emily Elizabeth Isaacs, 1962), *Robert Frost: A Collection of Critical Essays* (James M. Cox, 1962), *Robert Frost and John Bartlett: The Record of a Friendship* (Margaret Anderson, 1963), *Robert Frost: The Aim Was Song* (Jean Gould, 1964), *Robert Frost: A Backward Look* (Louis Untermeyer, 1964), *Poetry of Robert Frost: An Analysis* (John R. Doyle, Jr., 1965), *Frost* (Elizabeth Jennings, 1966), *Robert Frost* (Philip L. Gerber, 1966), *Frost: The Poet and his Poetry* (David. A. Sohn, 1967), *Robert Frost* (Elaine Barry, 1973), *Robert Frost: A Living Voice* (Reginald L. Cook, 1974), *Robert Frost: The Poet and His Critics* (Donald J. Greiner and Charles Sanders, 1974), *Fire and Ice: The Art and Thought of Robert Frost* (Lawrence Thompson, 1975), *Robert Frost* (Frank Lentriccia, 1975), *Newdick's Season of Frost: An Interrupted Biography of Robert Frost* (Robert Spangler Newdick, 1976), *Robert Frost* (Richard Poirier, 1977), *Frost: A Literary Life Reconsidered* (William H. Pritchard, 1984).

INTRODUCTION

Robert Frost is considered one of the foremost American poets of the twentieth century. His poetry has become so much a part of American culture that lines of it are often quoted with no knowledge of the original context. Although Frost did not write poetry aimed specifically at a young audience, the verses of "Stopping by Woods on a Snowy Evening" and "The Road Not Taken" have become a part of every American's childhood memory. His images were of nature and the life of rural New England, while his themes explored the fundamental questions of human existence and relationships and the topics of fear, confusion, and uncertainty. His hallmark was the use of simple, rustic language to meditate on the mysteries of life.

Frost is particularly noted for his mastery of form and rhythm, through which his poems evoke distinct New England speech patterns. In order to achieve this quality he termed "sound of sense," Frost structured his verse in strict metrical, rhyme, line, and stanzaic arrangements and experimented with conventional forms. His conversational farmer-poet persona and his use of iambic meter were both praised and dismissed by critics. Robert Graves observed, "Frost was the first American who could be honestly reckoned a master-poet by world standards . . . .Frost won the title fairly, not by turning his back on ancient European tradition, nor by imitating its successes, but by developing it in a way that at last matches the American climate and the American language."

BIOGRAPHICAL INFORMATION

Frost was born in San Francisco, but when he was eleven, after the death of his father, his family relocated to Lawrence, Massachusetts, where his grandparents lived. After he finished high school, he briefly attended Dartmouth College, but left to work at a variety of jobs, including teaching, mill work, and newspaper reporting. He self-published a book of his poems and had one poem published in a New York magazine. In 1895 he married Elinor Wylie, his high school sweetheart, and the couple became teachers at the private school established by Frost's mother. In 1897 he entered Harvard University as a special student, but left after 18 months because of illness. Shortly afterwards, Frost's grandfather gave him a farm in Derry, New Hampshire, where the growing family lived for 10 years, and where Frost entered one of the most artistically productive periods of his life.

In 1912, unable to interest conservative American publishers in his work and reduced to publication in obscure journals, Frost moved his family to England, following the example of two other frustrated and innovative American poets, Ezra Pound and T. S. Eliot. In England he continued to write prolifically and met others who were changing the course of literature, among them T. E. Hulme, William Butler Yeats, Ford Madox Hueffer, Edward Thomas, and, of course, Ezra Pound. Pound's review of Frost's first major collection, *A Boy's Will*, published in England in 1913, was the first important review of Frost's work to appear in an American journal. Frost's second collection of poems, *North of Boston*, considered by many critics to be his best, was published in England the following year.

When World War I broke out, Frost moved his family back to America to find that the American edition of *North of Boston* had been published. Supported by reviews from Pound and Amy Lowell, Frost soon became the acknowledged leader of the new poetry. During the next four years he published a third collection, *Mountain Interval* (1916), was elected to the National Institute of Arts and Letters, was named Phi Beta Kappa Poet at Harvard, became a professor at Amherst College, and was awarded the first of his 44 honorary degrees. For the next thirty years he taught part time in many colleges, returning often to Amherst, and lectured frequently at the Bread Loaf Writer's Conference in Vermont. Although he lectured, met with students, and occasionally taught a series of classes, his primary obligation was to write. He won the first of his four Pulitzer Prizes for *New Hampshire*, published in 1923, which contains two of his best known poems, "Stopping by Woods on a Snowy Evening" and "Fire and Ice."

During the last 15 years of his life, Frost was awarded a succession of honors and became a part-time diplomat. In 1954 he was sent to Brazil by the State De-

partment as a delegate to the World Congress of Writers; Vermont named a mountain after him; in 1957 the State Department sent him to London on a goodwill mission; in 1958 he was appointed Consultant in Poetry to the Library of Congress. He was inducted into the American Poet's Corner at the Cathedral of St. John the Divine in 1986, and was chosen Poet Laureate of Vermont by the State League of Women's Clubs. In 1961 he participated in the inauguration of John F. Kennedy as president of the United States by reading his poems "Dedication" and "The Gift Outright," the latter recited from memory because of his failing eyesight. He received the Congressional Gold Medal from President Kennedy in March of 1962. Unfortunately, on his return from an official mission to the Soviet Union in September of that year, he made some thoughtless remarks to the press about American liberalism and alienated the personal regard of the President.

Four months later, nearly 89 years old, Frost died. At his death, the public mourned the poet-farmer, the grandfatherly image that Frost had worked so hard to maintain. When biographers and scholars began to examine the truth of his life—his personal tragedies and failures, his depression and pain—there was much shock and disbelief. Many critics subsequently pointed out that Frost's fear and confusion could be seen clearly in his poetry, but his carefully cultivated persona had created a convincing mask. Frost's poetry stands as a remarkable artistic achievement, and later revelations of Frost's flawed humanity have done nothing to touch his status as one of the undisputed masters of modern American poetry.

MAJOR WORKS

Frost wrote scores of poems, many of them admired for their artistry and many loved simply for what they are. Among his most well known is "Stopping by Woods on a Snowy Evening," in which the speaker is faced with the decision of choosing between the unknown, represented by the wilderness, or the safe, mundane life, represented by the town. The ending is ambiguous, and for decades critics have debated the speaker's actions. Likewise, "The Road Not Taken" is a meditation on the difficulty of deciding on a course of action.

In "Mowing," one of Frost's earliest published poems, the speaker looks at his work in the field as a way of imposing order on the world. "The Mending Wall" is about separateness and community, using the image of repairs to a stone boundary wall. "Fire and Ice" compares humanity's strongest negative emotions to the elements of destruction. Other well known poems are the narratives "Death of a Hired Hand" and "Home Burial," "Birches," "Two Tramps in Mud Time," and the patriotic poem "The Gift Outright." Many critics consider "The Directive" to be one of Frost's best works, in which he speaks of poetry in a religious context as a momentary stay against confusion.

CRITICAL RECEPTION

Although Frost's reputation as a major American poet is secure, some critics express reservations about his artistry, citing such shortcomings as simplistic philosophy, stock sentiments, shallowness, and lack of universality. Most critics, however, praise the imagery, rhythmic qualities, dramatic tension, and synecdochical qualities of Frost's verse, and his poems are among the most widely studied and appreciated in American literature.

AWARDS

Among the many prizes Frost won for his poetry were four Pulitzer Prizes for poetry: for *New Hampshire* in 1924, for *Collected Poems* in 1931, for *A Further Range* in 1937, and for *A Witness Tree* in 1943. He won numerous gold medals, among them a unanimous resolution in his honor and gold medal from the U.S. Senate on his birthday March 24, 1950, and the Congressional Gold Medal in 1962. Other prizes included the Russell Loines Prize for Poetry from the National Institute of Arts and Letters in 1931, the Mark Twain Medal in 1937, the Gold Medal of the National Institute of Arts and Letters in 1938, the Gold Medal of the Poetry Society of America in 1941 and 1958, the Emerson-Thoreau Medal from the American Academy of Arts and Sciences in 1958, the Huntington Hartford Foundation Award in 1958, and the Bollingen Prize for poetry in 1963, just twenty-four days before his death. Frost also received honorary degrees from many colleges and universities.

AUTHOR COMMENTARY

Robert Frost with Richard Poirier

SOURCE: An interview in *Interviews with Robert Frost*, edited by Edward Connery Latham, Holt, Rinehart and Winston, 1966, pp. 229-36.

[Poirier]: When you started to write poetry, was there any poet that you admired very much?

[Frost]: I was the enemy of that theory—that idea of Stevenson's that you should play the sedulous ape to anybody. That did more harm to American education than anything ever got out.

Did you ever feel any affinity between your work and any other poet's?

I'll leave that for somebody else to tell me. I wouldn't know.

But when you read Robinson or Stevens, for example, do you find anything that is familiar to you from your own poetry?

Wallace Stevens? He was years after me.

I mean in your reading of him, whether or not you felt any. . . .

Any affinity, you mean? Oh, you couldn't say that. No.

Once he said to me, "You write on subjects." And I said, "You write on bric-a-brac." And when he sent me his next book, he'd written "S'more bric-a-brac" in it. Just took it good-naturedly.

No, I had no affinity with him. We were friends. Oh, gee, miles away. I don't know who you'd connect me with.

Well, you once said in my hearing that Robert Lowell had tried to connect you with Faulkner, told you you were a lot like Faulkner.

Did I say that?

No, you said that Robert Lowell told you that you were a lot like Faulkner.

Well, you know what Robert Lowell said once? He said, "My uncle's dialect—the New England dialect, *The Bigelow Papers*—was just the same as Burns's, wasn't it?" I said, "Robert! Burns's was not a dialect. Scotch is not a dialect. It's a language." But he'd say anything, Robert, for the hell of it.

I've been asking a lot of questions about the relationship of your poetry to other poetry, but of course there are many other non-literary things that have been equally important. You've been very much interested in science, for example.

Yes, you're influenced by the science of your time, aren't you? Somebody noticed that all through my book there's astronomy.

Like "The Literate Farmer and the Planet Venus"?

Yes, but it's all through the book, all through the book. Many poems—I can name twenty that have astronomy in them. Somebody noticed that the other day: "Why has nobody ever seen how much you're interested in astronomy?" That's a bias, you could say.

Would you agree that there are probably more good prizes for poetry today than there are good poets?

I don't know. I hate to judge that. It's nice for them—it's so nice for them to be interested in us, with their foundations. You don't know what'll come of it. You know the real thing is that the sense of sacrifice and risk is one of the greatest stimuli in the world. And you take that all out of it—take that away from it so that there's no risk in being a poet—I bet you'd lose a lot of the pious spirits. They're in it for the—hell of it. Just the same as these fellows breaking through the sound barrier up there, just the same.

I was once asked in public, in front of four or five hundred women, just how I found leisure to write. I said, "Confidentially—since there's only five hundred of you here, and all women—like a sneak I stole some of it, like a man I seized some of it, and I had a little in my tin cup."

Sounds as if I'd been a beggar, but I've never been consciously a beggar. . . . I've been a beneficiary around colleges and all. And this is one of the advantages to the American way: I've never had to write a word of thanks to anybody I had a cent from. The colleges came between.

Poetry has always been a beggar. Scholars have also been beggars, but they delegate their begging to the president of the college to do for them.

I was suggesting just now that perhaps the number of emoluments for poets greatly exceeds the number of people whose work deserves to be honored. Isn't this a situation in which mediocrity will necessarily be exalted? And won't this make it more rather than less difficult for people to recognize really good achievement when it does occur?

You know, I was once asked that, and I said I never knew how many disadvantages anyone needed to get anywhere in the world. And you don't know how to measure that. No psychology will ever tell you who needs a whip and who needs a spur to win races.

I think the greatest thing about it with me has been this, and I wonder if others think it: I look at a poem as a performance. I look on the poet as a man of prowess, just like an athlete. He's a performer. And the things you can do in a poem are very various. You speak of figures, tones of voice varying all the time.

I'm always interested, you know, when I have three or four stanzas, in the way I *lay* the sentences in them. I'd hate to have the sentences all lie the same in the stanzas. Every poem is like that: some sort of achievement in performance.

Somebody has said that poetry among other things is the marrow of wit. That's probably way back somewhere—marrow of wit. There's got to be wit. And that's very, very much left out of a lot of this labored stuff. It doesn't sparkle at all.

Another thing to say is that every thought—poetical or otherwise—every thought is a feat of association. They tell of old Gibbon; as he was dying he was the same Gibbon at his historical parallels. All thought is a feat of association: having what's in front of you bring up something in your mind that you almost didn't know you knew. Putting this and that together. That click.

Can you give an example of how this feat of association, as you call it, works?

Well, one of my masques turns on one association like that. God says: "I was just showing off to the Devil, Job." Job looks puzzled about it, distressed a little. God says, "Do you mind?" And, "No, no," he says, ("No," in that tone, you know: "No") and so on.

That tone is everything, the way you say that "no." I noticed that—that's what made me write that. Just that one thing made that.

*Did your other masque—**Masque of Mercy**—have a similar impetus?*

I noticed that the first time in the world's history when mercy is entirely the subject is in Jonah. It does say somewhere earlier in the Bible, "If ten can be found in the city, will you spare it? Ten good people?" But in Jonah there is something worse than that. Jonah is told to go and prophesy against the city—and he *knows* God will let him down. He can't trust God to be unmerciful. You can trust God to be anything but unmerciful. So he ran away and—and got into a whale. That's the point of that and nobody notices it. They miss it.

See, the masques are full of good orthodox doctrine. One of them turns on the thought that evil shows off to good and good shows off to evil. I made a couplet out of that for [the rabbis and Jesuits] in Kansas City, just the way I often do, offhand:

> It's from their having stood contrasted
> That good and bad so long have lasted.

Making couplets "off hand" is something like writing on schedule, isn't it? I know a young poet who claims he can write every morning from six to nine, presumably before class.

Well, there's more than one way to skin a cat. I don't know what that would be like, myself. When I get going on something, I don't want to just—you know. . . .

Very first one I wrote I was walking home from school and I began to make it—a March day—and I was making it all afternoon and making it so I was late at my grandmother's for dinner. I finished it, but it burned right up—just burned right up, you know. And what started that? What burned it?

So many talk (I wonder how falsely) about what it costs them, what agony it is to write. I've often been quoted: "No tears in the writer, no tears in the reader. No surprise for the writer, no surprise for the reader." But another distinction I made is: However sad, no grievance; grief without grievance.

How could I, how could anyone, have a good time with what cost me too much agony? How could they? What do I want to communicate but what a *hell* of a good time I had writing it?

The whole thing is performance and prowess and feats of association. Why don't critics talk about those things: what a feat it was to turn that that way and what a feat it was to remember that—to be reminded of that by this? Why don't they talk about that? Scoring. You've got to *score*. They say not, but you've got to score—in all the realms: theology, politics, astronomy, history, and the country life around you.

Do young poets send you things?

Yes, some—not much, because I don't respond. I don't write letters and all that. But I get a little, and I meet them, talk with them. I get some books.

I wonder what they're at. There's one book that sounded as if it might be good, *Aw Hell*. The book was called *Aw Hell*. Because "aw"—the way you say "aw," you know: "Aw, hell!" That might be something.

Most of the titles are funny. One is called Howl *and another* Gasoline.

Gasoline, eh? I've seen a little of it, kicking round. I saw a bunch of nine of them in a magazine in Chi-

cago when I was through there. They were all San Franciscans. Nothing I could talk about afterwards, though, either way.

When you look at a new poem that might be sent to you, what is it usually that makes you want to read it all or not want to read it?

This thing of performance and prowess and feats of association—that's where it all lies. One of my ways of looking at a poem right away it's sent to me, right off, is to see if it's rhymed. Then I know just when to look at it.

The rhymes come in pairs, don't they? And nine times out of ten with an ordinary writer, one or two of the terms is better than the other. One makeshift will do, and then they get another that's good and then another makeshift and then another one that's good. That is in the realm of performance; that's the deadly test with me. I want to be unable to tell which of those he thought of first. If there's any trick about it—putting the better one first so as to deceive me—I can tell pretty soon.

That's all in the performance realm. They can belong to any school of thought they want to, Spinoza or Schopenhauer, it doesn't matter to me.

You once saw a manuscript of Dylan Thomas's where he'd put all the rhymes down first and then backed into them. That's clearly not what you mean by performance, is it?

See, that's very dreadful. It ought to be that you're thinking forward, with the feeling of strength that you're getting them good all the way, carrying out some intention more felt than thought. It begins. And what it is that guides us—what is it?

Young people wonder about that, don't they? But I tell them it's just the same as when you feel a joke coming. You see somebody coming down the street that you're accustomed to abuse, and you feel it rising in you: something to say as you pass each other. Coming over him the same way.

And where do these thoughts come from? Where does a thought? Something does it to you. It's him coming toward you that gives you the animus, you know.

When they want to know about inspiration, I tell them it's mostly animus.

GENERAL COMMENATARY

Ezra Pound

SOURCE: "A Boy's Will," in *Robert Frost: The Critical Reception,* edited by Linda W. Wagner, Burt Franklin & Co., 1977, pp. 1-2.

[This review was originally published in Poetry *in 1913.]*

[*A Boy's Will*] is a little raw, and has in it a number of infelicities; underneath them it has the tang of the New Hampshire woods, and it has just this utter sincerity. It is not post-Miltonic or post-Swinburnian or post-Kiplonian. This man has the good sense to speak naturally and to paint the thing, the thing as he sees it. And to do this is a very different matter from gunning about for the circumplectious polysyllable.

He has now and then a beautiful simile, well used, but he is for the most part [simple]. . . . He is without sham and without affectation.

Amy Lowell

SOURCE: A review of "North of Boston," in *Robert Frost: The Critical Reception,* edited by Linda W. Wagner, Burt Franklin & Co., 1977, pp. 20-1.

[This review was originally published in New Republic *in 1915.]*

Mr. Frost is only expatriated in a physical sense. Living in England he is, nevertheless, saturated with New England. For not only is his work New England in subject, it is so in technique. No hint of European forms has crept into it. It is certainly the most American volume of poetry which has appeared for some time. I use the word American in the way it is constantly employed by contemporary reviewers, to mean work of a color so local as to be almost photographic. . . .

The thing which makes Mr. Frost's work remarkable is the fact that he has chosen to write it as verse. We have been flooded for twenty years with New England stories in prose. . . . [No hint of humor] appears in *North of Boston.* And just because of the lack of it, just because its place is taken by an irony, sardonic and grim, Mr. Frost's book reveals a disease which is eating into the vitals of our New England life, at least in its rural communities.

[We cannot] explain the great numbers of people, sprung from old New England stock, but not themselves living in remote country places, who go insane.

It is a question for the psychiatrist to answer, and it would be interesting to ask it with *North of Boston* as a textbook to go by. . . . Mr. Frost's is not the kindly New England of Whittier, nor the humorous and sensible one of Lowell; it is a latter-day New England, where a civilization is decaying to give place to another and very different one.

His people are left-overs of the old stock, morbid, pursued by phantoms, slowly sinking to insanity.

I have said that Mr. Frost's work is almost photographic. The qualification was unnecessary, it is photographic. The pictures, the characters, are reproduced directly from life, they are burnt into his mind as though it were a sensitive plate. He gives out what has been put in unchanged by any personal mental process. His imagination is bounded by what he has seen, he is confined within the limits of his experience (or at least what might have been his experience) and bent all one way like the wind-blown trees of New England hillsides.

He tells you what he has seen *exactly* as he has seen it. And in the word *exactly* lies the half of his talent. The other half is a great and beautiful simplicity of phrase, the inheritance of a race brought up on the English Bible. Mr. Frost's work is not in the least objective. He is not writing of people whom he has met in summer vacations, who strike him as interesting, and whose life he thinks worthy of perpetuation. Mr. Frost writes as a man under the spell of a fixed idea. He is as racial as his own puppets. One of the great interests of the book is the uncompromising New Englander it reveals. . . . Mr. Frost is as New England as Burns is Scotch, Synge Irish, or Mistral Provençal.

And Mr. Frost has chosen his medium with an unerring sense of fitness. As there is no rare and vivid imaginative force playing over his subjects, so there is no exotic music pulsing through his verse. He has not been seduced into subtleties of expression which would be painfully out of place. His words are simple, straightforward, direct, manly, and there is an elemental quality in all he does which would surely be lost if he chose to pursue niceties of phrase. He writes in classic metres in a way to set the teeth of all the poets of the older schools on edge; and he writes in classic metres, and uses inversions and *clichés* whenever he pleases, those devices so abhorred by the newest generation. He goes his own way, regardless of anyone else's rules, and the result is a book of unusual power and sincerity.

The poems are written for the most part in blank verse, blank verse which does not hesitate to leave out a syllable or put one in, whenever it feels like it.

To the classicist such liberties would be unendurable. But the method has its advantages. It suggests the hardness and roughness of New England granite. It is halting and maimed, like the life it portrays; unyielding in substance, and broken in effect.

Mr. Frost has done that remarkable thing, caught a fleeting epoch and stamped it into print. He might have done it as well in prose, but I do not think so, and if the book is not great poetry, it is nevertheless a remarkable achievement.

Robert Littell

SOURCE: "Stone Walls and Precious Stones," in *Robert Frost: The Critical Reception,* edited by Linda W. Wagner, Burt Franklin & Co., 1977, pp. 58-60.

[This review was originally published in New Republic *in 1923.]*

More than anything perhaps [the title poem of *New Hampshire*] resembles a journey across country in the company of a wise, shrewd, humorous person with an uncommon gift of common speech. . . . And at the end of the journey—or rather when the horse stops, for there is a lot more to see, we have been across a whole state, and overheard a race of men, and been amused, and informed, and disillusioned, and enchanted. The voice which talks to us does so in an easy, unhurried monotone, never dull, never lifted, never strained; now it is speaking prose, now doggerel, now verse, now poetry.

Maybe this is not [all] poetry. But does that matter? Or does it matter very much that so many of Mr. Frost's lines sound as if they had been overheard in a telephone booth. . . .

New Hampshire is just like an old, wandering stone wall. Made of human hands, it rests in the ground, or is partly buried there; it is never the same height in any two places. . . . So bends and wanders Mr. Frost's pithy, moving, garrulous, and invulnerable poem. . . .

Whatever Mr. Frost says, he means. Even his most prosaic lines are intended so to be. . . . His matter of factness in saying just what he means is a part of his virtue of never trying to say more than he means. If he doesn't use as much precious stone as we would like him to, if he uses too many plain ordinary boulders to fill in the chinks, it is because he knows that's the proper way to build his kind of a wall. . . .

[His] restraint, at its worst, verges upon caution; at its best, it produces clear and lovely poetry. Mr. Frost is a perfect example of the difference between reti-cence and reserve. He never holds back true feeling for fear of giving rein to false. He will tell you how fast his heart is beating, but he will not wear it upon his sleeve. . . .

All this applies to the Robert Frost of the title poem and the Notes. The Frost of the Grace Notes is a very different matter. Instead of the leisurely conversational pentameter straying over acres of time and country we have a number of delicate, economical, well-rounded poems, in the good old sense, poems with just and inevitable rhyme, with fragile cadences, with quick turns, with swift changes of mood. The stone wall architect has, in most of these poems, disappeared to give place to a sure and skilful jeweller. It is not so much that in these poems Mr. Frost has turned to another method. He has moved, emotionally, much closer to his subject. He is feeling things in a different way, which requires and inspires a different expression. The author of *New Hampshire* and the author of **"Stopping by Woods on a Snowy Evening"** are the same man, but in the latter case he is expressing emotion and not emotion plus amusement, interest, curiosity all at the same time.

Louise Townsend Nicholl

SOURCE: "New Hampshire," in *American Review,* Vol. 2, No. 6, November-December, 1924, pp. 679-83.

Frost is, I believe, the greatest, most truly major, poet in this country, bringing earth and sky closer than any other poet does, seeing sudden startling significance and holding it. Simple things are mysterious suddenly—and mysteries resolve into the natural, and curve about the earth. And man, who stands between the two, who *is* the two, is clothed with wondering wisdom, with loneliness and humor. That sudden shifting of the simple to the mysterious, the mysterious to the simple, is the unconscious mechanism of magic. Suddenly the absolute is brought near, made almost visible. Some new meaning, terrible and lovely and hardly understood, has been glimpsed, a small hitherto unnoticed piece of life has been set apart, distinctly, for all time.

"Poignant" is a word much overused; it will not do. But what is the word for that pageful called **"The Runaway"**—the poem about the little horse frightened in the growing darkness of his first snowstorm? That colt, out in weather he does not understand, in something which he does not even *know* is weather, maddened by it, wildly, frankly terrified. . . . Deliciously and obscurely the unknown is there, and all baffled conscious life running in circles to escape.

And yet Frost was simply writing about that colt, literally enough, telling exactly how it was, knowing only that or some reason the thing gave him the beautiful, unquenchable desire which poets know, to write a poem. When that desire is there strongly enough, the unknown absolute is there, though the poet himself may not know it until afterward, when he reads the poem over and has the ecstatic recognition of something beautiful and meaning more than he had thought.

No, Frost never sets out to be absolute. In **"A Star in a Stoneboat,"** for instance, he plays with the fanciful, exhausts the relative—is there any aspect of a star being picked up for a wallstone on which he doesn't ring the changes? And yet, at the last, we are left with the pathos, the vaguely intent compulsiveness, of human nature, the smallness of man on the earth under the heavens on a starry night. I wish I could quote it all; I will select:

> Never tell me that not one star of all
> That slip from heaven at night and softly fall
> Has been picked up with stones to build a wall.
> Some laborer found one faded and stone cold,
> And saving that its weight suggested gold,
> And tugged it from his first too certain hold,
> He noticed nothing in it to remark.
> He was not used to handling stars thrown dark
> And lifeless from an interrupted arc.

It isn't all poetry, people say. Great handfuls of it are nothing at all, they say. Well, I know what they mean, of course. Sometimes he doesn't "get going" until the last four lines or so of the poem, as, for instance, in **"The Census-Taker,"** and **"A Fountain, A Bottle, A Donkey's Ears and Some Books."** Personally, I never get dissatisfaction. I do not want him to take those last few lines and begin a lyric with them, as he might so easily do. What he has done he has done because he wanted to, because it was the right way, for him and for the thing he was writing about. It is to me always an adventure to see from what tough rock the flowers were wrested—to know the body of which some few lines are the heart. The two narratives mentioned above are not among the best ones in the book; when his best ones are concerned there can be no dissatisfaction anywhere. For in them he gives a shape to sound, and it is made new to us again that Frost is the poet who pioneered for us, and who is still practically alone, in the field of gathering up the cadences of conversation and letting their music, their sweetness, their inevitable rightness, come forth. Take, for instance, **"The Star-Splitter"** (the Brad McLaughlin poem). Here is the flow of life, the sweet-to-the-taste rhythm of joke and gesture and the hum of quiet existence and country nights. Quoting

will not show what I mean. But take the poem and get comfortable for your reading, and then drink it in. It gets to have the sound of small waves coming in. No other sound, as when one sits thus by the sea, can be imagined good. Take also **"Place for a Third,"** which is more like the narratives in an earlier book, *North of Boston,* in its almost unbearable starkness of New England life. Facts and emotions both are sunk deeply in the ground like rocks—ungarnished, there to stay.

Frost's lyrics are among the most perfect being written. **"Stopping by Woods on a Snowy Evening"** is already almost a classic example of the lyric, although others—**"The Aim Was Song," "Nothing Gold Can Stay," "Fire and Ice,"**—in this book, are also fit to be. **"Stopping by Woods"** has the inexhaustible quality which makes a poem enduring. . . .

The quality which is strong in all real poets of seeing the invisible, the telescope vision, crops out in Frost in many ways. Mysticism the quality might be called. The things he sees are various, but the way he sees them remains the same. He finds in New England, among other things, that strange efflorescence from harsh soil of the superstitious, the fearful, the hectically imagining—as see his witch studies and the legend of **"Paul's Wife."** He finds all beauty suddenly confronting him in that mysterious contact of human and animal consciousness, as in **"Two Look at Two."** . . .

And he sees that strangeness in the human spirit, that conflict between aspiration and some psychic drowsiness which would always hold it back. Perhaps never before has this been quite said, as it is in **"Misgiving."**

The mystery of a real poet, of any real artist, is insoluble; it comes down to the long vision, which connects. As he says in **"I Will Sing You One-O,"** about lying awake at night and hearing the clock strike one, a single stroke which had all the unified universe in it:

> Their solemn peals
> Were not their own:
> They spoke for the clock
> With whose vast wheels
> Theirs interlock. . . .

I can not feel that anyone who kneels at the well of Frost's poetry, unless he kneels entirely "wrong to the light," will fail to see a treasure shining whitely in the depths.

Harriet Monroe

SOURCE: "Robert Frost," in *Poets and Their Art,* revised edition, Macmillan Publishing Company, 1932, pp. 56-62.

[This essay was originally published in 1926.]

Perhaps no poet in our history has put the best of the Yankee spirit into a book so completely, so happily, as Robert Frost. [Ralph Waldo] Emerson, greatest of the early New England group, was a citizen of the world—or shall we say of the other world. [John Greenleaf] Whittier was a Quaker, with something of the Yankee thrift of tongue. [Henry Wadsworth] Longfellow was a Boston scholar, untouched by Yankee humor. [James Russell] Lowell had some of the humor, but he condescended to it, lived above it. Edwin Arlington Robinson came from New England, but his spirit did not stay there and his poetry escapes its boundaries. . . . But none of these is so completely the real Yankee, and so content to confess it in his poetry, as this "plain New Hampshire farmer." . . .

There are three or four facets of this local tang in Mr. Frost's art. One is the rural background—landscape, farms, animals. We have this more or less in all the poems, and specifically in a number—**"Birches," "The Woodpile," "The Mountain," "The Cow in Apple-Time," "The Runaway"** and others. And close to these are the poems of farm life, showing the human reaction to nature's processes—**"Mowing," "Mending Wall," "The Axe-Helve," "After Apple-Picking," "Putting in the Seed"** and others. Then there are the narratives or dialogues presenting aspects of human character: some of them dryly satirical, with a keen but always sympathetic humor, like **"The Code"**; others, **"Snow"** for example, broadly humane and philosophic: a few lit with tragic beauty—**"The Death of the Hired Man,"** the agonizing **"Home Burial,** the exalted and half-mystical **"Hill Wife."** And lastly we have the more personal poems, never brief confessional lyrics of emotion such as most poets give us—here Mr. Frost guards his reserves—but reflective bits like **"Storm Fear," "Bond and Free," "Flower-Gathering,"** or meditative monologues quaintly, keenly, sympathetically humorous, the humor veiling a peering questing wisdom. . . .

The poems of nature and of farm life all express delight, and some are ecstatic. The poet knows what he is talking about, and loves the country and the life. . . . His touch upon these subjects is sure and individual, the loving touch of a specialist. . . . And in the character pieces we feel just as sure of him.

When it comes to personal confession—to autobiography, so to speak—Mr. Frost refuses to take himself seriously. He has to laugh—or rather, he has to smile in that whimsical observant side-long way of his. This mood greets us most characteristically in *New Hampshire,* the long poem which, in painting a portrait, so to speak, of his state, establishes a sympathetic relation with himself, and paints, more or less consciously, his own portrait. That is, he presents a spare, self-niggardly, self-respecting, determined, uncompromising member of the sisterhood of states. . . .

New Hampshire and her poet both have character, as well as a penetrating, humorous and sympathetic quality of genius. They face the half-glance of the world, and the huge laughter of destiny, with pride and grit, and without egotism.

T. K. Whipple

SOURCE: "Robert Frost," in *Spokesmen: Modern Writers and American Life,* Appleton, 1928, pp. 94-114.

In the title-poem of *New Hampshire,* Robert Frost demurs at being thought a local poet: he says that his books are "against the world in general," and that to apply them more narrowly is to restrict his meaning.

This assertion Frost's readers outside New England are inclined to question. True, he is not local in the derogatory sense; he is not provincial. But to say that Frost is not a New England poet would be like saying that [Robert] Burns is not Scottish or that [John Millington] Synge is not Irish. For good and for evil his work is the distilled essence of New England, and from this fact spring both his marked limitations and his unique value. Frost himself, with his belief that "all poetry is the reproduction of the tones of actual speech," must admit that his language is local, that his diction and his rhythms bear much the same relation to the talk of New Hampshire farmers that Synge's bear to the talk of West Irish fisherfolk. But Frost's localism does not stop there: his characters and their life as he pictures it, the natural setting in which they live, the poet himself in his point of view and habit of mind, are all peculiarly local, for better and for worse. Only in so far as New England is not entirely unlike other regions and Yankees are not entirely inhuman, and in so far as poetry of marked excellence appeals to every one, can Frost claim to write for "the world in general."

Frost's district does not cover all New England even; it is confined to the inland, to the hilly farm country. And needless to say, he concerns himself only with the present, not with the New England of witches, Jamaica rum, the slave trade, reform crusades, and elevated philosophizing. His is the New England which most of us know only from the verandas of summer hotels, a land of great natural loveliness, with a sprinkling of uncomfortably quaint natives. . . . strange fragments of forgotten peoples, somehow more remote from us than the Poles and other immigrants who are settling the abandoned farms.

Frost himself, by saying that he writes "against the world in general," intimates that he considers his characters not essentially different from the normal, average run of humanity: but west of the Hudson he will find few to agree with him. To the rest of us, they look like very queer fish indeed. In brief, what ails them is their ingrowing dispositions. Not merely the famous New England reserve: it is a positive lack of frankness, an innate love of indirectness and concealment, which leads them not only to hide their own thoughts and feelings and motives, but to assume, naturally, that others do the same. Out of this tendency grows a suspiciousness, a tortuous habit of mind, which is a constant source of surprise to the more credulous and easy-going alien. To them, an act of kindness which other folk would think the sheerest matter of course seems so unnatural, so momentous, that it must be sedulously concealed. Even more striking is the meanness and the pettiness of these people. Not that they are unfeeling or frigid; on the contrary, they attach an excessive, often a morbid, intensity of feeling to the merest trifles. This makes them touchy, always with a chip on their shoulder, often close to hysterics. Most of them show an extraordinary capacity for dislike, hatred, and contempt—which may explain why New England has been the nursery of so many great reformers. . . .

Apparently, Frost is not so constituted that his reaction to a sense-impression is simple and direct, and in proportion to the force of the impression. His reaction bears no obvious and calculable relation to the stimulus; on the contrary, the relation of cause to effect is unpredictable, perhaps incomprehensible. It is a relation as incommensurate and arbitrary as that between pushing a button and turning on an electric light or ringing a bell. With him it is not only—not, I think, chiefly—sensuous pleasure that counts, but a subtle train of emotion and thought which the perception rouses in his mind. He is devoted to the fact, true—but because the fact is necessary to light the fuses of suggestion in his mind. A birch tree is to him not primarily an arabesque in black and white: it is fraught with hidden import. Conversely, he may be greatly moved by something quite devoid of sensuous appeal—a grindstone or axe-helve or woodpile—because to him it is tinged with hints of meaning that impart a feeling of the mysterious and the wonderful. And this is especially true if the perception is such as to excite the buried savage who sleeps within the most sophisticated of us. Consequently, in such a man's account of what he sees and hears we get sounds and sights not simply as they are, but on the one hand almost denuded of their physical beauty, on the other so transfigured that we see and hear them as it were through the shimmering veil of the more or less vague ideas and feelings which they have served to liberate.

[In] spite of his close observation and minute detail, [Frost] is not a markedly sensuous poet; in fact, he is markedly ascetic. . . . Though Frost deals by preference in the concrete, though his writing abounds in images that are sharp and specific, he does not luxuriate in sensuous gratification, in a frank relish for savor and color and sound. A mere reference to Keats and [Algernon Charles] Swinburne is enough to illustrate this point: there is no "purple-stained mouth," no "cloth of woven crimson, gold, and jet," no "lisp of leaves and ripple of rain" in Frost. Or perhaps the sensuous austerity is more in the expression than in the image itself. He all but eschews the appeal of musical sound, preferring the effect of talk to that of song; such lines as "The slow smokeless burning of decay" are conspicuous by their rarity. In his treatment of feeling also, . . . he is ascetic; his language seldom swells or rises; the emotion is conveyed by implication only, by economy and elimination. Consequently, a reader less abstemious by nature than Frost may make the mistake of thinking him severe and stark, even bleak and bare and cold.

[Frost] tells us little of his philosophy, for he is as chary with his reflection as he is with his feeling, preferring hints and implication to forthright statement. But he tells enough to show that his is a philosophy of attachment, of realization, of intuitive apprehension, of what [Walt] Whitman unpleasantly called "adhesiveness." . . . There can be no doubt of Frost's passion for experience; he calls himself "Slave to a springtime passion for the earth"; and he returns to the theme again and again—at the end of **"Birches,"** of **"Wild Grapes,"** and in his striking lines called **"To Earthward."** . . . He cannot take actuality for granted; he shows an almost bloodthirsty clinging to people and things. He never knows repletion; he is like a hungry man who never gets enough to eat.

How shall this paradox of Frost's asceticism and of his craving for experience be resolved? Would it be too fanciful to liken him to a newsboy gazing into a confectioner's window at Christmas time? Frost sees all the beauties of the world spread before him, but some mysterious agency prevents him from getting at them and absorbing them. . . . Perhaps it is the old transcendental streak which keeps him from a simple, naïve, unreflecting enjoyment of things, which suggests that a bird is not merely a song and a splash of color, but something mysteriously tinged with meaning, and which always sets up an inner experience to vie with, if not to outdo, the outer. . . . Whoever it was told Frost he always saw himself was a discerning critic, though I think it is more accurate to say that he sees the world, not himself, but the world only as reflected in his own temperament, and that, if he could, he would turn from reflections altogether and deal direct with actuality. But in spite of his wishes, the New England reserve, the New England tensity, will no more permit him to abandon himself freely to the world than to pour out his heart in unpremeditated verse. Always in his attitude there is a check or rigor which he cannot let go or relax; he cannot lose himself and be absorbed wholly by experience.

Yet, in trying to account for the vein of austerity which is always in Frost, apparently in spite of himself, I do not wish to overstress it. There is nothing gaunt or famished about him. Rather the reverse: his work, as contemporary American poetry goes, is remarkable for its solidity and completeness. He has come to better terms than most of our poets with his environment, and has had a better environment to come to terms with, and has profited by both circumstances. That may explain why . . . , though the tragedy of frustration is by no means absent from his writing, it is not set forth as the whole or even the norm of human life. Whatever may be Frost's limitations, he gives the impression of a wider and sounder and more many-sided development than that of any other living American poet.

Robert Frost's is preëminently a farmer's poetry. His familiarity with nature and with objects is not, for all his deservedly famous observation, that of the observer or spectator, but that of the man who has worked with them and used them. His acquaintance with them is more intimate and more intuitive than that of the onlooker. A grindstone to him is not a quaint object with rustic associations, but something which has made him groan and sweat; a scythe does not remind him of Theocritus but of the feel of the implement as he has swung it. Blueberries and apples are less connected in his mind with their color or their taste than with the process of picking them. . . . [As a poet] he is still the craftsman and the husbandman; he judges a poem by the same stan-

dards which he would apply to an axe or a hoe or a spade: it must be solid, strong, honest. And his own poetry meets the test, severe though it is.

[Frost's] work, to be sure, is severly restricted by the bonds of his own nature and by the lacks of his subject-matter. His is a poetry of exclusions, of limitations not only in area and in localism, but equally in temperament. . . . He has given us poetry with little music, little delight for the senses, little glow of warm feeling. He has introduced us to a world not rich in color, sound, taste, and smell, a world mainly black and white and gray, etched in with acid in deep shadow and fine lines and sharp edges, lighted with a fitful white radiance as of starlight. His predilection, among natural phenomena, for stars and snow is symptomatic. Even his people are etchings, or woodcuts—droll, bizarre, sometimes pathetic: when we see them crumple up, we know how they can suffer. But somewhere among their ancestors there was a snow man, and his essence runs in their veins, a sharper, keener fluid than common blood, burning and biting like snow water. Yet, like the etchings of the older masters and like the best of modern woodcuts, this poetic world of his has a good three-dimensional solidity. One cannot put one's finger through it.

And it has an even more valuable quality. Frost's poetry is among those useless, uncommercial products of New England which constitute her tenacious charm. It belongs with the silver birches and the bayberry, and it shares their uniqueness. It has the edged loveliness and the acrid relish and fragrance of every growth native to New England earth and air. It is the last flowering of the seeds blown to the Massachusetts coast by the storms of 1620. For it has about it the quality of the final and ultimate; it is an epitome. As perfect in its way as blueberries or wintergreen, what it lacks in nutriment and profusion it atones for like them in flavor. We may look elsewhere for our bread and meat; but nowhere else can we find in all its pungency that piquant aromatic raciness which is New England.

Richard Church

SOURCE: "Robert Frost," in *Eight for Immortality*, 1941. Reprint by Books for Libraries Press, 1969, pp. 27-40.

I am tempted to look upon [Robert Frost] as a major poet. A major poet is one who brings into a language and its poetry a new element of thought and experience, and a new twist of phraseology.

What is this new element which Frost has brought? It is difficult to define, because it is a quality of the man, of his whole personality and outlook on life. It is also something which is *local,* belonging to the people, the stock from which he springs. It is a characteristic of New England Puritanism, and its source may thus be traced back a long way until we find it originating in the Home Country, amongst the Quakers and Wesleyans of the eighteenth century. It is a complicated element (if that is not a contradiction in terms). It is a combination of quietism, piety with its underlying enthusiasm, suspicion of this world and especially of the world of man, self-restraint with its ever-imminent abandonment, humility with its threat of arrogance. There is a negativeness about these forces. They have a sort of dove-grey colour, like the cloak of a Quakeress. But how restful that colour is, how tender, how evocative of the latent beauty of all other hues with which it comes into contact! They represent a whole period of English history. It is that period which included the break away of the American branch, and established a community in New England more emphatic of the same power than the trunk from which it sprang.

Many sociologists to-day believe that this quality of quietism, of exerting authority by means of understatement, is doomed to extinction beneath the flood of barbaric noise brought in by the machine, the radio, and the dictator. I don't believe it. The United States, which is supposed to be the pioneer of latter-day hustle and go-getting, is saturated in this spirit of allusiveness, of understatement, of quiet emphasis. Examine the pages of the *New Yorker,* that hard-boiled humorous journal, and you will find that its technique has much in common with that which Robert Frost accentuated in English poetry thirty-five years ago. It is a native technique: that of the laconic Yankee. . . . Robert Frost is thus a spokesman of his own people. He is probably a more representative American than Walt Whitman. That is why his fame has not been a temporary one. His work needed only to be pointed out to the self-distrustful Americans, and they at once recognized it as something near home, something expressing their own habits, their own point of view, their own reaction to the society which they were still building, and the wild nature which they were still only beginning to subdue and to appreciate.

We all need to get things outside ourselves before we can see them and appreciate them. Robert Frost thus did his people as well as himself a service by leaving home and settling for a decade in Europe. Further, the scenery and the folk of England stirred something ancestral in him, waking his instincts to a fuller consciousness. He strengthened those instincts by means of a fine detachment, which enabled him to objectify the material from which his verse was made, and to give the result a universality without spoiling its local flavour.

[Simplicity] is the quality which most marks him. He has practised it until he can make it convey the most subtle ideas and emotions. . . . It is another aspect of his inherited puritanism; and the other outstanding feature of his work, its marvellous utilization of the laconic, is only another development of this same quality. And the discipline necessary for the constant refining down of a poetic nature to this purpose has added something else to that nature; a gift of humour; a humour wry, dry, sharp, but an eager participant in the process of unifying a personality.

That personality I have always found very much to my liking. There is no other poet to whom he can be compared. . . . Frost seems, for one thing, always to choose the disappearances of human life and of wild nature as symbols to fit his moods. His is the genius of shyness, and its abbreviated gestures may be overlooked by the reader who expects to find the fine exaggerations so common to poetry.

[There is, too, laughter] lurking in this poet's work. It is a serious laughter, folded over tenderness and love, ringing through his poems, toning down the high lights, lifting up the shadows, and intensifying that laconic monotone, at first strange to the ear, which becomes dearer and more entrancing by familiarity. And with this laughter, there trembles a note of passion, and deep understanding of the conflict of mind with heart, of man with woman, of humanity with the forces of life and death.

Laughter denotes detachment, and detachment denotes dramatic sense. Frost has that sense, and he uses it as [Robert] Browning did in a collection of narrative poems, each of which deals with a tense situation that he solves with humour, but sardonic humour that delights in revealing the subtlety of false endings, inconclusive endings, irrelevancies; devices which real life abounds in, but literature is shy of. But Frost loves such implicit criticism of human and natural affairs.

[His philosophy is: reject] nothing; but minimize it, in order to see it more roundly, and to locate it in its place in the chain of endless eventuality. So though his work is so quiet, it is not static. He pretends to step aside, as observer, from the universal mobility. But he also makes poetry out of that pretence. Indeed, it is the source of his laughter.

Malcolm Cowley

SOURCE: "Robert Frost: A Dissenting Opinion," in *A Many Windowed House*, Southern Illinois University Press, 1970, pp. 201-12.

[This essay was originally published in New Republic *in two parts in 1944.]*

We have seen the growth or revival in this country of a narrow nationalism that has spread from politics into literature (although its literary adherents are usually not political isolationists). They demand, however, that American writing should be affirmative, optimistic, not too critical, and "truly of this nation." They have been looking round for a poet to exalt; and Frost, through no effort of his own—but more through the weakness than the strength of his work—has been adopted as their symbol. Some of the honors heaped upon him are less poetic than political. He is being praised too often and with too great vehemence by people who don't like poetry, especially modern poetry. He is being presented as a sort of Sunday-school paragon, a saint among miserable sinners. And the result is that his honors shed little of their luster on other poets, who in turn feel none of the pride in his achievements that a battalion feels, for example, when one of its officers is cited for outstanding services. Frost's common sense and his "native quality" are used as an excuse for belittling and berating all his contemporaries, who have supposedly fallen into the sins of pessimism, obscurity, obscenity, and yielding to foreign influences; we even hear of their treachery to the American dream. Frost, on the other hand, is depicted as a loyal, autochthonous, and almost aboriginal Yankee. We are told not only that he is "the purest classical poet of America today"—and there is truth in Gorham B. Munson's early judgment—but also that he is "the one great American poet of our time" and "the only living New Englander in the great tradition, fit to be placed beside Emerson, Hawthorne and Thoreau."

But when he is so placed and measured against them, his stature seems diminished; it is almost as if a Morgan horse from Vermont, best of its breed, had been judged by the standards that apply to Clydesdales and Percherons. Height and breadth and strength: he falls short in all these qualities of the great New Englanders. And the other quality for which he is often praised, his utter faithfulness to the New England spirit, is hardly a virtue that they tried to cultivate. They realized that the New England spirit, when it stands alone, is inclined to be narrow and rigid and arithmetical. It has reached its finest growth only when cross-fertilized with alien philosophies. Hinduism, Sufism, Fourierism, and German Romanticism: each of these contributed its share to the New England renaissance of the 1850's. . . .

[Frost] is a poet neither of the mountains nor of the woods, although he lives among both, but rather of the hill pastures, the intervales, the dooryard in autumn with the leaves swirling, the closed house shaking in the winter gales (and who else has described these scenes more accurately, in more lasting colors?). In the same way, he is not the poet of New England in its great days, or in its catastrophic late nineteenth-century decline (except in some of his earlier poems); he is rather a poet who celebrates the diminished but prosperous and self-respecting New England of the tourist home and the antique shop in the old stone mill. And the praise heaped on Frost in recent years is somehow connected in one's mind with the search for authentic ancestors and the collecting of old New England furniture. One imagines a saltbox cottage restored to its original lines; outside it a wellsweep preserved for its picturesque quality, even though there is also an electric pump; at the doorway a coach lamp wired and polished; inside the house, a set of authentic Shaker benches, a Salem rocker, willow-ware plates and Sandwich glass; and, on the tip-top table, carefully dusted, a first edition of Robert Frost.

Peter Viereck

SOURCE: "Parnassus Divided," in *The Atlantic Monthly,* Vol. 184, No. 4, October, 1949, pp. 67-70.

Robert Frost's name is rarely heard among the exquisites of *avant-garde*. His poems are like those plants that flourish in the earth of the broad plains and valleys but will not strike root in more rarefied atmospheres. The fact remains that he is one of the world's greatest living poets. Frost, W. H. Auden, Wallace Stevens, and William Carlos Williams are the contemporary poets in America whose styles are most intensely original, most unmistakably their own. Of the four, Frost is the only one to be widely read in terms of general circulation and the only one who has never been adequately subjected to the Higher Criticism of the *doctores subtiles* of the Little Magazines.

On first reading, Frost seems easier than he really is. This helps account both for the enormous number of his readers, some of whom like him for wrong or irrelevant reasons, and for the indifference of the coteries, who become almost resentful when they can find no double-crostics to solve. Frost's cheerfulness is often mistaken as smug, folksy, Rotarian. This fact, plus his reputation for a solid New England conservatism, frightens away rebel youth and "advanced" professors.

In truth, his cheerfulness is the direct opposite of Mr. Babbitt's or even of Mr. Pickwick's. It is a Greek cheerfulness. And the apparent blandness of the Greeks was, as [Friedrich] Nietzsche showed in his *Birth of Tragedy,* the result of their having looked so deeply into life's tragic meaning that they had to protect themselves by cultivating a deliberately superficial jolliness in order to bear the unbearable. Frost's benign calm, the comic mask of a whittling rustic, is designed for gazing—without dizziness—into a tragic abyss of desperation. This is the same eternal abyss that gaped not only for the Hellenes but for such moderns as [Blaise Pascal, Søren Kierkegaard, Nietzsche, Charles Baudelaire, Franz Kafka]. . . . In the case of this great New England tragic poet, the desperation is no less real for being a quiet one, as befits a master of overwhelming understatements. His almost too smooth quietness is a booby trap to spring the ruthless doubt of the following typical Frostian quatrain:—

> It was the drought of deserts. Earth would soon
> Be uninhabitable as the moon.
> What for that matter had it ever been?
> Who advised man to come and live therein?

Let those who consider Frost obvious or superficial brood a bit upon the last line of **"Never Again Would Birds' Song Be the Same."** Consisting only of simple monosyllables yet subtly musical and full of "the shock of recognition," that concluding sentence is perhaps the most beautiful single line in American literature, a needed touchstone for all poets writing today. . . .

A word about his metrics and his diction. Frost is one of the few poets today who dare use contractions like "as 'twere" and "e'er." I don't care for this sort of thing, especially in a poet who makes a point of catching the idiom of everyday speech. But I don't let this annoying anachronism spoil my enjoyment of him. Equally old-fashioned, but this time in a better sense of the word, is the fact that his meters scan with a beat-by-beat regularity, usually in the form of rhymed iambic pentameters. In this connection, do not overlook his thoughtful preface [to **Complete Poems of Robert Frost**] on poetic techniques and meters.

Frost's stubborn conventionality of form makes many young poets and readers think his is also a conven-

tionality of meaning. On the contrary, he is one of the most original writers of our time. It is the self-conscious *avant-garde* rebels who follow the really rigid and tiresome conventions.

James G. Southworth

SOURCE: "Robert Frost," in *Some Modern American Poets,* Basil Blackwell, 1950, pp. 42-87.

Read chronologically, Mr. Frost's poetry, like that of every true genius, reveals the steady and almost imperceptible mutations demanded by inner necessity, not those arising from external causes. Mr. Frost has always been a truly intellectual poet: thoughtful, not bookish; independent, not a mere sounding board for others' thoughts. His intellectual qualities are as apparent in his images, rhythms, and forms as in the rational content. Few poets have ranged wider or deeper in their reading of the great works than he. . . .

One errs greatly to mistake restraint for coldness; or decorum for lack of passion. Mr. Frost's restraint is the natural reserve one associates with persons with generations of New England ancestry. When such persons are able to give freely they can give abundantly. It is no opening of the sluices to let through a trickle. An Englishman could better appreciate Mr. Frost than the American who linguistically is not a part of the small New England area. . . .

In Mr. Frost's earlier work . . . , the sensuous elements dominate but never obscure the rational; in mid-career the sensuous and rational are about evenly distributed; in his [late] work the purely rational gain a decided ascendancy. The emphasis changes, that is all. Both the sensuous and rational elements must be present at the beginning and persist to the end. Perhaps it would be truer to say that the sensuous elements in the later lyrics become subtler, are less of the surface than of the deeps. Since Mr. Frost brought his wares late to market this should be so. A man who publishes his first volume at thirty-seven must bring more than pure sensuousness if he expects to live. Mr. Frost is most sensuous in those subjects where persons are generally so, in their attitude toward love and nature. . . .

He looked for no basic change in the fundamental tenets of his faith, only a greater surety of their truth. . . . The purely contemplative life away from the world, however, was not enough. He knew that man needs man; not, however, as a means of escaping from himself, but as food for his thinking. He needs to observe him in his daily activities, he needs to ponder the meaning of death, and, even more, the aims of life. When these do not suffice, he needs to turn to a bruised plant, the earth, or to look into the 'crater' of an ant. . . . He needs the perspective possible through a telescope and accuracy of facts possible through a microscope, and the tolerance that sometimes comes from politics. Mr. Frost's vision is not restricted to one plane. He has looked up, into, and across others. Because he based his thinking on facts—'the fact is the sweetest dream that labour knows'—he has attained unto wisdom. . . .

Mr. Frost is strongly traditional; although he has little use for tradition as such. He is conservative in the finest sense of the word with a strong mixture of Yankee shrewdness and common sense. Each generation, he believes, must reexamine the customs by which it lives and discard the outmoded ones in order to keep vital those which are sound. . . . Not to do this keeps man from progressing; holds him, in fact, to the mental habits of a dweller in the stone age. This does not mean, however, that the poet believes a person should seize on every new and untried idea that passes by, or that he should discard a belief that happens to be out of fashion. Quite the contrary. . . .

[His] constant insistence on the necessity for vibrant awareness of the immediacy of life here and now and his unwillingness to escape from life constitute much of Mr. Frost's strength. Sensuous beauty may be enough in youth—a kiss from the beloved, a touch of a rose petal on the hand—but maturity (if it is to continue to grow) takes its nourishment from sterner stuff. . . .

There is no pretence at metaphysical profundity in Mr. Frost's poetry. There is only the profundity that springs from his wrestlings with the problems of life. If his answers differ little or only slightly from those found by others to the same questions, their validity is no less. The restatement of these answers in terms that enrich their communication is important. We have not only the ideas themselves, but Mr. Frost's passionate expression of his conviction and joy in those truths, in language that inspires the reader of his poems with a renewed conviction of the timelessness of basic ethical truths. Few modern poets have with so little ostentation assimilated the findings of science. . . .

Adequately to grasp the reaches of Mr. Frost's thought, one must understand his use of nature as metaphor. In the early work his images are drawn largely from the woods. The woods represent his

own inner nature and his withdrawal into them typifies his examination of himself. It is necessary, he repeats over and over, that a person must withdraw himself from the activities of life that absorb so large a part of one's time and make experiences from the sensations accompanying these activities. In his middle years references to the woods are less frequent. In . . . *Steeple Bush,* the metaphors from the woods have almost wholly given way to those drawn from the stars. The poet has turned from the problems of the personal to those of the universal and abstract. No modern poet has made the transition with more graciousness, because no one else possesses in such large measure the saving grace of humour, a humour which laughs through all cant and sham to the basic truths so far as man has yet been able to reach them. . . .

Because of the manner in which Mr. Frost has clothed his conclusions on life, he has at one time or other been called non-intellectual. This is, of course, to misunderstand him and his achievement. He is intellectual enough. As a poet, however, he is aware, as I have mentioned, of the value of colour. He is almost impressionistic in his concern for colour in his work. Because of his insistence on this quality—evident in his images, image-words, rhythms, and prosodic patterns, he achieves a correspondence with the reader otherwise impossible. The majority of his poems have an intellectual idea, but the idea is so transfused with emotion that it becomes knowledge and wisdom rather than cold fact. He knew, too, that wisdom came not so much from books as from an intelligent observation of life. He realized, too, as he grew older that although the colours of a poet's palette may become cooler, the emotion they evoke is no less profound. . . .

Mr. Frost's imagery never gives the impression of being tacked on or borrowed. It springs from his own observations of the world about him and, more frequently than a reader might suspect, from the world of literature, particularly from Shakespeare and some of the Latin poets. Nowhere is the poet's wholehearted absorption in nature more clearly revealed than in his dependence on nature for vivifying an impression from the world of people.

Randall Jarrell

SOURCE: *Poetry and the Age,* Knopf-Vintage, 1953, pp. 26-62.

Besides the Frost that everybody knows there is one whom no one even talks about. Everybody knows what the regular Frost is: the one living poet who has written *good* poems that ordinary readers like without any trouble and understand without any trouble; the conservative editorialist and self-made apothegm-joiner, full of dry wisdom and free, complacent, Yankee enterprise. . . . It is this "easy" side of Frost that is most attractive to academic readers, who are eager to canonize any modern poet who condemns in example the modern poetry which they condemn in precept; and it is this side that has helped to get him neglected or depreciated by intellectuals—the reader of Eliot or Auden usually dismisses Frost as something inconsequentially good that *he* knew about long ago. Ordinary readers think Frost the greatest poet alive, and love some of his best poems almost as much as they love some of his worst ones. He seems to them a sensible, tender, humorous poet who knows all about trees and farms and folks in New England, and still has managed to get an individualistic, fairly optimistic, thoroughly American philosophy out of what he knows; there's something reassuring about his poetry, they feel—almost like prose. Certainly there's nothing hard or odd or gloomy about it.

These views of Frost, it seems to me, come either from not knowing his poems well enough or from knowing the wrong poems too well. Frost's best-known poems, with a few exceptions, are not his best poems at all; . . . [one] can make a list of ten or twelve of Frost's best poems that is likely to seem to anybody too new to be true. Here it is: **"The Witch of Coös," "Neither Out Far Nor In Deep," "Directive," "Design," "A Servant to Servants," "Provide Provide," "Home-Burial," "Acquainted with the Night," "The Pauper Witch of Grafton"** (mainly for its ending), **"An Old Man's Winter Night," "The Gift Outright," "After Apple-Picking," "Desert Places,"** and **"The Fear."** . . . [So] far from being obvious, optimistic, orthodox, many of these poems are extraordinarily subtle and strange, poems which express an attitude that, at its most extreme, makes pessimism seem a hopeful evasion; they begin with a flat and terrible reproduction of the evil in the world and end by saying: It's so; and there's nothing you can do about it; and if there were, would *you* ever do it? The limits which existence approaches and falls back from have seldom been stated with such bare composure.

Frost's virtues are extraordinary. No other living poet has written so well about the actions of ordinary men: his wonderful dramatic monologues or dramatic scenes come out of a knowledge of people that few poets have had, and they are written in a verse that uses, sometimes with absolute mastery, the rhythms of actual speech.

Frost is that rare thing, a complete or representative poet, and not one of the brilliant partial poets who do justice, far more than justice, to a portion of reality, and leave the rest of things forlorn. When you know Frost's poems you know surprisingly well how the world seemed to one man, and what it was to seem that way: the great *Gestalt* that each of us makes from himself and all that isn't himself is very clear, very complicated, very contradictory in the poetry. The grimness and awfulness and untouchable sadness of things, both in the world and in the self, have justice done to them in the poems, but no more justice than is done to the tenderness and love and delight; and everything in between is represented somewhere too, some things willingly and often and other things only as much—in Marianne Moore's delicate phrase—"as one's natural reticence will allow." If some of the poems come out of a cynical common-sense that is only wisdom's backward shadow, others come out of wisdom itself—for it is, still, just possible for that most old-fashioned of old-fashioned things, wisdom, to maintain a marginal existence in our world.

Yvor Winters

SOURCE: "Robert Frost, Or the Spiritual Drifter as Poet," in *The Function of Criticism: Problems and Exercises,* Alan Swallow, 1957, pp. 157-87.

Robert Frost is one of the most talented poets of our time, but I believe that his work is both overestimated and misunderstood; and it seems to me of the utmost importance that we should understand him with some accuracy. If we can arrive at a reasonably sound understanding of him, we can profit by his virtues without risk of acquiring his defects; and we may incidentally arrive at a better understanding of our present culture.

Frost has been praised as a classical poet, but he is not classical in any sense which I can understand. Like many of his contemporaries, he is an Emersonian Romantic, although with certain mutings and modifications which I shall mention presently, and he has labeled himself as such with a good deal of care. He is a poet of the minor theme, the casual approach, and the discretely eccentric attitude. When a reader calls Frost a classical poet, he probably means that Frost strikes him as a "natural" poet, a poet who somehow resembles himself and his neighbors; but this is merely another way of saying that the reader feels a kinship to him and likes him easily. Classical literature is said to judge human experience with respect to the norm; but it does so with respect to the norm of what humanity ought to be, not with respect to the norm of what it happens to be in a particular place and time. The human average has never been admirable, and in certain cultures it has departed very far from the admirable; that is why in the great classical periods of literature we are likely to observe great works in tragedy and satire, the works of a Racine and a Molière, of a Shakespeare and a Jonson, works which deal in their respective ways with sharp deviations from the ideal norm; and that is why literature which glorifies the average is sentimental rather than classical.

Frost writes of rural subjects, and the American reader of our time has an affection for rural subjects which is partly the product of the Romantic sentimentalization of "nature," but which is partly also a nostalgic looking back to the rural life which predominated in this nation a generation or two ago; the rural life is somehow regarded as the truly American life. I have no objection to the poet's employing rural settings; but we should remember that it is the poet's business to evaluate human experience, and the rural setting is no more valuable for this purpose than any other or than no particular setting, and one could argue with some plausibility that an exclusive concentration on it may be limiting.

Frost early began his endeavor to make his style approximate as closely as possible the style of conversation, and this endeavor has added to his reputation: it has helped to make him seem "natural." But poetry is not conversation, and I see no reason why poetry should be called upon to imitate conversation. . . . The two forms of expression are extremes, they are not close to each other. We do not praise a violinist for playing as if he were improvising; we praise him for playing well. And when a man plays well or writes well, his audience must have intelligence, training, and patience in order to appreciate him. We do not understand difficult matters "naturally."

The business of the poet can be stated simply. The poet deals with human experience in words. Words are symbols of concepts, which have acquired connotation of feeling in addition to their denotation of concept. The poet, then, as a result of the very nature of his medium, must make a rational statement about an experience, and as rationality is a part of the medium, the ultimate value of the poem will depend in a fair measure on the soundness of the rationality: it is possible, of course, to reason badly, just as it is possible to reason well. But the poet is deliberately employing the connotative content of language as well as the denotative: so that what he must do is make a rational statement about an experience, at the same time employing his language in such a manner as to communicate the emotion which ought to be communicated by that rational understanding of the particular subject. In so far as he is able to do this, the poem will be good; in so far as the subject itself is important, the poem will be great. That is, a poem which merely describes a stone may be excellent but will certainly be minor; whereas a poem which deals with man's contemplation of death and eternity, or with a formative decision of some kind, may be great. It is possible, of course, that the stone may be treated in such a way that it symbolizes something greater than itself; but if this occurs, the poem is about something greater than the stone. The poet is valuable, therefore, in proportion to his ability to apprehend certain kinds of objective truth; in proportion as he is great, he will not resemble ourselves but will resemble what we ought to be. It becomes our business, then, to endeavor to resemble him, and this endeavor is not easy and for this reason few persons make it. Country conversation and colloquial charm are irrelevant to the real issue. . . .

Frost, then, may be described as a good poet in so far as he may be said to exist, but a dangerous influence in so far as his existence is incomplete. He is in no sense a great poet, but he is at times a distinguished and valuable poet. In order to evaluate his work and profit by it, however, we must understand him far better than he understands himself, and this fact indicates a very serious weakness in his talent. If we do not so understand him, his poetry is bound to reinforce some of the most dangerous tendencies of our time; his weakness is commonly mistaken for wisdom, his vague and sentimental feeling for profound emotion, as his reputation and the public honors accorded him plainly testify. He is the nearest thing we have to a poet laureate, a national poet; and this fact is evidence of the community of thought and feeling between Frost and a very large part of the American literary public. The principles which have saved some part of Frost's talent, the principles of Greek and Christian thought, are principles which are seldom openly defended and of which the implications and ramifications are understood by relatively few of our contemporaries, by Frost least of all; they operate upon Frost at a distance, through social inheritance, and he has done his best to adopt principles which are opposed to them. The principles which have hampered Frost's development, the principles of Emersonian and Thoreauistic Romanticism, are the principles which he has openly espoused, and they are widespread in our culture. Until we understand these last and the dangers inherent in them and so abandon them in favor of better, we are unlikely to produce many poets greater than Frost, although a few poets may have intelligence enough to work clear of such influences; and we are likely to deteriorate more or less rapidly both as individuals and as a nation.

John Ciardi

SOURCE: "Robert Frost: The Way to the Poem," in *Saturday Review,* April 12, 1958, pp. 13-15, 65.

Frost could not have known what a stunning effect his repetition of the last line [in **"Stopping by Woods on a Snowy Evening"**] was going to produce. He could not even know he was going to repeat the line. He simply found himself up against a difficulty he almost certainly had not foreseen and he had to improvise to meet it. . . .

It must have been in some such quandary that the final repetition suggested itself—a suggestion born of the very difficulties the poet had let himself in for. So there is that point beyond mere ease in handling a hard thing, the point at which the very difficulty offers the poet the opportunity to do better than he knew he could. What, aside from having that happen to oneself, could be more self-delighting than to participate in its happening by one's reader-identification with the poem? . . .

[The] human-insight of the poem and the technicalities of its poetic artifice are inseparable. Each feeds the other. That interplay is the poem's meaning, a matter not of WHAT DOES IT MEAN, for no one can ever say entirely what a good poem means, but of HOW DOES IT MEAN, a process one can come much closer to discussing. . . .

Once at Bread Loaf . . . I heard him add one very essential piece to the discussion of how [**"Stopping by Woods"**] "just came." One night, he said, he had sat down after supper to work at a long piece of blank verse. The piece never worked out, but Mr. Frost found himself so absorbed in it that, when next he looked up, dawn was at his window. He rose, crossed to the window, stood looking out for a few minutes, and *then* it was that **"Stopping by Woods"** suddenly "just came," so that all he had to do was cross the room and write it down.

Robert Frost is the sort of artist who hides his traces. I know of no Frost worksheets anywhere. If someone has raided his wastebasket in secret, it is possible that such worksheets exist somewhere, but Frost would not willingly allow anything but the finished product to leave him. Almost certainly, therefore, no one will ever know what was in that piece of unsuccessful blank verse he had been working at with such concentration, but I for one would stake my life that could that worksheet be uncovered, it would be found to contain the germinal stuff of **"Stopping by Woods"**: that what was a-simmer in him all night without finding its proper form, suddenly, when he let his still-occupied mind look away, came at him from a different direction, offered itself in a different form, and that finding that form exactly right the impulse proceeded to marry itself to the new shape in one of the most miraculous performances of English lyricism.

And that, too—whether or not one can accept so hypothetical a discussion—is part of HOW the poem means. It means that marriage to the perfect form, the poem's shapen declaration of itself, its moment's monument fixed beyond all possibility of change. And thus, finally, in every truly good poem. "How does it mean?" must always be answered, "Triumphantly." Whatever the poem "is about," *how* it means is always how Genesis means: the word become a form, and the form become a thing, and—when the becoming is true—the thing become a part of the knowledge and experience of the race forever.

Robert Penn Warren

SOURCE: "The Themes of Robert Frost," in *Selected Essays,* Random House, Inc., 1958, pp. 118-36.

A large body of criticism has been written on the poetry of Robert Frost, and we know the labels which have been used: nature poet, New England Yankee, symbolist, humanist, skeptic, synecdochist, anti-Platonist, and many others. These labels have their utility, true or half true as they may be. They point to something in our author. But the important thing about a poet is the kind of poetry he writes.

In any case, I do not want to begin by quarreling with the particular labels. Instead, I want to begin with some poems and try to see how their particular truths are operative within the poems themselves.

As a starting point I am taking one of Frost's best-known and most widely anthologized pieces, **"Stopping by Woods on a Snowy Evening."** . . . It will lead us to the other poems because it represents but one manifestation of an impulse very common in Frost's poetry.

The poem does, in fact, look simple. A man driving by a dark woods stops to admire the scene, to watch the snow falling into the special darkness. He remembers the name of the man who owns the woods and knows that the man, snug in his house in the village, cannot begrudge him a look. He is not trespassing. The little horse is restive and shakes the harness bells. The man decides to drive on, because, as he says, he has promises to keep—he has to get home to deliver the groceries for supper—and he has miles to go before he can afford to stop, before he can sleep.

At the literal level that is all the poem has to say. But if we read it at that level, we shall say, and quite rightly, that it is the silliest stuff we ever saw.

With [the] first stanza we have a simple contrast, the contrast between the man in the village, snug at his hearthside, and the man who stops by the woods. The sane, practical man has shut himself up against the weather; certainly he would not stop in the middle of the weather for no reason at all. But, being a practical man, he does not mind if some fool stops by his woods so long as the fool merely looks and does not do any practical damage, does not steal firewood or break down fences. With this stanza we seem to have a contrast between the sensitive and the insensitive man, the man who uses the world and the man who contemplates the world. And the contrast seems to be in favor of the gazer and not the owner—for the purposes of the poem at least. In fact, we may even have the question: Who is the owner, the man who is miles away or the man who can really see the woods?

[In the second stanza] we have the horse-man contrast. The horse is practical too. He can see no good reason for stopping, not a farmhouse near, no oats available. The horse becomes an extension, as it were, of the man in the village—both at the practical level, the level of the beast which cannot understand why a man would stop, on the darkest evening of the year, to stare into the darker darkness of the snowy woods. In other words, the act of stopping is the specially human act, the thing that differentiates the man from the beast. The same contrast is continued into the third stanza—the contrast between the impatient shake of the harness bells and the soothing whish of easy wind and downy flake.

To this point we would have a poem all right, but not much of a poem. It would set up the essential contrast between, shall we say, action and contemplation, but it would not be very satisfying because it would fail to indicate much concerning the implications of the contrast. It would be a rather too complacent poem, too much at ease in the Zion of contemplation.

But in the poem the poet actually wrote, the fourth and last stanza brings a very definite turn, a refusal to accept either term of the contrast developed to this point.

The first line proclaims the beauty, the attraction of the scene. . . . But with this statement concerning the attraction—the statement merely gives us what we have already dramatically arrived at by the fact of the stopping—we find the repudiation of the attraction. The beauty, the peace, is a sinister beauty, a sinister peace. It is the beauty and peace of surrender— the repudiation of action and obligation. The darkness of the woods is delicious—but treacherous. The beauty which cuts itself off from action is sterile; the peace which is a peace of escape is a meaningless and, therefore, a suicidal peace. There will be beauty and peace at the end of the journey, in the terms of the fulfillment of the promises, but that will be an earned beauty stemming from action.

In other words, we have a new contrast here. The fact of the capacity to stop by the roadside and contemplate the woods sets man off from the beast, but in so far as such contemplation involves a repudiation of the world of action and obligation it cancels the definition of man which it had seemed to establish. So the poem leaves us with that paradox, and that problem. . . . We must find a definition of our humanity which will transcend both terms.

James M. Cox

SOURCE: "Robert Frost and the Edge of the Clearing," in *The Virginia Quarterly Review*, Vol. 35, No. 1, Winter, 1959, pp. 73-88.

Frost has established himself securely in the position which Mark Twain created in the closing years of the last century—the position of American literary man as public entertainer. Frost brings to his rôle the grave face, the regional turn of phrase, the pithy generalization, and the salty experience which Twain before him brought to his listeners. He is the homespun farmer who assures his audiences that he was made in America before the advent of the assembly line, and he presides over his following with what is at once casual ease and lonely austerity.

Because the popularity surrounding Frost the public figure and hovering about his poetry has become the halo under which admirers enshrine his work, to many serious critics bent on assessing the value of the poetry this halo becomes a sinister mist clouding the genuine achievement.

Yet Frost's success as a public figure, rather than being a calculated addition to his poetic career, is a natural extension of it, and one way to approach his poetry is to see that the character who moves in the poems anticipates the one who occupies the platform. They are in all essentials the same character—a dramatization of the farmer poet come out of his New England landscape bringing with him the poems he plays a rôle in. To observe this insistent regional stance is to realize that Frost has done, and is still doing, for American poetry what [William] Faulkner has more recently accomplished in American fiction. They both have made their worlds in the image of their particular regions, and, moving within these self-contained and self-made microcosms, they have given their provincial centers universal significance. But while Faulkner has concerned himself with establishing the legendary Yoknapatawpha county and its mythical components, Frost has, from the very first poem of *A Boy's Will,* been engaged in creating the myth of Robert Frost, [the one Randall Jarrell calls, "The Only Genuine Robert Frost in Captivity"]. It is a myth with a hero and a drama.

The hero is the New England farmer who wears the mask, or better, the anti-mask of the traditional poet. But it is not a literal mask concealing the poet who lurks behind it; rather, it is a mode of being which releases the poetic personality in the person of a character who lives and moves.

It is Frost's ability to *be* a farmer poet which distinguishes him most sharply from [William] Wordsworth, with whom he is often compared. Wordsworth played the part of the Poet concerned with common man, but Frost has persistently cast himself in the rôle of the common man concerned with poetry. Such a strategy, while it cuts him off from the philosophically autobiographical poetry which Wordsworth built toward, opens up avenues of irony, wit, comedy, and dramatic narrative largely closed to Wordsworth. . . .

The haunting rhythms of **"Stopping by Woods on a Snowy Evening"** express the powerful fascination the woods have upon the lonely traveler, who, in the face of a long journey, descending night, and falling snow, pauses in the gathering gloom of the "darkest evening of the year," transfixed by the compelling invitation of the forest. . . . The poem is *about* the spell of the woods—the traveler's own woods, we want to say, but they are alien enough and belong to someone else enough for him to sense the trespass of his intent gaze into them at the same time he recognizes their sway over him. His heightened awareness

projects his concern for himself back to the representatives of civilization, the unseen owner of the woods and the horse in harness. Thus, the indifferent animal becomes, in his master's alerted imagination, the guardian who sounds the alarm which rings above the whispered invitation.

The poem *is* the counter-spell against the invitation, the act by which the traveler regains dominion of his will. . . . The logic of the rhyme scheme, in which the divergent third line of one stanza becomes the organizing principle of the next, is an expression of the growing control and determination described in the syntax. Thus, the first line of the last quatrain finally *names* the nature of the spell and also provides the term which is answered in rhyme by the poet's decision to refuse the invitation.

Seen in this light, the poem reveals what Frost means when he says that "every poem written regular is a symbol small or great of the way the will has to pitch into the commitments deeper and deeper to a rounded conclusion." . . . The poem in its totality is the image of the will in action, and the poet's spirit and courage convert words into deeds.

John T. Ogilvie

SOURCE: "From Woods to Stars: A Pattern of Imagery in Robert Frost's Poetry," in *The South Atlantic Quarterly,* Vol. LVIII, No. 1, Winter, 1959, pp. 64-76.

Together with **"Birches," "Mending Wall," "The Road Not Taken," "After Apple-Picking,"** and a dozen or so other familiar descriptive pieces, **"Stopping by Woods on a Snowy Evening"** is one of Robert Frost's most admired poems. The beginning poetry student in particular is likely to take to it, for quite understandable reasons: its diction is unpretentious and subtly musical; it presents an engaging picture and hints at a "story" without too much taxing the imagination; it is short and seemingly unambiguous. And the teacher, from his side, likewise welcomes the opportunity to present a poem that can be enjoyed purely for its visual and verbal interest without having to be subjected to a rigorous search for "hidden meanings." But, as experienced readers of this poem know, **"Stopping by Woods"** has a disconcerting way of deepening in dimension as one looks at it, of darkening in tone, until it emerges as a full-blown critical and pedagogical problem. One comes to feel that there *is* more in the poem than is given to the senses alone. But how is one to treat a poem which has so simple and clear a descriptive surface, yet which somehow implies a complex emotional attitude? To what extent and in what ways is one's experience of the poem different from, or the same as, the poet's experience? Can one's "feeling" about the poem be either proved or disproved, when so few footholds for interpretation are offered by the poem itself? Is *any* interpretation bound to be the result of "reading in" meanings of one's own?

These questions are too delicate to be acted upon hastily. Certainly, to construe the poem, as some critics have, as expressing a "humanistic" or "agnostic" view of life, or as projecting an unconscious "death-wish," is to impose a pretty heavy burden upon so brief and unassuming a lyric. Although it would be a mistake wholly to reject these interpretations, nevertheless it is unlikely that any one of them can be established as a conclusive reading solely on the evidence of the single poem. **"Stopping by Woods,"** I believe, represents one of those junctures where the critic must enlarge on his findings through searching comparisons with other of the author's productions. Taken in isolation, **"Stopping by Woods"** gives only a partial view (and for some readers possibly a misleading view) of what is actually an absorbing and central concern in Frost's poetry. The collaboration of a number of related poems is required to reveal this preoccupation in its entirety.

The visible sign of the poet's preoccupation—the word is not too strong—is the recurrent image, particularly in his earlier work, of dark woods and trees. Often, as in the lyric with which we have begun, the world of the woods (for such in effect it becomes), a world offering perfect quiet and solitude, exists side by side with the realization that there is also another world, a world of people and social obligations. Both worlds have claims on the poet. He stops by woods on this "darkest evening of the year" to watch them "fill up with snow," and lingers so long that his "little horse" shakes his harness bells "to ask if there is some mistake." The poet is put in mind of the "promises" he has to keep, of the miles he still must travel. We are not told, however, that the call of social responsibility proves stronger than the attraction of the woods, which are "lovely" as well as "dark and deep"; the poet and his horse have not moved on at the poem's end. The dichotomy of the poet's obligations both to the woods and to a world of "promises"—the latter filtering like a barely heard echo through the almost hypnotic state induced by the woods and falling snow—is what gives this poem its singular interest. If its "meanings" were more overt, it would be less interesting, less an authentically conveyed experience. The artfulness of **"Stopping by Woods"** consists in the way the two worlds are established and balanced. The poet is aware that the woods by which he is stopping belong to someone in the village; they are owned by the world of men. But at the same time they are *his,* the poet's woods, too, by virtue of what they mean to him in terms of emotion and private signification. . . .

In the lyrics of *A Boy's Will,* woods and trees foster a mood of youthful yearning and romantic furtiveness. In later poems, however, the mood perceptibly darkens. In **"The Sound of Trees"** and **"Misgiving,"** for example, trees and leaves are associated with thwarted desire. As they are swayed by the wind, their sound and motion suggest to the poet a longing to get away; but "a sleep oppresses them as they go" and they end by remaining, vaguely stirred, where they are. The poet himself desires the freedom to make "the reckless choice," to "set forth for somewhere," but by association we are led to believe that he will not do so. Though they are less congenial to him now, he will stay with the trees. In a still later poem, **"Bereft"** (*West-Running Brook,* 1928) leaves and wind conspire to remind the poet of his painful isolation. . . .

When reading through the *Complete Poems* (1949), one can see that at some undefined point in Frost's mid-career—roughly with *West-Running Brook* (1928) and *A Further Range* (1936)—his orientation begins to shift. He becomes more the "neighborly" poet who chats at length with his readers about the issues of the day, and less the objective dramatist and self-exploring lyricist of the earlier books. He becomes more outspoken about himself and about the world of men. He projects himself into the "further ranges" of politics, science, philosophy, education, and theology. "Ideas" as such become more important to him than the individual persons and objects of nature, the "specimens" of concrete life, so lovingly collected in *North of Boston* and *Mountain Interval.* The very manner of voice changes. Metaphorical indirection gives way to explicit generalizations. The forms of satirical discourse and epigram are introduced to convey his opinions more directly. The poet's old game of hide-and-seek is still evident but now is carried on more by means of a bantering verbal irony (e.g. **"A Drumlin Woodchuck"**).

Marion Montgomery

SOURCE: "Robert Frost and His Use of Barriers: Man vs. Nature toward God," in *Robert Frost: A Collection of Critical Essays,* edited by James M. Cox, Prentice-Hall, Inc., 1962, pp. 138-50.

The casual reader of Frost's poetry is likely to think of Frost as a nature poet in the tradition of Wordsworth. In a sense, nature is his subject, but to Frost it is never an impulse from a vernal wood. His best poetry is concerned with the drama of man in nature, whereas Wordsworth is generally best when emotionally displaying the panorama of the natural world. "I guess I'm not a nature poet," Frost said . . . in the fall of 1952. "I have only written two poems without a human being in them."

[We] may recall the epitaph Frost proposes for himself in **"The Lesson for Today"**: "I had a lover's quarrel with the world." This lover's quarrel is Frost's poetic subject, and throughout his poetry there are evidences of this view of man's existence in the natural world. His attitude toward nature is one of armed and amicable truce and mutual respect interspersed with crossings of the boundaries separating the two principles, individual man and forces of the world. But *boundaries* are insisted upon. . . . [Even in moments of affinity, or "favor,"] we shall always find the barriers which cannot be crossed. . . . Man is never completely certain that the earth, the natural world, returns his love.

From the publication of *A Boy's Will* down to the present time Frost has indicated a realization that nature, *natura naturata,* not only will, but sometimes seems intended to, hurt those who love it. The immediate natural world even seems to be moving toward chaos, intending to take man along with it if he isn't careful. But man has an advantage. . . . To sustain such injuries as nature inflicts "It's well to have all kinds of feeling, for it's all kinds of a world." And Frost expresses his all kinds of feeling toward the natural world. . . . [At] times he writes of the natural world in a cavalier fashion which Wordsworth would consider heretical. "You know Orion always comes up sideways," he says in **"The Star-Splitter,"** and he pokes fun at the seasons in **"Two Tramps in Mud Time."** It is no spirit of nature which sends Frost's rain or wind; he never sees in the natural world the pervading spirit which Wordsworth saw. . . . Frost makes his attitude toward nature clear when he says in **"New Hampshire"** that "I wouldn't be a prude afraid of nature," and again rather flatly, "Nothing not built with hands of course is sacred."

Frost at times speaks directly to objects in nature, as Wordsworth did. But what is high seriousness in Wordsworth is fancy or humor in Frost. Frost goes on at length in a Polonius-to-Laertes speech to his orchard, which he is leaving for the winter. Watch out for the rabbits and deer and grouse; they will eat you. And if the sun gets too hot before the proper season, you won't be bearing next summer. The final word is "Goodby and Keep Cold.". . . . [Even in] instances of direct address, . . . we never suppose that Frost feels the kind of brotherhood for natural objects that Wordsworth expresses through much of his poetry.

Always, to Frost, man differs essentially from other features and objects. . . . [There] is motion of natural objects and not emotion, human simile but not human feeling. In **"A Considerable Speck"** Frost says, after examining the microscopic creature, "Plainly with an intelligence I dealt." And in **"Departmental"** he seems to be interpreting the ants in human terms. But we make a mistake if we suppose that he would ascribe mind to the "microscopic item" in the first poem or human behavior to the actions of the ants in the second. The truth is that in each of these poems Frost is preparing the way obliquely for direct statement. In **"A Considerable Speck"** we have the final "No one can know how glad I am to find / On any sheet the least display of mind." And **"Departmental"** ends with the comment on the ants, "How thoroughly departmental." In the more direct poem, **"The Bear,"** we find "The world has room to make a bear feel free; / The universe seems cramped to you and me." Whenever Frost talks directly to or directly of natural objects or creatures, we feel that he is really looking at man out of the corner of his eye and speaking to him out of the corner of his mouth. In all these poems Frost is describing the animal and vegetable natures in man, not reading man's nature into the animal and vegetable worlds, as Wordsworth was inclined to do.

If Frost feels, as he seems to, that the natural world is impersonal, unfeeling, and at best animal creation, what does he think of its creator? In his early poetry he, like the people he refers to in **"The Strong Are Saying Nothing,"** holds his silence. He does not choose to make any sweeping statements about God any more than he does about nature or man. This has occasioned the belief among some critics that Frost is at best agnostic.

Frost's hesitancy in speaking dogmatically on the subject of the supernatural is due more to his acceptance of man's limitations and the acceptance of mystery in existence than to agnosticism. . . . He is quite ready to believe that which is appealing *if* it is also reasonable. Then he will express opinion. At the same time he is not willing to discard completely the appealing if it fails to be reasonable, knowing the fallibility of reason. He rather reserves judgment. Experience comes early, understanding later.

In his later years Frost, feeling more sure of what he thought was true, has spoken more freely of his views of God, as of man and the natural world. An indication of his broadening scope appeared in his book *A Further Range,* published in 1936, and finally, he has come to devote two of his latest works, *A Masque of Reason* (1945) and *A Masque of Mercy* (1947), to the question of man's relation to God. In *A Masque of Reason* Frost attempts to justify God's ways to man, which justification is that none is necessary. In this work Frost presents God in a rather familiar fashion, and this presentation of a somewhat undignified God has occasioned difficulty for many readers.

But Frost's presentation of a cavalier God is a deliberate device which points up the theme of the masque. . . . In this picture of God given in *A Masque of Reason* he is showing us not lack of reason or justice in God, but rather man's stubbornness and lack of understanding. It is like man, especially in our day, to see God "pitching throne with a ply-wood chair." It is like man to exclaim with Job's wife, "It's God. I'd know him by Blake's picture anywhere." As it has been the human error to read man into nature, so is it the human error to read man into God: and Frost's poem, satirical in its shrewd observation on this human fallibility, is concerned with this problem. Is man's reason sufficient to overcome the wall between himself and God? Job and Job's wife are after a rational explanation of man's predicament which will clarify everything and bridge the gap between the finite mind and the infinite. The theme of the poem, then, is that understanding is dependent not only upon reason, but upon faith as well, a faith which helps the finite mind accept the mystery its reason will not completely explain.

To Frost, the mindless world, despite its laws and patterns of cause and effect, lacks completeness. **"There Are Roughly Zones,"** the title of a poem says, but understanding man is created so that he may try to make the world complete. Man's hands and mind bring order to himself to the world around him. Having all kinds of feelings for this all kinds of a world, he is able to bring order to the natural world "by making a garden and building a wall. That garden is art." And the man who erects the wall and makes the garden is in the world for that purpose, not that he may expect to bring permanent order but that he may work out his own salvation. Frost's consistency in this view from early to latest publication is shown by the two masques and by a poem from his first publication, *A Boy's Will.* **"The Trial by Existence,"** which appeared in *A Boy's Will,* suggests that it is futile to attempt a complete explanation of why there are so many difficulties to prevent man's taking in and building his garden in the world. Man's real virtue, it argues, is to dare, to seek to

build the wall which allows the garden to flourish for a time. Frost concludes that it is not important in the final reckoning whether or not one has actually succeeded in erecting a great or small wall or in raising a great or small garden; man is not measured by his works.

Man, like Job, continually repeats, "The artist in me cries out for design," and design man tries to discover. The barrier between creator and created is maintained. God will not let man see completely into the life of things. To this barrier are added the limitations imposed on man by his reason, or mind, and his desire, or heart. Yet reason and desire arouse the complementary faith which helps man accept his situation and grow from that point of acceptance. For here is true understanding in man, the recognition through reason, and acceptance through faith, of man's limitations and of the belief in God as "that which man is sure cares, and will save him, no matter how many times or how completely he has failed," as Frost said in 1916.

Frost considers this would be a pretty desperate and meaningless situation but for man's own ability to erect and destroy barriers. . . . This concern with barriers is the predominant theme in Frost's poetry. The barriers fall into several categories. First of all there is the great natural barrier, the void between man and the stars, a barrier which man continually, and sometimes foolishly, tries to bridge in his attempt to escape his limited haunt. The very stars, because of their remoteness, reduce man if he confuses distance and size with his own nature.

But the remoteness of the stars is also something which man may lean his mind on and be stayed. What is more disturbing to man than the barrier of space is the barrier between man and the immediate natural world, for it is in this realm of desert places that most of man's "gardening" takes place. This is where the "breathless swing between subject matter and form" becomes most apparent. And it is the struggle in this sphere which reveals what men are.

Wordsworth in his early poetry tended to deny all barriers in his effort to become one with the great moving spirit of things, the soul of the world. He wanted to achieve the "abstract high singular" that Job's wife disparages in Frost's masque, to concern himself with the general idea rather than with the physical world. His approach was transcendental in that he denied the existence of barriers. For Frost there can be no such simplification of the problem of spirit and matter. Despite the necessity of maintaining one's garden against nature and of advancing it, there are certain limits which man cannot overstep, and one of them is the nature of physical existence. Frost has made no Platonic crosscuts to separate form and matter as Wordsworth did between 1798 and 1805. Existence is form plus matter to Frost, and any conflict in the world is conflict between such existences—form-and-matter man against form-and-matter world.

There is a fourth category of barriers in Frost's poetry—those between man and man. To Frost these barriers serve as framework for mutual understanding and respect. It is because of barriers that we understand each other, and, far from striving to tear them down as is the modern tendency, Frost insists on recognizing them. He even builds them wherever they seem necessary. The conflict caused by friction of personal barriers, "human nature in peace and war," is the subject of his most dramatic poetry.

The reader might suppose from ["**Mending Wall**"] that Frost does not particularly hold with the need for fences, but note that it is the narrator who "lets his neighbor know" when time comes to do the work. The narrator questions the necessity of the wall in an effort to make the neighbor think and come out of the darkness of mind he is walking in. Both men know that good fences make good neighbors, but only one of them knows why or that the wall is more than a barrier between neighbors. Something in the world doesn't like a wall between a man and the world or between a man and his neighbor. Something wants all walls down so that individual identity may be destroyed. The wise person knows that a wall is a point of reference, a touchstone of sanity, and that it must be not only maintained but respected as well.

Man's tendency, once he has brought what he understands as form to the semichaos of his world, is to try also to impose the form he understands on the mind of his fellow-men—to insist that they see as he sees. Since each man is an individual intended to discover his individuality by revealing or restoring order through his peculiar art—whether that art be the splitting of birch logs, the making of ax-helves, or the writing of poems about these activities—one thing he must remember: each man reveals form which is indwelling in the material with which he works. There are roughly zones which limit man's gardening, his restoration of order in his own image. The wood which the ax-helve is made from has its grain, and the artist reveals form within the limitations of that grain. If he does his job well, the ax-helve will bend in use without breaking. All the helve-maker may

boast of is his ability to reveal the form he has discovered in a particular piece of wood; his understanding of the form and his dexterity in revealing it mark his accomplishment. But when man imposes what he thinks should be the form of an ax-helve on a piece of wood whose grain will not allow the form, the first solid whack will split the finished helve. By showing the difference between a good and a bad helve, the French Canadian in "**The Ax-Helve**" argues against one man's imposing what he finds himself to be upon another man. The Canadian, it finally appears, is arguing that his children ought not to be forced to go to public schools where they will have themselves ground down to a form which is not in their nature.

Frost's view of man's nature, then, is consistent throughout his poetry. Each man is, in a sense, a stranger in this world, and so he remains. His is not to question why he is alone or why the world seems to be against him. He is to begin the breathless opening and closing of the mind, the hand, the heart, the eye upon the world, growing as he does so. As he grows he understands himself more, and as he understands himself he also understands more of the world and of his fellows. With understanding comes love which makes him respect the chaos of the world with which he is in conflict, the material with which he works. The same love makes him respect and accept differences between men also. He respects others' individual differences and expects that others will respect his. And he knows that those differences are not to be overcome by the "tenderer-than-thou // Collectivistic regimenting love / With which the modern world is being swept" ("**A Considerable Speck**"). That would be to reduce man to a numerical and animal problem, to make him no more than the other creatures who share the world of nature with him. . . . Scientific man has made so bold as to demonstrate the infallibility of natural laws and then has proceeded to measure himself against them. As long as there was man's fallibility, as long as he could bow to natural law, there was some distinction in being man.

In arguing man's distinction, Frost will not go to the two extremes offered by the philosophy of Plato on the one hand or the science of Democritus on the other. He will not accept pure spirit or idea as an explanation of man and a way out of the universe, nor will he accept the scientist's materialism measured with microscope and telescope as an alternate. Unhappy man tries both like a bear in a cage [in "**The Bear**"]:

He sits back on his fundamental butt
With lifted snout and eyes (if any) shut,
(He almost looks religious but he's not),
And back and forth he sways from cheek to cheek,
At one extreme agreeing with one Greek,
At the other agreeing with another Greek.

Once more [in **"A Masque of Mercy"**] Frost affirms that what is most important is the courage and not the accomplishment, the attempting and not successful completion. . . . St. Paul, the spirit of the New Testament, finally convinces Keeper that man is saved only by God's mercy, which man receives for having labored under injustice, his inability to overcome completely the barriers imposed upon him and the temporal nature of those barriers which man himself may erect. This is the only way to man's salvation, for if he had not labored thus his limitations would not allow that salvation. To Frost, God is still "that which man is sure cares, and will save him, no matter how many times or how completely he has failed." . . . Justice, Frost says, is only to the deserving, but mercy is for the underserving. And those who demand justice because of the limitations imposed upon them will receive justice; those who with courage in the heart move toward understanding through faith and reason may expect God's mercy.

Babette Deutsch

SOURCE: *Poetry in Our Time,* revised edition, Doubleday, 1963, pp. 65-8.

The people about whom [Frost] writes are usually of New England stock, folk who cultivate their rocky acres with stubborn courage and bear, until they break, the drudgery and isolation of their lot. His subjects are the common-places of the countryside: apple-picking, hay-making, the sleep of an old man alone in an old farmhouse, the cleaning of the pasture spring. His diction is simple and colloquial. . . . In the many instances where Frost allows some rural figure to speak for himself, his lapses into his own mannerisms are few. These dramatic monologues are spoken by people who might be his kindred or his neighbors. There is verisimilitude in their diction, whether the person speaking is the farmer who sees no reason for mending the wall between his apple orchard and his neighbor's pine grove; the farm woman whose mad uncle was housed in a home-made cage in the attic and who dimly senses his fate crawling toward her; the man and wife to whose kitchen the incompetent worn-out hired hand comes "home" to die; or either one of the middle-aging pair whose removal from the city to a farm invites scrutiny of the rewards of more than one

way of life and a glance at the chilling shadows that encroach on each. Frost has about as much to say of happy wooings and matings, of friendly encounters and generous neighborliness, as of the bleaker aspects of farm life. . . .

Frost's poems repeatedly remind us that the central fact in nature for himself and his kind is human nature. However interestedly he may observe such impersonal things as storms and stars, he is apt to relate his observations to some insight into humanity. Mankind has consecrated the earth for him, both as a poet and as a tiller of the soil. "Nothing not built with hands of course is sacred," he asserts. The hermit of Walden, for all his aloofness, would have understood what the poet meant. Certainly Frost's poetry, like Thoreau's prose, reveals not only an unshakable independence but also an intimate knowledge of the bases of existence ignored by the city dweller and a loverly patience with and delight in the natural scene. . . .

Frost's remoteness from things urban, his acceptance of the traditional forms, obviously ally him with the Georgians. Like that British group, he is closer to Wordsworth and John Clare and to the Dorcetshire poet of rural life, William Barnes, then to his contemporaries. . . . For the most part this verse ignores such features of contemporary life as the city and the slum, as it evades our confusions and anxieties. In this respect it differs markedly from poetry written after World War II by men who are again willing to employ traditional forms, to speak without raising their voices, to evoke the homely interior and the suburban scene.

Robert Graves

SOURCE: An introduction to *Selected Poems of Robert Frost*, Holt, Rinehart and Winston, 1963, pp. ix-xiv.

Frost was the first American who could be honestly reckoned a master-poet by world standards. [Edgar Allan] Poe, Longfellow, Whittier, and many more of his American predecessors had written good provincial verse; and Whitman, a homespun eccentric, had fallen short of the master-poet title only through failing to realize how much more was required of him. Frost has won the title fairly, not by turning his back on ancient European tradition, nor by imitating its successes, but by developing it in a way that at last matches the American climate and the American language.

Frost has always respected metre. When, during the *Vers Libre* period of the Nineteen Twenties and Thirties his poems were disdained as old-fashioned, he remarked disdainfully that writing free verse was like playing tennis without a net. The *Vers Librists,* it should be explained, had rebelled against a degenerate sort of poetry in which nothing mattered except getting the ball neatly over the net. Few games are so wearisome to watch as a methodical ping-pong tennis match in which each player allows his opponent an easy forehand return from the same court. The *Vers Librists,* therefore, abandoned the tennis-net of metre altogether, and concentrated on rhythm. But though metre is boring without rhythm, the reverse is equally true. A rhythmic manipulation of metre means—in this tennis metaphor—so placing your shots that you force the other fellow to dart all round his territory, using backhand, forehand, volley or half-volley as the play demands. Only the 'strain of rhythm upon metre' (Frost's own phrase), makes a poem worth reading, or a long rally in tennis worth watching. That you can't achieve much in poetry without, so to speak, a taut net and straight whitewashed lines, is shown by the difficulty of memorizing free verse; it does not fix itself firmly enough in the imagination.

Frost farmed for ten years among the well-wooded hills of Vermont. The four natural objects most proper to poems are, by common consent, the moon, water, hills and trees; with sun, birds, beasts and flowers as useful subsidiaries. It is remarkable that, among the ancient Irish, Highland Scots and Welsh, from whose tradition (though at second or third hand) English poetry derives most of its strange magic—the Muse was a Moon, Mountain and Water-goddess, and the word for poetic literature was always 'trees.' Bardic schools were built in forests, not in towns; and every letter of the alphabet had a tree name. Frost's most haunting poems, such as **"The Wood-Pile,"** **"Birches,"** **"An Encounter,"** **"Stopping by Woods on a Snowy Evening,"** are set in woods. The moon floats above, and water rushes down from every hill. The farmhouse in the clearing—unless it is staging one of those poignant country dramas which are his specialty—provides him with a convenient centre from which to saunter out and commune in thought with the birches, maples, hickories, pines, or wild apples. . . . Among trees, you are usually alone, but seldom lonely: they are companionable presences for those in love and, although Frost seldom uses the word 'love,' all his poems are instinct with it.

He reminds us that poems, like love, begin in surprise, delight and tears, and end in wisdom. Whereas scholars follow projected lines of logic, he collects his knowledge undeliberately, he says, like burrs that stick to your legs when you walk through a field. Surprise always clings to a real poem, however often it is read; but must come naturally, cannot be achieved by the cunning formula of a short story or detective thriller.

One good way of judging a particular poem . . . is to ask yourself whether the package contains anything irrelevant to its declared contents, and whether anything essential has been left out. I admit that even Frost lapses at times into literary references, philosophy, political argument and idle play with words: yet has any other man now alive written more poems that stand up to this packaging test? His chief preoccupation is freedom: freedom to be himself, to make discoveries, to work, to love, and not to be limited by any power except personal conscience or common sense.

Though Frost owns to the growing materialism of the United States, which stultifies the Founding Fathers' prayer for courage and self-control among those destined to occupy the land, he refuses to lament bygone times. The land, the tools, and the language are all still available, and he has himself proved how nobly they can be used. . . . A great part of the countryside has been scheduled for industrialization and, as everyone tells me, this is a critical, rather than a creative, age. But give thanks, at least, that you still have Frost's poems; and when you feel the need of solitude, retreat to the companionship of moon, waters, hills and trees. Retreat, he reminds us, should not be confused with escape.

Richard Eberhart

SOURCE: "Robert Frost: His Personality," in *Of Poetry and Poets,* University of Illinois Press, 1979, pp. 179-201.

[This essay was originally delivered as a speech in 1964.]

While Frost was integrated with what might be termed the rural life of his times, and wrote a sort of elegant pastoral, there is a question whether in future his relevance to the whole of life will increase or diminish.

[Perhaps] in the future Frost's vision will be pushed farther back in the past, in a sense, than would be expected, and he will be considered as dated and fixed to his times by the year 2000 as Longfellow is now for the most part only considered in relation to his times. This is a guess. A further guess is that a poet of comparable size in the near future, or in the far future, must be one who speaks not of country things, but holds a mirror up to the central doings, the goings and comings, the preoccupations and hazards of an almost totally urbanized population.

One reason why Frost is almost universally admired is that he believed in this world. He is skeptical of any other. He celebrates the possibilities of life as it is, its large and rich resources. . . .

When you read and make part of your consciousness and knowledge of life many of his poems, you may agree to a generalization that Frost stands firmly in this world and that his poems deal with an astute knowledge of others as well as of himself. He wants each of his poems to be in some way dramatic. He often told his audiences to note how different they are one from another. While he has deep personal lyrics, such as **"Stopping by Woods on a Snowy Evening,"** Frost never lets himself go in a piercing, self-revelatory, Romantic way as Gerard Manley Hopkins did.

Frost is a different kind of poet. His self-revelations are temporal and are embedded in poems showing human situations. He is not a confessional poet in the sense that Hopkins is a totally confessional one. Hopkins is committed to the Christian view. Frost is a secular poet, functioning and thriving in a Christian society.

Frost loved man as well as things. He does not turn away from mankind but speaks for it in some way in every poem. His great popularity is due in part to the love of life and of man, imperfect as they are. All readers can share in varying ways with this sympathy and this human understanding.

Frost was not a Platonist. He refused consciously throughout a lifetime to use the word "beauty" in his poetry. He was rooted in the here and now, the actual and the real, and it is easy to see that Frost belongs in the Aristotelian camp. He was not, of course, like Aristotle. Aristotle, while being almost everything else as a thinker, was not a poet. But Frost was also not at all like Shelley. It might be interesting for a moment to compare them. Shelley plucked poetry out of the air, as it were. He was protean, fertile, variable, quick, malleable. Frost is nothing like this. His poetry is rocklike, not ebullient; quiet, not wild; factual, not hallucinated; solid, not evanescent; relevant to things, not creating a dream world; rational, not irrational; well tempered, incapable of what the Greeks called divine frenzy; plausible, not an extremist; well grounded, not aerial; given to quatrains, couplets, and other set forms, not inventing new measures; recording man deep and sure, not strange and high.

The remarkable thing is that throughout his long, fruitful life Frost was able to write so many masterful poems, so consistently, and with so little deviation from the central excellence of his early work. He modestly said that he only wanted a few poems that men will not wish to get rid of; the few are, in fact, many. And no doubt men will be saying them "ages and ages hence." It may be that some of his attraction lies in the fact that urban man longs to remember a closer association he had with nature. . . . Certainly some of his attraction lies in the rare ability he has of appealing both to unsophisticated and to sophisticated readers of poetry. He cuts across all classes, is a classless poet. Children and young students can understand him; at the same time he appeals to the most learned men in many professions due to the subtlety of his thought. He is at once simple and profound. He has great range of interest and great breadth of technical resource. I have indicated repeatedly that his natural bias is in favor of this world; he engages us totally in what is commonly known and felt to be reality, and this may be his greatest gift. He is more of a realist than he is an idealist, as he is more a localist than an internationalist. But let me philosophize.

The brutal fact is that no man knows whether there is anything beyond death. This is a prime baffling fact of existence. Let us suppose that there is nothing to life but appearance, nothing to death but the appearance of death and therefore obviously no life after death. If this is the true state of things, then Robert Frost's poetry becomes more valuable than if this were not true. The fact that we do not know adds to the fascination of his ideas and to the potency of the poetical charge of his poems. For then we will have to admire him for his robust stronghearted resistance to any idea of life after death. We will have to salute him for persistent doubt.

However, a deep idea in the world is that there is something beyond it; a deep look at appearance will see right through it that there is something behind or beyond the realm of appearance; an idea as ancient and persistent as man is that there are ultimate mysteries beyond our mortality, that God exists, that there may be life after death. One generation of men rules that there can be no life on any other planet, another generation holds that the mathematical probabilities are that there must be life beyond what we can see.

There are notions of eternal recurrence in Oriental religions, the notion of Redemption in Christianity. If these ideas are true, if reality is not in appearances, but must include what does not appear, and if reason is not the highest faculty of man, but intuition is, then we are at liberty to adjust the value we set on Frost's poetry according to our own most intimate values.

Societies have a natural way of preserving their own images in literature. Frost is one of the vital poetic spokesmen of our time. Our society and our culture are sufficiently like his presentation of the meaning of life so that many Americans can read him with conviction.

Robert Frost is large in scope. He teaches us courage in the face of the enigmas of existence. We feel that he wears no mask and speaks the truth directly, and that his truth, if not the whole truth, is worthy of our serious, steadfast, and continuing love.

W. W. Robson

SOURCE: "The Achievement of Robert Frost," in *The Southern Review,* Vol. 2, No. 4, Autumn, 1966, pp. 735-61.

Frost's colloquialism is famous. It is also notorious, for in his anecdotal poems he can sometimes sink to an unparalleled flatness. But critics have sometimes misrepresented this quality of his work by overstatement, seeing in it the whole of his innovation. This does not do him justice. The most casual reader sees that Frost is colloquial; reading which is more than casual brings out how much of the "archaic" and "literary" language of traditional poetry he has retained. Thus no one familiar with Frost's work will find ["**The Silken Tent**"] uncharacteristic; yet to call it "colloquial" misdescribes it. So far from being the anecdotal jotting down of some incident of New England rural life, or a piece of gnarled rustic wisdom or country sentiment, it is a gracefully sustained literary fancy which (one might be inclined to say) could have come from an accomplished traditional poet. . . . [At first the poem] seems to belong with "literary" poetry; in its diction, syntactical organization, and structure—the careful and explicit working out of the central idea—it is obviously a "thing made," not a "happening," like a jewel, not like a pebble or a snowflake, as so many of Frost's typical poems seem to be. But "going slightly taut"—that is one's feeling about the poem: it is the reminder of the poet's formal control which here brings into un-

usual prominence Frost's usual firm grip on the sensory facts which provide the notation for his graceful compliment and comment; so that this delicate, consciously elaborated sonnet is, after all, of a piece with the most rugged of his poems. Frost's is a manner which can accommodate the literary and the artificial as well as other modes.

Frost's technical innovation is a notable one, guaranteeing him a place in the history of poetry. A question that naturally arises is how far it was solely *his* innovation; and a related question, whether it should be regarded primarily as an American contribution to the poetry of the common language, or seen more in the terms of English poetic history. It would be ludicrous to deny that Frost's poetry is American poetry, not only in its manifest subject matter, but in more impalpable qualities. But, as often, the definition of "English" as opposed to "American," in literary matters, is not simple. Notwithstanding the debt which American readers may perceive Frost to owe to Edwin Arlington Robinson, it seems clear that the development we note between the bulk of the poems in **A Boy's Will,** and the poems in **North of Boston,** has a vital connection with the work and study in which Frost joined with English poets in England. It was in the course of this association that Frost acquired a knowledge of other poetic experimenting, and a confidence in his own discovered "voice" in poetry, which enabled him in the long run to exert an influence and attain a status denied to the isolated poet of Gardiner, Maine. What seems unquestionable is that Frost, in whatever other ways American critics may want to describe him, cannot be considered altogether apart from the Georgian phase of English literary history. . . .

The question he cannot avoid is whether Frost has ever written a really considerable poem. This is not very different from the question whether he is a great poet; but a critic might be discouraged from asking that question, partly no doubt because of the vagueness of the category, but in the main because of Eliot's authoritative insistence, over the years, on the relative unimportance of surmises about "greatness" in comparison with considerations of "goodness" or "genuineness." Yet it seems a reasonable condition even of the good and genuine poet that he shall have a poem to offer us. The search for it surely takes precedence over the historical inquiry (in itself of some interest) how the "Georgian" poet of 1914 developed into the candidate for the status of American national poet—vacant since Whitman—which was urged for him when it began to be felt that Carl Sandburg somehow would not do. No amount of national appeal, country charm, regional flavor, or anecdotal personality can be a substitute for a poem; it is only in the world of the higher publicity and literary fashions that "poems," "poetry," a general poetical atmosphere, appear to compensate for the absence of a "Sailing to Byzantium," a "Cimetière Marin," a *Four Quartets.*

But it may be objected that Frost is not the kind of poet who invites description in terms of single masterpieces: that his claim to distinction is the impressive level maintained in a large body of work. In that case the question may be put in a different form, while remaining in essence much the same: what has he to say? what is the substance of his poetic achievement? And when we turn our attention to that question the frequent embarrassment of Frost's commentators is ominous. . . . But what is troubling, as we explore their commentaries, is the thinness which he and other writers on Frost seem to sense in their subject matter, and their apparent need to import some density into it by paraphrasing Frost's thought and considering Emerson, Thoreau, and a cultural tradition and habit of sensibility deriving from them. Of course this embarrassment of the commentators may reflect no more than the unsuitability of modern critical techniques, influenced by modern poetic fashions, to get hold of so traditional and unfashionable a poet. The kind of ironies, ambiguities, or "polysemy" to which those techniques are adapted—and which indeed, in some poets of academic provenance, they may have actually inspired—are not there. Nor is Frost the kind of poet congenial to erudite exegetes; he has not constructed an esoteric world system, or a scheme of private allusions; there is no code to be broken. To be an adequate critic, it would seem, all you need is a heart and feelings and a capacity for independent thoughts about your life and your world; ingenuity and tenacious industry are not only not enough, they are irrelevant and distracting. Hence the plight of the commentator. But to take this line is to come dangerously near the position of those admirers who have institutionalized our poet, removed him from the talons of criticism, by insisting (in effect) that the scope of his achievement is no more open to rational discussion than the goodness of maple syrup. This kind of protectiveness really insults him. Frost's work may well require a different critical approach or procedure from that appropriate to discussion of Yeats's, Eliot's, or Valéry's; but the same final considerations of value, substance, and interest are as relevant in appraising it as to theirs. . . .

The characteristic difficulty readers have with Frost is not "What does he mean?" but "What is the *point* of it?" Why has he chosen to crystallize *this* perception, rather than countless others? This kind of difficulty, it will be remembered, presented itself strongly—perhaps it still does—to Wordsworth's readers. But Wordsworth's little anecdotes, even if they do not always carry the charge of significance Wordsworth himself found in them, can be better understood in the context of Wordsworth's whole work—in the poems (by far the greater number) in which the poet speaks directly, not dramatically, sets out to communicate explicitly his thought or "message." Now Frost too speaks directly in the greater part of his poetry. And it will hardly be disputed that the quintessence of his work—his rarest and finest achievement—lies in the lyrical-reflective pieces in which he speaks with his own personal voice. But it is in that "personal" work also that we are most conscious, not only of limitations, but of weaknesses.

His principal weakness—the one that makes for the most doubt about his claim to high poetic rank—is monotony. This may be attributed in part to the very nature of his gift. What is represented by **North of Boston,** the achievement praised so warmly by Thomas and Pound, is of a kind that could be represented in comparatively few poems. How much of Frost's whole corpus (we cannot help asking) do we really need? His work calls out for anthologizing, as Wordsworth's, I think, does not. No one will doubt that Wordsworth wrote a great many mediocre poems, or worse, but we have to have *The Prelude,* and much else, before we can form a fair estimate of him. Frost's distinction seems only notably present in a few poems. His average—to speak bluntly—is rather dull. Johnson observes of Dryden that "he that writes much cannot escape a manner"; but "Dryden is always *another and the same.*" This could hardly be said of Frost, at least of the later volumes.

For there are dangerous temptations in a colloquial style, and Frost has often succumbed to them. The chief danger is self-indulgence. So far from making an effort to "escape a manner," he rather cultivates it. Old age can be the extenuation of much of the writing in **Steeple Bush,** where he seems at times to be maundering. But the same tendency can be observed in earlier work; Frost, like Hardy, seems to be a poet who, once he had formed his manner, stuck to it: there is no such technical (or personal) development as we find in a Rilke or an Eliot or a Yeats. This is both his strength and his weakness.

Arthur M. Sampley

SOURCE: "The Myth and the Quest: The Stature of Robert Frost," in *The South Atlantic Quarterly,* Summer, 1971, pp. 287-98.

Frost's conception of man's relation to an unpredictable universe is one which should especially appeal to men in the twentieth century. At a time when old values are being attacked by the thinking and unthinking alike, when the belief in God as the director of individual man's destiny is being questioned in theological as well as in secular circles, when the future seems filled with ominous perils which statesmen in their candid moments admit that they frequently lack the wisdom to avert, then Frost's myth of the individual dodging, at times retreating, but never cowering has a special appeal for men facing an uncertain and perilous world. Independence and courage such as Frost teaches may indeed have survival value.

The Times Literary Supplement

SOURCE: "Bad and Best," in *The Times Literary Supplement,* October 19, 1973, p. 1278.

The main difficulty in assessing, as in enjoying, Robert Frost is the extreme interdependence of his poetic virtues and vices. The agricultural canniness-within-canniness, the cracker-barrel philosophizing and the manly-coy flatness of tone yield so many dead acres it comes hard to admit these very qualities produce the best of the crop. And the best is so extraordinarily good, while so similar in *persona,* verse-method and aim, as to make the reader doubt whether the worst can be quite as bad as he thinks. Yet surely it is.

Which is not to say that Frost is a poet who does one thing either marvellously well or abysmally badly. He is a versatile writer, not only exploiting narrative, dramatic, lyric and argumentative forms in a wide variety of ways but accomplishing a multiplicity of effects. For instance, in addition to the major lyrics, **"The Death of the Hired Man"** is surely one of the best short stories of the century, **"The Witch of Coös"** and **"Paul's Wife"** important contributions to ghost and science fiction, and **"To Earthward"** a love poem that in tenderness, reach and music ranks with the best of the age. . . . [Views] have always been sharply divided on the point where the Frostian virtues, over-indulged, descend into self-caricature. . . . At [an] extreme of opinion on Frost's colloquial method is Yvor Winters's Johnsonian pronouncement that since poetry is very obviously not conversation, there is no virtue in its being conversational. That, in Frost's case, is surely wrong; his folksy tone may dilute and deaden longer poems, and it certainly makes for some heavy-handed satire, but it works to marvellous effect in many of the lyrics, especially when riding in unlikely harness with a very different sort of language: his own brand of high romantic rhetoric.

In a similar way Frost's craggy pragmatism and determinedly no-nonsense pose coexist with a habitual and unreigned mysticism. . . .

[Another] vulgarization that turns good Frost into bad [is] the over-exploitation of his genuine (and considerable) charm, the determination to please at all costs. The eagerness to displease is so prevalent in contemporary poetry that one feels Frost might be pardoned his more agreeable weakness; nevertheless it is a cloying defect and something more than that. . . .

[Ian Hamilton contends in the introduction to *Selected Poems*] that Frost, by hogging the stage with his honest-to-goodness homely old wiseacre act, obscured—and deliberately obscured—his true, unbeautiful and superbly treated subject. Whether or not Mr. Hamilton is entirely right in this (however phoney the *persona,* is it not often put to remarkable poetic uses?), he is surely correct, with Lionel Trilling, in identifying that subject as the terminal desolation of life, the futility at the root, with the poet "yearning for the conditions to be otherwise." At the still centre of Frost's world is a terrifying blankness, caught unforgettably in such pieces as **"Acquainted with the Night," "Neither Out Far nor In Deep"** and that extraordinary poem, **"The Most of It."**

Richard Poirier

SOURCE: *The Atlantic Monthly,* April, 1974, pp. 50-5.

[In] trying to place Frost in our cultural history, it is important not to lose sight of the most evident peculiarity of his career: unlike many of his great contemporaries in poetry—Yeats, Lawrence, Stevens, and Eliot—Frost was from the start a truly popular poet. Before he belonged to the profession of criticism, he belonged to the general public. He still does. It would be presumptuous, if it were even possible, to say that the Frost who enthralled readers and listeners across the nation was mostly a kind of front, that there is a "real" Frost underneath who can be reached only by those able to stand the pressures of supposedly uncharted depths. . . .

The attention [Frost asks for] is quite alien to the kind of reading we have been habituated to by most twentieth-century poetry and by most twentieth-century criticism of it. Usually, by close inspection of metaphors or of tones of voice, by recognition of philosophically or psychologically structured images, the reading moves gradually outward, the poem is expanded, techniques are translated into meanings. The line between the poem and mythology gradually becomes blurred; drama and voice become at last little more than a pretext—in a literal sense of that word.

Frost is a poet who obstinately resists that process. It's not too much to say that he writes *against* the disposition—poetic, critical, human—just described. This reluctance to reward the kinds of attention to which readers of Yeats and Eliot had become accustomed—quite aside from whether it ever gave a good picture of either Eliot or Yeats—would by itself be enough to make him both popular and unfashionable. But to compound the difficulty, the rewards Frost does offer require, I think, an even more strenuous kind of attention. Once you have decided, that is, to look for the remarkable power hidden behind the benign-ironic masks of his personality, you discover that Frost is quite without gratitude for small favors. He makes you work very hard indeed, simply to find out how much he's denying you by way of large significances. He will not let you have him as a poet in the style of Eliot or of Yeats; he will not let you even discuss him in the same terms. So that while, in the care you lavish upon him, you find yourself resolutely treating him like a very great poet, he is just as resolutely disqualifying the terms normally used to describe one. . . .

Frost, more than Eliot, is pleased enough with momentariness, with his quite extraordinary satisfaction in the poem as a human performance, in the poem as an exemplification of how to perform in the face of the confusions of life or the impositions of authority, including literary authority.

It is this that makes Frost so unique and his genius so hard to account for. It can only be accounted for by the most precise notation of *how* he performs, of how he momentarily achieves a stay in particular poems and particular lines, even particular feet. It is as if the world of other people and of things, including again other poets and poems, existed in a sound which is not his and to which he will succumb if he does not fashion a sound of his own. Each poem is an act of such confrontation starting from scratch and with a chance of his losing. In poem after poem, all that is other than himself is identified by sound, either seductive or threatening, either meaningful or brute. There is the sound of the wind and the rain, of trees in their rustling, of the scythe in the field, the cry in the night, the beating on a box by a lonely old man, the movement of a beast, the song of birds, the voice of a lover or her silence.

It is a commonplace of romantic poetry, this obsession with sound and its possible clues, with silence and its promise of visionary afflatus. But nowhere is the person who is vulnerable to these sounds and silences so often characterized not as a common man but as the common man who is a poet, a "maker" of poetry. . . .

Reuben Brower offers a good comment on **"Mowing"** when he says: "In feeling reverence and love in the common thing and act Frost renews the Wordsworthian sympathy between man and his world, but he does so in a decidedly American accent. The higher value for Frost is pragmatic, the fruit of action is *in* the moment."

The action *in* the moment is not only the acting dramatized by the poem but the poem itself as an enactment, an act of "earnest love." Many of the early poems, wherein I think one finds some of the psychological and structural source of all Frost's poetry, are about the relation of love to poetic vision and poetic making, of "making" it in all those senses. And they are also poems about sound and the danger of being silenced by failure in love. . . .

[The] biographical material doesn't tell us as much about the man as the poetry does. By that I mean that the poetry doesn't necessarily come from the experiences of his life; rather the poetry and the life experiences emerge from the same configuration in him prior to his poems or to his experience. Sex and an obsession with sound, sexual love and poetic imagination partake of one another, are in some sense the same. As he observes in **"The Figure a Poem Makes"** (again note that sense of the poem as an action, as not merely a "made" but a "making thing"), "The figure is the same as for love." And as he continues, the metaphors, without his even having to intend it, so central is the identification of making love and making poems, assume a peculiarly sexual suggestiveness. . . .

Hayden Carruth

SOURCE: "Robert Frost," in *Parnassus: Poetry in Review,* Spring-Summer, 1975, pp. 35-41.

["**Stopping by Woods on a Snowy Evening"**] is not Frost's best poem. . . . But it is a good poem, to my mind quite genuine, and its meanings and feelings, larger than any stated in the poem, do emerge indirectly but unmistakably from the arrangements of images, rhythms, sounds, and syntax; we all know this, and Frost knew it too. The story is told that he wrote the poem at dawn in a state of near-exhaustion, after working all night on a longer poem that wasn't going well. He wrote it easily and quickly. And it turned out to say more than he knew he was saying, which is just the experience that all of us who write poems recognize and long for. Frost longed for it too. He longed to repeat it. But his longing drove him to attempt the coercion of the experience by means of contrivance and conscious control.

I am certain that **"Stopping by Woods"** sprang from an actual experience of stopping by a woods, while [**"For Once, Then, Something"**] was entirely a studio performance with only a consciously contrived connection to any experience, probably a remote experience, of looking down a well. . . . [My] feeling is distinct and forcible. Perhaps in part it comes from the exact hendecasyllables, which are uncharacteristic of Frost and which usually convey a feeling of artifice in English. Perhaps also the well metaphor is simply too pat, too sentimental. But the poem itself reveals more, its strongest part is the opening sentence, really quite a good one, the syntax and sound patterns cast tellingly against the basic meter; which leads me to suspect that the poem's real, though hidden, occasion lay in those "others"—I wonder who they were?—who taunted Frost with his solipsism. That was the impetus; but it petered out, and after the first sentence the poem goes downhill rapidly. It becomes tendentious, almost peevish. . . . Then in the last line everything goes to pieces. The poet, in despair, *names* what his poem is about, "truth," thus committing the poet's cardinal sin; and at once the poem is destroyed, the labored metaphor of the well collapses. What lies at the bottom of the well is—is—is . . . but of course it *cannot* be named, that is the whole point, any more than the meaning of the snowy woods can be named. Yet Frost did it. He pushed and pressed and tried to coerce his poem. And he did it over and over again in other poems, many of them more substantial than this one.

Todd M. Lieber

SOURCE: "Robert Frost and Wallace Stevens: 'What to Make of a Diminished Thing'," in *American Literature,* March, 1975, pp. 64-83.

Frost was no more eager than any other poet to define poetry, but when he spoke about it he generally used such phrases as: "a way of grappling with life," "a little voyage of discovery," "a way *out* of something." All these phrases represent poetry not as entity but activity, and, more specifically, as "a way," that is, as method. In the essay **"Education by Po-**

etry,"** Frost suggests that in coming close to poetry the student enters the world of metaphor and, through metaphor, learns what it is to think: "it is just putting this and that together; it is just saying one thing in terms of another." He is not speaking of trivial comparisons but the most profound thinking humans engage in. "Unless you have had your proper poetical education in metaphor," he writes, "you are not safe anywhere. Because you are not at ease with figurative values: you don't know the metaphor in its strength and its weakness. You don't know how far you may expect to ride it and when it may break down with you. You are not safe in science; you are not safe in history." . . . The figure Frost uses to describe metaphor in this sentence is itself worth attending to: we "ride" our metaphors. Metaphor should be construed not merely as an identification of resemblance but as an instrument used to get somewhere, a tool for thinking, the vehicle, perhaps, on which the poet undertakes his "voyages of discovery." Poems become methods of moving toward new insights on the strength of the poet's figures.

Love, belief, and poetry. Frost . . . associates these three, and through that association he expresses the same vision of poetic activity that Stevens articulates in "A Primitive like an Orb" [see especially Cantos 4, 5, and 6]. Frost often used love as an analogy for poetry, as, for example, in saying that "the figure a poem makes . . . is the same as for love." . . . But love is more than an analogy for poetry; it is also Frost's name for the positive force that impels poetry, the energy behind all true thinking. In **"Accidentally on Purpose"** love is called the basic instinctual force that underlies "intention, purpose, and design" in the universe.

For Frost love and poetry function as twin figures of the creative activity in which man commits himself, with "passionate preference," to a certain tacit foreknowledge that he has and, by believing in it, brings it to fulfillment. In **"Education by Poetry"** he wrote that, in connection with learning about thinking, "the person who gets close enough to poetry, he is going to know more about the word *belief* than anybody else knows, even in religion nowadays". . . . Like the relationship of two people in love, the process of poetic thinking demands the act of "believing the thing into existence," and in poetry as in love one learns that the indwelling of the human spirit in its forms is essential to all creation and to all knowledge. Like Stevens, Frost came to see poems as individual embodiments of a single, central activity.

Frost's best treatment of the role of belief and commitment in establishing truth appears in **"Directive,"** a poem about returning to some basic source of wholeness and strength, "beyond confusion." It begins with an introspective journey through a landscape of desolation, marked by waste land imagery which makes it seem doubtful that this journey can lead in a valuable direction. Yet a guide appears, vague and phantom-like at first but increasingly more concrete and personal toward the end of the poem. By the final lines it is clear that the guide is the poet, and the source of wholeness he discloses is a fundamental power within the self. The poet is a guide to the life of the imagination, to the "broken drinking goblet like the Grail" taken from the children's "house of make-believe." . . . Like the teachings of Christ, poetic truth depends on commitment and faith. The power Frost guides us to in **"Directive"** is the power of belief in ourselves and our figures, the power of poetry itself as a method of thinking and knowing.

Roberta F. Sarfatt Borkat

SOURCE: "The Bleak Landscape of Robert Frost," in *The Midwest Quarterly,* Summer, 1975, pp. 453-67.

In the popular mind Frost appears in the guise of a gentle nature poet who writes poems which the common man can understand—poems free of those dreadful complexities and sexual allusions found in much modern poetry. How this image can persist in the mind of anyone who has read such a terrifying poem as **"Out, Out—"** I do not know. But most people have not read **"Out, Out—"** and others of its tone. When such appreciators encounter Lionel Trilling's theory . . . that their sweet cracker-barrel philosopher conceives of an essentially "terrifying universe," indignant sparks fly. These people have made Frost in their own image and cannot bear to have the mirror cracked.

To anyone who has read all of Frost's poems with an open mind, however, Trilling's conclusions become inescapable. Frost's landscape is bleak. His doctrine is disturbing. That doctrine appears most clearly in two poems which are central to an understanding of Frost, *A Masque of Reason* and *A Masque of Mercy.* . . . These poems were published in 1945 and 1947, when Frost was in his seventies and had had time to formulate his ideas about life. These poems are overtly doctrinal and should give us a good look at that bleak Frostian landscape.

A. Zverev

SOURCE: "A Lover's Quarrel with the World: Robert Frost," in *20th Century American Literature: A Soviet View,* translated by Ronald Vroon, Progress Publishers, 1976, pp. 241-60.

To picture American poetry of the 20th century without Robert Frost would be as difficult as picturing 19th century poetry without Edgar Allan Poe or Walt Whitman. Poe, Whitman and Frost represent the three high points in American poetry. The significance of each has long since been acknowledged unanimously and universally. Even people who have no interest whatsoever in verse know these names. . . .

A superficial reading of Frost's poetry may give the impression that he is an artist who has delved deeply into the law of eternal return: birth, flowering, death, new birth. Or an artist whose works are all authentic and autobiographical. Or an escapist philosopher, a Thoreau of the 20th century who has retreated from the soulless and cruel reality of the megalopolis and found refuge under the forest canopy of New England.

Each of these impressions is true and reveals some facet of Frost's poetic world. But let us try to read Frost not only as a poet who has given us marvellous examples of lyrical and dramatic poetry, but also as one who has left us with an uncommonly authentic artistic testimony of *our epoch.* In the stream of books on Frost issuing from his native land the poet's work is rarely viewed from such an angle. Yet such an approach might prove both important and useful. The fact is that Frost, like many other eminent writers, became a sort of legend in his lifetime, and his "public image," created by numerous critics, from the Georgians on down to the critics represented in Richard Thornton's anthology *Recognition of Robert Frost,* proved, it seems, to be rather distant from the essence of Frost as poet.

It is one thing to recognize an artist, but to understand his work is something far more difficult. Frost's earliest verses made it clear that here was a completely independent poet unlike any other. Frost was like an island, situated, it is true, not all that far from the mainland of American poetry, but separated from it by a sufficiently broad strait. It was necessary to understand what exactly distinguished Frost from his contemporaries. And the explanation was quickly found. Too quickly, in fact, for though it was based on actual features of Frost's poetic conceptions, it overlooked others, as a result of which Frost's creative temper was distorted. The explanation ran as follows: Frost in principle did not want to be a contemporary poet, did not want to respond to the "spirit of the times". . . .

Frost called poetry "an effort to explain life," by which, of course, he meant contemporary life. He did not write free verse and said that he would rather play tennis without a net than employ *vers libre,* but this does not in the least imply that Frost's metrical verse was the same as Longfellow's. He did not strive along with his contemporaries "to include a larger material," for often as a result of such efforts the poet "gets lost in his material without a gathering metaphor to throw it into shape and order." In comparison to T. S. Eliot or Carl Sandburg Frost was a poet of "narrow," local and always traditional material. But does that mean that Frost's "metaphor," in other words his poetic image, is equivalent to James Russell Lowell's "metaphors" or those of Edwin Arlington Robinson, a poet incomparably closer to Frost? Does this mean that Frost's "narrow" material does not reveal some absolutely new artistic qualities to the reader, or appear in an absolutely new artistic dimension?

Frost is too strikingly different from his New England predecessors for us to explain away these differences simply in terms of the creative individuality or uniqueness which nature bestows on any outstanding talent. It would be difficult to solve the "riddle" of Frost by examining his poetics from the inside, as a closed system. In the first decades of the 20th century the American poetic tradition was being rejuvenated, and here Frost had a decisive role to play. The American literature of those years was realistic, and Frost belonged to the aesthetic movement of his times, regardless of how traditional and "timeless" he may have appeared to be.

Here we approach the very essence of the problem. A realistic artistic system does not, of course, presuppose photographic fidelity in its reflection of the surrounding world. It presupposes above all an attempt to grasp the true laws of life, to penetrate the essence of life processes—social and individual, spiritual and psychological. It demands an objective view of the world. It entails not only a new aggregate of expressive means, but also a reconsideration of various aesthetic and philosophical categories which have determined the specific features of poetry in earlier periods, in particular romantic poetry.

For Frost the most important of these categories was understanding the people and the life of the people.

The romantic tradition lay at the foundation of his art, but as an artist of realistic bent he gave new meaning to a principal aspect of this tradition—the

way it reflected the people's life. For the romantics "the people" was an abstract and static spiritual substance. For Frost "the people" emerges as a category of historical existence. This was a great shift. Having apparently exhausted all its possibilities and now compromised in the "twilight interval," the romantic tradition received a powerful stimulus. Facing new aesthetic demands, the tradition proved its vitality, and the continuity of poetry was preserved.

In place of the mythologized and decorative "folk style" of the romantics Frost brought a peculiar artistic concept of "autochthony", to borrow the term from Mircea Eliade's *Myth, Dreams and Mysteries.* Speaking of "autochthony," Eliade implies a profound and frequently unconscious sense of belonging to the place: "men feel that they are *people of the place,* and this is a feeling of cosmic relatedness deeper than that of familial and ancestral solidarity."

This seems to be a relevant and true description of Frost's outlook too. In the context of literary history this "autochthonic" sense which is conveyed in his poetry is possibly Frost's greatest achievement. . . .

"I had a lover's quarrel with the world," Frost said of himself, and he could not have expressed himself more exactly, for his truly was a lover's quarrel, a recognition of life's drama which did not lead to a rejection of this life in the name of some ideal, nor to the setting up of his own, isolated world in contrast to the life around him. Yes, Frost belonged to this world, but he never looked at it through the rose-colored glasses of superficially understood patriotism. He saw this world in its true light and linked himself irrevocably to it. Otherwise he would have proved incapable of that organic understanding of the world's anxieties which so astonishes us in Frost's lyrics. The call of the city, luring us with its tawdry splendors, the lost harmony of man and the earth on which he toils, the growing mistrust and alienation between people who were once united by common cares, and the poet's unflagging feeling of belonging to that great body known as the People—all this we find in Frost and his remarkably, profoundly realistic panorama of the people's life.

Frost's comments on "two types of realist" are well known: "There are two types of realist—the one who offers a good deal of dirt with his potato to show that it is a real one; and the one who is satisfied with the potato brushed clean. I am inclined to be the second kind. To me, the thing that art does for life is to clean it, to strip it to form." Another of his statements on the same subject is less well known: "Instead of a realist—if I must be classified—I think I might better be called a Synecdochist; for I am fond of the synecdoche in poetry—that figure of speech in which we use a part for the whole." . . .

In his books this world was examined in a unique and profound manner, and the ideals to which Silas [in **"The Death of a Hired Man"**] adhered and which were so dear to Frost himself were far from being reactionary ("back to patriarchal simplicity") but rather democratic in character. Frost's realism and sincere democratic impulses made him the greatest American poet of the 20th century.

And a broad range of readers (not only in the poet's homeland) have long since acknowledged Frost, the real Frost—not as an intellectual dressed in homespun farmers' clothes, not as a conformist, not as an unthinking composer of idylls and pastorals, but as an artist who expressed the people's view on the complex, sharply contradictory world of America in the 20th century, one who believed in the people and shared their hopes, their democratic traditions and ideals. This is how he appears if we approach his work without prejudice.

David Bromwich

SOURCE: "Nedwick's Season of Frost," in *The New York Times Book Review,* January 16, 1977, pp. 4-5, 28.

Along with Whitman, Dickinson and Stevens, Frost has a place among the greatest of American writers. We know something about the lives of all these poets and they were all isolated souls. Dickinson was fierce in her detachment, Whitman troubled by it, Stevens at perfect ease. Frost is really in a different class: a more hateful human being cannot have lived who wrote words that moved other human beings to tears. . . .

There is a cant about "the dark Frost" and a cant about "Frost, the tragic poet." On the occasion of his 85th birthday Frost heard himself lauded, in an after-dinner speech by Lionel Trilling, as a bearer of bad tidings for civilization—as one who, like Sophocles, fulfilled the proper role of the poet. Frost was visibly shaken for days afterward. At last someone had called his bluff on the popular audience—and at a public ceremony. But he may have been shaken too because he had succeeded in yet another lie. Frost wrote out of the darkness in himself, and said so. He knew nothing else. But here was a critic of reputation, with enormous gravity and tact, calling that darkness a

universal condition and praising Frost for having revealed it. Once more he found himself where he wanted to be: before the others yet thoroughly hidden from their view.

What meaning, if any, does this life have for the art that came from it? Frost carried the dream of self-reliance farther than his heroes, Emerson and William James, would have dared, or wished. His recovery of his own axis was a project that had no end, and it made him the bleakest of lords. To realize this does not make his poems less astonishing. It does allow us to read them more truly and severely as what they are. At the end of **"To a Moth Seen in Winter"** Frost spoke for himself.

> You must become more
>   simply wise than I
> To know the hand I stretch
>   impulsively
> Across the gulf of well nigh
>   everything
> May reach to you, but cannot
>   touch your fate.
> I cannot touch your life,
>   much less can save,
> Who am tasked to save my
>   own a little while.

The lines can be read, many of us once read them, as a touching confession of humility and even modesty. But, if we think of Frost's own life, we can hear him biting off every word. He is signing off. As we survey 90 years for the most part so mean and so desperate, the artful and endearing "a little while" seems the only lie.

William H. Pritchard

SOURCE: "Deeper into Life: Robert Frost's Last Years," in *The American Scholar,* Vol. 53, Autumn 1984, pp. 522-32.

Robert Frost received his fourth Pulitzer for *A Witness Tree* in May 1943; he died in Peter Bent Brigham Hospital in Boston, in January 1963, at age eighty-eight. The final two decades of his life were those of a man whose productions as a poet, for the first time in his career, took a position secondary to his life as a public figure, a pundit, an institution, a cultural emissary. He had become the goodest greyest poet since Walt Whitman. *Steeple Bush* was published in 1947, and Randall Jarrell told the truth about it in the *New York Times Book Review* when he noted that "most of the poems merely remind you, by their persistence in the mannerisms of what was genius, that they are the productions of someone who once, and somewhere else, was a great poet"—although Jarrell rightly excepted **"Directive"** from his stricture. Frost did not see this review of *Steeple Bush* (his secretary, Kathleen Morrison, assured him that it was "all right"), but he did see one in *Time* that said the book "did nothing to enlarge his greatness." He promptly went into a tailspin, suffering pains in his wrists and chest. The review almost literally went to his heart; he was treated by a doctor who found no evidence of an attack, but who diagnosed the strain Frost was under and elicited from him the reasons for it.

It is fair to say that from that point on, his writing, or at least his publishing of poetry, became occasional rather than habitual. After the appearance of the *Complete Poems* in 1949, he managed to produce about one poem a year, and did so under the pressure of sending out his annual Christmas card, consisting of a new poem. But as the poems dried up, his reputation expanded. Let the poet be sent to Brazil and to Israel. Let him receive degrees from two ancient English universities. Make him poetry consultant at the Library of Congress. Let him read a poem at the inauguration of a president. Send him to the Soviet Union and let him talk with Premier Khrushchev. Make various films about him in which he pauses by a stone wall, or shoulders an ax, or putters around the stove in the kitchen of his Vermont cabin. Make sure that everyone knows America possesses, in Jarrell's phrase (from his essay "The Other Frost"), "The Only Genuine Robert Frost in Captivity."

It is difficult not to regard Frost's later years—in which the poems written were relatively few and relatively minor—with mixed feelings. The series of triumphs of the public figure may be celebrated for the honor they brought him; alternatively this increasing publicization may be regretted or even deplored. Surely there was something less than heartening in the spectacle of an old man being listened to too often, by too many people, most of whom cared little about poetry and cared about his only because they thought it wholesome country-American. At certain moments Frost spoke with candor and wry self-knowledge about what had happened to him, and on one such occasion, in an interview with Randall Jarrell at the Library of Congress in 1959, he mused on the difference between private and public, on what might be lost in moving from one realm to the other. "I'm a bad man to have around at a wedding," he said. "What begins in felicity and privacy, ends in publicity—and maybe really ends there. A wedding is the end of it." And he continued, thoughtfully: "What begins in felicity and a career like mine, you know, could end. . . . Someone might say mockingly,

what began in felicity and all the privacy and secrecy and furtiveness of your poetry is ending in a burst of publicity." Yet the fact was that over the course of his life he had devoted intense energy toward making sure that his work did not lack publicity, and of the most favorable kind.

Since on occasion he was able to view what had happened to him with perspective, even with a touch of irony (as in the play on the phrase "ends in publicity"), we should likewise be of two minds about his romance with fame and publicity. The weakness of the late poems is partly a matter of Frost's disregard for his own principles. After the eloquence with which, in the preface to Edwin Arlington Robinson's last book, he had insisted that poetry be left free to "go her way in tears," that her subject was "griefs, not grievances," *Steeple Bush,* a decade or so after the preface, was full of grievances against such phenomena as "the guild of social planners" (**"The Planners"**), or the revolutionary figure (in **"A Case for Jefferson"**) who wants America "made over new" ("He's Freudian Viennese by night. / By day he's Marxian Muscovite"), or against other prophets of disaster (one poem is titled **"The Prophet of Disaster"**). Frost felt compelled to respond to earthshaking world events like the dropping of the atomic bomb; but his response was so heavily underlined in its attempted playfulness that the reader fidgets uneasily. . . .

Yet to complain that Frost's late poems are inferior to the others is to indulge in the complacency one has identified in the poems. Instead, they should be put in their place, which is a small one, and seen as relatively weak manifestations of what on other fronts still revealed itself—never more so—as a quite unbelievable energy of performance.

Joseph Brodsky

SOURCE: "On Grief and Reason," in *The New Yorker,* Vol. 70, No. 30, September 26, 1994, pp. 70-85.

I should tell you that what follows is a spinoff of a seminar given four years ago at the Collège International de Philosophie, in Paris. Hence a certain breeziness to the pace; hence, too, the paucity of biographical material—irrelevant, in my view, to the analysis of a work of art in general, and particularly where a foreign audience is concerned. In any case, the pronoun "you" in these pages stands for those ignorant of or poorly acquainted with the lyrical and narrative strengths of the poetry of Robert Frost. But, first, some basics.

Robert Frost was born in 1874 and died in 1963, at the age of eighty-eight. One marriage, six children; fairly strapped when young; farming, and, later, teaching jobs in various schools. Not much travelling until late in his life; he mostly resided on the East Coast, in New England. If biography accounts for poetry, this one should have resulted in none. Yet he published nine books of poems; the second one, *North of Boston,* which came out when he was forty, made him famous. That was in 1914.

After that, his sailing was a bit smoother. But literary fame is not exactly popularity. As it happens, it took the Second World War to bring Frost's work to the general public's notice. In 1943, the Council on Books in Wartime distributed fifty thousand copies of Frost's **"Come In"** to United States troops stationed overseas, as a moralebuilder. By 1955, his *Selected Poems* was in its fourth edition, and one could speak of his poetry's having acquired national standing.

It did. In the course of nearly five decades following the publication of *North of Boston,* Frost reaped every possible reward and honor an American poet can get; shortly before Frost's death, John Kennedy invited him to read a poem at the Inauguration ceremony. Along with recognition naturally came a great deal of envy and resentment, a substantial contribution to which emerged from the pen of Frost's own biographer. And yet both the adulation and resentment had one thing in common: a nearly total misconception of what Frost was all about.

He is generally regarded as the poet of the countryside, of rural settings—as a folksy, crusty, wisecracking old gentleman farmer, generally of positive disposition. In short, as American as apple pie. To be fair, he greatly enhanced this notion by projecting precisely this image of himself in numerous public appearances and interviews throughout his career. I suppose it wasn't that difficult for him to do, for he had those qualities in him as well. He was indeed a quintessential American poet; it is up to us, however, to find out what that quintessence is made of, and what the term "American" means as applied to poetry and, perhaps, in general.

In 1959, at a banquet thrown in New York on the occasion of Robert Frost's eighty-fifth birthday, the most prominent literary critic at that time, Lionel Trilling, rose and declared that Robert Frost was "a terrifying poet." That, of course, caused a certain stir, but the epithet was well chosen.

Now, I want you to make the distinction here between terrifying and tragic. Tragedy, as you know, is always a fait accompli, whereas terror always has to do with anticipation, with man's recognition of his own negative potential—with his sense of what he is capable of. And it is the latter that was Frost's forte, not the former. In other words, his posture is radically different from the Continental tradition of the poet as tragic hero. And that difference alone makes him—for want of a better term—American.

On the surface, he looks very positively predisposed toward his surroundings—particularly toward nature. His fluency, his "being versed in country things" alone can produce this impression. However, there is a difference between the way a European perceives nature and the way an American does. Addressing this difference, W. H. Auden, in his short essay on Frost, suggests something to the effect that when a European conceives of confronting nature, he walks out of his cottage or a little inn, filled with either friends or family, and goes for an evening stroll. If he encounters a tree, it's a tree made familiar by history, to which it's been a witness. This or that king sat underneath it, laying down this or that law—something of that sort. A tree stands there rustling, as it were, with allusions. Pleased and somewhat pensive, our man, refreshed but unchanged by that encounter, returns to his inn or cottage, finds his friends or family absolutely intact, and proceeds to have a good, merry time. Whereas when an American walks out of his house and encounters a tree it is a meeting of equals. Man and tree face each other in their respective primal power, free of references: neither has a past, and as to whose future is greater, it is a toss-up. Basically, it's epidermis meeting bark. Our man returns to his cabin in a state of bewilderment, to say the least, if not in actual shock or terror.

Now, this is obviously a romantic caricature, but it accentuates the features, and that's what I am after here. In any case, the second point could be safely billed as the gist of Robert Frost's nature poetry. Nature for this poet is neither friend nor foe, nor is it the backdrop for human drama; it is this poet's terrifying self-portrait. . . .

While in **"Come In"** we have Frost at his lyrical best, in **"Home Burial"** we have him at his narrative best. Actually, **"Home Burial"** is not a narrative; it is an eclogue. Or, more exactly, it is a pastoral—except that it is a very dark one. Insofar as it tells a story, it is, of course, a narrative; the means of that story's transportation, though, is dialogue, and it is the means of transportation that defines a genre. Invented by Theocritus in his idylls, refined by Virgil in the poems called Eclogues or Bucolics, the pastoral is essentially an exchange between two or more characters in a rural setting, returning often to that perennial subject, love. Since the English and French word "pastoral" is overburdened with happy connotations, and since Frost is closer to Virgil than to Theocritus, and not only chronologically, let's follow Virgil and call this poem an eclogue. The rural setting is here, and so are the two characters: a farmer and his wife, who may qualify as a shepherd and a shepherdess, except that it is two thousand years later. So is their subject: love, two thousand years later.

To make a long story short, Frost is a very Virgilian poet. By that, I mean the Virgil of the Bucolics and the Georgics, not the Virgil of the Aeneid. To begin with, the young Frost did a considerable amount of farming—as well as a lot of writing. The posture of gentleman farmer wasn't all posture. As a matter of fact, until the end of his days he kept buying farms. By the time he died, he had owned, if I am not mistaken, four farms in Vermont and New Hampshire. He knew something about living off the land—not less, in any case, than Virgil, who must have been a disastrous farmer, to judge by the agricultural advice he dispenses in the Georgics.

With few exceptions, American poetry is essentially Virgilian, which is to say contemplative. That is, if you take four Roman poets of the Augustan period, Propertius, Ovid, Virgil, and Horace, as the standard representatives of the four known humors (Propertius's choleric intensity, Ovid's sanguine couplings, Virgil's phlegmatic musings, Horace's melancholic equipoise), then American poetry—indeed, poetry in English in general—strikes you as being by and large of Virgilian or Horatian denomination. (Consider the bulk of Wallace Stevens's soliloquies, or the late, American Auden.) Yet Frost's affinity with Virgil is not so much temperamental as technical. Apart from frequent recourse to disguise (or mask) and the opportunity for distancing oneself that an invented character offers to the poet, Frost and Virgil have in common a tendency to hide the real subject matter of their dialogues under the monotonous, opaque sheen of their respective pentameters and hexameters. A poet of extraordinary probing and anxiety, the Virgil of the Eclogues and the Georgics is commonly taken for a bard of love and country pleasures, just like the author of *North of Boston.*

To this it should be added that Virgil in Frost comes to you obscured by Wordsworth and Browning. "Filtered" is perhaps a better word, and Browning's dramatic monologue is quite a filter, engulfing the dramatic situation in solid Victorian ambivalence and uncertainty. Frost's dark pastorals are dramatic also,

not only in the sense of the intensity of the characters' interplay but above all in the sense that they are indeed theatrical. It is a kind of theatre in which the author plays all the roles, including those of stage designer, director, ballet master, etc. It's he who turns the lights off, and sometimes he is the audience also.

That stands to reason. For Theocritus's idylls, in their own right, are but a compression of Greek drama. In **"Home Burial"** we have an arena reduced to a staircase, with its Hitchcockian banister. . . .

I think you will agree that this is not a European poem. Not French, not Italian, not German, not even English. I also can assure you that it is not Russian at all. And, in terms of what American poetry is like today, it is not American, either. It's Frost's own, and he has been dead for over a quarter of a century now. Small wonder then that one rambles on about his lines at such length, and in strange places, though he no doubt would wince at being introduced to a French audience by a Russian. On the other hand, he was no stranger to incongruity.

So what was it that he was after in this, his very own poem? He was, I think, after grief and reason, which, while poison to each other, are language's most efficient fuel—or, if you will, poetry's indelible ink. Frost's reliance on them here and elsewhere almost gives you the sense that his dipping into this inkpot had to do with the hope of reducing the level of its contents; you detect a sort of vested interest on his part. Yet the more one dips into it, the more it brims with this black essence of existence, and the more one's mind, like one's fingers, gets soiled by this liquid. For the more there is of grief, the more there is of reason. As much as one may be tempted to take sides in **"Home Burial,"** the presence of the narrator here rules this out, for, while the characters stand, respectively, for reason and for grief, the narrator stands for their fusion. To put it differently, while the characters' actual union disintegrates, the story, as it were, marries grief to reason, since the bond of the narrative here supersedes the individual dynamics—well, at least for the reader. Perhaps for the author as well. The poem, in other words, plays fate.

I suppose it is this sort of marriage that Frost was after, or perhaps the other way around. Many years ago, on a flight from New York to Detroit, I chanced upon an essay by the poet's daughter printed in the American Airlines in-flight magazine. In that essay Lesley Frost says that her father and her mother were co-valedictorians at the high school they both attended. While she doesn't recall the topic of her father's speech on that occasion, she remembers what she was told was her mother's. It was called something like "Conversation as a Force in Life" (or "the Living Force"). If, as I hope, someday you find a copy of *North of Boston* and read it, you'll realize that Elinor White's topic is, in a nutshell, the main structural device of that collection, for most of the poems in *North of Boston* are dialogues—are conversations. In this sense, we are dealing here—in **"Home Burial,"** as elsewhere in *North of Boston*—with love poetry, or, if you will, with poetry of obsession: not that of a man with a woman so much as that of an argument with a counterargument—of a voice with a voice. That goes for monologues as well, actually, since a monologue is one's argument with oneself; take, for instance, "To be or not to be . . . " That's why poets so often resort to writing plays. In the end, of course, it was not the dialogue that Robert Frost was after but the other way around, if only because by themselves two voices amount to little. Fused, they set in motion something that, for want of a better term, we may just as well call "life." This is why **"Home Burial"** ends with a dash, not with a period.

If this poem is dark, darker still is the mind of its maker, who plays all three roles: the man, the woman, and the narrator. Their equal reality, taken separately or together, is still inferior to that of the poem's author, since **"Home Burial"** is but one poem among many. The price of his autonomy is, of course, in its coloration, and perhaps what you ultimately get out of this poem is not its story but the vision of its ultimately autonomous maker. The characters and the narrator are, as it were, pushing the author out of any humanly palatable context: he stands outside, denied reentry, perhaps not coveting it at all. This is the dialogue's—alias the Life Force's—doing. And this particular posture, this utter autonomy, strikes me as utterly American. Hence this poet's monotone, his pentametric drawl: a signal from a far-distant station. One may liken him to a spacecraft that, as the downward pull of gravity weakens, finds itself nonetheless in the grip of a different gravitational force: outward. The fuel, though, is still the same: grief and reason. The only thing that conspires against this metaphor of mine is that American spacecrafts usually return.

Brad Leithauser

SOURCE: "Great Old Modern," in *The New York Review of Books,* Vol. XLIII, No. 13, August 8, 1996, pp. 40-43.

As his book titles suggest, Robert Frost's poems abound in geological and geographical imagery—there's *North of Boston, Mountain Interval, New Hampshire, West-Running Brook, A Witness Tree* (one whose carved trunk records the boundaries of newly settled land), *A Further Range.* The connection between places and people—between the exterior and the interior landscape—is always close at hand in Frost's work, a point illustrated with dexterous affection in his dedication of *A Further Range* to his wife, Elinor:

> To E. F. / for what it may mean to her that beyond the White Mountains were the Green; beyond both were the Rockies, the Sierras, and, in thought, the Andes and the Himalayas—range beyond range even into the realm of government and religion.

So it's only fitting that Frost's long poetic career itself evokes a geological figure: a high, extensive plateau. We begin on relatively low if irregular ground—the apprentice work of *A Boy's Will* (1913), which was first published in London, during Frost's two-year English sojourn with his wife and four children. After that, the ascent is steep. What follows are six books remarkable for the consistent elevation of their excellence, before at last we descend into the scree and rubble of the final two volumes, *Steeple Bush* (1947) and *In the Clearing* (1962).

Those six central books constitute their own terrain—one of the most bewitching in all of American literature. They are a sort of pristine table-land where rock faces are burnished, where flora and fauna are plentiful and hardy, and where visibility can be preternaturally clear. This is a region where you proceed under the dazzling certainty that you're never very far from some unforgettable vista. You don't like the particular poem you're reading? Hike just a little farther—turn the page—and here's **"Stopping by Woods on a Snowy Evening"** or **"Birches"** or **"Hannibal"** or **"Fire and Ice"** or **"Nothing Gold Can Stay."** . . .

Frost's career embodies that happy paradox by which an artist who grows and advances inevitably conspires to betray his younger self: by replacing the merely good with the excellent, he effaces his earnest, earlier accomplishments. It would be much harder to call *A Boy's Will* apprentice work if what followed were not so commanding.

What is most striking with each rereading of *A Boy's Will* is how much of the mature Frost was present from the outset. Admittedly, judgments about Frost's early development can be complicated. He was nearly forty when his first book appeared and its poems reflect the work of a couple of decades. In addition, while completing *A Boy's Will* he was also amassing the manuscripts that would eventually materialize as his second and third collections. But questions of strict chronology aside, the leap in quality between *A Boy's Will* and his second book, *North of Boston,* is extraordinary—all the more so in that he progressed so far merely by refining rather than renouncing his techniques. It's no surprise that *A Boy's Will* voices many of the great thematic concerns of Frost's subsequent career (the threat of tragedy impinging on young lovers, his wavering between a need for approval and a hunger for solitude, his quest for corroboration of an innate optimism) as well as many of his characteristic tones (proud resolution, seasoned ruefulness, didactic grandeur). . . .

Such tastes naturally drew him to the sonnet, a form which, with its quatrains for building blocks, is literally foursquare. ("But before all," he requested, in a letter summarizing his literary tastes, "write me as one who cares most for Shakespearean and Wordsworthian sonnets.") The sonnet's characteristic movement toward compression, as exemplified in its final couplet, suited both the deductive bent of his mind, which habitually ventured from the particular example to the embracing principle, and the strategy of his rhetoric, which relished the journey from the colloquially offhand to the tightly epigrammatic. *A Boy's Will* opened with a sonnet, and others are sprinkled throughout his oeuvre. Robert Nye, editor of the valuable anthology *A Book of Sonnets,* has called Frost "perhaps the master sonneteer" of the century—a claim which, when all forty-some of his published and unpublished sonnets are considered together, seems indisputable. . . .

"The Master Speed," an affirmation of love's ability to overcome life's obstacles, was composed for the wedding of Frost's daughter Irma . . .

When viewed up close—with an eye to the concision of its phrasings, its fluency of rhyme and enjambment, its command of pacing—this Shakespearean sonnet is an astonishing feat. And no less astonishing when viewed from as far away as possible, just as though you'd never seen a sonnet before. While as artificial as any linguistic structure could be—this shipshape packet of a hundred-forty syllables, with its even apportionment of seventy stresses and its elaborate rhyme scheme rigging together every tenth syllable—it's also a natural spoken utterance. For this is precisely how all parents might speak to their children on their wedding days—provided, merely, that the parents could strip from their speech every last awkwardness and approximation, every little

stammering confusion and infelicity. I think it was Charles Lamb who once observed that he could write like Shakespeare if he only had the mind—which inspired a friend to add that, indeed, it was only the mind that was lacking. In his clarity and ease Frost, too, inspires a fatuous boast: we could all write like Frost, provided only we could all write like Frost. . . .

On the whole, Frost has been fortunate in his readers, having attracted over the years many sane and sensitive critics. Theirs has been an unusual task. Typically, the poetry critic's job is to present the poet in question as underappreciated and underread. In the case of Frost—the most beloved of all American poets—his defenders have worked to demonstrate that he has been embraced for all the wrong reasons. More than that of most poets, Frost criticism has progressed as a series of correctives. . . .

Even so, it's the nature of a corrective to overstate its arguments. Frost's defenders have been at such pains to establish the depth and subtlety of his thought that we can lose sight of one of his staple virtues: his lucidity. From the start, Frost aimed at the widest possible audience and much of what he wrote is as clear as glass. **"The Runaway," "A Patch of Old Snow," "The Most of It"**—a professor in American Studies is unlikely to pull anything more out of these poems, or appreciate them more richly, than would a good high-school student. Similarly, in pursuing the dark "other Frost" Jarrell sometimes takes a more dire view than the poems justify. The lovely **"Neither Out Far Nor In Deep"** (which Lionel Trilling considered possibly the "most perfect poem of our time") is surely not the blistering condemnation that Jarrell imagines. The poem meditates on humankind's innate attraction to the seashore—and to, by extension, all those spiritual thresholds toward which we peer so myopically. The poem concludes:

> They cannot look out far.
> They cannot look in deep.
> But when was that ever a bar
> To any watch they keep?

Jarrell observes that "it would be hard to find anything more unpleasant to say about people than that last stanza"—but isn't Frost looking with wry affection at others and at himself? Isn't he saying that, as seekers after the truth, we're to be commended for our immoderate appetites, rather than damned for our modest achievements? . . .

Few American poets have steeped themselves more thoroughly in Latin than Frost did. If the tales of New Englanders in *North of Boston* are homegrown affairs, they're also, as he noted, "in a form suggested by the eclogues of Virgil." (One can't help thinking, too, that what they are, or could have been, are beautifully produced radio plays, had America offered Frost anything comparable to the facilities the BBC has traditionally offered English poets.)

The book's annotations also address the issue of Frost's modernity. Seeking to shield him from the charge of being an old-fashioned writer—even a "retrograde artist"—a number of his defenders have stressed, again in a spirit of corrective, his intimate connection to various modern trends, especially the attempt to inject a more natural speaking voice into conventional metrics. There's a good deal of truth in the notion. Howard Moss was surely right in linking Frost's diction to Bishop's. He might equally have joined Frost to Richard Wilbur, Donald Justice, James Merrill, Amy Clampitt, Donald Hall, and to himself.

It's plausible, then, to place Frost squarely in a—if not the—central branch of modern poetry. This is in many ways our standard take on Frost: he becomes, like Hardy, a cagey modernist. Yet this is a corrected view that occasionally distorts as much as it clarifies—one that ignores, for instance, the notable degree to which Frost adhered to outmoded locutions. He was, it's worth recalling, a poet who some forty years after the appearance of *The Waste Land* could publish a couplet like "Tis a confusion it was ours to start / So in it have to take courageous part." He never shook off his liking for "twould" and "twixt" and "tween"—rather, he seems pointedly to have clung to such constructions, with a fidelity approaching fervent loyalty.

What exactly was Frost being loyal to? To a particular vision of the lyric poem, it would seem—one epitomized by Francis Palgrave's great nineteenth-century anthology, *The Golden Treasury*. When seeking to explain, many years afterward, what had inspired him in 1912, a year before **A Boy's Will** was published, despite very limited means, to move himself and his large family to England for a couple of years, Frost reported that he "had come to the land of the *Golden Treasury*. That's what I went for." The anecdote has a quaintly whimsical ring—Frost was a magnificent self-mythologizer. But like so much mythology it speaks its coded truth. The book was for him a talisman and touchstone—a volume he studied while a student, taught while a teacher, and during a long lifetime pressed upon his friends. "I *did* read that literally to rags and tatters," he once observed.

Palgrave served Frost as an exemplar, and Frost repaid that debt by composing verses that Palgrave's contributors could immediately have apprehended and appreciated. One can imagine Thomas Campion or Edmund Waller or Thomas Gray, resurrected from the grave, shaking his head in dismay at most of Frost's contemporaries. Marianne Moore was a wonderful poet, but Campion, Waller, Gray, et al., would have scrutinized her verse with befuddled disbelief. (Even W. H. Auden, though her near-contemporary and a ceaseless experimenter himself, reported that on first reading her poems, he "simply could not make head or tail of them.") Frost, though, they would have taken to.

If Frost the modernist ought to be acknowledged, so should Frost the sustainer of an expiring idiom. Ours is a critical age that bestows its highest praise on the innovator, as indicated by the wealth of terms that, although rooted in censure, have come to carry positive associations: rebel, subversive, iconoclast, maverick, nonconformist, insurrectionist. All are characterizations that have some applicability to Frost. But what is the approbatory term that would mark the complementary side of his achievement—that would honor the artist who extends beyond its expected life a beloved tradition? In this regard Frost is kin to an artist like Puccini (think of *Turandot*'s appearing in the same decade as Berg's *Wozzeck*) or to the Corot who went on producing calm, classical, marvelous canvases while Monet and Renoir and Pissarro were beginning to explode both the colors and the imagery of the traditional French landscape.

What is in fact so striking about Frost's old-fashioned touches is how *un*striking they seem. They feel oddly natural. For what Frost conveys in the aggregate is a sense of being thoroughly at ease in an essentially nineteenth-century armature. When reading the poems he produced in the Thirties—some of his finest work—I will occasionally find myself marveling at having just read past, untroubled, a "tis" or a "tween." If other poets of Frost's generation, and later generations, have chosen to work in conventional metrics, none has demonstrated quite the same blend of facility and fecundity. No one else in our century has been quite so at home in Palgrave's ideal, or has transported its tones and cadences so successfully into our own time. You might call Frost America's best nineteenth-century poet (and call Dickinson and Whitman, those stylistic oddballs, two of our best twentieth-century poets). In the long run, what's a mere hundred years, one way or the other?

And from where we now stand, with a few scant years to run before twentieth-century poets, too, are a thing of the past, it seems apparent that Frost represents both a vibrant tradition (a modernist effort to discover new ways of hitching form to a changing speech idiom) and the end of a line (a voice in whom Longfellow and Whittier and Bryant are heard as living heirs). At this point, it's impossible to imagine the emergence of another American whose work would ring so many echoes on our nineteenth-century poetic tradition. Hence, in any reading of Frost there's an elegiac burden—even when he is summoning up a spring thaw, or a foal, or a sunrise.

Frost's poetry strengthens over time. Whenever you go through the whole of it, you discover not only that the great poems have stayed great, but that since your last inspection one or two of the good ones have mysteriously elevated themselves. On my most recent go-round, the poem that overwhelmed me was one I'd hardly noticed before: **"Iris by Night,"** from *A Further Range.* It memorializes Frost's friend Edward Thomas, whom Frost never saw again after departing from England in 1915. Thomas died at the battle of Arras, in 1917.

"Iris by Night" recalls an evening walk with Thomas when the moonlight played various tricks—momentarily enfolding the two of them in a numinous spectrum. (Probably, they were witnesses to that rare phenomenon which meteorologists call a moonbow.) The poem is too long to quote in full, but it's worth digging up—indeed, would be worth digging up out of the side of a mountain, for this must be one of the most moving poems ever dedicated to friendship. The poem concludes on a mystical note, one of a fragile but infrangible union:

> And then we were vouchsafed the miracle
> That never yet to other two befell
> And I alone of us have lived to tell.
> A wonder! Bow and rainbow as it bent,
> Instead of moving with us as we went,
> (To keep the pots of gold from being found)
> It lifted from its dewy pediment
> Its two mote-swimming many-colored ends,
> And gathered them together in a ring.
> And we stood in it softly circled round
> From all division time or foe could bring
> In a relation of elected friends.

Frost scholarship in recent years also has been taken up with another sort of corrective: the rescuing of Frost from his authorized biographer. The late Lawrance Thompson's three-volume portrait was so saturated with bile that a mini-genre has since grown up devoted to exonerating Frost from the "monster myth." Well-intentioned as such efforts are, they look a little extraneous beside **"Iris by Night."** For a poem like this is manifestly the work of—there's no denying the notion—a true friend and a great heart. I wish we could all have the good fortune to befriend such a monster.

TITLE COMMENTARY

📖 *A BOY'S WILL* (1913)

William Morton Payne

SOURCE: A review of *A Boy's Will,* in *The Dial,* Vol. 55, No. 654, September 16, 1913, pp. 211-12.

A dream world of elusive shapes and tremulous imaginings is half revealed to our vision by the subdued lyrics which Mr. Robert Frost entitles *A Boy's Will.* It is a world in which passion has been stilled and the soul grown quiet—a world not explored with curious interest, but apprehended by the passive recipient. The sun does not shine, but the pale grey of twilight enfolds nature with a more gracious charm. The song called **"Flower-Gathering"** offers an exquisite example of the wistful and appealing quality of the author's strain.

> I left you in the morning,
> And in the morning glow,
> You walked away beside me
> To make me sad to go.
> Do you know me in the gloaming,
> Gaunt and dusty grey with roaming?
> Are you dumb because you know me not,
> Or dumb because you know?
>
> All for me? And not a question
> For the faded flowers gay
> That could take me from beside you
> For the ages of a day?
> They are yours, and be the measure
> Of their worth for you to treasure,
> The measure of the little while
> That I've been long away.

The desire of the solitary soul for companionship has rarely found such beautiful expression as it receives in this quotation:

> We make ourselves a place apart
>   Behind light words that tease and flout,
> But oh, the agitated heart
>   Till someone find us really out.

"Reluctance" is the poem that closes the collection—a lyric of lassitude with just a faint flicker of the spent fire of life.

> But through the fields and the woods
>   And over the walls I have wended;
> I have climbed the hills of view
>   And looked at the world, and descended;
> I have come by the highway home,
>   And lo, it is ended.
>
> The leaves are all dead on the ground,
>   Save those that the oak is keeping

To ravel them one by one
    And let them go scraping and creeping
Out over the crusted snow,
    When others are sleeping.

And the dead leaves lie huddled and still,
    No longer blown hither and thither;
The last lone aster is gone,
    The flowers of the witch-hazel wither
The heart is still aching to seek,
    But the feet question "Whither?"

Ah, when to the heart of a man
    Was it ever less than a treason
To go with the drift of things
    To yield with a grace to reason,
And bow and accept the end
    Of a love or a season?

If Mr. Frost's verses show the cast of melancholy, there is at least nothing morbid about it. In their simple phrasing and patent sincerity, his songs give us the sort of pleasure that we have in those of the *Shropshire Lad* of Mr. Housman.

O. W. Firkins

SOURCE: A review of *A Boy's Will,* in *The Nation,* New York, Vol. CI, No. 2616, August 19, 1915, pp. 228-29.

In Mr. Frost's **A Boy's Will,** criticism detects three elements: first, vigorous landscapes sketched, or scooped out, with a bold, free hand; second, feeling of a certain trenchancy and distinction; and, third, superadded interpretations. Of these three constituents the last seems wholly perfunctory. Mr. Frost is a poet by endowment; he is a symbolist only by trade. The meaning he personally attaches to landscape seems quite unrelated to the meaning by which he hopes to enlist the sympathies of his readers. His philosophy, in a word, is propitiatory; it is Mr. Frost's apologetic bow to a supposedly intellectual public, and I am uncourtly enough to wish that the obeisance had been withheld. When Mr. Frost's intellectual revenues come in his verse will profit by the circumstance, but I doubt if it profits in the least by his anticipation of his income.

One point of detail unrelated to Mr. Frost's essential claims deserves a passing comment. Under the title of each poem in the table of contents a few words indicative of its purpose are set, and these phrases, read seriatim, make up a single coherent paragraph. This is an artifice, no doubt, but, in my opinion, a pardonable and commendable artifice; if poets will be locksmiths, they should furnish keys. I object personally to researches into obscure poetic meanings, not merely from the healthy human disinclination to overwork, but from a sense that the faculties which the assessing of probabilities and the summing up of evidence call into play are destructive of the moods in which poetry is absorbed and enjoyed. To extract, and so to separate, the soul from the body is surely the wrong way of approaching an art whose basis is the idea that the two are inseparable. Mr. Frost's expedient impresses me as sensible and considerate.

The real value of these poems lies in the quality of their emotion. Their tone is sombre, but it is that youthful sombreness which is little more than a play of hide-and-seek with cheerfulness. The definition of the feeling is not always sharp, but, even in its vagueness, it exhibits a savor, a saltiness, a reaching and penetrating quality, which augurs well for this young writer's future. I regret that Mr. Frost should think it desirable to exhibit in many places a crabbed syntax and a jolting metre. I am not consoled for these asperities by the probability that they are intentional, for I do not subscribe to the theory that in our day, when the Muses are lethargic, they must be jostled before they can be made to dance. I content myself with this gentle and modest imprecation: May Mr. Frost mount high on the slopes of Parnassus in a wagon without springs!

NORTH OF BOSTON (1914)

Alice C. Henderson

SOURCE: A review of *North of Boston,* in *The Dial,* Vol. 57, No. 679, October 1, 1914, p. 254.

Mr. Robert Frost's new book of poems, **North of Boston,** leaves such a strong impression of men and women in the mind that one is led to think of it as a new novel rather than as a book of verse. This is a significant fact. Mr. Frost, using verse, and without in the least forcing the idea, has conveyed an impression of life such as might be conveyed by Mr. Henry James or Mr. Joseph Conrad in prose. Mr. Frost's first book of verse, **A Boy's Will,** was a volume of lyrics, fanciful, inventive, and with a certain whimsical twist, yet with very little of this more substantial quality. The sparse New England pasture with its outcropping granite boulders and the sparse New England character with its outcropping strata of close-grained, hard-headed practicality and its unexpected sunny levels of human idealism (the amazing Puritan compound)—these are both revealed through the sympathetic, kindly, but keenly humorous vision of Mr. Frost. Mr. Frost's feeling for nature is not romantic; nor is it realistic in an external sense. Rather it gives us a direct sense of the earth; that close connection between nature and man which is only gained by constant companionship or by that intimacy of toil in which the earth gives up only what is demanded of her. In cities we lose this sense of nature. Mr. Frost restores to us the direct primitive sense of the earth. A mountain, a field, or a wood exists for him as it exists in life. They are not shadowy, symbolic, or romantic shapes. They are real, they occupy space; they count as much as people count, and sometimes more, in a man's consciousness. Doubtless there will be many readers who will find Mr. Frost dull, and who will object to his verse structure. There is no denying that his insistent monosyllabic monotony is irritating, but it may be questioned whether any less drab monotony of rhythm would have been so successful in conveying the particular aspect of life presented. Mr. Frost is at his finest in his subtle delineation of Yankee heroics in **"The Code,"** in his whimsical humoresque, **"A Hundred Collars,"** in the drab tragedy of **"The Death of the Hired Man,"** and in the cold conflict of sundered temperaments revealed in the poem called **"Home Burial."** All these poems are too long to quote in full, and it would only misrepresent them to quote parts of them. So it must be flatly asserted that in the particular field Mr. Frost has chosen he is to be compared with Mr. John Masefield, Mr. D. H. Lawrence, and Mr. W. W. Gibson, the three English poets who are most eager in the attempt to express the gesture and the feeling of everyday life in something other than "the grand style."

Ezra Pound

SOURCE: "Modern Georgics," in *Poetry,* Vol. 5, No. 3, December, 1914, pp. 127-30.

It is a sinister thing that so American, I might even say so parochial, a talent as that of Robert Frost should have to be exported before it can find due encouragement and recognition.

Even Emerson had sufficient elasticity of mind to find something in the "yawp." One doesn't need to like a book or a poem or a picture in order to recognize artistic vigor. But the typical American editor of the last twenty years has resolutely shut his mind against serious American writing. I do not exaggerate, I quote exactly, when I say that these gentlemen deliberately write to authors that such and such a matter is "too unfamiliar to our readers."

There was once an American editor who would even print me, so I showed him Frost's **"Death of the Hired Man."** He wouldn't have it; he had printed a weak pseudo-Masefieldian poem about a hired man two months before, one written in a stilted pseudo-

literary language, with all sorts of floridities and worn-out ornaments.

Mr. Frost is an honest writer, writing from himself, from his own knowledge and emotion; not simply picking up the manner which magazines are accepting at the moment, and applying it to topics in vogue. He is quite consciously and definitely putting New England rural life into verse. He is not using themes that anybody could have cribbed out of Ovid.

There are only two passions in art; there are only love and hate—with endless modifications. Frost has been honestly fond of the New England people, I dare say with spells of irritation. He has given their life honestly and seriously. He has never turned aside to make fun of it. He has taken their tragedy as tragedy, their stubbornness as stubbornness. I know more of farm life than I did before I had read his poems. That means I know more of "Life."

Mr. Frost has dared to write, and for the most part with success, in the natural speech of New England; in natural spoken speech, which is very different from the "natural" speech of the newspapers, and of many professors. His poetry is a bit slow, but you aren't held up every five minutes by the feeling that you are listening to a fool; so perhaps you read it just as easily and quickly as you might read the verse of some of the sillier and more "vivacious" writers.

A sane man knows that a prose short story can't be much better than the short stories of De Maupassant or of "Steve" Crane. Frost's work is interesting, incidentally, because there has been during the last few years an effort to proceed from the prose short story to the short story in verse. Francis Jammes has done a successful novel in verse, in a third of the space a prose novel would have taken—*Existences in La Triomphe de la Vie.* Vildrac and D. H. Lawrence have employed verse successfully for short stories. Masefield is not part of this movement. He has avoided all the difficulties of the immeasurably difficult art of good prose by using a slap-dash, flabby verse which has been accepted in New Zealand. Jammes, Vildrac and Lawrence have lived up to the exigencies of prose and have gained by brevity. This counts with serious artists.

Very well, then, Mr. Frost holds up a mirror to nature, not an oleograph. It is natural and proper that I should have to come abroad to get printed, or that "H. D."—with her clear-cut derivations and her revivifications of Greece—should have to come abroad; or that Fletcher—with his *tic* and his discords and his contrariety and extended knowledge of everything—

should have to come abroad. One need not censure the country; it is easier for us to emigrate than for America to change her civilization fast enough to please us. But why, IF there are serious people in America, desiring literature of America, literature accepting present conditions, rendering American life with sober fidelity—why, in heaven's name, is this book of New England eclogues given us under a foreign imprint?

Professors to the contrary notwithstanding, no one expects Jane Austen to be as interesting as Stendhal. A book about a dull, stupid, hemmed-in sort of life, by a person who has lived it, will never be as interesting as the work of some author who has comprehended many men's manners and seen many grades and conditions of existence. But Mr. Frost's people are distinctly real. Their speech is real; he has known them. I don't want much to meet them, but I know that they exist, and what is more, that they exist as he has portrayed them.

Mr. Frost has humor, but he is not its victim. **"The Code"** has a pervasive humor, the humor of things as they are, not that of an author trying to be funny, or trying to "bring out" the ludicrous phase of some incident or character because he dares not rely on sheer presentation. There is nothing more nauseating to the developed mind than that sort of local buffoonery which the advertisements call "racy"—the village wit presenting some village joke which is worn out everywhere else. It is a great comfort to find someone who tries to give life, the life of the rural district, as a whole, evenly, and not merely as a hook to hang jokes on. The easiest thing to see about a man is an eccentric or worn-out garment, and one is godforsakenly tired of the post-Bret-Hartian, post-Mark-Twainian humorist.

Mr. Frost's work is not "accomplished," but it is the work of a man who will make neither concessions nor pretences. He will perform no money-tricks. His stuff sticks in your head—not his words, nor his phrases, nor his cadences, but his subject matter. You do not confuse one of his poems with another in your memory. His book is a contribution to American literature, the sort of sound work that will develop into very interesting literature if persevered in.

I don't know that one is called upon to judge between the poems in *North of Boston*. **"The Death of the Hired Man"** is perhaps the best, or **"The Housekeeper,"** though here the construction is a bit straggly. There are moments in **"Mending Wall." "The Black Cottage"** is very clearly stated.

MOUNTAIN INTERVAL (1916)

William Aspenwall Bradley

SOURCE: "Four American Poets," in *The Dial*, Vol. 61, No. 731, December 14, 1916, pp. 528-30.

Mr. Robert Frost has a touch of it [distinction] in more than one poem in his latest collection, *Mountain Interval*,—in **"The Oven Bird,"** for example:

> There is a singer everyone has heard
> Loud, a midsummer and a midwood bird,
> Who makes the solid tree trunks sound again.

It is for this purely sensuous quality, as well as for his genuine passion for nature, expressed through such wealth and delicacy of observed detail, that one most legitimately reads and admires Mr. Frost. There are, too, elements of deep divination in his art, where it touches complex human relations and reactions. But as a dramatic and narrative poet, his method is often unnecessarily cryptic and involved. Thus in **"Snow"** there is nothing sufficiently remarkable either in the incident itself, or in the resultant revelation and clash of character, to justify its long and elaborate treatment. But in **"In the Home Stretch,"** the poet is singularly successful in suggesting ghostly presences, in creating a veritable haunted atmosphere for the old New England farmhouse, akin to that produced by the English poet, Mr. Walter de la Mare, in "The Listeners." Mr. Frost is the one continuator at present of the "tradition of magic" in American poetry.

The New York Times Book Review

SOURCE: A review of *Mountain Interval*, in *The New York Times Book Review*, January 7, 1917, p. 2.

Robert Frost gives us a book full of rich contrast, clarity of vision, human appeal, and sharp revelation of character. We find a new lyric feeling in these later poems, tracing a warmer touch of life, a maturer sympathy, and a more memorable beauty.

His poems have deep spiritual insight and a serenity that is like soft wind flowing across snow-filled meadows. **"Birches"** and **"Putting in the Seed"** are full of a tranquil twilit beauty, and **"Hyla Brook"** and **"The Oven Bird"** are lyrics of superior quality. Mr. Frost writes of the region under Franconia Notch, lighting up rural New England with ruddy torch. In **"The Home Stretch"** and the dialogue **"Snow"** he shows an able narrative power.

Robert Frost is not a poet of wide, beautiful language—or fecund imagery. He describes colloquially the sections of the country that he is familiar with, but often his verse structure is uneven, rugged, and inchoate. Lines that should convey intelligent meaning, like

> A stranger to our yard, who looked the
> city,
> Yet did in country fashion in that there
> He sat and waited till he drew us out,

would lose none of their individuality by being constructed with greater care and conciseness, whereas many intrinsically fine effects are lessened by a certain inflexibility of speech, which is nevertheless probably so typical of New England that it is justifiable.

There are quite a few pleasing things in Mr. Frost's new volume. It is by no means momentous, but the fact that it contains the well-known **"Road Not Taken"** and the poignantly moving **"Sound of the Trees"** alone make the new collection interesting.

O. W. Firkins

SOURCE: "A Tryst with the Poets," in *The Nation*, New York, Vol. CIV, No. 2711, June 14, 1917, pp. 709-10.

Mr. Frost's title, *Mountain Interval,* is rather beautiful than auspicious; one is reminded that the intervals in mountains are depressions. The success of a first book is always a hardship for the second; but *A Boy's Will,* while plainly inferior to *North of Boston,* showed sufficient power and sufficient novelty in power to nourish the hopes of the poet's admirers. *Mountain Interval* will test their fortitude. The book, unquestionably, has its distinguished side. The moving combination of the strange and the commonplace, the tragical and the homespun, reappears. In two poems, **"In the Home Stretch"** and **"Snow,"** the old power takes the old path to a point over-topped by its earlier culminations. In **"Snow"** the setting is unforgettable, and the briefer speeches have a speed and lunge that dramatists might envy. A married pair telephone to an acquaintance (I insert "Man" and "Woman" for clearness):

> *Woman:* I hear an empty room—You know—it sounds
> that way. And, yes, I hear—
> I think I hear a clock—and windows rattling. No step
> though. If she's there she's sitting down.
> *Man:* Shout, she may hear you.
> *Woman:* Shouting is no good.
> *Man:* Keep speaking then.

> *Woman:* Hello! Hello! Hello!
> You don't suppose—? She wouldn't go out doors?
> *Man:* I'm half-afraid that's just what she might do.
> *Woman:* And leave the children?
> *Man:* Wait and call again.
> You can't hear whether she has left the door
> Wide open and the wind's blown out the lamp
> And the fire's died and the room's dark and cold?

This is attainment—effect foreseen and compassed. Too often Mr. Frost gropes a little, apparently seeks in the same breath to withhold meaning and convey significance, to attempt, by a device remotely suggestive of the youthful Maeterlinck, to convert a commonplace into an oracle through an intonation.

North of Boston exhibited a fine continence, pointing to an inner check in Mr. Frost capable of replacing that external authority which his innovations tacitly disowned. That check is lost in *Mountain Interval.* Mr. Frost has apparently read an endorsement of sheer boldness into a success which was actually the recognition of a fine equipoise between courage and restraint. The result has been to sanctify impulse; he has reached that beatific but parlous state when a poet mistakes shiftlessness for intrepidity. There is no harshness, no meanness, no rawness, in language or versification, that is not admitted to the eccentric pages of this undiscriminating volume. If Mr. Frost, of whom, even in his errors, I aim to speak respectfully, should contend that he heralds a new poetry, I can only suggest in reply that no man is bound to be more circumspect than the leader of a vanguard. It is, of course, imaginable, in the pranks of destiny, that our descendants may find pleasure in lines like these:

> It was not enough of a garden,
> Her father said, to plough;
> So she had to work it all by hand,
> But she don't mind now.

The forecast assuages one's longing for immortality.

NEW HAMPSHIRE: A POEM WITH NOTES AND GRACE NOTES (1923)

The New York Times Book Review

SOURCE: "Bards of New England and New York," in *The New York Times Book Review*, November 18, 1923, p. 6, 24.

Whether or not Mr. Robert Frost is America's leading poet is a question that need not be argued here. There are many who insist that he is, and even those who do not find themselves able to subscribe to the

Frost cult will hasten to admit that a new book of verse by this stalwart wielder of the pen is a literary event of no small magnitude, and that a poet of so many rugged and unique virtues, so many homely graces of style, should at least be widely read, even though he is not to be worshiped. And there can be little doubt that Frost is one of the most interesting figures in the modern field of American poetry. He suggests Wordsworth in more aspects than one. Like the Bard of Rydal Mount, his interest is in humanity seen against a background of nature; like him also he moves serenely, scorning all little men with little minds. If to one who reads superficially both Wordsworth and Frost seem to have little passion because their lines do not flash and blaze, it is because their passion is a fire smoldering too deep down for such eyes to see. On the other hand, Frost is not of Wordsworth's stature. Wordsworth could glimpse

> The light that never was, on sea or land.

and even if he could not quite grasp and hold it, he could at least make others believe they had glimpsed it too. Frost dreams of the light: he does not quite succeed in glimpsing it himself, or in making others glimpse it. But he comes near—very near.

The title of Mr. Frost's Autumn burgeoning is *New Hampshire: A Poem With Notes and Grace Notes,* the title piece being a blank-verse monologue of nearly a score of pages in length. The total number of poems in the volume is close to half a hundred. The book has something of an autumnal aspect; there are vivid colors here and there, like trees that stand out in their Fall dress against a hillside of brown or quiet green. For the most part, however, it is a monotone which greets the eye. And, at the risk of carrying the figure too far, it is a landscape mostly of rocks rather than a landscape of trees and foliage. One would not say that it is a forbidding landscape; but it is not a welcoming one. Every line of the book is authentic of the North, where nature shrouds herself in a veil that one must penetrate before her beauty and her calm majesty become apparent. Tennyson called the North "dark and true and tender." Robert Frost, from the outset of his career as a poet, has felt this, caught it, and ruggedly, at the same time delicately, portrayed it. And he has never been more successful than in the present book. Frost is a harmony of contradictions. He has just been likened to Wordsworth. And far as he would seem to be from Shelley, he is also like Shelley in one respect—he is ever on the quest of beauty, of intellectual beauty. But he searches (and finds) where Shelley would never have thought to look (and where he could never have found it if he had looked)—on the bare mountainside, on the leafless tree, in the narrowly bounded lives of farmer-folk in the State that "has only specimens," yielding nothing commercial.

> Just specimens is all New Hampshire has,
> One each of everything, as in a show-case,
> Which naturally she doesn't care to sell.

These "specimens" are one President ("pronounce him Purse"); one Daniel Webster, and "the Dartmouth needed to produce him"; one "Family"; and

> She has a touch of gold. New Hampshire gold—
> But not gold in commercial quantities.
> Just enough gold to make the engagement rings
> And marriage rings of those who owned the farm.
> What gold more innocent could one have asked for?

It is the key to the poem, to all the poems in the book, and to Robert Frost—just gold enough for the profounder uses of gold, not in quantities. *New Hampshire* is a philosophical utterance, but it is not a sermon, or, if it is a sermon, it is savored with a humor that is mellow without being acid; a humor Yankee in flavor but free of the Yankee twang. It's "restful," says the poet at the close, "just to think about New Hampshire":

> At present I am living in Vermont.

Among the "Notes and Grace Notes" are several short pieces—they seem too unconventional for the conventional term "lyric"—which stand out challengingly. It is unfortunate that this one, called **"Fire and Ice,"** is marred by the weakness of the line before the close:

> Some say the world will end in fire,
> Some say in ice.
> From what I've tasted of desire
> I hold with those who favor fire.
> But if it had to perish twice,
> I think I know enough of hate
> To say that for destruction ice
> Is also great,
> And would suffice.

And this one, **"Dust of Snow,"** is delicate with the sensitiveness of the poet to the minor touch in nature:

> The Way a crow
> Shook down on me
> The dust of snow
> From a hemlock tree
> Has given my heart
> A change of mood
> And saved some part
> Of a day I had rued.

This is the sort of thing any of us "might do," but the sort of thing none but a poet ever does do. Hence the reason for poets—and the need.

John Freeman

SOURCE: A review of *New Hampshire: A Poem with Notes and Grace Notes,* in *The Bookman,* London, Vol. LXVII, No. 397, October, 1924, pp. 47-8.

A contemporary reviewer is happily not required to determine the order of merit among those who practise an ancient art in a myriad different ways, else the difficulty of approaching modern American verse would indeed be great. There is however no need to be delicate in seizing on Mr. Robert Frost's latest volume, *New Hampshire: a Poem with Notes and Grace Notes,* and crying welcome to a work which is in its own "note" almost unique. It is because Mr. Frost gives us what nobody else gives us that his new poems are taken to our hearts immediately, with scarcely a question or protest from the shrewd and jealous brain; although later, when affection has been fed, it is the brain that sits down too and makes its fastidious feast.

Yet there are doubtless those who cannot receive simply what this poet gives us so simply, and object to his peculiar blank verse—so wilfully near to prose, but seldom only prose—and his undecorated, winter or early spring bareness. They have a distaste for anything so distinctly unlike a poetic diction as:

> It left the cellar forty years ago
> And carried itself like a pile of dishes
> Up one flight from the cellar to the kitchen,
> Another from the kitchen to the bedroom,
> Another from the bedroom to the attic,
> Right past both father and mother, and neither stopped it.
> Father had gone upstairs; mother was downstairs.
> I was a baby: I don't know where I was. . . .

and fail or refuse to hear the music which is like a sharp wind among cold, tall trees. There may be readers he will never reach, but there's an increasing number of those that find a natural strength and sweetness in this spare succession of sound and silence and, in the numerous characters of his poems, a touch of what is strange yet familiar, like a revelation in someone we have long known and seen hitherto in a dull customary light. To put it briefly, English readers may admire this American poet for many things, but not least for the touch of their own tongue, character and country in most of his writing.

There is another reason for gratitude. I think it was not long before the war that Mr. Frost visited England, made acquaintance with several English writers and then returned to America with lamentable abruptness, as suddenly as a swift leaves though summer still lingers. Among those English writers was Edward Thomas, to whom Robert Frost brought the magical, mysterious gift of liberation, unsealing—I do not know how—the spring of poetry which had for so long awaited freedom. Robert Frost had published but little verse, Edward Thomas had written none; it was the intimacy between the two, the discussion of verse—eagerness answering eagerness—that released the clear waters of Edward Thomas's poetry. But for something inflexibly independent in Thomas's spirit you might fancy that the response to his friend's finger was too perfect and too obvious—and indeed some of the earlier verses of the English poet (the whole came within a few months), are scarcely distinguishable from the American's. The truth is that the passion for rural and homely things—Crabbe's passion too, and Clare's—was shared by both writers; one spoke out of love, and out of love the other answered. For us at this moment the sign of the common interest and its acknowledgment may be read in Robert Frost's beautiful stanzas in the present volume **"To E. T.":**

> I slumbered with your poems on my breast,
> Spread open as I dropped them half-read through
> Like dove wings on a figure on a tomb
> To see, if in a dream they brought of you,
>
> I might not have the chance I missed in life
> Through some delay, and call you to your face
> First soldier, and then poet, and then both,
> Who died a soldier-poet of your race.

The war, he muses, "seemed over more for you than me"; but yet:

> How over, though, for even me who knew
> The foe thrust back unsafe beyond the Rhine,
> If I was not to speak of it to you
> And see you pleased once more with words of mine?

The slow movement of this, the ease and the weight are characteristic of Mr. Frost's work in other moods than elegiac; equally characteristic is the mildness of form—the rhyme binding the stanza so lightly as to be almost unnoticed. His deliberateness everywhere—a fault at times perhaps, if usually a virtue—secures him and enables him to write a beautiful tense lyric:

> Nature's first green is gold,
> Her hardest hue to hold.
> Her early leaf's a flower;
> But only so an hour.
> Then leaf subsides to leaf.
> So Eden sank to grief,
> So dawn goes down to day.
> Nothing gold can stay.

Nevertheless his more usual form is the laxer one of blank verse stooping near to prose. Splendours and honours are refused; sometimes his verse is humble and almost mean, but it is never degraded to rhetoric. He prefers under-statement, and instead of seeking harmony in variety he seems to prefer a homely monotony. He will not pretend or falsify, and so his lightest phrase has truthfulness and convincingness. Hence again even his monotony is pleasant, for it conveys with singular exactness the speaking tones of a firm masculine personality. It is for this reason that it sounds like a new voice among all that reach us across the Atlantic; and another reason, not less definite, is that Mr. Frost writes about *something,* deals with a solid and visible scene or situation, and is seldom if ever occupied with the aspiring, unrelated lyricism of many modern writers. Nothing could better illustrate his characteristic way than **"The Witch of Coös,"** from which I have already quoted. The subject is the groping of a skeleton which has crept up the stairs—the cellar-bones out of their grave climbing the stairs at midnight. The mother in the story knows whose are the bones that come so noisily up the stairs, and she tells, with a simplicity that is at once crude and humorous, how she had struck at them as they climbed, so that a hand was broken off and the finger-pieces slid in all directions; but still the climbing bones went stumbling up:

> I listened till it almost climbed the stairs
> From the hall to the only finished bedroom,
> Before I got up to do anything;
> Then ran and shouted, 'shut the bedroom door,
> Toffile, for my sake!' 'Company,' he said;
> 'don't make me get up; I'm too warm in bed.'
> So lying forward weakly on the handrail
> I pushed myself upstairs, and in the light
> (The kitchen had been dark) I had to own
> I could see nothing. 'Toffile, I don't see it.
> It's with us in the room, though. It's the bones.'
> 'What bones?' 'The cellar bones—out of the grave.'
> That made him throw his bare legs out of bed
> And sit up by me and take hold of me.
> I wanted to put out the light and see
> If I could see it, or else mow the room,
> With our arms at the level of our knees,
> And bring the chalk-pile down. 'I'll tell you what—
> It's looking for another door to try.'

She had opened then the attic door, and when the skeleton had passed through the door was nailed up and the bed thrust against the door so that, though the bones sometimes try to break through again and brush the door with chalky fingers, no one need worry. "Let them stay in the attic since they went there."

Is this poetry? The question has been asked and denied, but I cannot see the value of any definition which shuts out such things as **"The Witch of Coös."** And even the rigid traditionalists who may incline to reject it cannot refuse also the poems in which Mr. Frost has adopted the formal measures and modes of the lyric. His is the gift of making the most of both worlds, the visible and the invisible, each real and each precious, by being naturally at home in each. His reputation in America has been vastly enlarged during the last few years since the war, and this volume is sure to extend it again; for the new poems present characteristics which it is proper and indeed inevitable to call unique in modern poetry.

THE COLLECTED POEMS OF ROBERT FROST (1931)

Isidor Schneider

SOURCE: A review of *The Collected Poems of Robert Frost,* in *The Nation,* New York, Vol. CXXXII, No. 3421, January 28, 1931, pp. 101-02.

A reading of the **Collected Poems** can leave no doubt of Mr. Frost's importance. They have an appearance of obscurity, but what renders them difficult to first reading renders them also powerful and compact. The simplicity of their subject matter is never betrayed into coarseness or sentimentality. They constitute a body of poetry certain to enter into classic American literature.

However, since current reviews of this volume are all praise and no serious criticism is being attempted, I think it may be of interest to point out the limiting elements in Mr. Frost's work. There is a danger in too complete an acceptance of any man's achievement, a possibility of his influence becoming a catch-all for literary prejudice.

Mr. Frost, for instance, is singularly out of touch with his own time. Indeed, many poets who antedate him are more contemporary in spirit. It has, indeed, been Mr. Frost's wish to keep out of his own age and his own civilization. We may go therefore to his poetry for diversion and relief from our time, but not for illumination. Mr. Frost does not understand our time and will make no effort to understand it. When he essays to speak of it, as in the long poem **"New Hampshire"** (one of the poorest in the book and a sort of pudding of irrelevancies), he shows a surprising lack of comprehension. There, to the challenge of contemporary ideas, he replies with know-nothing arrogance, "Me for the hills where I don't have to choose."

In fact, Mr. Frost's work is weakest in ideas. His style is gnomic; it sounds impressively thoughtful and many sentences have the rounded conclusiveness of proverbs. But his thought, disengaged from the style, is often discovered to be no thought at all, or a banality. (I am far from agreeing with Mr. George Moore and other advocates of "pure poetry" that ideas are foreign to the nature of poetry. Shakespeare, Dante, Goethe, Milton, Donne, and Lucretius would have to be among the many poets sacrificed, and the purification of poetry would turn out to be its annihilation.) Mr. Frost has casual ambitions to be a philosopher in his poetry; and in these strivings he is not successful.

We may take for example the beautiful poem "**A Star in a Stone Boat.**" The star is a meteorite built into a stone wall. Mr. Frost follows it from its fall to the time a farmer finds it, handles it, puts it into a stone boat, and drags it to the wall he is building. We are given a marvelous sense of its weight and feel in the hands and the puzzled awe with which one looks at it. The concluding lines are perfect:

> Such as it is it promises the prize
> Of the one world complete in any size
> That I am like to compass, fool or wise.

These lines, summarizing as much of philosophy as the poem comes to, do not contain thought so much as a renunciation of thought. I doubt whether a poet of philosophic imagination could have given us a more satisfying poem. Nevertheless, this piece, so suggestive and so full of possibilities, shows how little the philosophic imagination is developed in Mr. Frost.

It is curious, therefore, that Mr. Frost should be so regularly praised for the thought content of his poetry. But there is a reason for it. The touch of philosophy in his writing is the commonest, most easily understood, most easily applied, most comforting form of thinking—renunciation. Mr. Frost adds to it no subtlety and no depths; when it occurs in his poems it is, despite the graces and novelties of his style, banality.

I dwell upon this because it is the one respect in which Mr. Frost clearly shows himself to be influenced. The influence is New England, the New England of other days. The individuality of his style is one of the valuable effects of this influence, for New England life and tradition have always encouraged intense individualism. But this individualism derives in part from renunciation. What a man renounces he is free from and in freedom he can be himself. Perhaps here lies an explanation of the individuality of Mr. Frost's style. He has made a renunciation of usual poetic subject matter and usual poetic effects, not pri-

marily for originality's sake, but in disdain of literary comforts. He has chosen instead to write of homely and country things, regarding them with his matchlessly keen observation and celebrating them with his almost painfully restrained eloquence. No doubt some deliberate and unnecessarily harsh lines are a further process of this renunciation.

Related to this lack of a developed and original philosophy is another lack. Mr. Frost's narrative poems are frequently poised upon a psychological situation. The satisfaction the poetry and the narrative give the reader often leaves him with the impression that Mr. Frost is an excellent psychologist. Now many poets have been good psychologists, as Freud has shown; but Mr. Frost as a psychologist does not get very far. He can describe sensations perfectly; in fact, such descriptions are among his finest achievements. But he does not reach beyond the sensation; and in a psychological narrative he does not reach beyond the fact. The interesting poem of the man who burned down his house to buy a telescope with the insurance money succeeds only in reporting a curiosity; the poem "**Maple,**" which attempts to describe the psychological effects of having an unusual name, stretches out to absurd length in the attempt and succeeds in doing no more than to supply the reader data for his own psychologizing.

No, the distinctions Mr. Frost achieves are not those of a thinker or a prober; nor does he need those. He has rounded out a poetic individuality of exceptional dignity; he has developed his descriptive powers to an accuracy so sensitive that his lines often have an effect of clairvoyance; and the patient, logical fulfilment of his metaphors gives his rhetoric an effectiveness achieved by very few poets besides him.

Mr. Frost's style is one of the most individual in all poetry and certainly the most individual of our time. The consciously aristocratic T. S. Eliot, with his almost selfish obscurities, the dazzlingly inventive E. E. Cummings, with all his inimitable experiments, sound like the generality beside him. It is impossible to describe this individuality because its most conspicuous elements, terseness and the use of plain words and the avoidance of metronomic rhythms, are characteristics of many other poets. One can only say that Mr. Frost writes in a manner wholly his own; and if he has been influenced in it at all, it is only in the individualism urged by the New England tradition.

The descriptive power of Mr. Frost is to me the most wonderful thing in his poetry. A snowfall, a spring thaw, a bending tree, a valley mist, a brook, these are brought not to, but into the experience of the reader. The method is simple and can be analyzed. What he describes is never a spectacle only, but an entire adventure. In **"Our Singing Strength"** we follow him disputing with birds a bit of roadway; in **"A Hillside Thaw"** we almost see him on his knees trying to feel with his hands the process of snow turning into water. With the sight and the act the emotional response comes naturally. The three fuse together and the experience comes whole to us. It is an effect rare even in the best poetry. This simultaneous description gives the reader almost a sensory instrument with which to share the perception; and since it is natural, anyway, for the reader to identify himself with the author, the result is to bring the reader into closer touch with this aloof poet than with many poets who directly seek such a companionship.

Metaphors as Mr. Frost uses them are more functional than they commonly are in poetry. Many poets have more abundance and more brilliance, but few have used metaphor so justly, so carefully, and so fully. It is worked in naturally and at length, becoming a part of the whole idea, not a mere illuminating flash. The most conspicuous example of this is **"A Hillside Thaw."** The first three lines announce the metaphor,

> To think to know the country and not know
> The hillside on the day the sun lets go
> Ten million silver lizards out of snow!

For most poets this would be sufficient. They would turn to other metaphors. But Mr. Frost continues it for thirty-two lines more, and we have a wonderfully complete sense of the coolness, swiftness, and liquidness of these snow lizards that the night will catch and hold, and the sun will again release in the next daylight.

There remains to make some estimate among the poems themselves. The later sections are much superior to the earlier, where the poems are frequently incomplete, beginning with promises of drama, of discoveries of thought that fail into unresolved and weak endings. This disappears in the later poems which, with the exception of the poem **"New Hampshire,"** are sound throughout. On the whole it seems to me that the longer lyrics are the most thoroughly satisfying of his poems. The narratives, although among the best in English poetry, suffer from the incompatibility found in all narrative poetry which attempts to be realistic—the rivalry of the poetic and the colloquial. The attempt to fuse the two seems to me doomed to failure; a noble failure, preferable to easier successes, but a failure nevertheless. It were better for a narra-

tive poem to be written wholly in poetic language, which, being complete and self-sufficient in its own terms, will sound natural, certainly more natural than when colloquialisms are inset and draw attention to their competing naturalness. A few of the very short lyrics in the book are inconsequential and, as in **"Fireflies in the Garden,"** tend to become cute. Mr. Frost seems to require space to express himself, for in a few lines his terseness and involution have the look of a mannerism.

In conclusion I wish to say again outright in words what I have already said by implication—Robert Frost is one of the great poets, one whose perceptions are among the most acute and the most personal in the whole range of literature. To this nearly every one of the poems written in his maturity bears witness.

A FURTHER RANGE (1936)

William Rose Benét

SOURCE: "Wise Old Woodchuck," in *The Saturday Review,* Vol. 14, No. 5, May 30, 1936, p. 6.

Two American poets of my time have possessed an integrity they wore so easily that no one could imagine them being otherwise. One is dead, Edwin Arlington Robinson, and one—we thank the gods—is still alive and writing with the same felicity and shrewd wisdom as of old. Of what does such integrity consist? One would say the chief element is being oneself. But then one really has to *be* someone in the first place. We soon find out what a man can do and how well he does it. But in the case of a major writer, the whole life becomes involved in the work. No matter how reticent he may be, or how objectively he may write, the whole man comes before us. A certain voice is speaking that is like no other. And that is not because he decides to adopt certain characteristics of style. His style grows out of his way of thinking and speaking. The commonplace, the specious, never achieve style. And no form of writing more betrays a man than the practice of what we call poetry.

Frost, I think, is a major poet, because he is, for one thing, a significant human being. He is definitely one certain kind of human being and has his own limitations; but he early decided to be his own man, and by so being he has developed his own special gift to the full. Probably there has only been one poet in the whole history of the world who could be all things to all men, and that was Shakespeare. Compared with that extraordinary phenomenon all other poets are minor, though all those we call major had their special gifts. But there is no use putting people into a pantheon too early, and it is of no particular importance, save to say that here is an American of whom we can rightly be proud as we are proud of Emerson, and that to me is saying a great deal.

But Frost is no transcendentalist. He is a close observer of the earth and the ways of man on the earth. When he first came into his own and wrote the line about "the highway where the slow wheel pours the sand" he demonstrated that he had the god-given faculty of reporting as a poet—of all beings at his best the most accurate—precisely what he saw. We have got used to that now, got used to his constantly opening our eyes to the things we overlook that he clothes with significance. He came before us quietly, with no blatancy, no fanfare, and at first we may have thought—we who were so romantic and so dramatic then—that it was commonplace. But how well he wears! No fuss and feathers. Just a man we like to listen to, because wisdom out of deep experience wells through his words.

So what?—says the young poet—you would have me become an admirable character first and all things poetic shall be added unto me? Unfortunately not. I am not forgetting the man of a craft. I suppose a thorough rascal might yet be a good stone-mason. That is a craft. So is verse. Frost is a craftsman of verse. But when verse somehow becomes poetry it certainly implies that you are not a rascal; at least, not a thorough one. Frost is a bit of a rascal at that. I think he is a bit of a rascal for being so intensely individual. But it is only that kind of rascality that gives tang to a man's work.

> Only where love and need are one,
> And the work is play for mortal stakes,
> Is the deed ever really done
> For Heaven and the future's sakes.

And what does he say in the brevities of "Ten Mills"?

> Let chaos storm!
> Let cloud shapes swarm!
> I wait for form.

At a time of the most extravagant experimentation in verse, that is the craftsman speaking. No, young poet, you must learn the trade and how to use the tools! But brilliant as your performance then may be, behind it must be your own stature. Make no mistake about that! Nor, it has been doubted, is a cubit added merely by taking thought. But don't involve me in metaphysics!

> They cannot look out far,
> They cannot look in deep.
> But when was that ever a bar
> To any watch they keep?

When we find a man who can look out far and look in deep, and at the same time express himself clearly, to say that we should be grateful is understatement.

Frost's way of writing sometimes looks so easy; it is only when you examine it closely and note the careful use of every word, which has now become second nature, and the way he has of stating anything with inimitable idiosyncrasy, that despair sets in. There have been some pretty good imitators, but they have not got far.

Why should I tell you what is in this new book? Read it! It is a small book, as books go; it is actually only the sixth book we have had from a man now with so large a reputation. And it is better worth reading than nine-tenths of the books that will come your way this year. In a time when all kinds of insanity are assailing the nations it is good to listen to this quiet humor, even about a hen, a hornet, or Square Matthew. Frost, as woodchuck, has been "instinctively thorough" about his burrow. Perhaps that is all it was from the first. Yet he has not only burrowed deep but sat often at the burrow-mouth to watch the great drift of the constellations. Wise old woodchuck! And if he has not got the whole "United States stated," he has got a good deal of life stated in original analogy and phrase. And if anybody should ask me why I still believe in my land, I have only to put this book in his hand and answer, "Well—here is a man of my country."

The Christian Science Monitor

SOURCE: "Mr. Frost Ranges Further," in *The Christian Science Monitor,* June 17, 1936, p. 14.

With the publication in 1913 of *A Boy's Will,* Robert Frost was recognized as one of the few authentic voices in America. Since that time his place in modern poetry has been particularly individual. He has had nothing to do with extreme fashions. His compass has been wide enough to embrace any form, but he has never quite allied himself with any movement. He has maintained a certain dignity, a quietude of thought, which have held him to the center of his road.

Thus, in his new offering, *A Further Range,* we find him still maintaining the "strong are saying nothing until they see." For him there are no "isms"; there is only man and his relation to nature and to his creator. And yet, strangely enough, the poet who has said, "most propaganda poetry is merely Marxian philosophy, thinly overlaid with verse," reveals himself, at this point in his career, as a propagandist. But with this difference: the Marxian poet is concerned with the philosophy of Marx, translated often into bad verse; Frost translates the philosophy of Frost into poetry.

A Further Range may seem, at first reading, a light book, a book of neat epigrams and homely wit. But a careful study is rewarding, for it contains much more than its surface may at times indicate. There are some poems here that the Frost of *North of Boston* might have written. But even these are a little more deeply penetrating, a shade more acute, perhaps, than even that excellent volume. In this section, for instance, we have a poem subtly comparing leaves with flowers. Again, the more familiar Frost shows himself in such poems as **"Desert Places," "They Are Welcome to Their Belief,"** and particularly, **"Iris by Night,"** which must stand as one of the most beautiful of the Frostian performances.

The indication that the poet had a double meaning in mind when he chose the title of his present volume is heightened and explained by his dedication, in which he says, " . . . beyond the White Mountains were the Green; beyond both were the Rockies, the Sierras and, in thought, the Andes and the Himalayas—range beyond range even into the realm of government and religion." Here indeed is a further range, not only of mountain but of thought, and yet the essential scene is unchanged, merely higher and more rarefied. Fundamentals have a way of remaining fundamentals. And one is able to go back to the first poem in Frost's first book and sum the whole matter up:

> They would not find me changed
> from him they knew—
> Only more sure of all I thought was
> true.

R. P. Blackmur

SOURCE: "The Instincts of a Bard," in *The Nation,* New York, Vol. CXLII, No. 3703, June 24, 1936, pp. 817-19.

It is a hard thing to say of a man grown old and honored in his trade, that he has not learned it. Yet that is what Mr. Frost's new volume, with its further range into matters of politics and the social dilemma, principally demonstrates. The new subjects, as they show

themselves poetic failures, reflect back and mark out an identical weakness in poems on the old subjects. It is a weakness of craft, and it arises from a weakness, or an inadequacy, in the attitude of the poet toward the use and substance of poetry as an objective creation—as something others may use on approximately the same level as the poet did. Mr. Frost is proud of his weakness and expresses it in the form of an apothegm at the close of the poem called **"To a Thinker."**

> At least don't use your mind too hard,
> But trust my instinct—I'm a bard.

If we may distinguish, and for more than the purposes of this review, a bard is at heart an easygoing versifier of all that comes to hand, and hence never lacks either a subject or the sense of its mastery; and a poet is in the end, whatever he may be at heart, a maker in words, a true imager, of whatever reality there was in his experience, and every resource of the mind must be brought to bear, not only to express his subject, to transform what Mr. Frost means by instinct into poetry, but also to find his subject, to know it when he sees it among the false host of pseudo-subjects. These are the labors of craft—in relation to which the bard's labors are often no more than those of a pharmacist compounding a prescription by formula. In the old bards we look mostly for history, in the modern for escape. Swinburne is the type of modern bard, Yeats of the modern poet. It may be that by accident a bard is also a poet—as Swinburne was; but a poet who writes with only the discipline of a bard writes unfinished poetry of uncertain level and of unequal value. That is the situation of Mr. Frost; and when, as now, he attempts to make poems of his social reactions without first having submitted them to the full travail of the poetic imagination, the situation becomes very clear.

More precisely, taking the longest and most "serious" poem in the book, **"Build Soil—A Political Pastoral,"** which is a blank verse dialogue between Tityrus the poet and Meliboeus the subsistence farmer, we find not poetry but an indifferent argument for a "one-man revolution" turned into dull verse. As bad religious poetry versifies the duty of an attitude toward God, bad social poetry versifies the need of an attitude toward society. Both the duty and the need may be genuine and deeply felt—it is our stock predicament and the great source of fanaticism and deluded action—but before either attitude can become poetry it must be profoundly experienced not only in intention but in the actuality of words. It is the object of craft, and only craft can secure the performance, to complete and objectify the act of experience. Craft in poetry is not limited to meter and rhyme, cadence and phrasing, gesture and posture, to any of the matters that come under the head of incantation, though it must have all these; for great poetry, craft is the whole act of the rational imagination. It must combine the relish and hysteria of words so as to reveal or illuminate the underlying actuality—I do not say logic—of experience.

Mr. Frost does not resort to the complete act of craft. His instincts as a bard do not drive him to the right labor, the complete labor, except by accident and fragmentarily, in a line here and a passage there. In a sense, his most complete and successful poems, the short landscape images where versification seems almost the only weapon of craft needed, are unfinished fragments. The good lines emphasize the bad, the careless, and the irrelevant, and make them intolerable; which is most often the case in activities which depend at critical points upon instinct. Instinct is only dependable in familiar circumstances, and poetry seldom reveals the familiar. A consideration of **"Desert Places,"** which is as good as any poem in the book, will show what I mean.

> Snow falling and night falling fast oh fast
> In a field I looked into going past,
> And the ground almost covered smooth in snow,
> But a few weeds and stubble showing last.
>
> The woods around it have it—it is theirs.
> All animals are smothered in their lairs.
> I am too absent-spirited to count:
> The loneliness includes me unawares.
>
> And lonely as it is that loneliness
> Will be more lonely ere it will be less—
> A blanker whiteness of benighted snow
> With no expression, nothing to express.
>
> They cannot scare me with their empty spaces
> Between stars on stars where no human race is.
> I have it in me so much nearer home
> To scare myself with my own desert places.

The same profound instinct that produced the first two stanzas of observation becoming insight allowed Mr. Frost to end his poem with two stanzas of insight that fails to reach the viable point of becoming observation. It may, practically, be a matter of bad rhyming in the fourth stanza, of metrical shapelessness in the third; but at the bottom, in so ambitious a poet as Mr. Frost, it must have been instinct that made the second pair of stanzas evade the experience forced into them by the first pair.

COME IN, AND OTHER POEMS (1943)

Alice M. Jordan

SOURCE: A review of *Come In,* in *The Horn Book Magazine,* Vol. XIX, No. 3, May-June, 1943, p. 172.

Selected from the seven volumes of published verse, the poems here assembled fairly represent the range of Robert Frost's art. No two persons ever make identical anthologies. This is Louis Untermeyer's choice for analysis and comment along the way. There is a brief chapter of biography, preceding the poetry, with its accompanying notes of clarification or emphasis. The book is perhaps designed as an introduction to Robert Frost for young people, and with the drawings, which are happy reminders of Robert Frost's New England, it will make a lovely gift.

Kirkus Reviews

SOURCE: A review of *The Road Not Taken,* in *Kirkus Reviews,* Vol. XIX, No. 2, January 15, 1951, p. 47.

An enlargement of the material contained in **Come In,** a selection of poems published in 1943, annotated with a running commentary. The word seems to be that young American poets, as well as Congress, have realized suddenly that Robert Frost, who has been with us for some time, is probably our greatest American poet. Mr. Untermeyer, who knew it all along, knows his subject. There may be those, however, who may object that Mr. Untermeyer's earnest commentaries obstruct poetry which speaks so wisely, obliquely yet directly. But others—in the majority—will welcome the hints, guides and appreciations. The poems are grouped roughly by subject and technique, and the introduction includes a biography and appreciation. The selection is representative and forty-nine new poems were added, although we missed the prophetic **"Once by the Pacific."** An agreeable tribute to the "no-singing" singer—of our land, our people, our legacy of wisdom.

IN THE CLEARING (1962)

Richard Wilbur

SOURCE: "Poems That Soar and Sing and Charm," in *New York Herald Tribune Books,* March 25, 1962, p. 3.

Tomorrow Robert Frost will be 88. This new collection of his poems will be published on his birthday.

In the Clearing has an epigraph borrowed from Frost's early poem, **"The Pasture"**—"and wait to watch the water clear, I may." This illuminates both the old poem and the new book, and it brings to mind something which Frost once said: "All we do in life is a clarification after we stir things up." And then there is a charming poem in the book called **"A Cabin in the Clearing."** It is a dialogue between the chimney smoke and garden mist which hover about a house encircled by forest, eavesdropping on the earnest talk of the couple within. The "clearing" of this poem is a little area of human coherence, a bit of the universe becomes a colony of mind. Frost's title, then, has to do with mind-activity, with clarification, with the penetration of nature by human thought and effort.

This is a high-spirited, high-minded book. Despite its Frostian skepticisms and paradoxes, it is sweepingly assertive, and ought to satisfy the sort of critic who values poetry for the philosophy which may be shaken out of it—as some children eat the Cracker Jack for the sake of the prize. A verse "frontispiece," excerpted from the long poem **"Kitty Hawk,"** argues that

> God's own descent
> Into flesh was meant
> As a demonstration
> That the supreme merit
> Lay in risking spirit
> In substantiation.

Or as Emerson put it in prose, "There seems to be a necessity in spirit to manifest itself in material forms." If men are considerably less than divine in apprehension, if they cannot create "One least germ or coal," nevertheless Frost holds that we, the only creatures who have "thoughts to think," are under divine orders to penetrate matter as far as we can, claiming it for intellect and imagination. The fall from Eden he sees as the "instinctive venture" of a creature designed to enquire, and he makes Jehovah say to Jacob (retracting a few of His recorded injunctions):

> Have no hallowing fears
> Anything's forbidden
> Just because it's hidden.
> Trespass and encroach
> On successive spheres
> Without self-reproach.

It may surprise some readers that Robert Frost should write a book full of the word "venture," a book whose longest poem celebrates unlimited reaching-out—soaring planes, soaring capsules, soaring thought. These attitudes seem hardly to suit with those of, say,

that great focal poem **"The Mountain,"** in which an earlier Frost advised a retreat from change, confusion, and "too much" generally into the coherence of local tradition. But after all there has been no fundamental change of mind: first and last, Frost's concern has been for wholeness of life and character, and he is now defending, by a new strategy and on a broader front, the Emersonian values he embraced. In late years, he has become more and more the conscience of his country, and taken upon himself the burden of its confusion: what certain of these poems are directed against is the fear that our society, cowed by its own dangerous powers and potentialities, will go back on those things in man which Frost sees as highest and most human.

"Ours is a Christian adventure into materialism," Frost said not long ago, and the political poems of *In the Clearing* all insist that Americans must see themselves not as ingenious materialists but as riskers of spirit in the realm of matter. **"America Is Hard to See"** reproaches Columbus with having, in his appetite for Cathayan gold, failed to recognize our continent as "The race's future trial place, / A fresh start for the human race." **"Our Doom to Bloom"** and **"The Bad Island—Easter"** attack the cynicism of welfare-state thinking while in **"How Hard It Is to Keep from Being King,"** King Darius is counselled to give his people "character and not just food." The lines **"For John F. Kennedy His Inauguration"** look to the new Administration not for an exacted benevolence but for courage, the pursuit of glory, the bold exercise of power, independence of the mob, and a spirit "answerable to high design." The effect of the whole book, as it bears upon the political poems, is to invest with idealistic vigor a number of ideas which, in earlier embodiments, may have seemed nostalgic, negative and ungenerous. It is a considerable clarification.

But what about the poems as poems? The percentage of "editorials," jokes, aphorisms, and humorous wisdom-verse is high, and of these the present writer prefers the long **"Kitty Hawk,"** which seems to ramble but ends as quite a structure of notions, and two delightful light pieces, **"In a Glass of Cider"** and **"The Objection to Being Stepped On."** Still, my reactionary taste is for the lyric and dramatic Frost, who in this volume happily persists. **"The Draft Horse"** is a sinister yet amusing symbolic poem on Frost's old theme of acceptance, and **"Questioning Faces"**—a six-line glimpse of an owl just missing a window-pane—is as ponderable as the densest haiku. As for the first four poems in the book, they are rightly placed, and every one a beauty. **"Pod** of the Milkweed," like Frost's brilliant sonnet **"De-sign,"** charges some insects and a flower with vast implications: in this case the implications have to do with waste and with the investment of spirit in matter. Of **"A Cabin in the Clearing"** I have spoken already. **"Closed for Good,"** a version of which appeared in **"Complete Poems,"** is here revised and shortened for the better. And this poem, **"Away!",** is perhaps the best of all:

> Now I out walking
> The world desert,
> And my shoe and my stocking
> Do me no hurt.
>
> I leave behind
> Good friends in town.
> Let them get well-wined
> And go lie down.
>
> Don't think I leave
> For the outer dark
> Like Adam and Eve
> Pull out of the Park.
>
> Forget the myth.
> There is no one I
> Am put out with
> Or put out by.
>
> Unless I'm wrong
> I but obey
> The urge of a song:
> I'm—bound—away!
>
> And I may return
> If dissatisfied
> With what I learn
> From having died.

That is a poem so perfectly dexterous as to seem easy: a gay, venturesome poem to go away by. But stay with us, Mr. Frost. Earth's the right place for happy returns, and may you have many more.

John Holmes

SOURCE: "He Has Told Us the Best He Knows About Life," in *The Christian Science Monitor,* Vol. 54, No. 104, March 29, 1962, p. 11.

The great poem in Robert Frost's new book is **"Kitty Hawk,"** perhaps the profoundest statement he has ever simplified into his kind of language, an ultimate in a lifetime's vision. That he means it as the chief piece we know at once, because he uses eighteen lines of it as **"Frontispiece,"** such a surge of hope and belief as his skeptical mind has never quite said aloud before.

His achievement in this poem is a curious and exciting study, because there have been preliminary published versions, and apparently the book has been delayed these five or six years till he could get it right. But it is right now, for him, and for our wider understanding of modern life. **"Kitty Hawk"** is a major poem, partly autobiographical, partly a far-fetched and successful identification with the Wright brothers' leap into air, mostly a grand gathering of the forces of American character.

There are all the other Frosts in this book, the rural Frost we fondly think is the only one; the topical Frost we are less accustomed to, but find deep and shrewd; the later political Frost, still wise and earthy; the mischievous, epigrammatic Frost; and the magical, the fabulous Frost that invents timeless tales; the direct-descriptive Frost; the ironic-tragic; and the Frost of the classical and American perspective in a responsible world-view.

The title of the book comes from a poem called **"A Cabin in the Clearing,"** sent out to his friends in 1951 as a Christmas greeting. It is a dialogue between Mist and Smoke, watching two human beings, and ends, "Than smoke and mist who better could appraise / The kindred spirit of an inner haze." Frost's way of saying that the spirit persists has always been metaphored in effort, as in the earlier **"Tree at My Window,"** by his naming this book *In the Clearing,* one feels the certainty of at least a clearing in the woods. Into this clearing we walk with him after a full life, as we did in **"Into My Own,"** in his first book. Unless I am too much stretching it, this sort of connection is one of many sensed in the cunning articulation of the book. A charming jacket-photograph shows a white-haired Frost with a finger at his lips, "Hush! . . . Listen! . . . "

Of course, the two Kennedy inaugural poems are included, not conspicuously. The longer one, which unfortunately and yet affectingly Frost could not read on the occasion, reads nobly and powerfully here, a call to glory, "a golden age of poetry and power." His intention, years in the making, is to bless government's recognition of the arts, including poetry, and his foresight was true; the Kennedys have done it. The 1942 poem, **"The Gift Outright,"** is reprinted. With this famous pair go **"America Is Hard to See,"** a longish one about Columbus, and shorter, lighter ones on the same theme. The strain of Frost the comprehensive, national elder counselor is in all these.

Among the apparently casual (but never underestimate this poet, especially when he is casual) couplets and bits at the back of the book is one called **"From**

Iron," He has often told the story in public. A huge ball of almost pure iron ore was mined in Sweden, and sent by the King to the United Nations, with the hope that it might be set up as a one-world symbol. An Indian representative of the UN, Ahmed S. Bokhari, called on Mr. Frost to invite him to write some lines to be done in bronze about this symbol. It must have tempted the poet. But he could not so perpetuate his approval of this oneness. All his thinking and writing had worked out the opposite concept. And so what the Indian delegate got, and all we get in this book, is a couplet, but it comes from the heart and center of all the poet's belief:

> Nature within her inmost self divides
> To trouble men with having to take sides.

Frost's last book of new poems was **Steeple Bush,** published in 1947; a long time, since. His assembly and demonstration of himself from the years between—and earlier—is of masterly and instructive interest. Here is **"Accidentally on Purpose,"** with its last quatrain,

> And yet for all this help of head and brain
> How happily instinctive we remain,
> Our best guide upward further to the light,
> Passionate preference such as love at sight.

Here are **"One More Brevity,"** about the Dalmatian; and **"Escapist—Never,"** concluding with "All is an interminable chain of longing"; and here, to my own delight, is the second longest poem in the book, **"How Hard It Is to Keep from Being King When It's in You and in the Situation."** It first appeared on one surprising Sunday in the *New York Herald Tribune* book section, and shortly thereafter in a hard-cover edition of 300 copies, in 1951.

This is Frost the parabalist. A King of old abdicates, but his son, to whom he offers the throne, declines the honor and leaves with his father. In another kingdom the ex-King becomes cook to a sovereign who first appreciates good food, then good advice, from his superior kitchen help. Excellence cannot hide itself; but the poem gives us the extra invention of the cook-King's son as poet. Here the didactic old arbiter Frost says what poetry is and isn't, should be and shouldn't be. Suddenly he is speaking of Carnegie grants, free verse, Whitman, Sandburg, and iambics, which he here defines:

> Regular verse springs from the strain of rhythm
> Upon a metre, strict or loose iambic.
> From that strain comes the expression *strains of music,*
> The tune is not that metre, not that rhythm,
> But a resultant that arises from them.
> Tell them Iamb, Jehovah said, and meant it.

This playfulness is a long passage for working poets, yet in the total structure of the book it is almost buried, one more of the gathered finalities. A first impression of the whole book might, in fact, be of miscellany. But the more one reads, and relates groupings of ideas, themes, and their cross-allusions, the more powerfully one is impressed that *In the Clearing* contains essences of most of the thoughts and convictions Frost ever had—with the great addition of **"Kitty Hawk."** Never underestimate Frost the book-planner.

And I must return to **"Kitty Hawk"** as a summation of the poet's thinking and as an almost documentary piece in our literary history. In 1894, Frost ran away from home in Massachusetts, wandered south aimlessly, found himself on the sands of Kitty Hawk and Nag's Head—of course, long before the Wrights—and returned to Lawrence, and marriage with his high school sweetheart, Elinor White. In all the later poems of temptation into the dark woods, he pulls back, but this once, and early, he ran recklessly and far.

Next, in tracing the poem's long evolution, we would have to point out epigrams, satires, and public talks in the 1930's, that were concerned with national and political party affairs; Frost the elder, the friend of Henry Wallace, the outraged critic of Franklin D. Roosevelt. But a little earlier, he had been invited by Herbert Hoover to the dedication of a memorial shaft at Kitty Hawk. This is the point when, by my guess, Frost began to want to identify himself with the Wrights, and the air age, and Washington, D.C.

He had never forgotten that he was on the scene, and he mightily strove, and mightily succeeds, in identification. He did meet the surviving Wright, and told him he had been there first. Wasn't it as important that a poet could fly off that beach as that a biplane could? This would be the poem's problem.

The first version was the 1956 Christmas pamphlet, 128 lines of three rapid, freely rhymed beats. In the 100th anniversary issue of the *Atlantic Monthly,* November, 1957, this became a 203-line Part I; the second half is mostly the same, the new part is first. The *Atlantic* version had a whole new Part II, of 219 lines.

In the final version, in this new book, Part I is subtitled, "Portents, Presentiments, and Premonitions," Part II, now lengthened to 289 lines, is subdivided as "Talk Aloft," "The Holiness of Wholeness," and "The Mixture Mechanic." Throughout the several expansions of the poem, the single-word changes, the line-omissions, the shifts of verse-paragraphs, and the long caring over the whole poem are strikingly evident. It was in this prolongation of the poem that Frost reached a depth of deliberation and insight that enabled him to put his own interpretative blessing on what has always made the American materialist uneasy.

"Kitty Hawk" is a manifesto, a major statement on American character and American achievement in mechanics, issued by our greatest modern poet, who has at last made his peace with science, which he has so long thought the enemy of poetry. He has brought about a magnificent, hard-won triumph; my rather arithmetical demonstration is meant only to prove the triumph. In this long poem, as in the seemingly artless combinations of the other poems, he has forgotten nothing of all he ever knew, he has managed to show off all the aspects of a lifetime's speculation, and told us the best he knows about life.

Lest anything or anyone be omitted, *In the Clearing* was published on Frost's 88th birthday Monday, and the dedication mentions Louis Untermeyer, Sidney Cox, and John Bartlett. A reminding line beneath the book's title is, "And wait to watch the water clear, I may," from the first poem in his first book. The title poem is dedicated to his publisher, Alfred Edwards. Even in **"Lines Written in Dejection on the Eve of Great Success,"** he prophesies Astronaut Glenn's orbit. He reached far back to a California memory of being swooped at but not carried off by an eagle, in **"Auspex,"** And he closes the book with a very simple poem about chopping down one maple tree, which will defeat neither nature nor himself. This small quiet image is summary: man active, nature ceaseless, neither one winning or losing, which is the core of Frost's belief.

Burton A. Robie

SOURCE: A review of *In the Clearing*, in *Library Journal*, Vol. 87, April 15, 1962, p. 1616.

Robert Frost has published a new book of verse and it was the pleasure of this writer some months ago to hear him speak one of the pieces at a small gathering in one of the Yale Colleges. Now upon reading the work in print (**"One More Beauty"** in which a transient canine becomes for one night the great star Sirius), it becomes blindingly clear how much the art is inseparable from the man. Frost, the poet and faithful lover of his world and country, needs no introduction or commendation from this reviewer. As ever, in these poems he is as much at home in the fields

and forests as in the mysteries of the universe and demonstrates in a wise, humble, not unhumorous way that he has come to terms with life. All have much to learn from and share with him. If ever there should be a Poet Laureateship in this country (and why not) his would be the certain honor.

STOPPING BY WOODS ON A SNOWY EVENING (1978)

Booklist

SOURCE: A review of *Stopping by Woods on a Snowy Evening*, in *Booklist*, Vol. 75, No. 9, January 1, 1979, p. 809.

The well-known lines of Frost's poem inspire Jeffers to a dreamily benign winter landscape: clean, soft, and shining from the heavily fallen snow and radiating an almost palpable serenity. In the heart of this pristine world moves Frost's narrator, realized here as a jovial, rotund old man, who pauses to savor deeply the special mood of the woods and to leave behind a jumble of seed and twiggy shelter for invisibly hovering wild creatures. Not since the artist's *Three Jovial Huntsmen* has her conception been so ambitious. Scenes are fully and carefully built, with each essentially black-and-white spread allotted a quiet infusion of color—a well-handled ploy that doesn't work against the book's careful unity. The visual interpretation preserves—even strengthens—the poem's underlying wonder; the only dispute is with the sweetening of some of the animals, the horse in particular. It's a book to slowly savor and share one to one.

Sharon Elswit

SOURCE: A review of *Stopping by Woods on a Snowy Evening*, in *School Library Journal*, Vol. 25, No. 6, February, 1979, p. 40.

Jeffers is comfortable with Frost's lyric. In soft pencil and pen washed with light orange, blue, and green, a man comes out of the snow, gets bigger and fades back into the swirling light grey storm. He is chubby, with a white beard, allusions to Santa unmistakable and regrettable. With comic spirit he rummages in the sleigh, rear sticking out and arms buried under the quilt; he falls down to make a snow angel and the forest animals flee his exuberance. Jeffers divides the lines, one and two per page, the way the poem might be read aloud. She speaks, with Frost, of the wonder of the woods, where just for a quiet moment, things are the way they seem. But in making the poem more accessible to younger children, she limits the traveler by giving him a reason to stop and a reason to go on—he leaves seed and hay for wild animals; his "promises" are to a family; perhaps he has other bundles to deliver. "Sleep" is not death here or the end of artistic struggle, but only itself, rest. And yet whatever dismay one feels at such definition, Jeffers does offer youngsters a fine first reading of Frost.

Bulletin of the Center for Children's Books

SOURCE: A review of *Stopping by Woods on a Snowy Evening,* in *Bulletin of the Center for Children's Books,* Vol. 32, No. 7, March, 1979, p. 114.

Although the picture book format indicates that this illustrated version of Frost's poem is best suited for a younger audience, there is really no age limit for good poetry, and many older readers should enjoy the illustrations; chiefly black and white and grey, the pictures of the trees and creatures of snow-stilled woods are touched briefly with the colors of an old man's clothing and the blanket on his sleigh. At times the color fades; that is, jacket or blanket may be left partly black and white. The pictures are realistic, save for one in which the artist has magnified snowflakes; although Jeffers has interpreted some of the poem (. . . "But I have promises to keep . . . " shows the man stopping at a house and being greeted by a woman and children) most of her delicate detail emphasizes the beauty of the woods in a frosted twilight.

Ethel L. Heins

SOURCE: A review of *Stopping by Woods on a Snowy Evening,* in *The Horn Book Magazine,* Vol. LV, No. 2, April, 1979, p. 182.

A beautiful picture book, handsomely designed, which is obviously an inspired creation. The illustrator, working with artistry and skill and reflecting both the wintry atmosphere and the natural serenity of the poem, has made double-page spreads in which intricate patterning is balanced by an elegant plainness of coloration: shades of gray upon white with only occasional touches of pale green, yellowish brown, and blue. An illustrator, like a composer, librettist, or choreographer, has the right, of course, to produce a highly personal interpretation of a literary work. But it is often questioned whether an explicit line-by-line pictorial representation of a lyrical—not

a narrative—poem may constrain a child's imagination and interfere with his or her response to poetic ambiguity—the spontaneous formation of images in the mind. Moreover, a spare but suggestive simplicity characterizes the famous poem; in Frost's volume *New Hampshire* it is one of a group of verses called Grace Notes, which contain some of his most haunting and quietly eloquent writing. The picture-book jacket states that a "kindly rotund figure . . . lends both humor and a Christmas feeling that should greatly enhance the enjoyment of the book." And it is precisely these additional elements—as well as a certain homely sentimentality that seem incongruous with the poet's essential reticence.

A SWINGER OF BIRCHES (1983)

Publishers Weekly

SOURCE: A review of *A Swinger of Birches,* in *Publishers Weekly,* Vol. 222, No. 17, October 22, 1982, p. 55.

More than an introduction in the usual sense, Fadiman's preface encourages readers to seek the deeper meanings in the late poet's works. As an illustrator, Koeppen also conveys nuances in words used with great care by Frost to make us think about what lies beyond the obvious in celebrating the joys of a swinger of **"Birches,"** for example. Superb paintings in full color accompany well-chosen poems—38 altogether—including **"The Road Not Taken," "The Gift Outright," "Stopping by Woods on a Snowy Evening"** and less familiar lyrics. Each confirms Fadiman's belief that Frost meant his poems to be "said," not merely read or recited but expressed as he himself insisted, as though in "talking" to a friend. A glossary that seems unnecessary is appended.

Margery Fisher

SOURCE: A review of *A Swinger of Birches,* in *Growing Point,* Vol. 22, No. 6, March, 1984, p. 4226.

With a title taken from one of the chosen poems, this selection for young readers show Frost's genius for using small incidents to express wider truths, and the inner strength, verbal and emotional, of poetry which he called 'a momentary stay against confusion.' Here are favourites like **'Mending Wall'** and **'The Runaway,'** illustrated in colour in a way that is unobtrusive but properly interpretative. The artist's landscapes often throw extra light on two or three poems printed in association, and one particular picture, of **'Tree at my Window,'** suggests both literal and figurative experience in the view of a boy looking out, in reflected image and actual appearance. A most approachable and timely selection for young readers from seven or so.

The Junior Bookshelf

SOURCE: A review of *A Swinger of Birches,* in *The Junior Bookshelf,* Vol. 48, No. 2, April, 1984, p. 82.

The poet, Robert Frost, was born in 1874 in America. He lived from 1912 to 1915 in England, and then returned to the countryside of New Hampshire. He died in 1963 with the reputation of being the most distinguished American poet of his day. The 38 poems in this book show how well-deserved that reputation was. The flowing beauty of the words express his deep love of the countryside with such sensitivity. The apparent simplicity of his appreciation of natural things covers a deep understanding of their ultimate purpose. Trees, animals, birds, stars, flowers, the weather—all these were inspiration for his talent.

An interesting and informative introduction to the book written by Clifton Fadiman will help readers to understand and appreciate the genius of the poet.

The artist certainly did. His colour illustrations are outstandingly lovely, especially the one complementing a short poem called **"The Runaway."** Exquisite flowers, delightful animals, natural settings, human figures, trees at all seasons, snow and sunshine—the variety is endless. Each page turned opens up a new beauty. His finely drawn black and white pictures are just as attractive.

This is a special book to be savoured and enjoyed by all poetry lovers.

📖 *BIRCHES* (1988)

Kirkus Reviews

SOURCE: A review of *Birches,* in *Kirkus Reviews,* Vol. LVI, No. 14, July 15, 1988, p. 1060.

Young has painted a lovely series of watercolors to illustrate one of Frost's most familiar and beloved poems, but the end result is a disappointment. Although pleasing in themselves, the watercolors don't illustrate the poem: they don't explain it, which is acceptable because explanation would probably be both obtrusive and unnecessary; but neither do they evoke its source: to see birches in northern New England is to experience black and white, blue and green, not Young's reddish browns and grays; nor has Young caught the gleam of the bark, the characteristic bend of these supple trees, or the way light filters through their leaves. Moreover, it's no kindness to the poem to chop it into two-and three-line fragments; as printed whole on the final two pages, the flowing, ruminative iambic pentameter generates a well-paced series of ideas and pictures in the reader's mind—a preferable way to appreciate Frost's images.

Nancy Palmer

SOURCE: A review of *Birches,* in *School Library Journal,* Vol. 35, No. 1, October, 1988, p. 152.

Frost's spare phrases conjure up vividly concrete mental pictures which are not reflected in Young's lovely, but often abstracted and incongruent, watercolors. In double-page spreads above the cream band that contains the few lines of text per page, Young's flowing atmospheric washes catch the New England landscape in all seasons and moods, but neither their sweeps and splotches not their impressionistic shapes that blur into precision get across that crucial central image of the bend of those trees toward earth. Their perspective is sophisticated and does convey something of the climb and descent imagery, but as a whole, the paintings provide a musical background rather than illumination of the poem. A literal interpretation isn't necessary, or perhaps even desirable, but there should be some congruence between art and text; and these softly frenzied abstractions tend to be disconcerting and dissonant. The full-color (but with an autumnal cast) pictures stand back; while adults may appreciate the non-interference with the text, children will find it distancing. The complete poem is reprinted at the end of the book, offering an intriguing contrast to seeing it page by page and illustrated. *A Swinger of Birches,* a collection of 38 Frost poems for young people, illustrated by Peter Koeppen, is much less dramatic artistically, but a better straightforward introduction to the poetry. Susan Jeffers's illustrations for the picture book edition of **"Stopping by Woods on a Snowy Evening"** offer a better example of expansion of the text without contradiction or confusion.

Ethel L. Heins

SOURCE: A review of *Birches,* in *The Horn Book Magazine,* Vol. LXV, No. 1, January/February, 1989, pp. 85-6.

Illustrating poetry can be a highly contentious artistic enterprise. Narrative verse by its very nature lends itself perfectly to the picture book form; but the reader's imagination may be constrained when the haunting ambiguity of a brief lyric poem, like **"Stopping by Woods on a Snowy Evening,"** is subjected to explicit pictorial representation. The artist has not illustrated **Birches** with literal images. Just as a composer or a choreographer can be inspired by a work of literature, Ed Young has made elegant, graceful paintings that are subtly analogous to the text. Descriptive and reflective, the poem speaks of the natural beauty of the birch tree and of the exuberant young "swinger of birches"—and ultimately of the poet's own heavenly aspirations while contentedly remaining earthbound. "I'd like to get away from earth awhile / And then come back to it and begin over . . . I'd like to go by climbing a birch tree, / And climb black branches up a snow-white trunk / *Toward* heaven, till the tree could bear no more, / But dipped its top and set me down again." Ed Young has never stereotyped his art; he is utterly versatile, meeting the challenge of each text with imaginative vision and consummate skill. Visually suggesting, rather than interpreting, the moods and nuances of meaning in the lines of poetry, the beautifully composed illustrations, with their muted seasonal colors and arresting, almost impressionistic variations in pattern and design, neither overwhelm nor attempt to explicate the superbly stated text; in their own way the paintings parallel the poetic experience.

CHRISTMAS TREES (1990)

Kirkus Reviews

SOURCE: A review of *Christmas Trees,* in *Kirkus Reviews,* Vol. LVIII, No. 18, September 15, 1990, pp. 1333-34.

Here, Frost's poem—in the form of a letter explaining why a farmer refuses to sell his trees to a city slicker—is illustrated in a casual, popular style that may have wide appeal but is careless in detail: the fence rails are suspended as if by magic; the kids wear galoshes on a crisp October day; and the sere landscape sprinkled with firs seems to be an unlikely blend of New England and the Northwest. It would be better to leave visualizing this fine poem to the reader's imagination.

School Library Journal

SOURCE: A review of *Christmas Trees,* in *School Library Journal,* Vol. 36, No. 10, October, 1990, p. 36.

In Frost's spare prose poem, written in 1916 as a "Christmas circular letter," a city man offers to buy a farmer's woods of balsam fir to sell back in the city for Christmas trees. While the farmer seems to consider the offer and an anxious extended family watches from the house and porch, the two men walk the hillside estimating how many trees might be cut. The city fellow reckons there are about a thousand trees for which he'll pay $30. The farmer figures that at three cents a tree, he could just about mail one to each of his friends if he could get one in an envelope. The text lacks child appeal, but the poetry and illustrations do blend perfectly to re-create a quieter time in this century. Rand's paintings contrast the city man's rigid purposefulness with the rumpled and relaxed posture of the farmer while displaying the rusty colors of the late fall Vermont countryside to splendid advantage.

THE RUNAWAY (1998)

Publishers Weekly

SOURCE: A review of *The Runaway,* in *Publishers Weekly,* Vol. 245, No. 51, December 21, 1998, p. 66.

With a muted palette of pastel and earth tones, Lang's serene illustrations of a New England landscape give Frost's haunting, potentially disturbing poem a happy ending. Walking in a snowfall, a girl and a woman who appears to be her mother spy a skittish colt frightened by the weather. As the animal bolts across a field, the poem's unnamed voice asks, "Where is his mother? He can't be out alone." Frost's concluding words leave the young horse's fate uncertain: "Whoever it is that leaves him out so late, / When other creatures have gone to stall and bin, / Ought to be told to come and take him in." Lang, however, answers the rhetorical question by introducing a concerned mare in the distance that takes her place by the frightened colt's side. Lang's collage-style spreads with large blocks of color are tranquil renderings of a seemingly sedate colt and do not effectively allow readers to experience the strength of Frost's words (to hear "the miniature thunder where he fled," for example). The poet suggests a colt fearful of the heavy snowfall, yet the illustrations convey a perfect pattern of spare white polka dots. Although the artist's interpretation may quell her audience, the artwork divests the poem of its drama and urgency.

Nina Lindsay

SOURCE: A review of *The Runaway,* in *School Library Journal,* Vol. 45, No. 3, March, 1999, p. 193.

In this successful picture-book adaptation of a Frost poem, a child watches a lone colt spooked by his first snowfall and comments, "Whoever it is that leaves him out so late, / When other creatures have gone to stall and bin, / Ought to be told to come and take him in." In an endnote on Frost, the poem is acknowledged as being a metaphor for "the impetuous spirit of youth." This metaphor is implied visually in Lang's illustrations. The bold, almost silhouetted figures of a girl and her dog watching the colt are rendered in matte colors with no or faint white outlining and evoke the cold, muted brightness of the early winter farm landscape. The artist frames the pictures so that the child's mother only occasionally appears at the periphery of the double-page spreads. The narrator seems to be the girl, who notices the colt's play and the fact that his mother isn't around, but who also plays in the snow unattended. Yet readers know that the child's mother is always at hand and, sure enough, Lang brings the mare to collect her young at the end. It is this visual layer to the text that makes this poem an appealing story for children. Lang makes her vision of this poem haunting enough to suggest new possibilities of interpretation as children grow up and mature.

Additional coverage of Frost's life and career is contained in the following sources published by the Gale Group: *Authors and Artists for Young Adults,* **Vol. 21;** *Concise Dictionary of Literary Biography, 1917-1929;* *Contemporary Authors New Revision Series,* **Vol. 33;** *Contemporary Literary Criticism,* **Vols. 1, 3, 4, 9, 10, 13, 15, 26, 34, 44;** *Dictionary of Literary Biography,* **Vol. 54;** *Dictionary of Literary Biography Documentary Series,* **Vol. 7;** *DISCovering Authors; DISCovering Authors: British; DISCovering Authors: Canadian; DISCovering Authors Modules: Most-studied Authors, Poets; Major 20th-Century Writers; Poetry Criticism,* **Vol. 1;** *Something about the Author,* **Vol. 14;** *World Literature Criticism.*

Lillian Hoban
1925-1998

American illustrator and author of picture books for preschoolers and beginning readers.

INTRODUCTION

Using simple pencil lines or a pen and ink wash, picture book illustrator Lillian Hoban has brought to life the charming characters of Frances the badger and Arthur the chimp as well as various human children and an assortment of other animals. She began illustrating picture books in collaboration with her husband, Russell Hoban, and together they crafted the charming series of books about Frances the badger. Frances is a very human badger child with very real problems and opinions. With the help of her loving parents, she always manages to get what she needs, if not always what she wants. Frances could have been created only by a loving parent, since she perfectly exhibits the behaviors of a happy child going through the normal conflicts of childhood, and, with her parents' encouragement, finding inventive solutions. Frances's face shows the expressions every parent knows. Hoban told *The Third Book of Junior Authors*, "I don't exactly use our children as models, but whether I'm drawing kids or animals I have them in mind, and the expressions on the face of Frances the badger have appeared on various small Hoban faces in our house."

Those expressions can also be found on the face of mischievous Arthur. These books are wholly Hoban's own as she both wrote and illustrated them. Among the other authors whose books she has illustrated, Miriam Cohen stands out as one she has worked with on many occasions, creating the images of the little boy Jim and his multi-ethnic first grade classmates. Critics enjoy Hoban's lively drawings and irrepressible characters, describing them as beguiling and filled with humor and the homely details of family life. Hoban enjoys what she does. She said, "I have just as good a time as a kid with a coloring book . . . I concentrate on getting the right feeling in the pictures. Sometimes I go mad with color separations, but most of the time I'm doing what I like best."

BIOGRAPHICAL INFORMATION

Hoban was born and raised in Philadelphia, Pennsylvania. Her family moved all over the city, and she

spent her spare time exploring whichever local library was nearest. She always wanted to be an illustrator. She took classes at the Graphics Arts Club where she met her future husband, author Russell Hoban. She received a scholarship to the Philadelphia Museum School and started classes there in 1942, the year after Russell began his. She studied there for two years, but left after her marriage in 1944. With Russell in the army, she moved to New York and gave up illustration to study modern dance with Hanya Holm. For many years she taught dance classes in New York and Connecticut and worked at a slenderizing studio. When the third of her four children was born, she gave up professional dance and returned to illustration, working with her husband on the picture books he was writing. Their first collaboration was *Herman the Loser* in 1961, and many others followed. She was soon illustrating books for other authors, and eventually began writing books herself. Among the many authors whose work she has illustrated are Miriam Cohen, Johanna Hurwitz, James Howe, Judy Delton, and her daughter, Julia Hoban. Hoban died of heart failure on July 17, 1998.

MAJOR WORKS

Hoban's best-known illustrations are for the charming series of books about Frances the badger written by Russell Hoban. Beginning with *Bread and Jam for Frances* (1964), in which Frances decides she will eat nothing but bread and jam ever again, until there is spaghetti and meat balls for dinner, the series continued with *A Baby Sister for Frances* (1964, Frances runs away under the dining room table), *A Birthday for Frances* (1968, Frances buys a present for her little sister using her own money), *Best Friends for Frances* (1969, Frances starts a No Boys Best Friends Club), *A Bargain for Frances* (1970, Frances learns about trust and friendship), and *Egg Thoughts and Other Frances Songs* (1972, Frances does not like eggs!)

In 1967, Hoban began illustrating what became a series of books for early readers written by Miriam Cohen. These book are about Jim, a first grader, and his experiences with his classmates. The first of these, *Will I Have a Friend?*, depicts the nervousness of a child's first day at school. This was followed by over a dozen more, among them *No Good in Art* (1980), which touches on how art is presented in school, *See You Tomorrow Charles* (1983), about the class adjusting to the new boy who is blind, and *It's George!* (1988), in which a mentally-challenged classmate proves himself. Critics liked the lively and colorful drawings of the children, and approved the depiction of a multi-ethnic class.

After illustrating so many books for others, it was only natural that Hoban would eventually try writing her own. Her first attempt was *Arthur's Christmas Cookies* (1971) about an energetic chimpanzee whose enthusiasm is greater than his skill. It was a successful first venture that led to another series of books, this time her own. Eight more Arthur books followed, to the delight of both critics and young readers: *Arthur's Honey Bear* (1974), *Arthur's Pen Pal* (1976), *Arthur's Prize Reader* (1978), *Arthur's Funny Money* (1981), *Arthur's Halloween Costume* (1984), *Arthur's Loose Tooth* (1985), *Arthur's Great Big Valentine* (1991), and *Arthur's Camp-Out* (1992).

AWARDS

In 1968 *Charlie the Tramp* (1967) won the Boys' Club Award, and in 1971 *Emmett Otter's Jug-Band*

Christmas (1971) won both the Lewis Carroll Shelf Award and the Christopher Award, Children's Category. Both books were written by Russell Hoban.

TITLE COMMENTARY

📖 *WILL I HAVE A FRIEND?* (1967)

Kirkus Reviews

SOURCE: A review of *Will I Have a Friend?*, in *Kirkus Reviews*, Vol. XXXV, No. 11, June 1, 1967, p. 640.

Brownstones outside the window, an integrated nursery school—"Will I have a friend?" asks Jim. "I think you will," says Pa. Jim is on the edge of things most of the first day, but at last someone speaks to him and they play together. All the normal activities of a quiet day at school are glimpsed in this tentative little story, reiterated with less skill (and cyclamen Negro faces) in the wash drawings. The details of toys and classroom and the cartoon-like figures of the children *are* fun to look at—a soft-sell initiation for newcomers, instant empathy for veterans.

Virginia Haviland

SOURCE: A review of *Will I Have a Friend?*, in *The Horn Book Magazine*, Vol. XVIII, No. 5, October, 1967, p. 581.

A beguiling book, especially for one who faces the experience of going to school. After Jim's father leaves him on the first day, with assurances that he will indeed have a friend there, Jim watches silently for a time, joins in giddy laughter over the bumping in "funny-tummies," and at last, in a rest period, discovers that he and neighbor Paul share a special interest. Lively full-color scenes of an integrated kindergarten engaging in familiar activities will make this a meaningful picture book for Head Start and other preschool story groups.

📖 *A BIRTHDAY FOR FRANCES* (1968)

Virginia Haviland

SOURCE: A review of *A Birthday for Frances*, in *The Horn Book Magazine*, Vol. XLIV, No. 5, October, 1968, pp. 552-523.

Followers of Frances, the badger child—in the United States and abroad—will be happy again. She reappears no less the real child, no less irresistible in her fourth story; her thoughts and actions attendant on giving little sister Gloria a second-birthday present are as appealing as the earlier domestic situations. Beguiling sketches and precisely the right words— with wonderfully amusing conversations—depict the preparations for Gloria's party and the celebration of the traditional ceremonies.

📖 BEST FRIENDS FOR FRANCES (1969)

Diane Farrell

SOURCE: A review of *Best Friends for Frances,* in *The Horn Book Magazine,* Vol. XLV, No. 5, October, 1969, p. 526.

Albert is having a "wandering day" (a day to do things girls can't—catching snakes and "a little frog work"). So Frances plays baseball with her little sister Gloria. But the next day when Albert is playing a "no girls game" with Harold, Frances organizes a "BEST FRIENDS OUTING NO BOYS." There are games, prizes, an enormous hamper of lunch. Albert, overcome by the size of the hamper, becomes a best friend; and everybody plays baseball—even Gloria. Text and pictures are full of the humor and the homely details of family life that characterize the stories of Frances the Badger and make them beloved by both children and adults. Frances herself is growing up; she sings as much but sulks less and attacks her problems with less reliance on adults.

📖 ARTHUR'S CHRISTMAS COOKIES (1972)

Kirkus Reviews

SOURCE: A review of *Arthur's Christmas Cookies,* in *Kirkus Reviews,* Vol. XL, No. 21, November 1, 1972, p. 1237.

Though Arthur the monkey can't hold a Christmas candle to last year's *Emmet Otter,* his problems in the kitchen offer recognition and amusement, and his solution might even provide beginning readers with inspiration for their own Christmas giving. As Arthur has spent his money and messed up a lamp he was making, the cookies are intended as a gift for his parents. But after all the mixing and baking, interspersed with some gentle jostling with his sister, and two friends, it turns out that he's used salt instead of sugar. What saves Arthur's project and the story is his realization, after a few tears, that the cookies (already shaped like trees, stars and bells) have the same ingredients as "play clay," so that by painting them different colors he can turn them into ornaments. The warmly colored pictures of Arthur's awkward labors help make this "a good present after all."

Ethel L. Heins

SOURCE: A review of *Arthur's Christmas Cookies,* in *The Horn Book Magazine,* Vol. XLVIII, No. 6, December, 1972, p. 581.

Violet and Arthur, two monkey siblings who talk and act much like their human cousins, are discussing the problem of buying Christmas presents for their parents. Arthur has recklessly squandered his pocket money, so he volunteers to make Christmas cookies in his sister's toy oven. Just as he is collecting the ingredients, several of their friends drop in; advice and suggestions are freely and loudly offered; and in the general hubbub, poor Arthur puts salt instead of sugar into the batter. Alas! The cookies bake as hard as rocks; but all is not lost, for he has made clay cookies—Christmas angels, stars, and bells; and gaily painted, they become perfect tree ornaments. Amusing pictures accompany an I Can Read Christmas tale, told with real humor, which is always delightful to find in so simple a text.

📖 THE SUGAR SNOW SPRING (1973)

Kirkus Reviews

SOURCE: A review of *The Sugar Snow Spring,* in *Kirkus Reviews,* Vol. XLI, No. 6, March 15, 1973, p. 316.

"It's sugar snow. Spring's just around the corner," the Easter Bunny tells Oscar when he pulls him from a deep bootprint. But the winter looks grim for the Mouse family after father Everett disappears and young Oscar is forced to make his rounds alone— wearing a back pack made from a scrap of old feedbag. In trying to steal straw from the barn for the expected new baby, Oscar is nearly captured by the cat Ethel, but everything works out on Easter Sunday when the bunny delivers jelly beans and tiny chocolate Easter eggs, Dr. Pfeffer-Mouse delivers a tiny baby mouse and a now stout Everett delivers himself home after eating his way out of a feed bin. Sugary melodrama with just enough of Hoban's spry humor to make it palatable for tiny readers.

Ethel L. Heins

SOURCE: A review of *The Sugar Snow Spring,* in *The Horn Book Magazine,* Vol. XLIX, No. 3, June, 1973, pp. 265-66.

Probably because of their size and vulnerability, mice—in shamelessly anthropomorphic stories—are enormously appealing to young children. In a fantasy for early readers, Henrietta Mouse worriedly awaits the springtime arrival of her new baby. Everett, her husband, usually a good provider, has mysteriously vanished; Oscar, her son, is hard-pressed to outwit Ethel, the watchful barn cat, and to bring home a bit of food and some straw to plait into a baby basket. It is sugar snow time—"'when it snows after the sap starts running in the maple trees. . . . It means spring is just around the corner.'" In its bleakest hour, the mouse family is saved by the Easter Bunny, who first restores Everett safely to his home and then leaves an Easter basket for the tiny new arrival. Pictures in three colors illustrate the miniature drama, emphasizing the cat-and-mouse skirmishes as well as the atmosphere of snug domesticity.

TOUGH JIM (1974)

Harriet Groner

SOURCE: A review of *Tough Jim,* in *School Library Journal,* Vol. 21, No. 5, January, 1975, p. 38.

This is an average story about Jim who decides to come to his class costume party as a strongman. When his teacher leaves the room for a moment, the third grade bully, Zoogy, enters and picks a fight with Jim. In the shuffle, Jim's helmet falls over his eyes; he crashes about; and accidently knocks Zoogy into the wastebasket. Lillian Hoban's delicately toned watercolors enliven the bland story with their humorous details (the boy who is dressed as fried chicken is especially good). An adequate choice for reading aloud to youngsters who will remember Jim and his first grade friends.

ARTHUR'S HONEY BEAR (1974)

Publishers Weekly

SOURCE: A review of *Arthur's Honey Bear,* in *Publishers Weekly,* Vol. 205, No. 21, May 27, 1974, p. 65.

We met and fell in love with the chimpanzee brother and sister, Arthur and Violet, in *Arthur's Christmas Cookies,* an earlier I Can Read Book. This sequel is equally delightful. Arthur and Violet plan a Tag Sale of their outgrown toys and playthings. They put price tags on all their pictures, rocks, marbles, a yo-yo, old maid cards, a hula-hoop—on everything except Arthur's Honey Bear. Arthur knows he's too old for a stuffed toy but Honey Bear is special. When the chimp's friend Wilma offers 50[00a2] for the bear, Arthur reluctantly agrees to sell, but Wilma changes her mind when she finds that gift-wrapping is not included. After the sale, Violet makes Arthur an offer he can't refuse but he's disconsolate until he and his sister arrive at a happy compromise.

Booklist

SOURCE: A review of *Arthur's Honey Bear,* in *Booklist,* Vol. 70, No. 22, July 15, 1974, p. 1253.

If growing up means selling your favorite stuffed toy, Arthur—of *Arthur's Christmas Cookies*—is unprepared. Although he won't admit it, he is relieved when no one buys the ragged Honey Bear at his personal spring-cleaning rummage sale. He finally—and grudgingly—sells Honey Bear to his little sister, but later makes the happy discovery that he is now Honey Bear's uncle and can once again openly lavish warmth on his toy. Lillian Hoban's intimate, charming, and sparsely worded text supported by her characteristically expressive color drawings of a monkey-child in the throes of discovering the tie that binds.

Beryl Robinson

SOURCE: A review of *Arthur's Honey Bear,* in *The Horn Book Magazine,* Vol. L, No. 4, August, 1974, p. 371.

Arthur decided to have a tag sale to dispose of his old toys. With his sister Violet helping, he blithely attached prices to all of his toys until he came to his beloved Honey Bear. Then, he tried several delaying tactics to keep Honey Bear for himself. But the machinery for the sale had been set in motion, and he finally had to yield to Violet's offer to buy Honey Bear for "'thirty-one cents, my coloring book, my crayons, and half a box of Cracker Jack with the prize still in it.'" However, with the same resourcefulness that had enabled him to turn his cookie-making fiasco into a great triumph in *Arthur's Christmas Cookies,* he found a way to honor his agreement with Violet and still keep a close relationship with Honey Bear. The little chimpanzees are completely captivating, childlike, and convincing in motivations and actions; and Arthur's solution to a problem that has been faced in some way or other by many a small child is both logical and satisfying. A delightfully illustrated I Can Read Book with flavor, suspense, a good plot, and a fresh situation.

ARTHUR'S PEN PAL (1976)

Beryl Robinson

SOURCE: A review of *Arthur's Pen Pal,* in *The Horn Book Magazine,* Vol. LII, No. 4, August, 1976, p. 392.

In a third I Can Read story about the engaging chimpanzees, mild rivalry between Arthur and his little sister Violet is ended satisfactorily after Arthur admits that although he can beat Violet at Indian wrestling, she can beat him at jumping rope. Furthermore, since she can't do karate like his pen pal Sandy—who, to his great surprise, turns out to be a girl and a karate champion—he is never knocked down like Sandy's big brother. Realistic details of family relationships will be recognized and enjoyed as will the satisfying warmth that pervades the conclusion. Appealingly illustrated, the story is wise as well as entertaining.

Zena Sutherland

SOURCE: A review of *Arthur's Pen Pal,* in *Bulletin of the Center for Children's Books,* Vol. 30, No. 1, September, 1976, p. 11.

Another story about that beguiling child in chimpanzee form, Arthur. Here he wistfully contrasts his sister Violet, who squabbles and teases, with the sibling relationship enjoyed by his pen pal, Sandy. Sandy has a big brother who does karate with him. They Indian wrestle. All that little Violet can do is skip rope. Then Arthur discovers that Sandy is a girl, that she beats her brother at karate. Suddenly Violet seems satisfactory to him, and he writes his pen pal a letter that boasts of Violet's prowess at skipping Red Hot Pepper and double loop-the-loop. A conventional view of sex roles, but a very funny one, is given in a story told very simply, with dialogue that is truly childlike and pictures that capture the busy enthusiasm of childhood.

Marjorie Lewis

SOURCE: A review of *Arthur's Pen Pal,* in *School Library Journal,* Vol. 23, No. 1, September, 1976, pp. 100-01.

Anthropomorphic Arthur and his little sister Violet in a pleasant, warm lesson in which Arthur, a small male-chauvinist chimp, is forced to change his views when he discovers that his pen pal, with the unisex name of "Sandy," whose talent in karate and playing the drums Arthur envies, is really a girl. Pre-schoolers and beginning readers, as well as adults, will find the shock of recognition here both satisfying and amusing: Arthur's "bath" contrasted with Violet's orderly scrub, Arthur's pocket contents, the jump rope contest between Arthur and Violet, and the despair of their elderly chimp-lady baby sitter all bear the talented mark of Hoban's good ear and eye for the details of a young child's world—its triumphs, disappointments and preoccupations. The lesson is palatable rather than didactic and the characters ingratiating rather than cute. Arthur's discontent and Violet's small-sister predicaments should chasten chauvinists and suit Sisters everywhere.

STICK-IN-THE-MUD TURTLE (1977)

School Library Journal

SOURCE: A review of *Stick-in-the-Mud Turtle,* in *School Library Journal,* Vol. 23, No. 9, May, 1977, p. 74.

A warmly illustrated story on a familiar theme. Lillian Hoban's **Stick-in-the-Mud Turtle** is envious of new neighbors who have such luxuries as a "shiny motor boat that went putt-putt around the pond" and shoo-fly pie whenever they desire it, but finds the grass actually isn't greener in the mudhole on the other side of the pond. The new neighbor children are rude and rough. When their visit to their new neighbors ends, they are happy to go home to their homemade toys and Mother Turtle's special treat—"super dooper double delicious shoo-fly pie."

Zena Sutherland

SOURCE: A review of *Stick-in-the-Mud Turtle,* in *Bulletin of the Center for Children's Books,* Vol. 30, No. 10, June, 1977, p. 159.

Ten turtle children and their parents live contentedly in their mudhole, taking sunbaths at the front door, rowing about in a hollow log, using what's at hand for entertainment. When a new turtle family moves next door, the older residents (save for wise father) are envious of the motorboat, the fancy water toys, etc. But the new turtle children are prone to bully and tease, the motorboat is noisy and pollutes the air, and the older family soon comes to appreciate the pleasures of the simple life. The "make-do" theme is commendable, but the equating of possessions with unpleasant behavior seems overdrawn; otherwise the book is adequate fare for Hoban's usual audience. The family relationships are realistic, there's enough action in pictures and text, and the pictures have a gentle appeal. Although issued as a book for beginning independent readers, this seems more appropriate for a preschool audience. What it lacks is the humorous and affectionate insight that is in the *Arthur* stories, the creation of a character with whom children can identify.

The Horn Book Magazine

SOURCE: A review of *Stick-in-the-Mud Turtle,* in *The Horn Book Magazine,* Vol. LIII, No. 4, August, 1977, pp. 434-435.

Fred the turtle wasn't impressed when a new turtle and his family moved into the mudhole across the pond, but Fred's wife and children were. For the newcomer was making renovations, and his children had fancy water toys. "But Fred didn't say anything. He just opened his mouth and caught another fly"; whereupon Mrs. Turtle called him "'a STICK-IN-THE-MUD turtle!'" Invited to visit the new family, Fred's wife and children had to bear the brunt of the aggressive conduct of the newcomers as well as the noise and smoke of their motor boat, and they were glad to return to the quiet simple joys of their mudhole. A hint of didacticism, in keeping with the traditional moralism of the anthropomorphic animal fable, is well-hidden beneath the humor of the situation; and the unpretentious line drawings enlivened by pastel color washes suggest the art employed by Arnold Lobel in his sagas of Frog and Toad.

📖 *I MET A TRAVELER* (1977)

Betsy Hearne

SOURCE: A review of *I Met a Traveler,* in *Booklist,* Vol. 74, No. 1, September 1, 1977, pp. 41-42.

Among several expository novels about Israel written by American visitors, this stands out as having taken a step beyond purposeful experience of the country to create a unique situation and set of characters. While there is still the inevitable enumeration of what a sabra's breakfast consists of, it is dropped subtly into a climactic scene in which young Josie confronts her mother after being left alone all night.

The basic problem is that Josie is often left alone—to face a school she hates and a country in which she feels strange—while her independent, artistic mother carries on another in a long string of affairs. Josie secretly plans to amass enough money to buy tickets for herself and her Russian-immigrant mother substitute, Mira, straight home to snowy Connecticut. But Mira marries a friendly puppeteer, and Josie must learn that she can't turn the clock back to childhood. The personality of Jerusalem is well delineated as is that of a refreshingly imperfect mother-daughter team.

The Horn Book Magazine

SOURCE: A review of *I Met a Traveler,* in *The Horn Book Magazine,* Vol. LIV, No. 1, February, 1978, pp. 45-7.

An author-illustrator long associated with books for young children has written her first full-length novel. The story is built around several of the near-clichés of contemporary realistic juvenile fiction: a perceptive girl, physically and psychologically displaced by her parents' divorce, awkwardly straddling the gulf between childhood and adolescence, and a spirited but embarrassingly unconventional mother. Yet the exotic setting and the well-seasoned mixture of unusual characters offset any trendy elements. Josie and her mother have left their big suburban house in Connecticut, and after traveling to Europe, they end up, almost accidentally, in Israel. The mother, a painter, is blissful in Jerusalem; she is stimulated by the atmosphere and feels a kinship with other Jews in the exciting young country. Since she is often away from home, deep in an affair with Boris, a concert pianist, the child is wretchedly lonely. Because Josie knows no Hebrew, she goes to an English-language missionary school and yearns for her old home and a "good plain normal American school." Then Mira, a newly arrived Russian emigré, provides her with an interest in life; and somehow the eleven-year-old and the elderly woman—who speak no common language—fashion a warm and loving companionship, and Josie is drawn into the circle of Mira's lively friends. Eventually the girl and her mother grope toward an understanding of each other's desperate needs; and the end of the year finds them leaving for America—but not before Josie has developed a heady affection, "like a secret singing in the blood," for the "pale gold city" encircled by "tawny wrinkled hills." A glossary of the Hebrew words used in the text would have been helpful.

Zena Sutherland

SOURCE: A review of *I Met a Traveller,* in *Bulletin of the Center for Children's Books,* Vol. 31, No. 8, April, 1978, p. 128.

Josie, eleven, tells the story. She's come from high suburbia to Jerusalem with her divorced mother, who emerges as one of the more unpleasant maternal figures of contemporary fiction. Mom avers love, but she gives Josie neither her time nor her understanding, being too busy with her current love affair. Josie has communication problems, since she can't speak Hebrew; she has no friends except an elderly Russian emigrée, who thwarts Josie's plans for them to run away to the U.S. together when she marries. Mom finally decides to go back, but it seems less in response to Josie's need than because she's wearied of her Boris. There's some tough talk, some acid remarks about Daddy ("Mom says the kids are bastards because she and Dad never got a divorce,") and his present ménage, and some variety given by Josie's involvement in puppet shows, but the book's story line is overshadowed by information about Jerusalem; the local color is, however, vividly evoked, as is the frustration and isolation of a lonely only child.

MR. PIG AND SONNY TOO (1977)

Booklist

SOURCE: A review of *Mr. Pig and Sonny Too,* in *Booklist,* Vol. 74, No. 2, September 15, 1977, p. 201.

Mr. Pig is all that a good, likable pig should be: he's rather sloppy, very fat, and quite unassuming. Sonny pig is all that a son should be: he tries to help his dad learn to skate, encourages his attempts to lose weight and tidy up, and finally gets Mr. Pig to the church on time for the elder's own wedding. While all this is going on, readers are treated to some most amusing little scenes of slapstick, silliness, and sentimentality, packaged in a smooth, colorful text. The author's illustrations are both quaint and lively, if a little muddy in hue.

Publishers Weekly

SOURCE: A review of *Mr. Pig and Sonny Too,* in *Publishers Weekly,* Vol. 212, No. 22, November 28, 1977, p. 50.

Hoban's four stories about Pig father and Pig son are going to be enjoyed by little ones who are starting to read on their own. The illustrations delight the eye as they show Mr. Pig, Sonny and papa's friend, Miss Selma, wearing human clothes and living in tastefully decorated homes. The adventures, wildly impossible, are the kind that kids cotton to. In the first tale, Mr. Pig's problem is that Miss Selma has invited him to an ice-skating party but he can't skate. Sonny's efforts to teach his clumsy dad are futile but Pig senior gets a reward anyway. In each of the tales, Mr. Pig turns adversity into triumphs, with Sonny's help or in spite of it. In the last piece, Miss Selma and Mr. Pig marry at last, after nutty complications that almost cancel the wedding.

School Library Journal

SOURCE: A review of *Mr. Pig and Sonny Too,* in *School Library Journal,* Vol. 24, No. 4, December, 1977, pp. 58-9.

The first three easy-to-read stories and the light-hearted watercolor illustrations in *Mr. Pig and Sonny Too* by Lillian Hoban are appealing though contrived. **"Ice Skating," "Exercise,"** and **"A Special Pig"** abound with humorous situations as lazy Mr. Pig and his son find themselves in unexpected adventures and misadventures. However, the last story, **"The Wedding,"** featuring the stereotypic reluctant bridegroom (Mr. Pig) and the patient, understanding, willing-to-put-up-with-anything bride ("She never got angry, though Mr. Pig was late to his own wedding."), is a lot less amusing.

Zena Sutherland

SOURCE: A review of *Mr. Pig and Sonny Too,* in *Bulletin of the Center for Children's Books,* Vol. 31, No. 6, February, 1978, p. 96.

Four short stories for the beginning independent reader are illustrated with cheerful pictures in soft shades. The protagonists are father and son, and it is the son who is the sensible character; Mr. Pig is always in trouble or indulging himself or procrastinating: a porcine fuss-pot. He decides to exercise and winds up eating; he has a disastrous and funny skating lesson; he picks daisies and is chased by bees; he pokes about and makes excuses when he's supposed to be getting to a wedding which proves to be his own. (Presumably Sonny has lost his mother through death rather than divorce?) The stories have action and humor, and as smooth a narrative flow as can be achieved with prose that is so simple.

TURTLE SPRING (1978)

Kirkus Reviews

SOURCE: A review of *Turtle Spring,* in *Kirkus Reviews,* Vol. XLVI, No. 6, March 15, 1978, p. 303.

When Mrs. Turtle calls out that there is a strange bump under the lettuce bed, it's not long before all the little turtles are running around shouting that there are bombs under their beds. The youngsters spend a spring day trying to decide what to do about the matter, but they are repeatedly interrupted and distracted by instances of the season's new life: baby snails, ducklings, chickadees, mayflies, marsh marigolds. Then POW! goes the bomb in the lettuce bed, and out come "ten little new little dear little turtle children . . . fresh out of their eggs, and new as the spring, and all peeping sweetly in soft turtle voices." "All the old little turtle children" are pleased as punch with their new siblings; readers with less tolerance for the chirpy will regret that the bomb turned out to be such a dud.

Booklist

SOURCE: A review of *Turtle Spring,* in *Booklist,* Vol. 74, No. 16, April 15, 1978, p. 1357.

When Mrs. Turtle finds a "very strange bump" in the garden, her children, misinterpreting, set out to do something about the "bombs under the beds." But spring is in the air—no one can think right or stick to a job for long. The animals around them constantly break their train of thought, and flowers and butterflies distract the turtle youngsters. The emergence of a new batch of turtle babes from the bump-bomb solves the mystery. "I knew I buried those eggs in the garden," says mother Turtle, "but I told them not to hatch till fall." Amusing and mildly celebratory, the story unfortunately meanders—a bit too much in the spirit of spring. Still, it may help readers through those trying, warm school days.

School Library Journal

SOURCE: A review of *Turtle Spring,* in *School Library Journal,* Vol. 24, No. 9, May, 1978, p. 81.

In **Turtle Spring** Lillian Hoban captures the spirit of the fertile season with spry illustrations of just-born ducks, worms, chicks, and peepers. En route to discovering what rests in the mound in her garden soil, Mrs. Turtle and her young meet with other species

hatching and coming to life. After this series of births it comes as no surprise that the mysterious bump harbors a batch of baby turtles, welcomed with " . . . always room for ten more."

ARTHUR'S PRIZE READER (1978)

Kirkus Reviews

SOURCE: A review of *Arthur's Prize Reader,* in *Kirkus Reviews,* Vol. LXVI, No. 22, November 15, 1978, p. 1244.

The running argument engaged in here by chimp siblings Arthur and Violet has obvious easy-reader relevance: Violet, out to win the first-grade reading contest, insists that she can read, and Arthur says she can't handle hard words. Arthur too is in a contest, selling Super Chimp comics so he can win dinner for two with King Kong—he ridicules Violet when she picks up the ad and sounds out "dinner for two at your fav-or-ite rest-au-rant." Violet of course proves correct—but verification is artificially postponed till the end. There is no dinner for two anywhere as Arthur doesn't win, but there are ice-cream sodas for two at Violet's favorite ice-cream store—her prize for being the best first-grade reader. The plot is predictable and the prevailing competitiveness unfortunate, despite the made-to-order situation.

The Horn Book Magazine

SOURCE: A review of *Arthur's Prize Reader,* in *The Horn Book Magazine,* Vol. LIV, No. 6, December, 1978, pp. 635-36.

The difference between reading and comprehension is the comic catalyst for the latest escapades of Arthur, the captivating chimp. Displaying the older child's typical supercilious attitude toward a little sister's initial reading efforts, he ignores Violet's perceptive interpretation of the Super Chimp Comics sales contest, convinced that the prize is a dinner for two with King Kong. The result of his misapprehension is a comedy of errors for the reader—if not for Arthur. Convincingly childlike in structure and situation, the book conveys a universal humor through an easy-to-read vocabulary. The bright three-color illustrations are a felicitous accompaniment to the jaunty narrative.

Booklist

SOURCE: A review of *Arthur's Prize Reader,* in *Booklist,* Vol. 75, No. 8, December 15, 1978, p. 693.

Little sister Violet triumphs again, though more directly and amiably than in *Arthur's Pen Pal.* Although she's just learned to read, she tries to point out an error in Arthur's decoding: the prize for selling the most Super Chimp Comics is not dinner for two with King Kong. Arthur brushes Violet aside, telling her she can't read hard words. He finds selling comics unrewarding work, reads the fine print, and resignedly watches Violet tramp off to win a first-grade reading contest, sharing the prize with her brother. Throughout, Violet embodies child wisdom in an unstuffy way, while Arthur and others are quite as convincing. Bonus One: a book about the thrill of first reading. Bonus Two: easier to read than the previous *Arthur.*

LOST IN THE MUSEUM (1979)

Booklist

SOURCE: A review of *Lost in the Museum,* in *Booklist,* Vol. 75, No. 12, February 15, 1979, pp. 931-32.

The teacher's direction to stay together during their museum visit is quickly forgotten when Danny suggests he'll show Jim and a few others the dinosaurs. The sight of the huge, bony beasts frightens Jim, however, and they decide to return to the group. Danny leads the way but becomes lost, and it's Jim who eventually braves the vast array of rooms and corridors to find the teacher. Her reproof to the wanderers is in loud letters, "IF WE ALL STAY TOGETHER, NOBODY WILL GET LOST," but Hoban tempers this with an arm around the shoulder and a gentle smile. The final page finds class and teacher enjoying hot dogs in the museum cafeteria. The excitement of the visit is captured in simple words and attractive full-color pictures bustling with child actions and reactions, making this a splendid read-aloud prior to a primary grade field trip.

Kirkus Reviews

SOURCE: A review of *Lost in the Museum,* in *Kirkus Reviews,* Vol. XLVII, No. 6, March 15, 1979, pp. 321-22.

When our old friends in [Miriam] Cohen's first-grade class go to the museum, Danny splits to see the dinosaur and is followed by Jim, Willy, Sammy, Paul, and George—and Cohen puts down the girls again (as in *Tough Jim,*) by having Anna Marie and Sara

start after them calling "Come back! You'll get lost!" Jim does get them all lost when he bolts in fear before the tyrannosaurus, but later, when he finds the teacher on his own, he wins the other children's "Jim was brave! He went to find you!" Cohen makes the least of the experience with the teacher's "Yes, Jim was very brave. But next time, remember—IF WE ALL STAY TOGETHER, NOBODY WILL GET LOST." But while we're on that level, we might just as well question why any teacher would take a whole first-grade class to the museum without an adult helper. Hoban's chipmunk-cheeked children are as appealing as ever and her double-page views of Jim alone under a vast gray whale are wonderfully expressive. But Cohen does have a tendency to overemphasize the lesson, while her continued stereotyping of the little girls speaks for itself.

The Horn Book Magazine

SOURCE: A review of *Lost in the Museum,* in *The Horn Book Magazine,* Vol. LV, No. 2, April, 1979, pp. 181-82.

A field trip to the Museum of Natural History provides the basis for another story of the adventures of an engaging first-grade class. The situation is one readily comprehensible to young children, who can understand the curiosity which precipitates a problem when, despite teacher's admonition, a clutch of youngsters breaks away from the group and becomes lost in the dinosaur display. Then Jim, more apprehensive than his classmates about the fiercely smiling skeleton, volunteers to find their teacher. His quest contains the right balance of humor and suspense to maintain interest until the happy reunion. Teacher is as understanding as she is resourceful, for she praises Jim's bravery but, without becoming pompous, manages to interject a salutary warning against future independent explorations. Lovingly portrayed in colored illustrations, the children are eager, rumpled, and comfortably familiar; the background details are shown from a first-grader's point of view.

HARRY'S SONG (1980)

Publishers Weekly

SOURCE: A review of *Harry's Song,* in *Publishers Weekly,* Vol. 217, No. 4, April 11, 1980, p. 78.

Little Harry Rabbit may suggest to young readers that he's a lazy type, fated to suffer like the carefree insect in the fable, "The Grasshopper and the Ant."

Harry sits outside the rabbit hole and sings all day long while his brothers wear themselves out stocking up provender for the long winter ahead. No matter how much they natter and nag, Harry keeps singing, until Mom comes out to bring everyone home. Taking a last long look at the waning day, Harry obeys. And now comes the time when the small one's contribution to the supplies is explained. In the dark and cold, Harry cheers everyone with his song of a summer day. Lush, lovely illustrations in Hoban's inimitable style round out a charming package.

Kirkus Reviews

SOURCE: A review of *Harry's Song,* in *Kirkus Reviews,* Vol. XLVIII, No. 6, March 15, 1980, p. 360.

While the other animals busily prepare for winter, little Harry Rabbit blithely sings his summer song ("Rows of leafy lettuces. . . . Plump pods of sweet peas. . . . "). And the more the others rail at him and rebuke him ("It's a good thing all your brothers are hard-working rabbits"), and the longer he stays put in the darkening, increasingly chill day, the more one wonders—admiringly, fearfully—at his obduracy, at his possible fate? Then—for this is in the Margaret Wise Brown tradition—Harry's mother calls him to come home. He hops into the den where his brothers are stowing away grain and greens and twigs, and adds his contribution to the winter store—in his delighted mother's words, "the song of a perfect summer day." A tender but not mushy tidbit, becomingly illustrated with resolute animals (including welcome reminders of Peter Rabbit) and visions of summer plenty.

Zena Sutherland

SOURCE: A review of *Harry's Song,* in *Bulletin of the Center for Children's Books,* Vol. 33, No. 10, June, 1980, pp. 191-92.

On a chilly fall day, Harry Rabbit is bemusedly composing a summer song, rich and golden, while his mother calls to him and the other creatures urge him to join their busy preparations for the long winter ahead. "Harry is a dumb bunny," says Mr. Fieldmouse. "He doesn't know enough to come in out of the cold." Harry goes on singing of "bees buzzing in the honey-heavy air," and all the others urge him to gather food. When he does come home, his siblings are sorting and storing food, but Harry's mother is delighted, since he's brought home the song of a perfect summer day to carry them all through the winter,

and he gets a hard bunny hug. This is very much like Lionni's *Frederick,* the story of a fieldmouse who gathered words about the golden sun of summer while the other mice were gathering grain, and who warmed them with his memories of summer warmth when winter came. The illustrations are more vernal (often the paintings are flower-framed) and less humorous than most of Hoban's work.

MR. PIG AND FAMILY (1980)

Kirkus Reviews

SOURCE: A review of *Mr. Pig and the Family,* in *Kirkus Reviews,* Vol. XLVIII, No. 23, December 1, 1980, p. 1517.

It's hard to work up any fellow-feeling for the flabby-wide-mouthed Pig family. The first episode in this sequel to **Mr. Pig and Sonny Too** concludes with the family agreeing that "as long as we're together it will always feel like home"—but in the story it's Mr. Pig's armchair and teapot that make anyplace seem like home. Another episode starts cute as Mr. Pig throws different seeds and water together in a hole in the ground, planting vegetable soup. But his next move is a regression: told the proper way to plant seeds, "all in a row," he rolls up and down in the seeds and the mud to distribute them. One gives up hope when his new wife tells Mr. Pig that his son Sonny will have a half-brother and Mr. Pig commences to worry about what the "other half" of the baby will be. Giving animals the limited understanding of children is a standard device, but gross householder Mr. Pig is just too dumb and too piggish for patience.

Zena Sutherland

SOURCE: A review of *Mr. Pig and Family,* in *Bulletin of the Center for Children's Books,* Vol. 34, No. 5, January, 1981, p. 95.

It's a happy second marriage for Mr. Pig; his new wife, Selma, has all the common sense he lacks. Unable to decide whether to stay at Selma's house in town or his place in the country, Mr. Pig accepts his son's suggestion that they alternate. The newlyweds keep changing their minds about what to take along, and finally overload their cart and have an outdoor tea party when it breaks down. The second tale is about silly Mr. Pig's love of eating, the third about his deficiencies as a gardener, and in the last he gets muddled when his wife says she's going upstairs to have a baby and Sonny will soon have a half sister or brother. Mr. Pig is too foolish to be believable, but the stories are pleasant nonsense, and palatable experience for the beginning independent reader. The illustrations are cozy line and wash pictures that slightly extend the text.

Booklist

SOURCE: A review of *Mr. Pig and Family,* in *Booklist,* Vol. 77, No. 12, February 15, 1981, p. 814.

Mr. Pig's new wife and his son look upon his foibles good-naturedly, as will readers, who will enjoy a view of a close-knit family and its appealingly naive "head of household." The third of four anecdotes finds Sonny advising his father on the proper planting methods for a vegetable garden. Admiring his work—a pool of water into which seeds are being stirred—Mr. Pig counters, "I'm not planting a garden . . . I'm planting vegetable soup." And when Mrs. Pig goes upstairs to have a baby, Mr. Pig worries: Sonny is going to have a half sister or brother, but what will the other half be? Readers who chuckled over **Mr. Pig and Sonny Too** will get no less from its sequel, which has the bonus of putting a "second-time-around" family in a positive light. With the author's familiar, earthy illustrations.

NO GOOD IN ART (1980)

The Horn Book Magazine

SOURCE: A review of *No Good in Art,* in *The Horn Book Magazine,* Vol. LVI, No. 4, August, 1980, p. 393.

Upset by the criticism he received from his art teacher in kindergarten ("'dear, your man has no neck. . . . You ought to make your grass with *thin* lines.'"), Jim is afraid to paint in first grade. His new art teacher encourages everyone. The class's enthusiasm is contagious, and Jim finally risks doing a painting and meets with approval. Obviously written in praise of good art teachers, the story has a less dramatic plot than do the earlier stories about Jim and his classmates, but the multiracial classroom is energetic and appealing. The cartoonlike illustrations do not provide much ethnic differentiation, and skin color is the main clue. But the pictures have action, humor, and, appropriately for the story, lots of color.

ARTHUR'S FUNNY MONEY (1981)

The Horn Book Magazine

SOURCE: A review of *Arthur's Funny Money,* in *The Horn Book Magazine,* Vol. LVII, No. 5, October, 1981, p. 531.

Once again Violet comes to the aid of her big brother Arthur in the fifth easy-to-read book about the two likable chimps. Violet is having trouble with a math problem, and she seeks help from Arthur. Arthur, however, is having his own difficulties: He does not have enough money to buy a Frisbee team T-shirt and cap. With help from Violet, Arthur sets up a bike wash and eventually—after many frustrations and setbacks—makes the necessary money to buy the outfit and some licorice as well. The candy gives Arthur an idea, and he uses the five licorice sticks to help Violet understand her math problem. But as the problem is worked out, Arthur slowly realizes what the outcome will be—one piece for him, four for her. The cheerful illustrations clearly show the expressions of the appealing brother and sister.

Zena Sutherland

SOURCE: A review of *Arthur's Funny Money,* in *Bulletin of the Center for Children's Books,* Vol. 35, No. 4, December, 1981, p. 69.

Arthur and his little sister Violet, those beguiling chimpanzees, again work out a problem in cooperation and sharing; this time Arthur is stumped by simple arithmetic, which as usual he won't admit. He's trying to earn money to buy a shirt and cap like those the other members of the frisbee team have, and at Violet's suggestion, he sets up a bike-wash business. The colorful, casual drawings have vitality and humor, and they're a nice match for the light, ingenuous tone of the simply written text.

School Library Journal

SOURCE: A review of *Arthur's Funny Money,* in *School Library Journal,* Vol. 28, No. 4, December, 1981, p. 74.

More monkey business with Arthur and Violet in **Arthur's Funny Money** by Lillian Hoban. This time out, Arthur is trying to make enough money to buy a team shirt and cap, and Violet is trying to work out an "if I have five peas and you take three . . ." number problem. The money-earning machinations have a familiar ring, but the simian siblings remain funny and realistically endearing in both text and pictures. Kids will have fun keeping track of Arthur's alternating income and expenses and enjoy Violet's quick-witted twist on her number problem.

NO, NO, SAMMY CROW (1981)

Booklist

SOURCE: A review of *No, No, Sammy Crow*, in *Booklist*, Vol. 77, No. 13, March 1, 1981, p. 964.

Sammy Crow remains unruffled in the face of warnings and accusations from family and neighbors; he knows he's old enough for school, yet he won't stop "nice-ing" his blanket and sucking his thumb. But bird snatchers force the issue. Sammy's big sister Sheila gets a threatening note and, leaving the egg she is keeping warm for her mother, goes to the rescue. "Help us get the blanket if you want your brother back," yell the Robin boys, whose own mother has forcibly separated them from their nice-ing objects. Sheila helps Sammy instead, and on return to the nest he sacrifices his blanket to save the now-cold egg. It hatches momentarily and, not without justice, the newborn takes to the blanket with relish. If there is a moral here, it has to do with hanging on to what's really important, to which Sammy, with his salvaged bit of blanket fluff, will attest in the end. The clipped and honest talk of real children creates an instant relationship between readers and characters. Hoban opts for bright spring colors to further freshen a lively, pithy story.

Kirkus Reviews

SOURCE: A review of *No, No, Sammy Crow*, in *Kirkus Reviews*, Vol. IL, No. 9, May 1, 1981, p. 568.

To rev up the familiar topic of a child who's almost ready for school but won't give up his blanket, Hoban first of all makes Sammy a crow. She gives him an older sister Sheila who teases him about "nice-ing" his blanket, and she gives them both a little adventure when Mrs. Crow goes off for tea with Mrs. Robin, leaving Sheila to egg-sit and keep an eye on Sammy. (The human family pattern is convenient for the story, but it makes the crow casting seem all the more arbitrary.) Poor Sheila, stationed on the egg, is faced with a dilemma when Sammy is crow-napped and needs help—but Hoban makes a silly performance of this with Sheila's "Oh, yaawwk! Ma told

me not to let the egg get cold, so this crow won't go! . . . Oh, aawk aawk aawk. Ma told me to keep an eye on Sammy, and now the Crow-Getters have got him, so this crow's got to go!" The crow-getters turn out to be the Robin boys, who want Sammy's blanket because their mother has taken theirs away. Between them Sheila and Sammy punch out and tie up the robins and return in time for Sammy to wrap his blanket around the "shivering" (actually hatching) egg. The story ends in a neat solution for Sammy's habit, but the whole contrivance seems forced and over-elaborate. Still, too much yaawking may be preferable to the pallid too little we get in most treatments of the problem.

Zena Sutherland

SOURCE: A review of *No, No, Sammy Crow*, in *Bulletin of the Center for Children's Books*, Vol. 35, No. 11, July-August, 1982, p. 208.

"Ma," Sammy's older sister tattles, "Sammy is sucking his thumb and nice-ing his blanket again." In that one sentence, Hoban sets the stage for what is to come: sibling conflict, and a young creature that clings to babyish ways. Mrs. Crow points out that the Robin boys don't nice *their* blankets any longer; Sammy Crow retorts that it's because Mrs. Robin took their blankets away from them. Sammy's maturation and a change in brother-sister relationships come when the Robin boys attack Sammy while his mother is away and his sister is egg-sitting. She comes to Sammy's rescue, they rout the blanket-snatchers, they go back to find the egg has hatched, and Sammy nobly turns his blanket over to the nestling, winning commendation from sister and mother, who do not know that Sammy has kept a very small piece of his blanket in his pocket and is secretly nice-ing it. Hoban's illustrations of animals are never quite as engaging as those she does of children, but they are adequate, and the story has some vitality.

READY … SET … ROBOT (1982, WITH PHOEBE HOBAN)

Kirkus Reviews

SOURCE: A review of *Ready . . . Set . . . Robot*, in *Kirkus Reviews*, Vol. IL, No. 9, May 1, 1981, p. 568.

Without much of a story, this depends mainly on the concept of a little-boy robot, the built-in suspense of a race, and the strangeness of the different "zones"

Sol-1 passes through as he competes with other robot children in the race. For "human" interest, Sol-1 has a robot sister, a robot dog, Big Rover, and a robot mother who scolds him about his untidy room. Because of the mess, Sol-1 misplaces his power pack and goes off to the race with Big Rover's instead. This slows him down, but his sister and the dog fly to his rescue in time to ensure his victory. Despite the minimal plot, Hoban's suggestive, softly colored space scenes please the eye, tempt the imagination, and evoke the moods each new zone or predicament calls for.

School Library Journal

SOURCE: A review of *Ready . . . Set . . . Robot!* in *School Library Journal,* Vol. 28, No. 9, May, 1982, p. 81.

It's **Ready . . . Set . . . Robot!** when a vaguely Artoo-Detoo looking robot named Sol-1 enters the Digi-Maze race not realizing that his power pack and his dog's have become mixed up. This leads to trouble when he enters the Outer Zone of the maze where his solar cap can't function, but his charged-up dog arrives to pull him to light and victory. Lillian and Phoebe Hoban create a story that works well as science fiction, integrating technological terms naturally, loading it with action and yet maintaining very human personalities. The cheat-to-win ethic that caps the tale almost spoils its good features, however. Lillian Hoban's pencil, ink and wash illustrations capture a futuristic tone, but the action can be difficult to distinguish sometimes, amongst the patterns and pencil strokes.

Booklist

SOURCE: A review of *Ready . . . Set . . . Robot!* in *Booklist,* Vol. 78, No. 18, May 15, 1982, p. 1262.

Undoubtedly, many will hail the debut of a Hoban mother-daughter team; but just as surely, readers who don't recognize that auspicious name will eagerly investigate a book whose cover suggests that both racing and robots await within. The metallic personage who figures in the story does indeed win—not only a harrowing space race, but the affections of readers as well. Young Sol-1's ingenuity is admirable, and his messy home habits, though they threaten to cost him the race, are comfortingly familiar to most youngsters. One can nearly forgive an occasional tampering with humanoid nature and the rules of fair play in the context of an enjoyable adventure into cyber-

netic fantasy for an audience that can't seem to get enough of that type of thing.

📖 *IT'S REALLY CHRISTMAS* (1982)

Kirkus Reviews

SOURCE: A review of *It's Really Christmas,* in *Kirkus Reviews,* Vol. L, No. 17, September 1, 1982, p. 995.

This year's sentimental mix of mice and Christmas deals with Gamey Joe, so called because he's born with a game leg, a little shorter than the other. But he is almost called "Christmas Joe" because he's born in the attic among the stored-away Christmas decorations and wrapped by his mother in cotton snow. "When will it really be Christmas?" he asks her later; and she answers, "When mouse feet squeak on the frosty ground and snow drifts over the land and the brightest star of all shines in the sky." Then when the attic mice are warned that the noise of their scampering may cause the people to send the cat up, Gamey Joe learns another definition of Christmas. The mice could quiet their tread with soft slippers, if they had the material to make them, and Gamey thinks of his cotton snow. He's reluctant to give it up, but does so after a tiny white mouse appears to him and whispers "If you give, you will have, and it truly will be Christmas." So he gives and gives once more when he stops up a noisy roof leak with his precious tinsel. But that project results in a bad fall, an ailing Gamey . . . and his recovery when the other attic mice give him the Christmas he's been looking for. Running on the roof ("mouse feet squeaking on the frosty ground"), they drop fluffy bits of their cotton-snow slippers ("snow drifting over the land") past his window. "Yes, Gamey, yes," they chorus, "It really is Christmas at last." It's really pure treacle.

Booklist

SOURCE: A review of *It's Really Christmas,* in *Booklist,* Vol. 79, No. 2, September 15, 1982, p. 116.

A Christmas story that doesn't even take place at Christmas, yet is gently satisfying and especially suitable for sharing aloud. Born in a box of Christmas decorations, baby mouse Gamey Joe (so called because of a bad leg) spends most of his waking minutes longing for the December holiday to come. When he falls while fixing a leak in the ceiling, his family nudges him back to health by devising a

Christmas in July, and he learns the meaning of "If you give, you will have, and it truly will be Christmas!" Softly colored illustrations, boxed with ribbon frames, contain detailed, enticing drawings that set a tone deserving that much overused word, *charming*.

Zena Sutherland

SOURCE: A review of *It's Really Christmas*, in *Bulletin of the Center for Children's Books*, Vol. 36, No. 2, October, 1982, p. 27.

Soft-hued paintings, more detailed and romantic than Hoban's usual work, illustrate a gentle, sentimental story about a very young lame mouse who longs for Christmas because he was born in a box of Christmas decorations and loves to play with them. Twice the mouse, Gamey Joe, gives up his precious playthings to help the other mice, both times in order to keep the attic quiet (tinsel to plug a noisy drip from the roof, cotton snow to make slippers) so that the cat won't be sent up there. A fairy mouse had told Gamey Joe, "If you give, you will have, and it truly will be Christmas." And when Gamey Joe is very ill, it is his own acts of kindness that lead to a way for others to help him; that's how Christmas comes in midsummer to the mice in the attic. A little sugary, the story is nicely structured and told, and the wee protagonist should be appealing to the read-aloud audience.

SEE YOU TOMORROW, CHARLES (1983, BY MIRIAM COHEN)

Catherine Wood

SOURCE: A review of *See You Tomorrow, Charles*, in *School Library Journal*, Vol. 29, No. 8, April, 1983, p. 98.

[Miriam] Cohen's story is full of good intentions, but they are not enough to support this book. Charles, a new boy in the first grade class, is blind and his classmates are in the process of learning to become comfortable with his disability. True-to-life dialogue captures the varying attitudes of the lively group of children as they interact among themselves and with Charles. A patient teacher supports the children throughout. Unfortunately, the illustrations are weak. Charles wears a dull-witted expression and a vacant smile a great deal of the time, while his classmates' faces exhibit a wider range of emotions. Cardigans and fluffy dresses clothe all the girls and striped jerseys and overalls clothe all the boys. This and their similarly executed features make the children an undistinguishable mass. As the text is comprised only of dialogue, these illustrations do not help to identify the already confusing voices we hear speaking.

The Horn Book Magazine

SOURCE: A review of *See You Tomorrow, Charles*, in *The Horn Book Magazine*, Vol. LIX, No. 4, August, 1983, pp. 429-30.

In another visit to the first-grade class the author and the illustrator again demonstrate their sensitivity to the feelings of young children. This time the class has been joined by a new student—Charles, a blind boy. Everyone initially tries to help him, overemphasizing his handicap and treating him too gingerly. "'don't say, "Look what I made,"' Anna Maria admonishes Jim. "'Charles can't see.'" But during recess when Charles and two other children get trapped in the school's dark basement, Charles is the one who leads them to safety; so that by the end of the book he has the children's respect rather than their sympathy. Nondidactic, effective dialogue fills the book, and brightly colored illustrations of the multiracial class capture the lively personalities of its members.

THE LAZIEST ROBOT IN ZONE ONE (1983, WITH PHOEBE HOBAN)

Kirkus Reviews

SOURCE: A review of *The Laziest Robot in Zone One*, in *Kirkus Reviews*, Vol. LI, No. 3, February 1, 1983, p. 119.

Lazy because he hasn't done his homework or weeded the garden, little Sol-1 of last year's *Ready . . . Set . . . Robot!* has also lost his dog Big Rover. He and little sister Sola must find the dog by Down Time; and to make the search less like work, Sol-1 decides to enlist his friends in a "search party." But they too have homework to do and gardens to weed, and Sol-1 ends up helping them so they'll be free to search. It's in helping friends Arla and Fax retrieve their cat Power Puss from atop a metal windmill that Sol-1 also finds Big Rover. Now his friends will weed his garden while he does his homework— and Mama-Sol, told of his deeds, says with a hug, "It is nice when robots work together." That the characters are robots and the scene outer space has no intrinsic bearing on the mundane plot. On the other hand, you never forget these conditions, what with Lillian Hoban's amorphous violet-hued backgrounds, Sol-1's controls humming and his lights flashing when he arrives at an idea, and so on. Kids attuned to zappy space wars will find this pretty tame; for beginning readers the borrowed space-age glamour might suffice.

School Library Journal

SOURCE: A review of *The Laziest Robot in Zone One*, in *School Library Journal*, Vol. 29, No. 9, May, 1983, p. 88.

Lazy robot Sol-1 ends up working very hard in the course of searching for his lost dog—catching giant puff weeds in a space garden, sinking to the bottom of the solar pond as a robot-thermometer, climbing up to the blades of the wind station to rescue Power Puss. His friends then help Sol-1 with his work, and afterwards they all "danced until Down Time." Children will like the homey high tech of it all, the occasional dry humor and the familiarity of parental nagging which even robots can't escape. The purples, greens, yellows and pinks of the illustrations, with their computer grid borders and robot brigades add to the fun—with greater clarity and distinction than their earlier *Ready . . . Set . . . Robot!*

Booklist

SOURCE: A review of *The Laziest Robot in Zone One*, in *Booklist*, Vol. 79, No. 18, May 15, 1983, p. 1224.

Children fascinated by robots will find the second in this series still fresh territory for easy-reading books. Sol-1 is a lazy little robot who likes to put off his chores. One of his tasks is walking his dog, Big Rover, but when he finally gets around to doing it, Big Rover has disappeared. The little robot wants to find his dog, though looking for him seems like lots of work. So Sol-1 organizes a search party, but he manages to spend so much time helping his friends with their projects they almost don't get around to the task at hand. Big Rover is finally located; he has chased Power Puss up a windmill, and a brave Sol-1 proves he can be quite energetic when it's in a good cause. The presence of some technological terms will not deter robot lovers. The pictures, done mostly in pink, yellow, and purple, are futuristic without being mechanical.

THE DAY THE TEACHER WENT BANANAS (1984, BY JAMES HOWE)

Publishers Weekly

SOURCE: A review of *The Day the Teacher Went Bananas*, in *Publishers Weekly*, Vol. 226, No. 5, August 3, 1984, p. 67.

Versatile [James] Howe's latest invention is a real rib-tickler, illustrated in full color by Hoban, the unbeatable portrayer of small fry like the gaggle of first-graders featured here. One of them confides gleefully the results of crossed wires that give them a "new teacher," a gorilla, and ship the real teacher to the zoo. The students' lessons in the new math include taking off their shoes and socks and counting on their toes. The drills in writing are even more fun. Although teacher says nothing, just grunts, he is inspiring and very amiable. When the embarrassed principal arrives with the bona fide pedagogue and the gorilla leaves for the zoo, it's a sad parting. But the author figures out a way to end the daffy tale with a neat, happy twist.

Catherine Blanton

SOURCE: A review of *The Day the Teacher Went Bananas*, in *School Library Journal*, Vol. 31, No. 4, December, 1984, p. 72.

In [James] Howe's slight but imaginative story, a mix-up places a gorilla and a new teacher in the wrong places, and the class of children find that the gorilla is a fine teacher. They learn to count on their toes and swing on trees before the error is matter-of-factly righted, and the following day the class goes to the zoo to have lunch with their favorite teacher. Pastel pencil drawings on large pages with an ample amount of white space show lots of children involved in monkey business, giving the book a sense of openness, movement and fun. The story harmlessly pokes fun at the teacher, a theme universally acclaimed by the younger crowd. Kids will go bananas over . . . *Bananas*.

ARTHUR'S HALLOWEEN COSTUME (1984)

Zena Sutherland

SOURCE: A review of *Arthur's Halloween Costume*, in *Bulletin of the Center for Children's Books*, Vol. 38, No. 1, September, 1984, p. 7.

Disappointed because other children are going to a school party dressed as ghosts just as he is, Arthur feels he will neither win a prize for originality nor will he frighten anyone. By the time Arthur has spilled ketchup on his sheet, acquired a wig from the trash can and a few other accessories, it is clear that he has a costume that is unique. He doesn't know what it is, but an admiring older student announces that Arthur is the Spirit of Halloween. Arthur, as those addicted to earlier books about him know, is a chimpanzee. This hasn't the same kind of humor as the earlier books; here it's more slapstick/disaster than invested in personalities and relationships, but the humor is right for the beginning independent reader, and the Halloween setting has appeal.

The Horn Book Magazine

SOURCE: A review of *Arthur's Halloween Costume,* in *The Horn Book Magazine,* Vol. LX, No. 5, September-October, 1984, p. 588.

"'This is my worst Halloween,'" remarks Arthur glumly early on October thirty-first. Not only has he accidentally splattered ketchup on his ghost costume and misplaced his school notebook, but his sister Violet has informed him that she knows three *other* kids planning to be ghosts. Then, searching desperately through the trash barrel for his schoolwork, Arthur comes across a few choice additions to his costume—although, unfortunately, the tuna-scented rug that makes a perfect wig also makes Arthur popular with the local cats. So off to school he goes, harassed by an eager feline following and annoyed because everyone misinterprets his costume. At last, however, another student gives his masquerade a name that surprises and satisfies everyone, including Arthur. Written simply, the story has ample humor and subtly conveys his frustrations and trepidations. Pleasing colored drawings depict the wide-eyed chimps in their Halloween regalia.

📖 ARTHUR'S LOOSE TOOTH (1985)

Booklist

SOURCE: A review of *Arthur's Loose Tooth,* in *Booklist,* Vol. 82, No. 4, October 15, 1985, p. 342.

Arthur might be the bravest chimp in the world, but a cut lip reduces him to wails. Still, his posture is all bravado when his sister Violet—who isn't afraid of a little blood—asks him to accompany her upstairs because it's dark. Arthur's biggest problem, however, is how to get rid of his loose tooth in order to eat the taffy apples that the baby-sitter is preparing for a

special treat. If he pulls the tooth out, there will be blood; will he be brave enough to weather such a crisis? Violet demonstrates her bravery at going outside in the dark to get sticks for s'mores; so Arthur thinks up a trauma-free way to get rid of his tooth and then bravely readies himself for the task. The picture of brother-sister competition is apt; so are Hoban's charcoal drawings in which chimp-child Arthur seems as real as any little boy. An engaging story that has a firm hand on the foibles of early childhood.

School Library Journal

SOURCE: A review of *Arthur's Loose Tooth,* in *School Library Journal,* Vol. 32, No. 4, December, 1985, p. 109.

The latest chimp tale starring Arthur and his little sister Violet centers around bravery. Violet is afraid of the dark but willing to risk going outside at night to find a stick to roast marshmallows. Arthur poohpoohs her fears but finds himself scared to pull out his loose front tooth because there will be blood. After his usual spell of self-pity, Arthur pulls it together and pulls it out, via the old string on the doorknob trick. The loose-tooth theme will attract kids, as will the play-by-play of Arthur's superhero persona, Captain Fearless, who bombs around the house wreaking havoc. Hoban's chimps are in good form here; there's lots going on in addition to the continuing realistic brother/sister relationship, and the presence of the no-nonsense babysitter adds a refreshing crispness to the interactions. The pencil-and-wash pictures are chimpier than ever and do a great job of capturing a range of all too human emotions. Go for it.

📖 THE CASE OF THE TWO MASKED ROBBERS (1986)

Kirkus Reviews

SOURCE: A review of *The Case of the Two Masked Robbers,* in *Kirkus Reviews,* Vol. LIV, No. 18, September 15, 1986, p. 1448.

Another entertaining *I Can Read,* this time a mystery with a clever twist at the conclusion, from veteran Hoban.

Two masked detectives (raccoons) disguise themselves as the two masked burglars who have stolen Mrs. Turtle's eggs from the bank, hoping to catch the real culprits—and find two sets: the crows, and, in a smart maneuver, the turtles themselves, who this year have absconded with their own eggs before the crows could find them. Well sprinkled with such easy but enthralling words as hold-up and shoot-out, plus a nice bit of parent-child interplay: "' . . . will [they] be angry because we sneaked out?' 'Maybe . . . at first . . . but when they hear how we found the eggs, they will be very proud.'" A solid contribution to the easy-reader shelf.

School Library Journal

SOURCE: A review of *The Case of the Two Masked Robbers*, in *School Library Journal*, Vol. 33, No. 4, December, 1986, p. 123.

Arabella and Albert Raccoon decide to track down the robbers who stole Mrs. Turtle's eggs. After a run-in with a snake and a couple of cagey crows, the twins have enough clues to figure out that the Turtles themselves have staged the heist in order to fool the gluttonous crows. Hoban's raccoons are an engaging pair, although lacking the charm of her chimp siblings, Arthur and Violet. Arabella tends to be the bravery and brains of the outfit, a nice role model turnabout, while Albert makes an indignant victim when shaken down (literally) by the nattily-clad crows. The pencil and wash illustrations, in magentas, greens, and golds, are vintage Hoban—clearly and distinctly drawn figures with real expression and homey woodsy detail. The mystery plot is just clever enough to keep readers guessing and surprised at the end, although not so difficult that it's impossible to figure out. Solid, although not the tops.

Betsy Hearne

SOURCE: A review of *The Case of the Two Masked Robbers*, in *Bulletin of the Center for Children's Books*, Vol. 40, No. 6, February, 1987, p. 108.

Raccoon twins Arabella and Albert solve the mystery of who stole the eggs Mrs. Turtle deposited at Meadow Marsh Bank. After sneaking out at night disguised as the robbers—a vague plan at best—the twins pick up clues from a snake and two crows and conclude that it was the turtles themselves who staged a robbery to fool the crows, who annually eat the eggs. This has an element of suspense and some inviting illustrations set in easy-to-read format, but the plot is too farfetched and forced to be more than an exercise.

SILLY TILLY AND THE EASTER BUNNY (1987)

Kirkus Reviews

SOURCE: A review of *Silly Tilly and the Easter Bunny*, in *Kirkus Reviews*, Vol. LIV, No. 24, December 15, 1986, p. 1860.

Seasonal tales are always popular with the Early I Can Read Book fan, and this one adds humor of a kind to amuse young readers.

Silly Tilly Mole is so excited about the imminent arrival of the Easter Bunny that she gets flustered and forgets what she is doing (looking for the glasses on her forehead, making tea to offer the visitor, etc.). This is the kind of silliness that five-and six-year-olds find funny. Some may have mixed feelings about the ageism/sexism/handicapism involved in poking fun at absent-minded, nearsighted, little old ladies, but the humor is not unkind and the book is dedicated to "all grandmothers."

Hoban is very good at writing these simple stories. In spite of the slight plots possible at this level, she manages to make her characters seem real and to find both humor and music in their conversation. An unexceptional but pleasant book, good for swelling the shelves for beginning readers.

Publishers Weekly

SOURCE: A review of *Silly Tilly and the Easter Bunny*, in *Publishers Weekly*, Vol. 231, No. 3, January 23, 1987, p. 71.

Lovable Silly Tilly Mole frequently forgets to remember things—she can't see because she forgot to remember that her glasses are perched high on her head. So when she smells jelly beans on the wind, she knows that she must have forgotten to remember Easter. A thump at the door makes her think that the Easter Bunny has arrived, and she makes him tea. Actually, she makes the tea for a chair, which she has mistaken for the Easter Bunny. And she dons a flowerpot, which she believes is her Easter bonnet. But all ends well for a creature as dear as Silly Tilly, who's bound to become a favorite. Hoban's watercolor pictures are looser here than in her other works, joyfully free in Easter Egg pastels; through them readers get glimpses of Tilly's world, with the thumps and bumps and objects that she so happily misinterprets.

School Library Journal

SOURCE: A review of *Silly Tilly and the Easter Bunny,* in *School Library Journal,* Vol. 33, No. 2, May, 1987, p. 119.

Tilly Mole wakes up one morning, smells jelly beans in the wind, and remarks to herself, "'It must be Easter.'" Easter it is, but that's the only thing Tilly gets right during the morning. She keeps forgetting to remember what she's about: looking for her glasses, which are pushed up onto her forehead, she bumps into a chair and thinks it's the Easter Bunny; she goes to make tea, but forgets what she went to the stove for, and she puts a flower pot on her head as an Easter bonnet. So it goes, with the forgetful Tilly muddling one thing after another, till she finally manages to sit down to tea and jelly beans with the Easter Bunny. Kids will get a laugh out of Tilly's goofs, which *are* genuinely gently funny, and smack their lips over the basket the Bunny brings. It's a pleasure to see Hoban's pencil and wash soft line drawings in full color; their bright pinks, yellows, lavenders suit Tilly's silliness and the story's season.

IT'S GEORGE! (1988, BY MIRIAM COHEN)

The Horn Book Magazine

SOURCE: A review of *It's George!* in *The Horn Book Magazine,* Vol. LXIV, No. 2, March-April 1988, p. 191.

[Miriam] Cohen's first-graders are featured here in their seventeenth story. The smartest person in the class is Anna Maria, who calls George "'d-U-M'" because he can't write, causing Danny to refuse to work with him on a project. George, of course, has other strengths: he is best at taking care of the class hamster and feeding the fish. But one day George makes the four o'clock news: while on a daily visit to a seventy-nine-year-old acquaintance, George plays a large part in saving the man's life when his friend falls from his rocker and can't get up. A special assembly brings praise from the principal: "'This young man knew just the right thing to do. He saved his friend's life.'" The helpful message that one can feel special and be appreciated for things other than classroom knowledge will be easily grasped and taken to heart. While the book breaks no new ground, the satisfying plot, coupled with Hoban's cheerful watercolor paintings depicting the now familiar multiethnic class of first-graders, will be enjoyed for its positive message.

Publishers Weekly

SOURCE: A review of *It's George!* in *Publishers Weekly,* Vol. 233, No. 4, January 29, 1988, p. 430.

That well-loved class of first-graders is delightful in another adventure, this one starring George. He's one of the slowest members of the class when it comes to spelling, handwriting and special projects. But George is a careful and attentive keeper of the classroom hamster and fish. Sometimes the other kids are impatient with him and even Anna Maria calls him "D-U-M"! Then one day, George doesn't come to school—and the first-grade class doesn't find out why until they watch the afternoon news on TV. George had stopped to visit an elderly friend on his way to school, and when the friend became ill, George called 911 and got help. The formerly scorned first grader is now a classroom hero. [Miriam] Cohen and Hoban's collaboration once again perfectly captures the essence of that all-important first year of school, with a zingy text and comic classroom pictures.

Jane Saliers

SOURCE: A review of *It's George!* in *School Library Journal,* Vol. 34, No. 7, March, 1988, p. 161.

George is not "smart" at writing or at thinking up projects. As irrepressible Anna Maria announces decidedly, "You can't *get* smart. You just are or you aren't." But George has other strengths. He knows the right way to take care of the animals in his classroom. He also knows how to save the life of his elderly friend by telephoning the emergency number. Much to the delight of his classmates, George's quick thinking is spotlighted on the afternoon TV news. A follow-up assembly and newspaper photograph affirm George's special gifts. [Miriam] Cohen once again shows her sensitivity to the varieties of children's strengths and struggles as they adjust to school. Her children are real and individual. Anna Maria has forgotten that she called George D-U-M and happily proclaims, "He's in *my* class." Hoban's sketchy full-color watercolors capture the multiethnic first graders in all of their activities and interaction. In tune with the text, Anna Maria's proud pose with George is a marvel of self-assurance. Another on-target story from a sensitive author/illustrator team.

📖 *ARTHUR'S GREAT BIG VALENTINE* (1989)

Publishers Weekly

SOURCE: A review of *Arthur's Great Big Valentine*, in *Publishers Weekly,* Vol. 235, No. 2, January 13, 1989, p. 90.

Arthur's best friend Norman ripped his jacket while they played Tarzan; now Norman will not let Arthur belong to his secret club. It's Valentine's Day, and feeling friendless, Arthur refuses to make a valentine for Norman. He turns down an invitation to a party when he learns that Norman will be there, and spends his time writing verse in the snow: "Valentines are stupid. / Some people get many. / I don't care / if I never get any." Then Norman's little brother Tony confides that Norman has made a Valentine for Arthur. That changes everything; Arthur reciprocates by making a huge Valentine in the snow by Norman's house. This is somewhat protracted for such a slim idea, and it's unfortunate that rather than initiating a truce, Arthur's actions are only in response to Norman's. Still, Hoban's drawings are characteristically full of charm, and fans of the Arthur books will find this a heart-warming addition to the series.

Martha Rosen

SOURCE: A review of *Arthur's Great Big Valentine*, in *School Library Journal,* Vol. 35, No. 6, February, 1989, p. 71.

This is a lovely valentine from Hoban to all beginning readers, many of whom are already fans of Arthur the monkey and his wise little sister, Violet. A minor squabble with his best friend, Norman, has left Arthur all alone this wintry Valentine's Day. Although Violet generously offers to join him, she is distracted by the arrival of her friend, Wilma, who has brought invitations to a big Valentine's party. Arthur declines because Norman will be there. But Norman's little brother, Tony, saves the day, and the two best friends are reunited. Wilma's party is a special celebration of fun and friendship. In this welcome addition to a popular series, Hoban's lively, colorful illustrations add humor and meaning to the text. Arthur's early "I-don't-care" attitude to being left out is believable, but not forced. This title will warm up any snowy, blustery day, and it should be particularly useful where holiday titles for this age group are in demand.

Booklist

SOURCE: A review of *Arthur's Great Big Valentine*, in *Booklist,* Vol. 85, No. 13, March 1, 1989, pp. 1198-99.

Arthur is back, wanting to celebrate Valentine's Day, but frustrated because he's on the outs with his friend, Norman. It doesn't help Arthur's mood that his sister Violet is busy making and receiving lots of valentine cards. A reconciliation between the two boys occurs—Norman brings Arthur a valentine, and Arthur writes a message in the snow. Similar in look and feel to the other Arthur easy-to-reads, this has mostly one-syllable words to attract new readers and a warm tone for those who enjoy the kidlike concerns of this popular hero.

📖 *I'M GONNA TELL MAMA I WANT AN INGUANA* (1990, BY TONY JOHNSTON)

School Library Journal

SOURCE: A review of *I'm Gonna Tell Mama I Want an Iguana*, in *School Library Journal,* Vol. 11, No. 11, November, 1990, p. 104.

A collection of 23 poems about everyday happenings and objects. Accompanied by Hoban's warm, sprightly drawings, the poems describe the events from the point of view of young children and include such activities as taking a dog to the vet, walking on the beach, watching a sunset. The vocabulary and images are accessible to young readers without being condescending, making this a fine choice as a read-aloud or a read-alone.

The Horn Book Magazine

SOURCE: A review of *I'm Gonna Tell Mama I Want an Iguana*, in *The Horn Book Magazine,* Vol. LXVII, No. 2, March-April, 1991, pp. 211-12.

Although the majority of the twenty-three verses in this sprightly compilation are humorous views of the world from the perspective of the young child, some offer metaphorical glimpses of beauty, as in **"Sunset"**: "Day took the pennies / from her pocket, / melted them all, / and poured them / over the hills." The varied subjects include grasshoppers, frog eggs, jellyfish, and birds, as well as onomatopoeic commentaries on topics real and imaginary. **"Skeleton Train,"** with its rhythmic refrain—"Clackety-clack goes the skeleton train. / Clackety-clack down the skeleton track"—would be a fine choice for choral recitation at Halloween time. Lillian Hoban's illustrations, reminiscent of those she has so engagingly created for Miriam Cohen's well-known series about Jim and his classmates, add a comfortably familiar note to what is sure to be a popular collection.

WAITING FOR NOAH (1990, BY SHULAMITH LEVEY OPPENHEIM)

The Horn Book Magazine

SOURCE: A review of *Waiting for Noah*, in *The Horn Book Magazine*, Vol. LXVI, No. 3, May-June, 1990, p. 328.

A grandmother recounts to her grandson Noah the often told tale of how she spent a wintry day waiting for the news of his birth. She recalls that she pruned berry canes, baked cookies, shined pots, and dreamed of all the things they would do together someday. Now, on a summer day, Noah eats the berries from those same brambly canes and excitedly waits to hear the part of the story about the phone call in the middle of the night asking, "Is this *Noah's* Nana?'" They hug each other, and together they answer, "'Oh yes, it is!'" Lillian Hoban's illustrations for this simple story are filled with warmth and affection.

Anna Biagioni Hart

SOURCE: A review of *Waiting for Noah*, in *School Library Journal*, Vol. 36, No. 7, July, 1990, p. 63.

Nana tells Noah the story of the winter day her son called to say that Noah's mother had gone into labor. Now that he's a toddler, Noah loves to hear this special story time and again; his face shines with pleasure and anticipation on every page. Hoban's pastel crayon drawings are particularized enough to make the two characters interesting in themselves, while allowing readers to ask for their own coming-into-the-world stories. Details of cats, countryside, and kitchen add to the story's warmth and honest sentiment, and the warmed reds and oranges of the art convey Noah's delight at his arrival and his place in the world. An excellent addition to preschool collections.

SILLY TILLY'S THANKSGIVING DINNER (1990)

Luann Toth

SOURCE: A review of *Silly Tilly's Thanksgiving Dinner*, in *School Library Journal*, Vol. 36, No. 9, September, 1990, p. 205.

Silly Tilly's memory is playing tricks on her. It's Thanksgiving day and she "forgot to remember" that she planned to have dinner for all her friends. After a series of mishaps, she unwittingly distributes her recipe cards instead of the invitations. Tilly naps by the fire and awakens at dinner time realizing that no feast has been prepared, just as her friends arrive— each with a delicious dish in hand. Hoban's sprightly, colorful watercolors and endearing cast of animal characters make this simple story an easy-reading holiday treat.

Booklist

SOURCE: A review of *Silly Tilly's Thanksgiving*, in *Booklist*, Vol. 87, No. 4, October 15, 1990, p. 446.

Like the first book about a beguiling old mole—*Silly Tilly and the Easter Bunny*—the sequel revolves around Silly Tilly's tendency to forget. When her glasses fog up (befuddled Mr. Bunny sat on them), Tilly sends out recipe cards instead of invitations for a Thanksgiving dinner. Even though she forgets to cook and falls asleep, the party is saved because her animal guests arrive with their favorite dishes. Watercolors in vibrant autumn hues accentuate this comedy of errors with quirky characterizations and fine brushwork.

WILL YOU BE MY VALENTINE? (1993, BY STEVEN KROLL)

Booklist

SOURCE: A review of *Will You Be My Valentine?* in *Booklist*, Vol. 89, No. 10, January 15, 1993, p. 921.

Following the classic formula—boy meets girl, boy loses girl, boy gets girl—this picture book tells of troubled romance among the jungle gym crowd. When the teacher announces that each child will take another's name out of a hat and make a valentine for that person, Thomas is thrilled to have chosen the name of his favorite girl, Gretchen. But does Gretchen care for Thomas? Not much, at least not until she comes over to his house to play. Gretchen's fickleness, even on Valentine's Day, dismays Thomas, but readers counting on a happy ending will not be disappointed. Hoban's colorful, child-like illustrations capture the shifting emotions of early childhood with finesse.

Mollie Bynum

SOURCE: A review of *Will You Be My Valentine?* in *School Library Journal,* Vol. 39, No. 5, May, 1993, pp. 87-8.

A preschool teacher instructs her students to each make a valentine for another classmate. Thomas draws Gretchen's name and while she is his favorite girl in the class, the feeling is not mutual. In fact, Thomas and Gretchen do not share many interests, it seems, until his mother arranges for a Saturday play date at his house. While incredibly predictable, the story offers positive ways that young children can resolve differences. The gentle text, combined with Hoban's charming illustrations, is a surefire winner for the picture-book set, not just for Valentine's Day, but as a model for forging friendships at any age.

ARTHUR'S CAMP-OUT (1993)

Booklist

SOURCE: A review of *Arthur's Camp-Out,* in *Booklist,* Vol. 89, No. 13, March 1, 1993, p. 1239.

Cheerful line-and-watercolor artwork illustrates this episodic story from Hoban's Arthur series. Whiling away a spring day, the young chimp puts down his little sister Violet's bits of nature lore as "baby science," and decides to go on a field trip without her "to collect frogs and worms and snakes—slimy things that you would not like." When Violet's friends invite her for a girls-only camp-out, he annoys them by offering to come along to protect them. Rebuffed, he decides to do a little solo camping instead. After a series of misadventures, a wet, tired, hungry, and humbled Arthur joins the girls around their campfire after all. Not the best of the series, but still a pleasant excursion for Arthur's many fans.

Sharron McElmeel

SOURCE: A review of *Arthur's Camp-Out,* in *School Library Journal,* Vol. 39, No. 4, April, 1993, p. 96.

In this ninth story about the chimp and his family, Arthur tells Violet that her knowledge of walking-sticks and cocoons is "baby science." After all, he has been on field trips and collected specimens. The siblings get permission from their babysitter to go on their own field trip and meet up with friends Mabel and Wilma. They invite Violet to go camping with them. Arthur offers to go along to protect them, but Mabel informs him that she is in charge. Arthur goes on his own camp-out and finds himself out of breath, out of food, tired, and alone at the edge of a pond. He follows a scent and finds the campers gaily roasting hot dogs and singing songs. Arthur finds out that girls not only know how to camp but they know something about science as well. Hoban's watercolor illustrations are as refreshing as the tale, which will not only amuse young readers but also give them food for thought as well. One of Hoban's best "Arthur" tales.

The Horn Book Magazine

SOURCE: A review of *Arthur's Camp-Out,* in *The Horn Book Magazine,* Vol. LXIX, No. 5, September-October, 1993, pp. 633-34.

Arthur reveals his vulnerability and gets his comeuppance in the ninth story about the chimpanzee. After smugly telling his sister Violet that because she is afraid of slimy things, she cannot accompany him on a camping trip. Arthur goes on to have a wet, food-less, and terror-filled night. Convincing dialogue; bright pencil, crayon, and watercolor illustrations; and a satisfying conclusion—complete with Violet's unobtrusive ecology lesson on the importance of bats—round out this latest entry in the popular series.

Wilson Library Bulletin

SOURCE: A review of *Arthur's Camp-Out,* in *Wilson Library Bulletin,* Vol. 68, No. 10, June, 1994, p. 129.

Seasoned author Lillian Hoban tells a silly story in ***Arthur's Camp-Out.*** The chimp's fans will grab this four-chapter narrative, in which Arthur seizes the moment but wisely capitulates and graciously joins the crowd. The bored youngster itches for a vacation activity and decides on a collecting expedition, concurrent with a three-girl camping trip.

Given the premise, any reader who's sat through a couple of seasons of sitcoms can guess what fate befalls Arthur. By the middle of Chapter Two, he exemplifies the "klutzy guy" syndrome. (The giveaway is his "Maybe I can protect you" line, which the gutsy girls immediately reject.) Everything goes wrong on Arthur's woodsy venture. He collects specimens (none of which willingly crawl into his jars), and nature just about collects him. After he fends off bats and mosquitoes, he ends up joining the girls at their campfire.

Arthur does keep his cool and the reader's sympathy. Neither gender loses or wins—the girls don't gloat, and even bossy Mabel, who sasses Arthur at the outset, diplomatically holds her tongue. The girls do flaunt their scientific knowledge, and facts about forest creatures slip easily into the narrative. Hoban's color paintings show Arthur's struggles, as the open-mouthed kid survives the humorous encounters with local fauna.

📖 *A PLANT CALLED SPOT* (1994, BY NANCY J. PETERAF)

Booklist

SOURCE: A review of *A Plant Called Spot,* in *Booklist,* Vol. 90, No. 12, February 15, 1994, p. 1093.

Teddy wants a pet of his own, a pet whose affection he can claim exclusively. His mother patiently explains that their current pets favor particular family members because of the care the animals receive from them. Teddy, on the other hand, clearly mistreats the pets. A compromise is reached when Mother brings Teddy a seedling houseplant. Despite his disappointment, he gives it a pet name. In tending Spot, Teddy learns to care for the animals as well, bargaining with them to behave in exchange for proper food and attention. In a satisfying ending, Spot rewards his master with a superb bloom. Hoban's line-and-wash drawings cleverly capture Teddy's Jekyll-and-Hyde behavior—from endearing wheedler, skilled at "working" his mother, to impish tormentor of family pets. The repetitive structure of the text, simple dialogue, and close coordination of illustration and narrative make this a good choice for beginning independent readers as well as younger listeners.

Publishers Weekly

SOURCE: A review of *A Plant Called Spot,* in *Publishers Weekly,* Vol. 241, No. 11, March 14, 1994, p. 72.

Expressive, pastel-colored drawings and a simple, repetitive text convey the story of Teddy, who longs to have a pet of his own. Teddy's family already has a dog, a cat and a rabbit, but the animals avoid Teddy because he mistreats them. Finally, Teddy's mother buys him a plant. "You don't look like a very good pet to me," Teddy says hesitantly. "But since you're all my mother will let me have, I think I'll name you Spot." As Teddy begins to care for Spot, he also learns how to appreciate his pets and to treat them with tenderness; by the time Spot has bloomed, so has Teddy. Hoban's sweet-natured illustrations add humor to Peteraf's first book, which—a little chirpily—reminds children that all living things need care and respect.

📖 *LIKE ME AND YOU* (1994, BY RAFFI AND DEBI PIKE)

Alexandra Marris

SOURCE: A review of *Like Me and You,* in *School Library Journal,* Vol. 40, No. 8, August, 1994, p. 152.

Each page of this simple book introduces a child from a different country either mailing, writing, or reading an airmail letter. Hoban's characteristic drawings have few details but show distinctive national features, landmarks, or dress. The repeated refrain ties them all together: "And each one is much like another. / A child of a mother and a father. / A very special son or daughter. / A lot like me and you." Unlike Raffi's *Down by the Bay, Shake My Sillies Out,* and *Baby Beluga,* this title is best suited to one-on-one sharing with an adult who can expand upon the concept and extend the minimal text.

📖 *I NEVER DID THAT BEFORE* (1995, BY LILAN MOORE)

Kathleen Whalin

SOURCE: A review of *I Never Did That Before,* in *School Library Journal,* Vol. 41, No. 10, October, 1995, p. 128.

[Lilian] Moore's newest poetry collection offers 14 selections based on young children's everyday experiences, with subjects like **"Monkey Bars," "New Sneakers,"** and **"Kittens."** The images and rhymes are obvious ("My new sneakers / want to / run. / They want to race / every / one"); the cozy lines never quite become the original viewpoint that is poetry. Hoban's exuberant mixed-media drawings capture the youngsters in action.

📖 *ARTHUR'S BACK TO SCHOOL* (1996)

Booklist

SOURCE: A review of *Arthur's Back to School,* in *Booklist,* Vol. 93, No. 2, September 15, 1996, p. 253.

In the tenth *I Can Read Book* about Arthur and Violet, there's a lunch-box mix up on the first day back at school. Arthur is confused, and so, at times, is the reader about who has whose lunch box and which snack is where. The subplot is more interesting, even if it is messagey: all the children get so excited that they misbehave on the school bus, and the principal has to make them see the reasons for safety rules. As always Hoban's colorful cartoon drawings of the eager chimpanzee characters are wonderfully humorous and affectionate, without trace of condescension.

Sharon R. Pearce

SOURCE: A review of *Arthur's Back to School,* in *School Library Journal,* Vol. 42, No. 9, September, 1996, p. 180.

The engaging little chimp is back for his 10th adventure. This time Arthur and his sister, Violet, are waiting for the school bus when Norman arrives with a lunch box exactly like Arthur's. After some excitement on the bus and at school (where school-bus safety rules are discussed), it is finally time for a snack. Arthur and Norman have inadvertently switched lunch boxes and Arthur's cookies are gone. In classic heartwarming style, Violet shares her cookies and they all have a great first day of school. The soft-focused, warm watercolors will be recognized by Hoban's many fans. The topic is timeless and of great appeal to this age group. The characters may be welcomed back or met for the first time. A surefire selection for the first day of school.

BIG LITTLE OTTER; BIG LITTLE LION (1997)

Kirkus Reviews

SOURCE: A review of *The Big Little Otter,* in *Kirkus Reviews,* Vol. LXIV, No. 23, December 1, 1996, p. 1738.

Hoban has created a honey of a board book (as well as its companion, *Big Little Lion,* that addresses the timeworn complaint of youngsters who believe they aren't being treated like the big kids they wish they were. Otter endures his mother's cleaning licks and her solo hunting for dinner (they munch away on what look like boiled crabs), but what he really wants is to join in the hunt ("I'm not a baby, Mama. I can fish for supper, too"). He demonstrates his diving, flipping, and spinning talents, and says, "I'm a big little otter!" The simple text comes with illustrations that captures the otter's friendly, curious face; readers will wish they could reach in and give him a good scratch behind the ear. Hoban is perfectly in tune with the yearnings of preschoolers.

Publishers Weekly

SOURCE: A review of *Big Little Otter* and *Big Little Lion,* in *Publishers Weekly,* Vol. 244, No. 1, January 6, 1997, p. 74.

Lillian Hoban spotlights independent-minded baby animals in two board books, *Big Little Otter* and *Big Little Lion.* In the first book, soft, aquatic scenes winningly depict the spirited, playful otter fishing and diving ("I can fish for supper, too!" he tells Mama Otter). The little lion, likewise, doesn't want to be his mother's baby: he wants to run and roar.

SILLY TILLY'S VALENTINE (1998)

Kirkus Reviews

SOURCE: A review of *Silly Tilly's Valentine,* in *Kirkus Reviews,* Vol. LXVI, No. 25, November 15, 1997, p. 1708.

A third holiday adventure about the absentminded mole and her friends. Tilly "forgets to remember" lots of things, such as why February 14 is a special day, how slippery snow is, and that she has cupcakes in the oven. On this Valentine's Day, it's snowing so hard that Tilly's glasses become clouded, so there's more silliness resulting from her poor vision. Her friends Mr. Mail-Mole and Mr. Bunny help her out of these difficulties, and they eventually have a jolly Valentine's celebration. This has inconsistencies for an I Can Read: The dialogue makes use of contractions erratically; commas are occasionally omitted in places where standard usage requires them, e.g., to set off the word *too,* and at the ends of some lines of poetry. Still, easy-to-read holiday stories are always in demand, and this one is, if unexceptional, fairly harmless.

Lisa Gangemi

SOURCE: A review of *Silly Tilly's Valentine,* in *School Library Journal,* Vol. 44, No. 22, February, 1998, p. 85.

Tilly the mole is back for her third adventure in this beginning reader. Here, she is so excited about snow falling that she forgets all about Valentine's Day. Mr. Bunny hints that there is something in her mailbox, but when she checks it out, her glasses are so covered with snow that she doesn't see the valentines sticking out. Mr. Bunny finally comes back to visit Tilly and wipes her glasses off so she can find her holiday cards. Hoban's simple text and trademark illustrations make this story a fine addition for easy-reader collections. Fans of Hoban's Arthur the chimp, and of Frances the badger, will enjoy Tilly's escapades.

☐☐ *ARTHUR'S BIRTHDAY PARTY* (1999)

The Horn Book Magazine

SOURCE: A review of *Arthur's Birthday Party,* in *The Horn Book Magazine,* Vol. LXXV, No. 1, January, 1999, p. 63.

Arthur the chimpanzee is planning a birthday party. After defensively putting down the "babyish" ideas of younger sister Violet, Arthur settles on the idea of a gymnastics party, where there will be prizes and he will win. Norman and Wilma and Violet *et al* enthusiastically throw themselves into practicing for the big day, with Arthur out of sorts because they are all too busy practicing to play with him. On the day of the party, Arthur performs wonderfully—but so do all his friends. Fortunately for Arthur, although Norman is best on the trampoline and Wilma and Violet are the best team, Arthur gets the prize for "best all-around gymnast." "'Just like I said I would!' yelled Arthur." Hoban manages to pull off the unusual feat of a complete and empowering absence of grown-ups by setting the book outside—mostly in the vicinity of Arthur's play structure and yard—so that the presence of adults somewhere inside is reassuringly implicit. The happy resolution is not at all bland: there are some realistic sibling tensions and less than selfless impulses along the way. A welcome, and perhaps last, addition to the series.

Blair Christolon

SOURCE: A review of *Arthur's Birthday Party,* in *School Library Journal,* Vol. 45, No. 2, February, 1999, p. 84.

Hoban continues her successful series with this fast-moving story with lots of child appeal. Arthur is planning his gymnastics birthday party. He begins by showing off his athletic prowess in front of his little sister Violet and her friend Wilma. At his party, he plans to win the prize for best all-around gymnast. In fact, he brags so much it's a wonder that Arthur's friends even show up on the special day. At the party, however, all of the guests win a prize for their stunts, and Arthur is bestowed the honor he coveted. Hoban uses simple words and straightforward sentence structure in this easy reader. Longer words such as "trampoline" and "gymnastics" have obvious picture clues and are repeated frequently. Here, the artist uses more colorful pastels than in her earlier books. Action-filled pictures of various sizes appear on every double-page spread. Birthdays have always been a favorite theme of new readers and they will be happy to celebrate with this little chimpanzee.

Booklist

SOURCE: A review of *Arthur's Birthday Party,* in *Booklist,* Vol. 95, No. 14, March 15, 1999, p. 1337.

Looking forward to a gymnastics competition at his birthday party, Arthur imagines that each of his friends will win a prize for a particular skill, and that he will win the prize as the best all-around gymnast. The week before the party, Arthur is disappointed that his friends are too busy practicing gymnastics to play with him. Even sister Violet and her friend Wilma are planning a secret performance. It's worth it, though, when everyone at the party performs to perfection, and sure enough, Arthur is named the best overall gymnast. Softly shaded pencil drawings, brightened with watercolor washes, illustrate the story with style. Another rewarding story in the series featuring this beloved chimpanzee and his friends.

Additional coverage of Hoban's life and career is contained in the following sources published by the Gale Group: *Contemporary Authors,* Vols. 69-72; *Contemporary Authors New Revision Series,* Vols. 23, 169; *Major Authors and Illustrators for Children and Young Adults*; and *Something about the Author,* Vols. 22, 69, and 104.

George MacDonald
1824-1905

Scottish author of novels, short stories, and poetry for adults and children.

Major works about the author include: *George Mac-Donald and His Wife* (Greville MacDonald, 1924), *The Golden Key: A Study of the Fiction of George MacDonald* (Robert L. Wolff, 1961), *George Mac-Donald* (Richard H. Reis, 1972), *The Harmony Within: The Spiritual Vision of George MacDonald* (Roland Hein, 1982), *George MacDonald* (Michael Phillips, 1987), *George MacDonald's Fiction: A Twentieth-Century View* (Richard H. Reis, 1989).

INTRODUCTION

George MacDonald is credited with being the first writer of fantasy with spiritual overtones, thereby opening a new genre in literature. Although he claimed his writing was not for children, but for the "childlike," many of his fantasy works and fairy tales have become classics of children's literature. His fantasies have never been out of print since they were first published over a century ago, and several of them have been republished many times, an inspiration to generations of illustrators. His children's books all have a strong undercurrent of spirituality, not surprising since he believed that his primary calling was to be a minister. He believed that the highest spiritual aspiration was to become consciously like an innocent child, that children have the ability to overcome all evil, and that there is an absolute necessity for free choice and childlike belief. His work exemplifies his understanding of the process of spiritual conversion—the ongoing spiritual process of birth, maturation, and future state—the lifelong activity of becoming a child.

Influenced by the German author Novalis, Mac-Donald's fairyland turns conventions upside-down in order to satirize them, taking traditional fairy tales and giving them a twist. For example, *The Light Princess* (1867) is cursed, not with sleep, but with a lightness of mind that makes her incapable of seriousness, even in the face of tragedy. Although his children's

fantasies are clearly symbolic, MacDonald insisted that they were not allegorical. He uses a recurring grandmother figure, modeled on his own grandmother, to represent God or the Holy Spirit, and his stories always contain some focus on death.

Unlike most female characters in Victorian literature, MacDonald's girls have strong characters and exhibit qualities of bravery and practicality usually assigned to boy characters. This attitude towards women was among the unorthodox and forward-thinking ideas that got him into trouble with the church. It has been said that in his ideas and personal philosophy, he was well ahead of his time. Among his friends he counted Mark Twain, with whom he once collaborated (although the book was never published), and Lewis Carroll, whose *Alice in Wonderland* was published with the enthusiastic encouragement of the Mac-Donald children.

BIOGRAPHICAL INFORMATION

MacDonald was born in Scotland near the city of Aberdeen. His mother died when he was eight years old, and he was raised on the family farm by his loving father and strict Calvinistic grandmother. He inherited tuberculosis from his mother and was troubled by it all his life. Lonely and introspective, he attended King's College at Aberdeen University to study chemistry, natural philosophy, modern literature, and languages. After graduating in 1845 with an M.A., he worked as a tutor while he wrestled with his spiritual doubts. Feeling strongly that he was called to be a preacher, he returned to school at Highbury College in London and received his divinity degree in 1850. That same year he was called to be the Congregational pastor at Arundel in Sussex, England. In 1851 he married Louisa Powell, an accomplished and strong-minded woman, with whom he had eleven children and adopted two more. His literary career was launched at his marriage with a poem he wrote for her as a wedding gift. His first collection of poetry was published in 1857 and brought him public recognition. His first major work, *Phantastes*, published in 1858, was highly praised by most critics and marked the advent of MacDonald's experimentation with the literary parable.

MacDonald's unorthodox views and departures from doctrine made him unpopular as a clergyman, and the church fathers kept lowering his salary in an attempt to make him quit. He finally did so, even though he believed that the ministry was his calling. He wrote, lectured, and did odd jobs until he received a professorship at Bedford College in Bedford, England, one of the first colleges for women. He later resigned in protest of outside examiners. Finally, writing became his livelihood. *David Elginbrod* (1863) was the first of his many popular Scottish romances. He edited and wrote for a children's magazine named *Good Words for the Young*, and two of his classic works, *At the Back of the North Wind* (1871) and *The Princess and the Goblin* (1872) were serialized in it. In 1872 MacDonald made a successful tour of America, then in 1877 he moved to Italy to live because the climate dramatically improved his health. He lived there for the remainder of his life, entertaining his many friends and admirers, some strangers to him, and enjoying his wife's organ recitals. In the late 1890s he suffered a possible stroke, and in his last years he was withdrawn and silent. He died at the age of 80, and his ashes were buried in Italy. In 30 years he had written over 50 books and sold millions of copies, although he never received payment for many editions of his work.

MAJOR WORKS

The Light Princess is MacDonald's version of the Sleeping Beauty fairy tale. Cursed at her christening with lightness of body and lightness of temperament, the princess is unable to be serious about anything, not even war or death or the misery of the poor. She has weight in the water and enjoys the feel of swimming. The prince who loves her sacrifices his life so that she can have her lake, but when she fully realizes his sacrifice, she weeps for him, thus breaking the spell. With her lightness gone, she is ready to assume the gravity of adulthood and its responsibilities, and the prince offers to teach her to walk. Many critics have focused on the sexual implications and symbolism in this tale, but others have insisted that MacDonald was concerned more with spiritual maturity than sexuality.

In *At the Back of the North Wind* MacDonald brings to life his belief in the corresponding and interpenetrating worlds of the natural and supernatural. Although it is a long story with a plot considered too complicated for most children, it has nonetheless become a classic chronicling little Diamond's passage through illness to death. Critics find of most interest MacDonald's treatment of death as a comforting friend, the North Wind, and the way he depicts Diamond's ordinary life in conjunction with his dream world encounters. When the child flies away at night with the North Wind, time disappears, and what becomes most important is his relationship with her, more so than the moral decisions he makes along the way.

Possibly MacDonald's best-known work, *The Princess and the Goblin* is the story of the Princess Irene and her friend, the poor boy Curdie. The goblins under the earth want to kidnap the princess and force her to marry the son of the goblin king so that they can rule both the earth and the underworld. Curdie saves her and earns the king's blessing. In the sequel, *The Princess and Curdie* (1883), Curdie once again saves the kingdom, and this time wins the hand of the princess. The spiritual significance of the story, however, is much deeper, and critics view it as a parable in which MacDonald explores, among other ideas, the concept of belief on several levels, including belief in one's own experiences. G. K. Chesterton wrote about this book, "I, for one, can really testify to a book that has made a difference to my whole existence, which helped me to see things in a certain way from the start; a vision of things which even so real a revolution as a change of religious allegiance has substantially only crowned and confirmed."

CRITICAL RECEPTION

Although most of his romantic fiction is forgotten today, MacDonald's work was very successful in his own time; his poetry was considered well enough and his Scottish romances were extremely popular. His fantasies, however, much admired by his contemporaries and by those who had grown up reading his works, are still in print. Among his admirers were W. H. Auden, who said that MacDonald was one of the most remarkable writers of the nineteenth century, and G. K. Chesterton, who called him one of the three or four greatest men of the nineteenth century. According to critics, his work inspired many prominent literary figures, among them T. S. Eliot, J. R. R. Tolkien, and C. S. Lewis, creator of the Christian allegory for children "The Chronicles of Narnia," who wrote of MacDonald, "I have always claimed that he was my master. I fancy I have never written a book in which I did not quote from him."

AUTHOR COMMENTARY

George MacDonald

SOURCE: "The Fantastic Imagination," in *A Dish of Oats: Chiefly Papers on the Imagination and on Shakespeare,* 1893. Reprint by Norwood Editions, 1977, pp. 313-22.

Were I asked, what is a fairytale? I should reply, *Read* Undine: *that is a fairytale; then read this and that as well, and you will see what is a fairytale.* Were I further begged to describe the *fairytale,* or define what it is, I would make answer, that I should as soon think of describing the abstract human face, or stating what must go to constitute a human being.

Many a man, however, who would not attempt to define *a man,* might venture to say something as to what a man ought to be: even so much I will not in this place venture with regard to the fairytale, for my long past work in that kind might but poorly instance or illustrate my now more matured judgment. I will but say some things helpful to the reading, in right-minded fashion, of such fairytales as I would wish to write, or care to read.

Some thinkers would feel sorely hampered if at liberty to use no forms but such as existed in nature, or to invent nothing save in accordance with the laws of the world of the senses; but it must not therefore be imagined that they desire escape from the region of law. Nothing lawless can show the least reason why it should exist, or could at best have more than an appearance of life.

[Man] may, if he pleases, invent a little world of his own, with its own laws; for there is that in him which delights in calling up new forms—which is the nearest, perhaps, he can come to creation. When such forms are new embodiments of old truths, we call them products of the Imagination; when they are mere inventions, however lovely, I should call them the work of the Fancy: in either case, Law has been diligently at work.

His world once invented, the highest law that comes next into play is, that there shall be harmony between the laws by which the new world has begun to exist; and in the process of his creation, the inventor must hold by those laws. The moment he forgets one of them, he makes the story, by its own postulates, incredible. . . . Suppose the gracious creatures of some childlike region of Fairyland talking either cockney or Gascon! Would not the tale, however lovelily begun, sink at once to the level of the Burlesque—of all forms of literature the least worthy?

"You write as if a fairytale were a thing of importance: must it have a meaning?"

It cannot help having some meaning; if it have proportion and harmony it has vitality, and vitality is truth. The beauty may be plainer in it than the truth, but without the truth the beauty could not be, and the fairytale would give no delight. Everyone, however, who feels the story, will read its meaning after his own nature and development: one man will read one meaning in it, another will read another.

A genuine work of art must mean many things; the truer its art, the more things it will mean. If my drawing, on the other hand, is so far from being a work of art that it needs THIS IS A HORSE written under it, what can it matter that neither you nor your child should know what it means? It is there not so much to convey a meaning as to wake a meaning. If it do not even wake an interest, throw it aside. A meaning may be there, but it is not for you. If, again, you do not know a horse when you see it, the name written under it will not serve you much. At all events, the business of the painter is not to teach zoology.

But indeed your children are not likely to trouble you about the meaning. They find what they are capable of finding, and more would be too much. For my part, I do not write for children, but for the childlike, whether of five, or fifty, or seventy-five.

A fairytale is not an allegory. There may be allegory in it, but it is not an allegory. He must be an artist indeed who can, in any mode, produce a strict allegory that is not a weariness to the spirit.

The best thing you can do for your fellow, next to rousing his conscience, is—not to give him things to think about, but to wake things up that are in him; or say, to make him think things for himself. The best Nature does for us is to work in us such moods in which thoughts of high import arise. . . . Nature is mood-engendering, thought-provoking: such ought the sonata, such ought the fairytale to be.

"But a man may then imagine in your work what he pleases, what you never meant!"

Not what he pleases, but what he can. If he be not a true man, he will draw evil out of the best; we need not mind how he treats any work of art! If he be a true man, he will imagine true things; what matter whether I meant them or not? They are there none the less that I cannot claim putting them there!

If a writer's aim be logical conviction, he must spare no logical pains, not merely to be understood, but to escape being misunderstood, where his object is to move by suggestion, to cause to imagine, then let him assail the soul of his reader as the wind assails an aeolian harp. If there be music in my reader, I would gladly wake it. Let fairytale of mine go for a firefly that now flashes, now is dark, but may flash again. Caught in a hand which does not love its kind, it will turn to an insignificant, ugly thing, that can neither flash nor fly.

The best way with music, I imagine, is not to bring the forces of our intellect to bear upon it, but to be still and let it work on that part of us for whose sake it exists. We spoil countless precious things by intellectual greed.

If any strain of my "broken music" make a child's eyes flash, or his mother's grow for a moment dim, my labour will not have been in vain.

GENERAL COMMENTARY

James Moffatt

SOURCE: "George MacDonald," in *The Bookman*, London, Vol. XXIX, No. 170, November, 1905, pp. 59-61.

To George MacDonald this power of finding one's true place, or of being at home with God, was given in the knowledge of God's Fatherly love, which constituted the crown and substance of religion.

An early critic has noted the recurrence of "floating" in his pages. It is the writer's expression for a Wordsworthian passivity and receptivity of soul, his phrase for a gentle, mystical belief in the universe as a constant action of God upon the human spirit. One of his heroes, in conversation upon the joys of deep-sea fishing by night, "dwelt especially on the feeling almost of disembodiment, and existence as pure thought, arising from the all-pervading clarity and fluidity, the suspension, and the unceasing motion." This sensation of yielding to a spiritual tide in the universe is one of George MacDonald's cardinal emotions. But it is merely the reverse side of an active sense of responsibility. His sense of a vocation is really expressed in terms of the hills. He is generally on the mountain path. The relationship of master and pupil, the magnetism of aspiration, and the influence of strong natures over weaker, or of sane characters over morbid girls and boys, are favourite themes of his prose. Like his beloved Wordsworth, he is always going up into the hills, and expecting to be followed, from the sleeping streets and dark valleys of conventional existence. Nor is the quest in vain, as he was never tired of expounding to disappointed or sceptical natures. . . .

This mounting trait or tendency dominates his verse especially, even in those passages where he shows traces of the very fault which he detected in the lines of T. T. Lynch, an excess of fancy over imagination. To some readers, as to the late Principal Geddes, Dr. MacDonald's poetry will always appeal at least as forcibly as his novels, but mainly as devotional reading. Others will be content to pronounce his mind primarily poetic, and among these was his shrewd, sympathetic critic who wrote under the pseudonym of "Henry Holbeach." W. B. Rands, with all his keenness and eagerness of spirit, was curiously alike at many points to George MacDonald. Both had to outgrow the narrow religious life of a Puritan community, though Graveley was probably uglier than anything the Scottish author had to experience, and though the latter remained Christian in a far more devout and distinctive sense than the Englishman's semi-political instincts allowed. Both combined a zeal for propaganda with a zest for parabolic compositions and for children's verse, though the one wrote for, the other about, children. Both had the fantastic touch, and each was a true student of English literature. But George MacDonald's permanent verse will probably be for the most part what he wrote out of that vein of devotional simplicity, reflective rather than passionate, which recalls the delicate, rare gifts of Crashaw, Donne, and Vaughan. There is more serenity than blood in it, however. A ripe calm marks nearly all his choicer verse and those passages of prose where his poetic feeling shimmers through. His mind was intense rather than comprehensive; but it was fundamentally an intensity of vision, not of passion, and as the years went on a certain diffuseness spread over his writing, till his pages came more and more to breathe the fragrance of a noble, sensitive, unworldly spirit, rather than the impact of a keen intellect or the masculine ardour of an artist. The music is stronger than the momentum, the brooding faculty outdoes the thirst for truth, and vitality is subordinate to elevation. . . .

Hence, it may be, the increasing prominence of the evangelist in the author. At the head of his works in prose fiction stand the four Scottish novels, *Robert Falconer, Alec Forbes, David Elginbrod,* and *Sir Gibbie,* whose praise is, or used to be, in all circles. Here George MacDonald is himself. He has stories to tell, and he tells them. The occasional glints of dry humour, the animation, the veracious delineation of the Scots peasantry, from cottars to students, from stonemasons to schoolmasters, the keen and subtle grasp of middle-class character, and the masterly use of dialect, prevent the writer's moral interests from transgressing artistic limits. It is a small thing to say that they are masterpieces of their class. No doubt, they mirror, as they helped to promote, the growth of Christianity beyond the strait orthodoxy of Scottish Calvinism in the last century. The author takes no pains to conceal his aim, yet there is self-detachment enough to preserve the story's life. He is a "novelist" in the original sense of the phrase, an innovator, a speaker of new things, a seeker for "oracles in the hills," conscious of himself and of his design even in his most objective novels. But, for one thing, the excellences of these stories in no way depend upon their original religious setting; and, for another thing, a good novel may be the vehicle of some propaganda, as *Caleb Williams,* or even *Rasselas,* out of scores of instances, may serve to prove. It is not until we come to *Malcolm* and *The Marquis of Lossie,* or to lesser books like *Castle Warlock* and *Donald Grant,* that the stream of incident, especially in *Donald Grant,* is hopelessly clogged with the water-lilies of comment and disquisition. . . .

"Dear Friends," the novelist observes, "I am beginning a new book like an old sermon; but, as you know, I have been so accustomed to preach all my life, that whatever I say or write will more or less take the shape of a sermon." Even in his children's stories he is often sinking through the subject into a deeper topic. There, however, the didactic mannerism

perhaps does not matter quite so much. But worthy youths like Malcolm and Cosmo almost answer to Fred Vincy's definition of a prig. They present all and sundry with their opinions, and this pedantry clings to them even in their love-making. Sometimes lapses of this kind are due to an excess of sentimentalism in the author; but more often they appear to be the result of a deficiency in humour. For George MacDonald's humor, which is never exuberant, is of sayings rather than of situations. It seldom acted as an artistic principle, otherwise he would have escaped many a breach of symmetry and several plunges into what the profane would bluntly term bathos. Form is sacrificed to matter, needlessly. A thought is overdeveloped, a dialogue is little more than an essay cut into blocks of conversation. Or, as at the close of *The Marquis of Lossie,* the story parts company with real life altogether.

Allied to these defects are others of a minor nature. George MacDonald, for example, shared with Galt an inconvenient predilection for melodramatic features in a plot, and as unconvincing a treatment of the aristocracy. The former flaw is native to writers of sentiment. . . . [I]t is pre-eminently by the truth and charm of these Aberdeenshire transcripts that one would wish George MacDonald to be judged as a novelist, or even appreciated as a heartening religious force.

Greville MacDonald

SOURCE: *George MacDonald and His Wife,* Dial Press, 1924, pp. 324-61.

[It must] have been quite in the early sixties that my father discovered his gift for lighter, imaginative narrative. For now and again, in place of a lecture he would read or recite a fairytale—particularly *The Light Princess.* All the fairy stories comprised in the little volume, *Dealings with the Fairies* . . . had been written before the end of 1863, and appeared first in the novel, *Adela Cathcart* . . . as setting for them. *The Light Princess,* written on a long scroll, perhaps with some idea of making its form accord with vocal delivery, should be defined rather as a *jeu d'esprit.* It hardly compares with the other fairy stories which were expressly written for little people. . . .

Good Words for the Young made its first appearance in 1869. . . . [The magazine] was too good to succeed, in spite of contributors such as Charles Kingsley, William Gilbert, W. R. S. Ralston, and George

MacDonald. It reawakened, however, my father's surest gift of faerie-allegory, and produced *At the Back of the North Wind,* with like-inspired illustrations by Arthur Hughes. Of all my father's works, this remains the "best seller." Its secret here again lies in its two-world consciousness. A child no more grasps intellectually its exalted symbolism than he reflects upon Form's relation to its indwelling Idea when he runs to his mother with a primrose because of its beauty. Yet in both cases a lasting impression of the story's and the flower's place in the Divine Economy remains, consciously or not. One need not ask what the rose means if its sweetness pierces the veil and gives taste of the joy that "will never pass into nothingness."

James Moffatt

SOURCE: "George MacDonald's Scottish Tales," in *The Bookman,* London, Vol. LXXII, No. 430, July, 1927, pp. 219-20.

"Of course it is very good indeed, yet will one ever want to read it again?" That was D. G. Rossetti's remark about "The Angel in the House." I fear it has proved a true anticipation. Our age has moved away from the sentimentalism of Coventry Patmore's poem; it does not hold us. My edition is the cheap and convenient one in Cassell's National Library, in which so much good literature was brought within the reach of poor persons in last century, but I cannot read "The Angel in the House" with any sustained interest. Now it appeared just before the first of George Macdonald's stories, which Cassells have reprinted in this attractive shape. Here we have an enterprising effort to provide for a new generation which is supposed to possess an interest in these tales of Scotland, written over fifty years ago. The question is: will the novels retain their flavour? Rossetti's query is quite fair. It may be put to anyone who is reading a book for the first time, and I dare say some asked it long ago when they read George Macdonald's new romances of the North. If so, the answer is that many will. It is years since I read them. I took them up in this new dress, half afraid lest the glamour would have gone, but it has not gone altogether, even in an age when the taste for novels has so materially altered. "Crime in a black coat is what appeals most strongly to the popular imagination," said Anatole France. It does appeal to many; a corpse in the first chapter stirs and catches our unregenerate interest. So does romance in foreign lands, the blood-quickening tale of some less civilised existence away from easy chairs in Middlesex. So does the propaganda novel, oddly enough, though

its vogue is surely nearing a close. And yet George Macdonald holds his own in spite of all this, to which he is serenely indifferent. . . .

Macdonald's tales are also drenched in dialect, but less awkwardly, and his pages occasionally help the reader by introducing the English equivalent in brackets. "Gi'en ye had hard hoo Mistress Cattanach flytit (*scolded*) at me 'cause I wadna gie't to her! You wad hae thocht, mem, she was something no canny—the w'y 'at she first beggit, an' syne fleecht (*flattered*), an' syne a' but banned and swore." So Malcolm to Mrs. Courthope. Or, again, Mrs. Bruce to little Annie in *Alec Forbes,* telling her that she cannot have a candle to light her up the dark stairs to her room: "Can'le! Na, na, bairn! Ye s' get no can'le here. Ye wad hae the hoose in a low (*flame*) aboot oor lugs (*ears*). I canna afford can'les. Ye can jist mak' a can'le o' yer han's, and fin (*feel*) yer gait up the twa stairs." And so the shivering little maid had to crawl up the dark stairs to her rat-infested garret, driven by the Spartan rule of the shopkeeper's wife. No, the dialect is not a real difficulty here; it is racy of the soil and adds to the flavour of the novels.

They are mostly set in the Gordon country, up in Strathbogie. Indeed he intended to call *Alec Forbes The Little Grey Town,* after Huntly. They are novels of a district, of a definite country life with its hatred of the Campbells, its clan-feuds, its Calvinism, its queer streaks of piety and humour, and its mixture of grim hardness and sentimental love-making. David Elginbrod reproduces memories of the author's home and particularly of his father. But its English and London scenes introduce F. D. Maurice by way of variety, and the novel gives a caustic account of spiritualism as practised in those days, when mesmerism was repelling and fascinating men like Macdonald by its eerie revelations of a world beyond their conventional psychology. The strong figure in *Alec Forbes* is Mr. Cupples, and the life of a poor, keen student at the University of Aberdeen is depicted with rare skill. In Mr. Cupples drink and genius are mixed. It is a novel in which there is less of the sentimental *motif* than in the later tales, and this is one recommendation, though most readers prefer *Robert Falconer,* if only for the vital little boy Shargar. Macdonald was good at boys of the wild, eager type. He took this hint from Richter, but he worked it out along his own lines.

Lads at college, lads loving books, lads breaking away from traditional views about religion, lads falling in love with ladies above them in station, these are the themes which come more to the front than ever in the other three novels. In *Malcolm* the hero's grandfather is a fierce Highlander: "He's the quaietest, kin'liest auld man! that is, providit ye say naething *for* a Cawmill, or *agen* ony ither hielanman." So Malcolm to Lady Florimel, who by the way is not one of the author's successes. Fishing folk abound in this novel and in its sequel, *The Marquis of Lossie,* where we meet a wild-tempered horse Kelpie. *Sir Gibbie* has a girl Ginevra, who again is more of a mouthpiece for the author than a real character; but it is wonderful how he still contrives to use the old materials freshly in this tale. *Sir Gibbie* has not had the popularity of its predecessors, but a reader who is trying Macdonald for the first time might be safely advised to take up *Alec Forbes* and then *Sir Gibbie*; they represent two facets of the author's mind distinctively.

Sentiment and sensationalism are blended in these tales. Macdonald is a storyteller, and he loves to construct a plot with some revelation about the birth of the hero which alters things at the end, or to introduce some exciting episodes, fights and brawls, which vary the flow of the story. It is in the description of local life that he excels however. The change of life in the North has rather added to the interest of these tales, for they preserve a vigorous, odd country life that has passed away, and preserve it in a classical form. No one entered so thoroughly into its quaint features as George Macdonald. He is at his best when he is drawing these village and fishing folk, old and young, good and less good, telling the story of their loves and hates and clashing in kirk and cottage and even in castle.

The old story about Coleridge and Lamb will occur to the reader of these novels. "Charles, did you ever hear me preach?" "I never heard you do anything else," Lamb is said to have retorted. Well, Macdonald is generally preaching; when he gets the chance—and often he makes the chance—he drops moral observations. It is one flaw of his characterisation that he turns some men and women into pipes for his thoughtful observations upon life in general, and that he sometimes interrupts a tale by lifting the pulpit finger in admonition. Still, it is good moralisation. "She would have taken the whole world to her infinite heart, and in unwisdom coddled it into corruption. Praised be the grandeur of the God who can endure to make and see his children suffer." George Macdonald was a peaceable Christian, but he has small comfort for pacifists and sentimentalists. It was the fashion in those days to convey ethical and religious teaching through fiction, and he shares George Eliot's love of interlacing aphorisms with action. "Obligation is a ponderous roll of canvas which Love

spreads aloft into a tent wherein he delights to dwell." "The power of enjoying the present without anticipation of the future or regard of the past, is the special privilege of the animal nature and of the human nature in proportion as it has not developed beyond the animal. Herein lies the happiness of cab-horses and tramps." "The increase of examinations in our country will increase its capacity and diminish its faculty." "The poetic element has its share in the most common pugfaced man in creation; and when he is in love, what of that sort there is in him, as well as what there is of any sort of good thing, will come to the surface as the trout do in the balmy summer evenings. Therefore let every gentle maiden be warned how she takes such manifestation of what is in the man for the man himself." "I fancy that when they die many will find themselves more at home than ever they were in this world." These are the sort of things that one picks up in reading the Scots novels of George Macdonald. But then they are set in good literature. Stories like these cannot be written in this hurrying age. They require a soil of their own, and that soil was Macdonald's by inheritance and possession. He worked it out thoughtfully, and if he did write sometimes with a facile pen, yet his tales tell still. We are in debt to the enterprising spirit of Messrs. Cassell for putting these novels again within reach of the public; they were too individual to be forgotten, and too full of good narrative and racy characterisation to be neglected by lovers of sound fiction.

G. K. Chesterton

SOURCE: "George MacDonald," in *G. K. C. as M.C.: Being a Collection of Thirty-Seven Introductions,* edited by J. P. de Fonseka, Methuen & Co. Ltd., 1929, pp. 163-72.

I for one can really testify to a book that has made a difference to my whole existence, which helped me to see things in a certain way from the start; a vision of things which even so real a revolution as a change of religious allegiance has substantially only crowned and confirmed. Of all the stories I have read, including even all the novels of the same novelist, it remains the most real, the most realistic, in the exact sense of the phrase the most like life. It is called *The Princess and the Goblin.*

When I say it is like life, what I mean is this. It describes a little princess living in a castle in the mountains which is perpetually undermined, so to speak, by subterranean demons who sometimes come up through the cellars. She climbs up the castle stairways to the nursery or the other rooms; but now and again the stairs do not lead to the usual landings, but to a new room she has never seen before, and cannot generally find again. Here a good great-grandmother, who is a sort of fairy godmother, is perpetually spinning and speaking words of understanding and encouragement. When I read it as a child, I felt that the whole thing was happening inside a real human house, not essentially unlike the house I was living in, which also had staircases and rooms and cellars. This is where the fairy-tale differed from many other fairy-tales; above all, this is where the philosophy differed from many other philosophies. I have always felt a certain insufficiency about the ideal of Progress, even of the best sort which is a Pilgrim's Progress. It hardly suggests how near both the best and the worst things are to us from the first; even perhaps especially at the first. And though like every other sane person I value and revere the ordinary fairy-tale of the miller's third son who set out to seek his fortune (a form which MacDonald himself followed in the sequel called *The Princess and Curdie*), the very suggestion of travelling to a far-off fairyland, which is the soul of it, prevents it from achieving this particular purpose of making all the ordinary staircases and doors and windows into magical things.

Dr. Greville MacDonald, in his intensely interesting memoir of his father which follows, has I think mentioned somewhere his sense of the strange symbolism of stairs. Another recurrent image in his romances was a great white horse; the father of the princess had one, and there was another in *The Back of the North Wind.* To this day I can never see a big white horse in the street without a sudden sense of indescribable things. But for the moment I am speaking of what may emphatically be called the presence of household gods—and household goblins. And the picture of life in this parable is not only truer than the image of a journey like that of the Pilgrim's Progress, it is ever truer than the mere image of a siege like that of The Holy War. There is something not only imaginative but intimately true about the idea of the goblins being below the house and capable of besieging it from the cellars. When the evil things besieging us do appear, they do not appear outside but inside. Anyhow, that simple image of a house that is our home, that is rightly loved as our home, but of which we hardly know the best or the worst, and must always wait for the one and watch against the other, has always remained in my mind as something singularly solid and unanswerable; and was more corroborated than corrected when I came to give a more definite name to the lady watching over us from the turret, and perhaps to take a more

practical view of the goblins under the floor. Since I first read that story some five alternative philosophies of the universe have come to our colleges out of Germany, blowing through the world like the east wind. But for me that castle is still standing in the mountains and the light in its tower is not put out.

All George MacDonald's other stories, interesting and suggestive in their several ways, seem to be illustrations and even disguises of that one. I say disguises, for this is the very important difference between his sort of mystery and mere allegory. The commonplace allegory takes what it regards as the commonplaces or conventions necessary to ordinary men and women, and tries to make them pleasant or picturesque by dressing them up as princesses or goblins or good fairies. But George MacDonald did really believe that people were princesses and goblins and good fairies, and he dressed them up as ordinary men and women. The fairy-tale was the inside of the ordinary story and not the outside. One result of this is that all the inanimate objects that are the stage properties of the story retain that nameless glamour which they have in a literal fairytale. The staircase in *Robert Falconer* is as much of a magic ladder as the staircase in the *Princess and the Goblin*; and when the boys are making the boat and the girl is reciting verses to them, in *Alec Forbes*, and some old gentleman says playfully that it will rise to song like a magic Scandinavian ship, it always seemed to me as if he were describing the reality, apart from the appearance, of the incident. The novels as novels are uneven, but as fairy-tales they are extraordinarily consistent. He never for a moment loses his own inner thread that runs through the patchwork, and it is the thread that the fairy great-grandmother put into the hands of Curdie to guide him out of the mazes of the goblins.

The Times Literary Supplement

SOURCE: "Menander's Mirror: Princesses and Goblins," in *The Times Literary Supplement*, No. 2134, December 26, 1942, pp. 627-28.

The Victorians specialized in children. Their method was to take you on their knee and explain. Even George MacDonald moralized, but his moralizing was for all men, not for the nursery only. When Curdie's parents were inclined to be over-ambitious for him, MacDonald's comment was:—

> The good, kind people did not reflect that the road to the next duty is the only straight one, or that, for their fancied good, we should never wish

our children or friends to do what we would not do ourselves if we were in their position. We must accept righteous sacrifices as well as make them.

This is, certainly, a blemish on any story, but it is not the intolerable blemish that it would have been if it had been addressed to children as such; therefore, like most of MacDonald's personal interventions, it was pardonable—a thing to skip if you could, to pass through and forget if you stumbled into it, at any rate not an insult, not an Olympian patting on the head, and not, thank heaven, that vilest thing of all—a facetious pinching of the cheek! George MacDonald was very far from being a great writer; he was too mild, he lacked intensity, his arrows were designed for the gentler purposes of archery, he had no lightnings in his quiver; but he had two saving gifts, denied to all hack writers "for" children: that his writing bore the impress of his personality—he wrote with joy and not with his tongue in his cheek; and that he took his own story seriously, gave himself to it, was lost in it, describing, for example, each turn of the Princess and Curdie's underground escape from the goblins with an accuracy, a visual detail, a care for fact that entitles him to at least a corner of Defoe's mantle. Very little a sentimentalist, an honest story-teller, George MacDonald, though neither giant nor poet, had an evocative power extremely rare among writers "for" children. Why? After many years, during which the book has slept on its shelf, the Princess's ceiling is still remembered. Look for the marvellous passage, the source of so many and such enduring visions:—

> The ceiling of her nursery was blue, with stars in it, as like the sky as they could make it.

What was marvellous in that? Nothing. Nothing, perhaps, except—except that you knew George MacDonald was not making things up for your benefit, was not painting the ceiling to your taste. It was the Princess's ceiling; he had seen and liked it; he was saying so. . . .

What seems to be necessary—since it can be the salvation of even such a minor prophet as George MacDonald—is that the writer of a book that children can make their own should not self-consciously grovel to what he supposes to be the childish taste of a child. If, while writing, he is altogether unaware of children, so much the better; it is then that the rare miracles happen; but, if this is impossible, let him at least acknowledge that, in imaginative range, children, though they differ from him, are not less than he, and free his mind of patronage. They love facts, they love fantasy, they understand ritual; they are not

frightened in their own lives by the terrors of the forest or deceived in their own values by an enchantress. They can pass through tragedy unscathed, they can rejoice in the naturally incongruous (which has nothing whatever to do with the thick vulgarism of farce); the laughter they give to a clown is the same that they give to a kitten. But their supreme enchantments are grave ones and their supreme pleasures are found in the intensity, the pressure and the sweep of narrative. Of course what it all comes to is what all criticism comes to in the end—style. And style, whatever else it may or may not be, implies two things: individualism and taste. If there be any who do not know what those words mean they had better join the army of those who now produce mass-entertainment for the "juvenile" market. They will make their fortunes. Meanwhile, we may wonder how it was that one man who epitomized in himself all the virtues of a writer for children—a genius for telling and skipping, sadness, romance, plainness, valiance, lightness and seriousness of heart—how it was that Goldsmith, who left a masterpiece in every other kind, omitted this. He was the man for the deliberate miracle that should have given us all a key to this critical mystery, which, for want of an absolute standard, remains a mystery still.

C. S. Lewis

SOURCE: A preface to *George MacDonald: An Anthology,* by George MacDonald, 1946. Reprint by Macmillan Publishing Co. Inc., 1947, pp. xxi-xxxiv.

Most myths were made in prehistoric times, and, I suppose, not consciously made by individuals at all. But every now and then there occurs in the modern world a genius—a Kafka or a Novalis—who can make such a story. MacDonald is the greatest genius of this kind whom I know. But I do not know how to classify such genius. To call it literary genius seems unsatisfactory since it can coexist with great inferiority in the art of words—nay, since its connection with words at all turns out to be merely external and, in a sense, accidental. Nor can it be fitted into any of the other arts. It begins to look as if there were an art, or a gift, which criticism has largely ignored. It may even be one of the greatest arts; for it produces works which give us (at the first meeting) as much delight and (on prolonged acquaintance) as much wisdom and strength as the works of the greatest poets. . . . It gets under our skin, hits us at a level deeper than our thoughts or even our passions, troubles oldest certainties till all questions are reopened, and in general shocks us more fully awake than we are for most of our lives.

It was in this mythopoeic art that MacDonald excelled. And from this it follows that his best art is least represented in this collection. The great works are *Phantastes,* the *Curdie* books, *The Golden Key, The Wise Woman,* and *Lilith.* From them, just because they are supremely good in their own kind, there is little to be extracted. The meaning, the suggestion, the radiance, is incarnate in the whole story: it is only by chance that you find any detachable merits. The novels, on the other hand, have yielded me a rich crop. This does not mean that they are good novels. Necessity made MacDonald a novelist, but few of his novels are good and none is very good. They are best when they depart most from the canons of novel writing, and that in two directions. Sometimes they depart in order to come nearer to fantasy, as in the whole character of the hero in *Sir Gibbie* or the opening chapters of *Wilfrid Cumbermede*. Sometimes they diverge into direct and prolonged preachments which would be intolerable if a man were reading for the story, but which are in fact welcome because the author, though a poor novelist, is a supreme preacher. Some of his best things are thus hidden in his dullest books. . . . I am speaking so far of the novels as I think they would appear if judged by any reasonably objective standard. But it is, no doubt, true that any reader who loves holiness and loves MacDonald—yet perhaps he will need to love Scotland too—can find even in the worst of them something that disarms criticism and will come to feel a queer, awkward charm in their very faults. (But that, of course, is what happens to us with all favorite authors.) One rare, and all but unique, merit these novels must be allowed. The "good" characters are always the best and most convincing. His saints live; his villains are stagey. . . .

In making this collection I was discharging a debt of justice. I have never concealed the fact that I regarded him as my master; indeed I fancy I have never written a book in which I did not quote from him. . . . It must be more than thirty years ago that I bought . . . the Everyman edition of *Phantastes*. A few hours later I knew that I had crossed a great frontier.

Louis MacNeice

SOURCE: "The Victorians," in *Varieties of Parable,* Cambridge at the University Press, 1965, pp. 96-101.

MacDonald's main problem was that of the mystical poets, how to express the Ineffable, and like many mystical poets he tries to do this by piling up sensuous detail (notice particularly the use he makes of precious stones). But even in MacDonald, especially in the children's books, we find, . . . the flat prosy statement or the touch of humour which serve as correctives to what might seem overlush or overjewelled. Thus the Bunyanesque note is struck in *The Princess and Curdie* when he is describing a corrupt society: 'There were even certain quacks in the city who advertised pills for enabling people to think well of themselves, and some few bought of them, but most laughed, and said, with evident truth, that they did not require them.' And in *The Golden Key,* where the hero and heroine, Mossy and Tangle, are enabled to communicate with the beasts, birds and insects, we hear the Andersen note: the squirrels, for instance, turn out to be kind, 'but the bees were selfish and rude, justifying themselves on the ground that Tangle and Mossy were not subjects of their queen, and charity must begin at home, though indeed they had not one drone in their poorhouse at the time.' But these are minor matters: what is unique in MacDonald is his passionately spiritual attitude to the universe and his prolific invention of symbols to embody it. It should be noted that with him, as with Kingsley but much more so, the stories involve very serious moral issues, which are contingent not on Law but on Grace. . . .

MacDonald does not talk about God, let alone Christ, in his parable writing. . . .

MacDonald's course requires a very unusual gift of sheer invention, which fortunately he possessed. A few of his minor creations appear arbitrary and therefore fail to pull their weight—some of his monsters, for instance, might have been knocked up by Hieronymus Bosch on an off day—but on the whole the stream of invention flows astonishingly fresh without any sign of failing. . . . I think MacDonald's extraordinary supernatural females compare very well with either Gretchen or Goethe's Virgin Mary. . . . They are the conferrers of magical gifts, and so are these strange creations of MacDonald's such as the Old Lady in *The Princess and the Goblin* who can be seen only by those who have faith and who then sometimes appears as a beautiful young lady. Other examples are the beautiful old women in *Phantastes* and *The Golden Key,* and Mara, the daughter of Adam and Eve, in *Lilith.*

These creatures, who are neither goddesses nor angels nor enchantresses nor fairies but something of all four, exist in a way outside normal time but slip into our time or allow us to slip into theirs, in order to do their good works—and they are all indefatigable workers. The other world to which they belong seems to be ruled by the two great principles of Love and Death—what C. S. Lewis rightly calls 'a good death.' These worlds are entered from ours by something in the nature of a conjuring trick. In both *The Princess and the Goblin* and *Lilith* the approach is made through an attic reached by a long flight of stairs. . . . [T]hese attics are the counterpart to the cellars in the former book and to the subterranean passages, especially those inside mountains, which are always appearing in MacDonald. Both sets of images represent things outside the compass of the normal reasoning mind: some admirers have claimed that MacDonald, like Ibsen, was one of the few people of his time to pay due attention to the Unconscious. . . .

MacDonald's moral view of the universe means that his heroes and heroines have to develop and they usually do it the hard way. MacDonald talks about Fairies and Fairy Land as freely as Barrie but in attitude as in vision he is poles apart from him: MacDonald would never tolerate Peter Pan or, for that matter, Wendy. There are indeed Peter Pan-like children in *Lilith* but the hero sees that their growth has been arrested and feels that it is his mission to cure this. MacDonald's heroes have not only to prove themselves through action, like Tom in *The Water Babies,* they have also to achieve a spiritual evolution. This involves paradoxes which are nearly all variants on the Christian paradox that one must lose one's life to save it.

Maurice Sendak

SOURCE: "The Depths of Fantasy," in *Book Week— The Washington Post,* July 24, 1966, pp. 14-15.

George MacDonald was a novelist, poet, mythmaker, allegorist, critic, essayist, and, in everything, a preacher. One of the towering and mystifying figures of Victorian literature, he wrote well over 50 books, of which only two, *At the Back of the North Wind,* and *The Princess and the Goblin*, are still widely read. His main forte was fantasy—his remarkable power, in the words of W. H. Auden, to "project his inner life in images, events, beings, landscapes which are valid for all." For admirers of MacDonald, such as myself, his work has something of the effect of an hallucinatory drug. Finishing one of his stories is often like waking from a dream—one's own dream. The best of them stimulate long-forgotten images and feelings—the "something profound" that borders frustratingly close to memory without quite ever reaching it. . . .

The Lost Princess strikes a very different note from MacDonald's earlier fairy tales. There is a falling off,

not of creative power but rather of his faith in moral power. This is a harsh, angry tale whose magic, unlike the pure crystal fantasy of MacDonald's earlier stories, is black, erratic, and appears finally to be nearly impotent against the forces of evil.

The Lost Princess and *The Princess and Curdie* are the last major fairy tales MacDonald wrote for children, and in both of them joyfulness of the early tales has been replaced by a grim, apocalyptic gloom. Magic is powerless against evil, which partially triumphs in *The Lost Princess* and at the end of *The Princess and Curdie* sweeps everything before it. The two heroines of *The Lost Princess* are the very opposite of the lovely Princess Irene of *The Princess and the Goblin.* Unlike Rosamond and Agnes, Irene believes completely in her great-great-grandmother, who lives at the top of the staircase; she puts herself unquestioningly in her care and follows wherever her magic thread leads. Those who admire MacDonald for Irene and for Diamond, the gentle boy of *At the Back of the North Wind,* might very well be put off by the harshness of *The Lost Princess.* That would be a pity, for despite the sharp change of mood from the earlier fairy tales, *The Lost Princess* abounds in MacDonald's wildly beautiful imagery. There are the familiar unearthly landscapes, the subtlety and seriousness with which he analyzes his characters' thoughts and feelings.

Best of all, there is MacDonald's extraordinary evocation of the dream, as astonishing and as true as ever. Beyond providing the personal motif of his works, the dream offered MacDonald freedom to examine his emotions behind a screen sufficiently remote and fantastic to safeguard his mid-Victorian audience from shock. Even more important, he shared the views of the early German Romantic writers, particularly Novalis and E. T. A. Hoffmann, whom he most admired. These pre-Freudian artists rebelled against the prevalent attitude that dreams were merely the meaningless rumblings of the brain. They equated dreams with emotional truths and imagination, and Novalis contended that life would have meaning only when it attained the spiritual, poetic truth of the dream. Rosamond, the lost princess, only begins to find herself in the mood—or dream—chambers of the Wise Women.

MacDonald might have ended *The Lost Princess* with one of his favorite questions, from Novalis, a quotation he used as an epigraph for his first great fairy tale for adults, *Phantastes,* and which make up the closing words of his last book, the dream romance *Lilith*: "Our life is no dream, but it should and will perhaps become one."

Denis Donoghue

SOURCE: "The Other Country," in *The New York Review of Books,* Vol. IX, No. 11, December 21, 1967, pp. 34-36.

On October 14, 1863, Charles Dodgson, soon to become Lewis Carroll, visited his friends the Mac-Donalds at their home, Elm Lodge, Heath Street, Hampstead. During the afternoon he took a photograph of George MacDonald and his eldest daughter, Lilia. It is a curious picture. Lilia is as sweet as any of Lewis Carroll's heroines, even if she is a little too old to be perfect. But her father, reading to her in the garden, is caught with a haunted look, as if his text were the quintessence of dust and the garden a charnel-vault. The picture is probably misleading. There is nothing in the available reecord to suggest that MacDonlad was much possessed by doom. Visits to Elm Lodge, according to Carroll's diary and other sources were always genial occasions. Often they included private theatricals, once *Pilgrim's Progress,* again *Polyeuctus.* On formal occasions the company was always interesting and sometimes fine. Carroll noted, after a later visit: "Met Mr. Clemens (Mark Twain) with whom I was pleased and interested."

George MacDonald was born in 1824 at Huntly, Aberdeenshire. He went to Aberdeen University and was ordained to the Trinity Congregational Church in 1850. His sermons were considered unsatisfactory because they did not contain enough doctrine, and after three years he resigned to become a lay preacher. He spent some years in Manchester before moving to London, where he made his living as writer, with some aid from a Civil List pension in his later years. From 1855 to the end of the century he wrote poems, sermons, allegories, novels of Scotland, and fairy tales. He died in 1905. His most celebrated stories are ***At the Back of the North Wind*** (1871), ***The Princess and the Goblin*** (1872), and ***The Princess and Curdie*** (1883). ***The Golden Key*** is not as widely known as these, but its particular pleasures are now, happily, available again.

Appropriately, George MacDonald and Lewis Carroll were friends, but their writings have little in common. No wonder the photograph is odd. Carroll's art is Nonsense, MacDonald's is fairy-tale: the difference is fundamental. In *The Field of Nonsense* Elizabeth Sewell gives the rules of the Carroll game. The first rule is that Nonsense is a closed system, which delights in minding its own business. Part of this business is to exclude many respectable consider-ations and values which, outside the system, are properly acknowledged. In Nonsense, Miss Sewell observes, "all the world is paper and all the seas are ink." So the touch of nature which makes the whole world kith and kin destroys, in Nonsense, the whole pack of cards. True, the Mock Turtle was once a Real Turtle, but that was in another country, and besides, we are playing "a game, to which emotion is alien." The aim of Nonsense is "to make the mind create for itself a more orderly universe," more like symbolic logic, that bachelor science, to be precise. Telegrams and anger are replaced by numbers, progressions, one and one and one and one and one. The effects are bound to be insidious, subversive, considered from any standpoint in the sensual world, and the perpetrator is bound to be manic. Perhaps George MacDonald saw these effects when he faced the camera, despite the domestic props, the book, and Lilia's hand on his shoulder. In his own fiction there are numbers, but they are always amenable to other persuasions, love, fear, the desire and pursuit of the good. There are also dreams, but dreams are important in MacDonald's fiction only for their influence upon the quality of the dreamer's waking hours, his decisions and actions thereafter.

So the motive for fairy tale is the motive for metaphor, the exhilaration of change. You like metaphor, Wallace Stevens says in an exemplary poem, when you want things to change, when you particularly want them to change to you, as if a cripple were to sing. The particular change that MacDonald wanted was a change of character, as he wanted people to be different by being better. This is the flow of feeling between his sermons, metaphors, novels, and fairy tales. Metaphor is the shortest way of getting out of Manchester, the quickest answer to the Industrial Revolution. Some of the evidence is contained in **"A Manchester Poem,"** one of his most revealing compositions. "Slave engines utter again their ugly growl," he says, but every "marvellous imperfection" points ahead to "higher perfectness than heart can think." The strange feature of the poem is that it is so deeply committed to metaphor and change that Paradise itself, because it is the End, is deemed to be improper. To MacDonald it was far more important, because far more human, to travel hopefully than to arrive. He turns away from first and last things, preferring drama to eschatology. Value is embodied in action, striving, change; to arrive is to make metaphor redundant:

> Man seeks a better home than Paradise;
> Therefore high hope is more than deepest joy,
> A disapointment better than a feast,

And the first daisy on a wind-swept lea
Dearer than Eden-groves with rivers four.

The problem is to endow the Good Life with the right metaphors of action. In several stories we hear of "the place where the end of the rainbow stands," clearly the same place as "the back of the North Wind" and "the country from which the shadows come," but there is always a suggestion that this place is worthy because of the aspiration, the energy, it engenders; and that its finality is its defect. Heaven is inferior to Nature, MacDonald goes to the brink of implying, because Heaven is changeless and Nature is always changing. His parishioners were right, MacDonald's sermons are short of doctrine.

Emerson is relevant. In the fourth section of the long essay on Nature he says that Nature gives us, one of many gifts, an ethical vocabulary. Every word we use to express a moral fact, "if traced to its root, is found to be borrowed from some material appearance." For instance, "*right* means *straight*; *wrong* means *twisted . . . transgression,* the crossing of a *line*." Later, as if anticipating T. S. Eliot's theory of the "objective correlative," he says:

> Every natural fact is a symbol of some spiritual fact. Every appearance in nature corresponds to some state of the mind, and that state of the mind can only be described by presenting that natural appearance as its picture.

This is the rationale of the fairy tale. The supernatural tinge which Emerson gives to his descriptions of Nature is more evident in him than in MacDonald, but even to MacDonald the strongest justification of a change of character is featured in the constantly changing appearances of Nature. Magic is the equivalent of all the possibilities of ethical change, brought together in a single dramatic power. The epigraph to Emerson's essay reads:

> A subtle chain of countless rings
> The next unto the farthest brings;
> The eye reads omens where it goes,
> And speaks all languages the rose;
> And, striving to be man, the worm
> Mounts through all the spires of form.

Darwin is good medicine. In Emerson and in MacDonald Nature is also featured as discipline, because she contains and therefore presumably knows all the answers. MacDonald's *The Lost Princess* is often read as a moral tract, the point being that children should never be pampered. But its power as a story depends upon MacDonald's sense of natural forces working behind or beneath the maxim; forces far in excess of the moral occasion, but working in its be-

half. North Wind has more business in hand than merely to push Diamond or Old Sal in the right direction. The point about Princess Rosamond and the shepherd-child Agnes in *The Lost Princess* is only incidentally that they are both spoiled brats. Rather, it is that their young lives are perverse and unnatural, because deprived of the discipline of natural power. This is what the Wise Woman knows, so she takes the children away for their own good. Nature is a foster parent, better than the original. MacDonald's stories reach far and wide and deep because, especially in *The Golden Key* and the Curdie books, they imply a lively set of forces which can get out of hand, at least for a time.

Here again MacDonald differs from Lewis Carroll. William Empson, as usual, makes a good point about the Alice books. Carroll shared the Wordsworthian feeling that children are wiser than us because they are "in the right relation to Nature"; being right about life, the young girl can afford to be independent. Perhaps we might add that this independence is Carroll's way of urging a certain disengagement from Nature's apron-strings. If the child is right, to start with, there is no need to keep fussing. MacDonald was inclined to fuss. He believed that adults are better than children because they have been active longer. Lying in Abraham's bosom is not enough. The narrator is a good teacher because he is gifted in reading natural signs, alive to the metaphorical possibilities and the force they contain. The only advantage children have is that the likelihood of becoming adults still stretches ahead of them. There is a right way, there is a wrong way, children must be taught the difference. So MacDonald saw his work as the collusion of an adult with Nature for the guidance of children, bringing them along. "The whole system of the universe," he says in one of his sermons, "works upon this law—the driving of things upwards towards the centre." Everything in his books is on the move, because to stop is to despair. Battles are great occasions, especially in *The Princess and Curdie* where the King's forces include the great Uglies and the birds, all striving for the Good. The books are Sermons on the Mount. Diamond reaches for the sky. Curdie, attacked by a flock of birds, is defended by Lina, an animal on its way to become a child. The worm strives to be man. Much of MacDonald's symbolism is based on this figure: stairs, winding paths, mountains, excelsior, excelsior. The only way to live, moment by moment, is in aspiration. With the right metaphors, conspiring with natural change, we can then enjoy what he calls in *Sir Gibbie* "the holy carelessness of the eternal *now*." Magic is Faith. When Curdie has let himself become stupid and insensitive, killing harmless things like pigeons, Nature rebukes him:

> Suddenly everything round about him seemed against him. The red sunset stung him; the rocks frowned at him. . . .

The only safe way is humility, which reconciles high and low.

There is a passage in *The Princess and Curdie* which seems to refute this symbolism but, in fact, confirms it. When Curdie reaches the castle he sees the great staircase and he knows that to reach the tower he must go further. The narrator takes the occasion to say that "those who work well in the depths more easily understand the heights, for indeed in their true nature they are one and the same. . . . " The goblins are evil and their home is underground, but the miners are good because they work well in the depths, the King's servants. If the King's palace is at the top of the mountain it is necessary to redeem the lower places. MacDonald does this by an ethic of content, Christian humility. Curdie is a good miner, so "from knowing the ways of the king's mines, and being able to calculate his whereabouts in them, [he] was now able to find his way about the king's house." The social equivalent comes later when the Lady of Light says to Peter: "I am poor as well as rich . . . I, too, work for my bread. . . . "

Mostly, this pastoral consolation is given in familial images. There is an especially ingenuous poem called **"The Golden Key,"** in MacDonald's *Parables,* about a boy, caught in a storm, trying to find the golden key. Darkness falls, he goes home, his mother kisses him, and

> *Soon, things that are and things that*
> *seem*
> *Did mingle merrily;*
> *He dreamed, nor was it all a dream,*
> *His mother had the key.*

The available force is called Love, a word which MacDonald pays extra because, like Humpty Dumpty, he makes it do a lot of work. North Wind is Mother. "Love makes everything lovely," MacDonald writes in *Alec Forbes*; "hate concentrates itself on the one thing hated." To Emerson the spirit of Nature is Father; to MacDonald, Mother. Either way, there can be no final evil. In MacDonald's stories the local evils are considerable, especially when they are our own construction, like Mr. Vane's house which falls upon him in *Lilith*. *At the Back of the North Wind* is par-

ticularly keen in its suggestion of the power of darkness. Among MacDonald's stories it is the one which most vigorously implies the world of Industrial Revolution, crying for Love, metaphor, and the Factory Acts. Sal the gin-crone and the drunken cabman stay in the mind longer than North Wind's ostensible cruelties, which are rationalized in the usual way. When North Wind is rebuked by Diamond for sinking the ship, she tells him that behind the cries from the drowning ship she hears the sound of a far-off song in which every cry is reconciled. Diamond does not protest. At the end of *Phantastes* MacDonald says that "what we call evil is the only and best shape which, for the person and his condition at the time, could be assumed by the best good." Ideally, evil consumes itself; as the goblins, trying to flood the King's palace, are drowned in the flood. When the people in *The Princess and Curdie* choose a bad King, he plunders the mountain for gold, and the mountain, caving in, destroys the palace. Then there is nothing. The country is given back to the wild deer, "and the very name of Gwyntystorm . . . ceased from the lips of men." But the deer will strive upward, presumably, in their season.

It is customary to say, with Professor Tolkien, that "Death is the theme that most inspired George MacDonald." But it is a hard point to establish. His work is not very Grimm. Besides, he could always treat death as he treated evil, taking the harm out of it. *The Golden Key* is the classic text. The action of the book is the convergence of the boy Mossy and the girl Tangle. For a long time their stories are separate. They meet, about halfway through the book, only to lose each other again. Tangle's adventures bring her to meet an air-fish, then the Old Man of the Sea, the Old Man of the Earth, and a naked child who turns out to be the Old Man of the Fire. "Follow that serpent," the Man of Fire says, "He will lead you the right way" . . . to the country from which the shadows come. Meanwhile Mossy, who has found the key, is searching for the appropriate lock. After sundry incidents he meets the same Old Man of the Sea. "You have tasted of death now," the Old Man says, "Is it good?" "It is good," Mossy answers, "It is better than life." "No," the Old Man says, "it is only more life." Eventually Mossy finds the keyhole in a rock, and when he opens the lock he comes upon Tangle. They climb out of the earth into the rainbow, "going up to the country whence the shadows fall." True, the story can be glossed as MacDonald's refusal to think of his favorite metaphors languishing in the Fortunate Fields, their work done. If life loses the name of action it loses itself, and to MacDonald no prize, however Elysian, is worth the loss. So it is natural for him to think of death as merely more life, carrying the figures of action beyond the grave. The Old Man of the Sea is the guardian of this idiom.

Of the other books, *The Princess and Curdie* is unusual in its impression of finality, writing "Finis." More often we are meant to hear: "To be Continued in our Next." This is the impression of *The Golden Key*, as of *North Wind* and *The Lost Princess*. MacDonald is happiest, after all, in the "sensuality of the shade," working, acting, choosing. His most characteristic work is a form of cooperation, participation in natural energies which are deemed to be already working in the field. Think of that serpent, in *The Golden Key*, which the Man of Fire creates to lead Tangle to the shadowy place. The dramatic invention at that point in the story, so easy and fluent, implies full confidence in the metaphorical resources of Nature and confidence, hardly less full, in the poetic imagination, Metaphor, metamorphosis, invention, Nature as the Aeolian lyre: the imaginative unity of MacDonald's work relies upon these fictions. Thinking of these figures we think of literature according to Coleridge, who in "The Aeolian Harp" invokes *"the one Life within us and abroad, / Which meets all motion and becomes its soul."* The idiom is sufficiently active to suit MacDonald, and may be allowed to stand as another gloss.

Richard H. Reis

SOURCE: *George MacDonald,* Twayne Publishers, Inc., 1972, pp. 17-30, 75-105.

The chief problem inherent in an examination of MacDonald's accomplishment is that, while he wrote poems, conventional novels (for which he was most famous in his lifetime), criticism, and in nearly every other imaginable genre, his claim to a permanent place in English literature must probably rest upon his few fantastic, visionary, or symbolic works, for both children and adults. Of paramount interest, from the point of view of literary history, is the fact that such symbolic literature was decidedly "out of style" in the Victorian period when MacDonald wrote. The period was the golden age of the realistic novel and the prose essay, but not of symbolic fiction; MacDonald was one of the few writers of his time who practiced the latter art, which has in the twentieth century become far more important than it was in the nineteenth. Only fairy tales, of which MacDonald is a master, had much importance in Victorian England as symbolic literature.

The adult world wanted novels, so MacDonald wrote them because he had to make his living as a writer.

Yet George MacDonald's literary profession was in a sense only a secondary calling; primarily, he thought of himself as a preacher, a moralist, even a divine. Denied an "official" pulpit because of his unorthodoxy, MacDonald chose to give his message to the world in fiction which was consciously didactic. The result was a series of rather bad (though very popular) novels and a few interspersed masterpieces of symbolic literature, a genre to which didacticism is perfectly suited. . . .

As an author of fairy tales, which are unfortunately not often taken seriously as literature, MacDonald has largely maintained a reputation undimmed by the shifts in taste which have obscured his popularity as a novelist. The fairy tales continue to sell and to be reissued; in fact, editions of *The Princess and the Goblin* and *The Princess and Curdie* have been published within the past few years, under the sponsorship of Auden and Lewis. Even the novels, ignored by most literary historians nowadays, are still read, especially in Scotland, where the dialect works have always been popular.

Finally, another sign of revived interest in MacDonald's works is the publication of a full-length study by Robert Lee Wolff entitled *The Golden Key: A Study of the Fiction of George MacDonald.* Professor Wolff's book is uneven and at times unsound, but its appearance provides additional evidence that MacDonald is not forgotten yet. Unfortunately, Wolff's volume, largely biographical and psychoanalytical in its orientation, is of little critical value. Wolff's insistence upon treating literature as a half-inadvertent revelation of an author's psychic troubles is interesting doctrinaire Freudianism that should not be mistaken for literary criticism. It is to be hoped, however, that the appearance of this rather sensational study will stimulate the slow current revival of interest in George MacDonald.

II. MacDonald's Life

Although Greville MacDonald's exhaustive biography of his father has relieved me of any obligation to chronicle MacDonald's life at length, it does seem appropriate to review the facts of his career briefly. The son's biography is, naturally, the source of most of these facts; and it is sufficiently authoritative not to require correction. *George MacDonald and His Wife* is invaluable as a source of information, as a repository of letters unpublished elsewhere, and, to a lesser extent, for its earnest but rather inexpert critical commentary. I must stress, however, that the biography displays the faults of many such works by the sons of notable fathers. Greville MacDonald insists that his father was the best writer and wisest man who has ever lived and that he has been maligned and misunderstood by the ignoramuses who fail to concede the point. It is very likely, indeed, that there may have been some glossing over of useful facts in the son's anxiety to portray the father in the best possible light. This filial piety seems to have inspired Robert Lee Wolff's speculative efforts to throw some light upon the darker places in MacDonald's psyche.

Details of MacDonald's early life are of greatest significance for a critical understanding of his works. Many of his novels, especially, are in part autobiographical; and, as is often the case with autobiographical writers, the novels focus on his upbringing and on his earliest encounters with the world of practical affairs. Therefore, we need to know that MacDonald was born in Huntly, Aberdeenshire, in 1824, and that he grew up there and in nearby Pirriesmill, where his father established a somewhat larger farm not long after George was born. His boyhood was set in a traditional rural atmosphere, compounded of Calvinist hellfire, oatcakes, horsemanship, agricultural virtues, and exploration of neighborhood ruins and wildernesses. Reminiscences of such adventures, portrayed with vigor and immediacy, occur again and again in MacDonald's most convincing realistic novels, constituting a large part of his charm as they do of Dickens's. It should not be supposed, though, that MacDonald's own family was conventionally Calvinistic: his father was a nonsectarian Christian of the sort which values the Bible more than what anybody says about it. Nevertheless, the prevailing sternness of Presbyterian Scotland was always there, an oppressive, ubiquitous force.

Greville MacDonald maintains that George's father was infinitely noble and that his relations with his son were exemplary. C. S. Lewis adds that this rare rapport between father and son must account for MacDonald's ideal of the transcendent Fatherhood of God. George, if we are to believe Greville, never asked his father for anything without getting what he asked; for he never asked for anything undeserved or unobtainable. Lewis correlates this enviable if improbable circumstance with one of George's remarks on prayer: "He who seeks the Father more than anything He can give, is likely to have what he asks, for he is not likely to ask amiss." Lewis adds that "the theological maxim is rooted in the experience of the author's childhood. This is what may be called the 'anti-Freudian predicament' in operation." Robert Lee Wolff, on the other hand, who refuses to believe anything of the sort, remarks: "I leave to students of

Lewis the job of explaining his triumphal assertion of MacDonald's freedom from Freud." As an apostle of Freud, Wolff insists that MacDonald must have suffered from an involved sort of Oedipus complex, disturbed by the fact that MacDonald's mother died when he was eight. According to Wolff, the father could not substitute for the mother's tenderness, nor for her sexual attractiveness. Since nothing of this sort can, of course, be found in Greville MacDonald's biography, Wolff looks for confirmation in the novels and insists that he finds it everywhere. He proposes, without factual evidence, that MacDonald, unable to resolve his Oedipal wishes, nurtured a lifelong fantasy of sleeping with his mother.

At sixteen MacDonald entered a public school in Aberdeen, winning a bursary (scholarship) to the University of Aberdeen a year later, in 1840. At the university he embarked upon a scientific curriculum, but in 1842 he ran out of money and had to leave school to accumulate some savings. It is quite possible that the temporary rustication was due, in part at least, to some degree of overindulgence in alcohol and at the city's brothels, although again Greville MacDonald naturally does not discuss the question. But in *Alec Forbes of Howglen* (1865), a largely autobiographical novel, MacDonald clearly implies that his hero fell into a deplorable course of hinted-at vice while at the university.

Whatever the reason for MacDonald's leaving his studies in 1842, that summer one of the most important events of his life certainly occurred. According to Greville MacDonald, his father "spent some summer months in a certain castle or mansion in the far North, the locality of which I have failed to trace, in cataloguing a neglected library. . . . The library, wherever it was, and whatever its scope, added much to the materials upon which his imagination worked in future years." While it is often unwise to interpret passages of ostensible fiction as autobiographical, Greville MacDonald does not hesitate to cite from *The Portent* (1864), one of his father's romances, a description of his experience in this northern library; the passage, which follows, is almost certainly autobiographical: "I found a perfect set of our poets, perfect according to the notion of the editor and the issue of the publisher, although it omitted both Chaucer and George Herbert. . . . But I found in the library what I liked far better, many romances of a very marvellous sort, and plentiful interruption they gave to the formation of the catalogue. I likewise came upon a whole nest of the German classics . . . ; happening to be a tolerable reader of German, I found these volumes a mine of wealth inexhaustible."

The English poets, the literature of romance, the works of the German Romantics-these are the most profound and permanent influences upon Mac-Donald's own works. Together they set in motion his change from an ordinary young Scotch scientist to a religious mystic and votary of the imagination. As Lewis suggests, the profound effect of this experience can be traced throughout MacDonald's works: "The image of a great house seen principally from the library and always through the eyes of a stranger or a dependent (even Mr. Lane in *Lilith* never seems at home in the library which is called his) haunts his books to the end. It is therefore reasonable to suppose that the 'great house in the North' was the scene of some important crisis or development in his life."

The same experience, whatever its nature, figures in the lives of almost every protagonist in MacDonald's most autobiographical novels; but no explicit account of what happened that summer exists. Professor Wolff is sure that MacDonald must have fallen in love with the daughter of the house but that she eventually dropped him because she thought his social status inferior. Such circumstances do appear now and then in the novels; but Wolff, although he makes a plausible case, builds upon conjecture. Wolff adds that this experience caused MacDonald to develop a permanent and neurotic hatred for rich noblemen, basing this conclusion upon the fact that aristocratic villains are found in most of MacDonald's stories. Wolff conveniently chooses to ignore the equally indisputable fact that upper-class villains are a staple of Victorian fiction, often no doubt designed to appeal to a lower-class reader's jealousy—a commercial consideration which MacDonald, who needed the widest possible market, surely would not ignore. In any case, MacDonald always depicts libraries as places of high excitement, sources of thrilling secrets, the settings for dramatic encounters between heroes and villains or for love scenes.

When MacDonald returned to the university in 1843, he entered a period of inward ferment and outward gloom, marked by religious doubts; and he also began writing Romantic poetry after the manner of Byron. His studies prospered and he received his master's degree in chemistry and in natural philosophy (physics) in 1845. Several years of indecision followed, during which MacDonald earned a meager living as a private tutor in Fulham, a district of southwest London. Several of his heroes, who also spend some years as tutors, usually undergo at the time spiritual crises. Precisely what inward struggles MacDonald went through we do not know, but he de-cided sometime in 1847 or 1848 to become a minister. Probably a good deal of his personal religion had been worked out by this date.

Also during this period he met Louisa Powell, to whom he became engaged in 1848; but they could not afford to marry. In the fall of 1848 MacDonald entered Highbury College, London, a struggling Congregationalist divinity school, to study for the ministry. Just after he graduated in 1850, new problems arose before he could take over his first parish in Arundel, Sussex. In December he was stricken with the first of his serious tubercular attacks; thereafter, his lungs troubled him. MacDonald's father died of a tubercular bone infection; his two beloved brothers succumbed while young; and the disease killed in childhood four of MacDonald's eleven children. In later years, he grimly referred to tuberculosis as "the family attendant."

While he was convalescing, difficulty arose between him and Louisa Powell. From Greville MacDonald's perhaps deliberately obscure account, Louisa resented the fact that the mystic considered earthly love as inferior and as perhaps contradictory to his love of God. Whatever the exact nature of the crisis, it led to his starting work on his first major literary attempt, a long dramatic poem entitled *Within and Without* (not published until 1855). The work, which presents an account of a love misunderstanding presumably similar to his own, displays most of the faults of his poetry—a smooth facility of versification combined with a lack of the vigor of expression found in his best fiction. Reading MacDonald's poetry is often a pleasantly musical experience in which the reader has trouble remembering or caring about what has been said.

By the time MacDonald assumed the ministry of the church at Arundel in the spring of 1851, his trouble with Louisa was resolved, and the marriage took place. At about the same time came the first of his published works, a translation of *Twelve Spiritual Songs of Novalis,* which was privately printed in Edinburgh. It is important to note that at this time MacDonald was only an occasional writer; he considered his true calling the ministry. Soon enough, however, he was forced to make literature his career, somewhat against his will.

In May, 1853, came the deciding crisis of George MacDonald's life. He was forced to resign his pulpit under pressure from his congregation, the elders of which resented his unorthodoxy. Presumably, they were shocked at his preaching that the heathen would be saved. Though suddenly unemployable in his profession, MacDonald felt that his vocation was genuinely a summons from God and, like Jonah's, inescapable. But he now had no money, and he had a wife and an infant daughter to support. This blow and his economic need, and his determined reaction to each, decided MacDonald's fate. He resolved to earn a living as a writer if he could and to incorporate into his works the urgent religious message which he felt called upon to disseminate, pulpit or no pulpit. For most of the rest of his life he had to live by writing, supplementing his slender income with whatever odd jobs and subsidies he could find. In addition to his literary work, he lectured, wrote hack reviews, edited a children's magazine while it lasted, and later was the impresario of dramatic performances acted by himself and his family.

MacDonald's literary career began painfully and slowly. Not until 1855 could he find a publisher for **Within and Without**, and the growing family's poverty meanwhile was extreme. But the poem's appearance promptly started him on the way to the reputation and popularity which he consolidated during the succeeding decade. Charles Kingsley wrote to him; Lady Byron, the poet's widow, became his friend and patron. She was a moral and religious uplifter and philanthropist; her gifts and bequests to the MacDonald family actually kept them from starvation until the father's writing began to produce an income of sorts.

Phantastes, his first prose book and the first of the symbolic works, appeared in 1858. It was generally ignored or abused, although several fairy stories of about the same time were better received. The first of MacDonald's conventional novels, **David Elginbrod**, was published in 1863 and immediately became celebrated for the epitaph of the hero's ancestor:

> Here lie I, Martin Elginbrodde:
> Hae mercy o' my soul, Lord God;
> As I wad do, were I Lord God,
> And ye were Martin Elginbrodde.

The rest of MacDonald's life is not so important to his fiction as his early years, for his religious and artistic consciousness never changed appreciably through the remaining decades of his life. Already in **Phantastes** and **David Elginbrod** he was a mystic of a sort, had worked out the tenets of his personal religion, and had displayed a mastery of symbolic technique scarcely equalled in his era. In realistic fiction he never needed to improve upon **David Elginbrod**, nor did he especially try. It was popular, it paid, it got its message across; its author was satisfied—no doubt too easily.

During the 1860's, **David Elginbrod** was followed by a rush of realistic novels in the same mode, usually but not always written partly in lowland Scots dialect. MacDonald's reputation, friendships, and family multiplied steadily. By 1872 he was sufficiently famous to capitalize upon his renown with a lecture tour in the United States. In thus following the example of Dickens, he netted over a thousand pounds. Meanwhile, MacDonald was befriended by John Ruskin and was intimately involved in Ruskin's strange love affair with Rose La Touche. For a time Rose lived with the MacDonald family, which was charged by her parents with the girl's protection. According to Greville MacDonald, his father even went so far as to interrogate the more famous man, including a frank question as to Ruskin's potency.

In 1873 MacDonald was granted a civil list pension of one hundred pounds a year by Queen Victoria, and he acquired a residence at Bordighera in the Italian Riviera, where he wintered thereafter for the sake of his lungs. His novels, which continued to come out almost annually through the 1880's, were increasingly popular. From time to time, whenever he got far enough ahead of his bills to afford a sure failure, he indulged his less popular taste for fantasy, and he went on writing fairy tales for children which are still classics.

MacDonald became a close friend of "Lewis Carroll," who had his doubts about the value of *Alice in Wonderland* and tested it on the MacDonald children, accepting their favorable verdict before trying to publish it. Upon Tennyson's death in 1892, MacDonald was apparently considered for the laureateship on the basis of the considerable body of poetry which he had by then produced; but the idea never received very serious support, and the vacant post went to Alfred Austin—hardly a better poet than MacDonald.

The frequency of MacDonald's publications understandably began to decline by 1890, when he was sixty-six years old. His last work, the story **Far Above Rubies,** appeared in 1898. In 1897 MacDonald's chronic eczema became severe and damaged his health generally; in 1900 he apparently suffered a stroke and lost the power of speech. After a long illness George MacDonald died in 1905, leaving behind him a record of grim struggles, of the nobility with which he bore them, and of the reverence in which he was held by everyone who knew him.

From time to time, MacDonald produced short fairy tales for children, mostly to be featured in *Good Words for the Young,* a magazine which he edited for a while early in his professional career. Some of these little stories are rather wooden and trivial in both conception and execution, written as they were under the pressure of printers' deadlines and without waiting for inspiration to strike; but the fact is that most such works are very good indeed of their kind; for, even with a deadline looming over him, MacDonald was capable of astonishing brilliance, charm, and subtlety. Most of these shorter works for children were, in time, collected into anthologies, of which the earliest was entitled *Dealings with the Fairies* (1867).

The Light Princess, longest and one of the most fascinating of MacDonald's shorter fairy stories, is remarkable both for its humor and for what appears to be, in the humorous context, a rather incongruous sexual motif. In this tale, a princess is deprived at birth by a nasty witch of her "gravity." MacDonald puns on the word by having the princess lose both her weight and the ability to take anything seriously. Her chief pleasure is to swim in a lake nearby, where she seems to have weight of a sort and to be free of the inconvenience of forever floating up to the ceiling unless held down. When a prince falls in love with the princess and joins her in her swims, the witch resolves to spoil the girl's new-found happiness. With the aid of a snake, the witch tunnels beneath the lake and begins to drain its water through a hole in the bottom that has been drilled by the malevolent serpent. Simultaneously, all the springs and rivers of the kingdom stop giving water, all rain ceases, and a drought threatens. Indeed, the drainage of the lake can be stopped only if some man will plug up the hole with his body; and, in the manner of all fairy-tale heroes, the prince volunteers. As the lake begins to refill, it threatens to drown the hero. For a while, the princess cannot take even this martyrdom seriously; but, just as the prince is about to drown, she screams in terror and pulls him from the hole. Her action breaks all of the spells: she regains her weight, she weeps for days, and the springs are restored.

As Robert Lee Wolff remarks, "some psychoanalysts would no doubt have a field day with this story." Sexual symbolism is easy to unearth and impossible to ignore—the phallic snake, the man's plugging the hole with his body, and so forth—but it need not be insisted upon. The Wasteland motif, so familiar to the twentieth-century consciousness since Eliot's poem was written, is also present, with its implicit equation between vegetative and sexual sterility. Here, the drought is identified with the absence of tears, and thus with the child's inability to face the troubles of life with the "gravity" of adulthood.

The entire story is, in fact, a parable of puberty. When the princess has married her prince, MacDonald pictures her looking back nostalgically to her gravityless childhood: "It was a long time before she got reconciled to walking. She had always drifted lightly through the air until that time. But the pain of learning was quite counterbalanced by two things, either of which would have been sufficient consolation. The first was that the Prince himself was her teacher; and the second was that she could tumble into the lake as often as she pleased." Perhaps this reference is to the relative sexual license of the married state, just as the entire story is designed to convince children that sooner or later childhood's frivolity must be abandoned for the sake of mature seriousness, which has its own rewards, . . .

In another remarkable story for children, *The Golden Key,* a boy and a girl set out separately on journeys to fairyland, meet on the way, go through a series of odd adventures both together and apart, and at the end are apparently united in the Other World. . . .

The important point about *The Golden Key* is not its sexual undertones but its vastness of scope. In it, MacDonald manages to incorporate a great many of the salient ideas which he expresses in his sermons and essays and to utilize nearly every device in the repertoire of symbolic technique.

The tale lacks the coherence of *The Light Princess*; instead, it is what Auden calls a "chain adventure story." From an apparently vast store of invention, MacDonald throws into the story many incidents which are intriguing in themselves but which would not subvert the plot (if it can be called that) if one or the other were omitted, and which are related to each other only by the fact that they happen to the same two characters, Mossy and Tangle. Each such adventure is described in a delicate, evocative, haunting style which contrasts remarkably with that of the pedestrian, conventional novels. . . .

MacDonald wrote four book-length fairy stories for children, and all but one of them continue to be popular in the twentieth century. Of *The Princess and the Goblin*, which is generally considered the best of these, Auden says that it is "the only English children's book in the same class as the Alice books." This volume contains one of MacDonald's favorite settings, a house with mysterious chambers and corridors; and also has its parallel: a mountain honeycombed with tunnels and subterranean rooms, in which there are two separate networks, one inhabited by human miners, the other by a brood of vicious goblins. The goblins are the enemies of the Princess, and Curdie is a miner's son who rescues her from their plot to destroy her. High up in the palace there lives a wise old fairy godmother (called a fairy grandmother by MacDonald for the sake of variety), in whose room there is a symbolic light which G. K. Chesterton chooses to regard as the light of God, but whose meaning MacDonald carefully refuses to delimit by defining it.

Neither the plot nor the particular incidents can be regarded as very remarkable; but the image of the castle with underground chambers and with a holy force in the attic stays with the reader. . . .

Unlike the other full-length children's stories [*At the Back of the North Wind*] has a very real setting, though the events are not "realistic" in the ordinary sense of the word. The setting is London sometime during the middle of the nineteenth century, and the characters are mostly poor people.

Little Diamond, the child-hero, is so very good and innocent that most worldly folk think him absent-minded or even feeble-minded. In this respect, he is like some of the saintly children of the novels, such as Sir Gibbie or the children in *Guild Court*. Little Diamond's parents are a London cab-driver and his wife; his best friend is Old Diamond, the cab-horse after whom he was named. Among Diamond's London friends is a little girl who sweeps crossings for the gentry, and whose earnings are stolen by her mother to buy gin. (The crossing sweeper is one of the most outrageous social institutions of the nineteenth century's brutal perversion of laissez-faire economics and "survival of the fittest": the sweepers were waifs, usually orphans, cast into the city streets to earn pittances by sweeping horse-droppings from the paths of gentry who wanted to cross at street corners without soiling their precious trouser-cuffs and hems.) The setting in general is comparable to the first part of Charles Kingsley's *Water Babies,* which was published eight years earlier and which may have suggested the idea to MacDonald; but, whereas Kingsley's chimneysweep suffers the cruelties of slaving for the owners of English country houses, Diamond and the little girl undergo the complementary cruelties of the city. As does Kingsley, MacDonald takes his child from a bitter life in this world to another, better existence through the door of ostensible "death."

Perhaps the most remarkable thing about *At the Back of the North Wind* is that MacDonald is trying, in fact, to justify death, that most inscrutable of the ways of God, to children. Diamond falls ill and nearly dies when exposed to the North Wind in winter through a crack near his bed over the stable. His coma is explained as the result of the fact that his spirit is journeying to the "hyperborean regions," an idea taken from Herodotus. The North Wind, personified as a woman who takes Diamond on a sort of guided tour through her domains, is also the force which brings death. . . .

After coming so near death, Diamond recovers temporarily, but he then has a relapse and dies. MacDonald tries to explain to his child readers that death is not an end but a departure to another place which is a good deal more pleasant than the poverty in which Diamond had "lived." Here we have, perhaps, a seminal difference between the children's classics of the nineteenth century and the wishy-washy stories fed to the children in our own time: a hundred years ago a MacDonald *faced* the bitter fact of death and made his readers face it, while the authors of children's stories today seem, with a well-meaning but rather fatuous effort, to avoid subjecting their readers to "traumas"; and they expend their efforts in *denying* the reality of life's grimmer side.

And *At the Back of the North Wind* has a most peculiar attribute of plot, besides its bluntness of implicit content, to distinguish it from most saccharine books for children. Diamond, perhaps uniquely among the child-heroes of fairy tales, comes back again into this world after having had a glimpse of the Other World after death. This oddity is something present in *At the Back of the North Wind* that is absent from the otherwise similar *Water Babies* of Charles Kingsley (in which there is likewise a dual this-world, other-world setting and a blunt facing of death). The idea of trips to the other world sandwiched between returns to this is, as we shall see, typical of MacDonald and of some symbolic significance.

The least known of MacDonald's full-length stories for children, and the only one not still in print, is called *A Double Story.* (This work causes a certain amount of confusion because it appears under a number of titles other than the original one: *The Wise Woman, The Lost Princess,* and *Princess Rosamund.*) Anticipating Mark Twain's *The Prince and the Pauper* (1882), it concerns a spoiled Princess and an almost equally coddled peasant girl who are exchanged for each other through the therapeutic influence of a Wise Woman. Both of the little girls are duly chastened by the experience and eventually resume their original places with gratitude. Although the plot is ingeniously worked out, *A Double Story* is marred by the sort of nonfunctional sermonizing which similarly weakens many of the novels but is usually absent from the imaginative works. For some unfathomable reason, however, C. S. Lewis ranks this story among MacDonald's great works."

Glenn Edward Sadler

SOURCE: "An Unpublished Children's Story by George MacDonald," in *Children's Literature,* Vol. 2, 1973, pp. 18-34.

There is hardly a nineteenth-century writer of fairytales and stories for children and adults who has undergone a greater eclipse of popular reputation than has George MacDonald (1824-1905), praised in 1924 by G. K. Chesterton as being "a Saint Francis of Aberdeen" and by his son Dr. Greville MacDonald as having a "spiritual genius whose art was so rare that, had he confined himself to poetry and purely imaginative story-telling, he could not have been almost forgotten." MacDonald's "fairy-tales and allegorical fantasies were epoch-making," claims his son, "in the lives of multitudes, children and parents alike, and still are widely read." For all of this, MacDonald has been neglected but not entirely forgotten. At least half a dozen or so of his stories have gained free entrance into the Palace of Classics: *At the Back of the North Wind,* 1871 (possibly his most famous); *The Princess and the Goblin,* 1872, and *The Princess and Curdie,* 1883, which have assured his fame; *The Wise Woman,* 1875; and his two adult faerie romances, *Phantastes,* 1858, and *Lilith,* 1895, fairytales, parables and fantasies which are currently in print. (A first edition copy of his classic collection, *Dealings with the Fairies,* illustrated by Arthur Hughes, 1867, commands an extremely high price, even in worn condition.) In the midst of a revived interest in the ancient art of myth-making, and of symbolic literature, particularly folklore and fairy-tales, there is reason to believe that the general reader will be joining again the literary critic—as C. S. Lewis and W. H. Auden have done—in pursuing more of MacDonald's "working genius," his canny ability to cross successfully over the hazardous modern age barriers into Faerie and to spin wonder out of a night in the woods. "I do not write for children," insisted George MacDonald, "but for the childlike, whether of five, or fifty, or seventy-five." No dictum about the intention of writing (or enjoying) books for children could be more necessary, demanding or rewarding than MacDonald's.

Jack Zipes

SOURCE: "Inverting and Subverting the World with Hope: The Fairy Tales of George MacDonald, Oscar Wilde and L. Frank Baum," in *Fairy Tales and the Art of Subversion: The Classic Genre for Children and the Process of Civilization,* Wildman Press, 1983, pp. 97-133.

George MacDonald's life was filled with struggles against social conservatism, religious orthodoxy, and commercial capitalism. Though the types of socio-religious changes he desired were never realized in his day, he never lost his hope and zest for reform: the beastliness of civilization was to be countered by uncovering and perfecting the divine qualities of humankind—despite the corrupting influences of society. . . .

No matter what form his writing took, MacDonald was bent on spreading his socio-religious convictions to large audiences. Indeed, he wrote over forty volumes of prose and poetry and became one of the most successful novelists and popular lecturers of his day. Like Dickens, he wanted to expose the deplorable material conditions and unjust social relations in England during the period of industrialization. Building the Empire meant breaking the backs of common people, and he demanded reforms. However, he never argued for a radical transformation of the hierarchical structure of society and government. Influenced by his agrarian upbringing, his politics were more inclined to take the form of safeguarding the natural rights and autonomy of individuals whose own responsibility was to create the moral and ethical fibre of good government. . . .

It is interesting to note that MacDonald's social and political views generally took a more conventional form in his realistic novels than in his fairy tales for children. Writing in the fantastic mode apparently freed him to explore personal and social problems to a degree that fostered his radicalism and innovation. It is generally acknowledged that MacDonald's major historical contribution to literature is in the area of fantasy and children's literature. In particular the fairy tale nurtured his religious mysticism and fundamental beliefs in the dignity of men and women whose mutual needs and talents could only be developed in a community that was not based on exploitation and profit-making. Since MacDonald felt that dreams were like religious epiphanies and that fairy tales were symbolically related to dreams, he endowed their symbolical constellations with social-religious values to convey messages without sermonizing in a laborious manner.

Between 1864 and 1883 MacDonald made his views known to children in various ways. He edited a magazine entitled *Good Words for the Young* (1868-1872), in which several fairy tales appeared including his most famous one *The Light Princess.* He published four book-length fairy tales: *At the Back of the North Wind* (1871), *The Princess and the Goblin* (1872), *A Double Story* (1874-5) also known as *The Lost Princess,* and *The Princess and Curdie* (1883). In addition he incorporated some fairy tales in novels such as *Adela Cathcart* (1864), published them collectively as in *Dealings with Fairies* (1867) or individually as separate books. In each case MacDonald consciously sought to enter into the fairy-tale discourse on manners, norms, and values and to transform it. More than any of the classical writers before him, MacDonald's perspective on the socialization of children contradicted the accepted version of discipline and punishment of the British civilizing process. Indeed, the patterns and configurations of his tales clearly display a tendency to negate the institutionalized and established forms of raising children.

As a Christian mystic, MacDonald believed in the perfection of humankind and maintained that each individual could achieve a supreme state in this world. It is not just 'divine individualism' which MacDonald preached but the necessity to develop compassion for other human beings and nature. Implicit is a notion of utopia in most of his fairy tales: the utopian impulse can be realized in the here and now if one is receptive to God who makes his will known through all earthly creation. . . .

If we compare MacDonald's fairy tales with many of the prudish and pious ones of his day, it becomes apparent that he was arguing against the conventional rules of pedagogy and strict Christian upbringing. He shunned upper-class dictums of an authoritarian nature, and his fairy tales shift and expand attitudes toward children by moving 'God' from a transcendental place to within the child: the divine is to be discovered inside and through the imagination. Such a different perspective on socializing children demanded a reformulation of the norms, values, and social relations, the use of fantasy to mirror the ossification of English social and religious standards. To grasp MacDonald's utopian critique conveyed through his fairy tales, I want to deal with three of his more prominent shorter pieces, *The Light Princess* (1864), *The Golden Key* (1867), and *The Day Boy and the Night Girl* (1879) and two of his major longer narratives, *The Princess and the Goblin* (1872) and *The Princess and Curdie* (1883). The pattern in each one of these fairy tales is similar. There is never one hero, rather there are always male

and female protagonists, who learn to follow their deep inclinations, respect each other's needs and talents, and share each other's visions. Together they overcome sinister forces which want to deprive them of possible happiness and the realization of an ideal community. In contrast to all his poems, novels, and essays, MacDonald forgoes the pathos and the rhetoric of sermonizing in the name of God. Though his Christian mysticism may be behind the ideological perspective of each narrative, his very use of unique and bizarre fairy-tale symbols imbue his stories with a touch of the unorthodox. The moral rebel in MacDonald led to a playful experimentation with conventions to undermine them and illuminate new directions for moral and social behavior.

The Light Princess (1864) like his tale *Little Daylight* (1867) is a parody of *Sleeping Beauty* and *Rapunzel,* and, for that matter, it reflects MacDonald's disrespectful attitude toward traditional folk and fairy tales. MacDonald realized that the symbolism of most of the traditional tales points to a dead end and prevents children from glimpsing their special relationship to the divine within and beyond them. It is striking that he does *not* see his point of departure for the fairy-tale discourse in the works of Grimm or Andersen but largely in those of the German romantics, particularly the fascinating stories of Novalis. . . .

The plot of *The Light Princess*, still in wide circulation today, is well known. A king and queen are without child. When they eventually have one, they insult the king's own sister, Princess Makemnoit, a witch by trade, by not inviting her to the christening. As is to be expected, the insulted witch casts a spell on the baby daughter by destroying her gravity. The princess soars and floats when she wants to walk and is difficult to control because she is light-bodied. When she becomes 17, she learns the pleasure of swimming, gains a sense of gravity, and also meets a young prince, who is willing to sacrifice himself so she can pursue her passion for water. Only by using himself as a plug to stop the water in the lake from disappearing (another spell cast by the witch) will she have enough water to swim. When it dawns upon her that the prince is dying for her, she tries to save him, breaks the spell by bursting into a passion of tears, and finds her gravity.

The irreverent tone of the story not only places the convention of traditional fairy tales in question but also the very style of aristocratic life. For instance, the king is a banal figure, a 'little king with a great throne, like many other kings.' The royal metaphysicians, Hum-Dru and Kopy-Keck, are fools. Even the typical prince is mocked. MacDonald winks his eye and debunks aristocratic language and codes, and yet, there is a serious side to the light comedy. From the beginning, after the bewitchment, the princess, court, and the implied reader of the tale are faced with a problem: how to provide gravity for the princess who does not have her feet on the ground and could cause continual havoc in the kingdom. The major theme of the tale concerns social integration, but—and this is significant—gravity (social responsibility and compassion) cannot be imposed or learned abstractly. It is gained through passion and experience, and it is also liberating. Once the princess touches water, she develops a veritable passion for it because she can control her own movements, and she can share her pleasure with the prince. Moreover, she overcomes her egocentrism by realizing her pleasure is not worth the death of a beloved human being. Through her relation to the prince, who is self-sacrificing and tender in the mold of traditional fairy-tale females, she develops social empathy, and her learning to walk after the spell is broken, though painful, can be equated to the difficult acceptance of social responsibility.

Of course, one could argue that MacDonald leaves the aristocratic social structure unchanged—a system which harbors authoritarianism and that the princess seems to achieve her 'gravity' or identity through the male hero. These were clearly his ideological preferences and weaknesses from a political point of view. It should be pointed out, however, that MacDonald was more interested in the reformation of social character and was convinced that all social change emanated from the development of personal integrity not necessarily through political restructuring and upheaval. This belief is why he stressed ethical choice and action through intense quests and experience. Moreover, in *The Light Princess,* his female protagonist does not become dependent on the prince, who is a 'softy.' Rather she gains certain qualities through her relationship with him just as he benefits from the encounter. There is more sensitive interaction between two unique individuals than traditional role-playing at the end of the tale, a special configuration which MacDonald was to develop in all his narratives.

For instance, in *The Golden Key* the young boy Mossy goes in pursuit of treasure at the end of the rainbow only to learn that the real 'riches' in life are those experiences which amount to self-knowledge. In part he learns this from Tangle, a maltreated 13-year-old girl, who runs away from home out of fear. Both are brought together in the middle of fairyland by the mysterious grandmother (a kind of mother nature), and she instills them with courage so that they bravely embark on a quest for the keyhole of the golden key, which had already been found by Mossy at the end of the rainbow. On their way they become separated and undergo various experiences with the old men of the sea, earth, and fire. Eventually, after enduring all kinds of trials, they are reunited before the country whence the shadows fall. Ageless they move toward their conception of paradise.

At the basis of MacDonald's utopia is the perfect social and sexual relationship. Mossy and Tangle are companions. Once lost in fairyland, as we the readers become lost in this highly symbolical and complex tale, everything depends on how we read the symbols, how receptive and appreciative we are to nature and the challenges of life. Mossy and Tangle have their own unique adventures and impressions while seeking the keyhole (another obvious voyage of sexual exploration). Their mystical and sensual experiences form the bedrock of their growth. Their diligence is rewarded not through material riches but through entrance to another world which promises the fulfillment of their intuitions.

This pattern of self-exploration, symbolical trips toward inner realms that can help create understanding of other people and the outside world is depicted in a variety of intriguing ways in MacDonald's other tales, *The Carasoyn, Little Daylight,* and *Cross Purposes.* The fairy tale, however, which is by far MacDonald's most unusual portrayal of mutual respect and interdependence between men and women is the provocative narrative of *The Day Boy and the Night Girl* (1879). MacDonald creates a witch named Watho, who has a wolf in her mind, and her uncontrollable appetite to know everything leads her to experiment indiscriminately with human beings. She invites two ladies to her castle named Aurora and Vesper, and she uses her magical powers to have them give birth to children. After the births the two women flee the witch in dread. Watho keeps the boy Photogen and the girl Nycteris in separate parts of the castle and exposes one only to darkness and the other only to light. In fact they each develop a respective fear of their opposites, night and day. It is only later during their adolescence that the two of them chance to meet and discover that Watho's means of raising them has crippled them. Therefore, Nycteris offers to be Photogen's eyes in darkness while she teaches him to see, and there is an amusing scene in which MacDonald addresses the entire problem of regimentation and sex-role conditioning:

> He wished she would not make him keep opening
> his eyes to look at things he could not see; and

every other moment would start and grasp tight hold of her, as some fresh pang of terror shot into him.

'Come, come, dear!' said Nycteris, 'you must not go on this way. You must be a brave girl, and—'

'A girl!' shouted Photogen, and started to his feet in wrath. 'If you were a man, I should kill you.'

'A man?' repeated Nycteris, 'what is that? How could I be that? We are both girls—are we not?'

'No, I am not a girl,' he answered; '—although,' he added, changing his tone, and casting himself on the ground at her feet, 'I have given you too good reason to call me one.'

'Oh, I see!' returned Nycteris. 'No, of course!—You can't be a girl: girls are not afraid—without reason. I understand now: it is because you are not a girl that you are so frightened.'

Photogen twisted and writhed upon the grass.

This delightful reversal is only one aspect of MacDonald's endeavor in this narrative to depict what he calls 'the arrogance of all male creatures until they have been taught by the other kind.' In the course of events Nycteris and Photogen realize that they have a great deal to learn from each other, and this realization gives them the power to overcome the witch. Their relationship becomes a synthesis in which light can be found in darkness and darkness in light.

This fairy tale is perhaps MacDonald's most outspoken statement on child-rearing. Watho's castle, personality, and treatment of the children assume symbolical forms of school, rigid teacher, and arbitrary programming. Against this system MacDonald pits the painful but meaningful exploration of two human beings who gradually recognize that their essence and autonomy depend on the interdependence of all things. Photogen and Nycteris come to revere the totality of nature by developing a receptivity to what they fear most. The confrontation with fear, however, enables them to see anew, to rethink and refeel their surroundings so that they gain ultimate pleasure from their senses and begin building a world commensurate with their ideals. MacDonald shuns Victorian prudery, as he did in almost all his fairy tales, and projects the symbolical sexual play and intercourse which can prepare the way for a wholesome union of the sexes.

MacDonald believed firmly that individuals could be 'civilized' in a natural way to attain a devout reverence for the nature and needs of all living creatures, but he also had grave doubts as to whether people as a whole, that is, society, could attain the level of 'civilization' which separate individuals could. Here his notion of civilization was in direct contradiction to the class-bound civilization process of England, and his two book-length fairy-tales, *The Princess and the Goblin* and *The Princess and Curdie,* demonstrate to what extent he went against the Victorian grain. In the first narrative the Princess Irene is plagued by goblins who want to kidnap her and destroy her father's kingdom. She is protected by her omniscient and mysterious grandmother, who endows her with the fortitude and sensitivity necessary to cope with her enemies. Furthermore, she is aided by a brave miner's son named Curdie, who literally undermines the sinister plans of the goblins and puts an end to their kingdom. In the sequel, Curdie is in danger of becoming a 'beastly character' until summoned by the majestic grandmother. He then realizes that he was on the verge of becoming decrepit, and the grandmother sends him on a mission to help the father of Princess Irene because he is being poisoned by corrupt officials. On his way to the city of Gwyntystorm, Curdie organizes a squadron of forty-nine strange creatures and misfits, who ironically return order and justice to the community. Curdie marries Princess Irene, but they have no children. When they die, the people choose a new king who is interested mainly in mining for gold, and the people become corrupt and dissolute once again. Their self-destructive tendencies lead to the destruction and disappearance of the city.

Not a very happy end for a fairy tale, and one must ask why MacDonald wrote such a book in 1883, his very last one for children. Had he become pessimistic? Or, was this a warning to children? Was this MacDonald's way to keep the utopian impulse alive in his readers by pointing to the dangers of slumbering—not keeping one's creative sensitivities active in a religious way? There are indications that the two narratives taken as a whole expressed MacDonald's sober optimism: humanity must raise itself from a beastly state to form the utopian society and must constantly exercise creative and moral powers to pursue the ideal society. Otherwise, there will be a return to barbarianism. . . .

It is obvious that this was MacDonald's perspective, too. Writing about late nineteenth-century England, he deplored the materialistic behaviour of the majority of people and the corruption of government. The relationship between Curdie and the princess is intended to be exemplary and provocative for young readers. In fact, MacDonald depicts the experiences and growth of the two protagonists to mirror all that was wrong in English society. Princess Irene's communion with the other world—her mystical and creative powers—is distrusted by her governess and everyone around her. To a large extent, her behavior and views are the opposite of how children in Victorian England were socialized to behave. Even Curdie is suspicious of her and expresses doubts about her sanity and character until the very end of the first book. These doubts continue in the sequel, and because of them it seems that Curdie might become an ordinary, crass miner, insensitive to other people and the world around him. However, his love and admiration for the tiny princess is such that a spark of his great potential is still alive, and, through his imagination, he comes to symbolize all that *should be* but *could not be*—the coal miner/King's efforts in behalf of humanity are lost on a society in quest of power and wealth.

MacDonald himself never ceased deploring the evils of social influences which interfered with the natural and sublime endeavors of human beings to become perfect. Early in his life he grasped the importance of the German romantics' aesthetic critique of philistine society, and he drew out the mystical religious essence while still defending the powers of the imagination and creative artist. At the point where he entered the fairy-tale discourse for children in England, he could not help but be influenced by social reform movements and the ideas of Dickens and Ruskin. From 1864 to 1882 he made a major effort to expand the discourse of fairy tales and to shift the perspective from the legitimatory voice to one critical of the civilizing process. His works were just the beginning: 'classical' fairy tales were about to acquire a new quality of conscious social protest.

Leona W. Fisher

SOURCE: "Mystical Fantasy for Children: Silence and Community," in *The Lion and the Unicorn*, Vol. 14, No. 2, 1990, pp. 37-57.

To many adult Western readers, the word "mystical" suggests hermits, monks, the medieval cloister, the isolated inner experience of religious ecstasy and mystery, while the literary genre of "fantasy" implies knights, pilgrims, travel, supernatural trappings, and heroic activity. The tradition of mysticism is individual and inward; fantasy, communal and active.

Mystical *writing* would therefore seem a contradictory concept, since the moment of mystical insight or religious ecstasy requires long silent preparation and resists linguistic description. . . .

Adult fantasy, particularly heroic fantasy, is perceived to be a much more expressive and public entity than mystical writing. Yet like the mystics in the religious tradition, its heroes customarily stand alone in the world. . . .

Even in children's nonmystical fantasies, like *Alice's Adventures in Wonderland* or *The Phantom Tollbooth*, the heroes must discover who they are essentially by themselves.

But there is a genre of children's literature that transcends the radical subjectivity of these other forms by grafting children's natural companionability onto the root of visionary writing. . . .

Far from seeing this genre as marginal or supplementary to "domestic" fiction in the canon (works like *Little Women* or, more recently, Cynthia Voigt's series of adolescent novels), I would argue that the texts included in this tradition are central to the Western mainstream—both spiritually and culturally. Spiritually, they represent the child's need to come to a personal understanding of deep and enduring questions about time, God, and moral behavior—but in a context that is neither institutionalized nor individualistic. Culturally, they incorporate middle-class values associated with the development of the nuclear family since the eighteenth century into a child-centered context—one that excludes adults because they are too static, unimaginative, set in their ways. . . .

A child (or two) may be the protagonist(s) in mystical fantasy, but no human patriarchal figure controls the action or the outcome: cooperation and sociability take precedence over individualism or authoritarian power. The relationships among the increasingly mature children thus comes to represent an idealized (and reconstituted) family in which knowledge and morality are achieved supernaturally rather than through a scheme of social rewards and punishments. . . .

George MacDonald's *At the Back of the North Wind*, which C. S. Lewis admired, may be the earliest experiment with mystical fantasy. Although the book remains as shadowy and other-worldly as its protagonist, little Diamond, it is a paradigm of mystical fantasy; the techniques MacDonald invented and used to portray his Christian message can help us to foresee later, more complete examples of the form. His central contribution to mystical fantasy is his focus on silence or inexpressibility, his demonstration that language is inadequate and can never accurately convey his character's (or the author's) fundamental moral insights. Silence speaks with greater eloquence than speech. . . .

Retaining his sense of the mystery and the inadequacy of language also helps MacDonald to ward off accusations of sentimentality or oversimplification; he is able to maintain the necessary separation between the skeptical adult and the innocent child. While in separating the child from the adult world, he gives the child access to a transcendent, private, secret realm, he also empowers one adult—the narrator—to act as translator of the boy's experiences and interpreter of their significance for us. Thus mystery and authority are combined; the adventures of the child are validated not arbitrarily by an omniscient author standing outside the text, but by a dramatized narrator whose "reality" we accept.

Judith Gero John

SOURCE: "Searching for Great-Great-Grandmother: Powerful Women in George MacDonald's Fantasies," in *The Lion and the Unicorn,* Vol. 15, No. 2, 1991, pp. 27-34.

It would be a mistake to call MacDonald a feminist; the magnificent and powerful female characters he created cannot quite escape their Victorian heritage. The value, for a feminist reader, of studying MacDonald's work, is not in his feminism (or his lack of it); rather, his work is valuable because it offers women a new perspective for their search. In MacDonald's fantasies, mothers, especially great-great-grandmothers, are ageless, powerful, and eternal. Although these female characters infrequently step over the bounds of strict Victorian propriety, they easily become part of our fantasy search for our own forebears. The wary reader, stepping carefully between male fantasy and wish fulfillment, will find that MacDonald's fantasy grandmothers do offer us some insight into the male understanding of the female mystique. It is in his effort to understand women that MacDonald proves most valuable to our own search.

. . .

MacDonald borrows this woman of ancient wisdom from many well-known folk tales. She is the wise old hag who offers aid and advice to many characters. In many legends she is a fairy disguised as an old woman, but often she is mortal, and it is her age that gives her the wisdom to help the hero. MacDonald frees his old women from the ravages of time and gives them the knowledge to change the world and create a better place to live. These may indeed be women who fulfill male fantasies. But they also fulfill the fantasies of women. When Yolen created her characters, she created women who act and react to other women; she created women who belong to

sisterhoods—both evil and good. She removed male influence from the equation. Jane Yolen's women fulfill a more important role in our search, perhaps, than MacDonald's, but it is his vision and his fantasies which helped women to understand that a sisterhood of shared experience stands behind many of the tales which have been inverted by male writers. MacDonald was able to do something marvelous and rare; he was able to reach across barriers. In his attempt to find his own mother, he offered to women characters that which we have been denied—women who care for and genuinely like each other.

Michael Mendelson

SOURCE: "The Fairy Tales of George MacDonald and the Evolution of a Genre," in *For the Childlike: George MacDonald's Fantasies for Children,* edited by Roderick McGillis, The Children's Literature Association and The Scarecrow Press, Inc., 1992, pp. 34-49.

When we turn to the fairy tales, we find much of MacDonald's mature ideology reflected in these stories. But if MacDonald augments the fairy tale with his own intellectual and theological concerns, he also handles the basic narrative formula of the fairy story with a good deal of reverence. This blend of tradition and personalization is clearly in evidence in MacDonald's first fairy tale, *The Light Princess* (1864), a story based on "Sleeping Beauty" but with a bit of Hoffmann's "Princess Brambilla," a dash of Andersen's comic didacticism, and a good deal of original inventiveness thrown in as well. This eclecticism is, in itself, a good example of the break that modern, written fairy tales have made with the traditional, oral ones. For as Max Lüthi has repeatedly explained, early storytellers, while willing to transform particular motifs within traditional tales, did not seek to create a personalized tale connected specifically with any identifiable dogma. But after the gentrification of the tales by Perrault and the French romanceurs after the "invention of childhood," and after the Romantic deification of originality, the traditional formulas are continually put to work in the service of a particular author's compelling interests. Like Andersen some decades before him, and unlike the Grimms, MacDonald is no literary archeologist working to uncover the bedrock of the tale; rather, he is interested in how he can adapt shards from earlier material into a new vessel capable of containing the wine of his own message. It is this process of individualizing that I am calling "modernization" and that *The Light Princess* illustrates so well.

The story itself is based on a pun: the "light princess" is both without gravity of body and without gravity or seriousness of mind. As in the case of "Sleeping Beauty," the princess's condition is the result of a witch's curse, though the circumstances surrounding this curse are interestingly modified. In Perrault's version, a king and queen try unsuccessfully for some time to have a child. The same is the case here, but borrowing another introductory motif from Hoffmann, MacDonald makes his king and queen opposites in temperament, with the king as a dour, selfish monarch who blames his lighthearted wife for their lack of an heir. Moreover, in a variation of his own, MacDonald makes the evil witch the king's sister, whose dark disposition is really just an aggravated version of his own peevish self-centeredness. The christening curse, then, while on the one hand a traditional introductory trope, is also (in this instance) an extension of the marital discord (originally expressed in their childlessness) between a somber king and a queen who is good-natured but given to joking. The king's sister (that hidden/neglected part of his heritage who is—according to convention—overlooked at the critical moment) shows up at the christening to condemn the couple with an infant who paradoxically conjoins the polarities of both parents: i.e. an excess of her mother's levity and an extreme case of her father's self-absorption. The king responds to the revelation of the curse by claiming that "she can't be ours!"; but she most emphatically is theirs, and in a graphic, symbolic way that only a fairy tale could render. The critical question, as posed by MacDonald's reworking of the formulaic introduction, is whether romantic love is to prosper in this kingdom in a way it has not with this king, and whether the king's daughter will somehow learn to temper the extremes and harmonize the conflicts of her emotional inheritance.

The light princess is condemned by her curse not only to weightlessness, but also to a prolonged period of childishness—a time analogous to Sleeping Beauty's extended incubation. When the king's army is slaughtered, the princess laughs; when the king storms at her, she claps her hands in glee; and, most tellingly, when she encounters a beggar, she breaks out in "violent hysterics." One of the Chinese Metaphysicians at court is not far off when he says that "she cares for nothing here; there is no relation between her and this world." MacDonald is playing with language here (much after the fashion of his friend Lewis Carroll), since her lack of gravity literally threatens to lift the princess "out of" this world; but in essence the princess's condition *is* one of disconnection with the lives of those around her. As in

the case of her aunt, the Witch Makemnoit, this absolute egocentrism threatens to lead her into a kind of emotional hysteria. As she grows up, her giggling turns to a sort of maniacal glee, and we see her "furious," "exploding," even "frantic" with laughter. All this is the dark side of her levity, the result of a life in which all that is unpleasant is suppressed and all compassion is denied. So the difficulty is not simply the prolonged adolescence that besets Sleeping Beauty and Snow White and makes of those stories "parables of puberty"; rather this problem (or better: this additional complication that MacDonald has grafted onto the traditional parable) is the more fundamental, ageless one of the inability to get outside one's self, to empathize with rather than to laugh at one's companions, to feel pity and fear, as well as glee. . . .

As we might expect, the practical conflict facing a fairy tale princess with this condition is, how is she going to respond to the love of the inevitable prince charming? All Sleeping Beauty and Snow White had to do was lie there and wait for him to come—eventually. But how, asks our author, a princess who has no gravity can fall into anything, much less love, is "a difficulty, perhaps THE difficulty." And so when the prince dutifully arrives, the problem here, in contrast to the traditional tale, is decidedly not one of adolescent sexual reserve. We soon find the princess (who reclaims her physical gravity once she is in water) taking long, sensual swims in the moonlight with her suitor, swims that begin as she climbs into his arms and they jump together from a cliff into the dark, warm water below. These scenes of plunging and swimming are so remarkably sensual that no critic yet has been able to desist from waxing psychoanalytical in response to them. And yet, MacDonald tells us that "whenever the prince . . . began to talk to the princess of love, she always turned her head and laughed." Not until she is faced with the possibility of tragedy will the princess's implacable comic mask crack and the possibility first of real tears, and then of real love open up within her.

At this point in the story, MacDonald breaks fully with his narrative precursors and exhibits the imaginative exuberance that C. S. Lewis claimed was his most notable literary quality. We speed through a series of scenes that illustrate with graphic precision how the princess is threatened by Makemnoit from a secret cave beneath the lake, how the White Snake of Darkness is conjured up and begins to suck the lake dry, and how the selfless prince plugs the leak with his body. The exact significance of this original sequence is itself submerged in a fascinating multiplicity of potential interpretations. What we can assert with some assurance is that the provocative combination of imagistic precision with an uncertainty of semiological reference is a hallmark of traditional tales. And indeed, in his own essay on **"The Fantastic Imagination,"** MacDonald insists that the fairy tale functions not so much "to convey a meaning" as "to wake" one. So while Robert Lee Wolff is undoubtedly correct when he notes that it is impossible to ignore the Freudian symbolism of these scenes, with the white snake sucking at the inverted breast of a restorative lake, it is also impossible to distill the language of action and imagery that MacDonald employs in this mythopoetic episode into any discursive, didactic concept.

Suffice it to say, then, that the draining of the lake is an objective correlative for the princess's emotional sterility; as MacDonald puts it, she "felt as if the [evaporating] lake was her soul drying up within her," turning her airy heart "first to mud, then to madness." Having been grounded, so to speak, by her own distress, she is next called to compassion by the martyrdom of the prince, which draws up from within her an untapped wellspring of emotion and tears. Finally outside her own vault of egocentrism, the princess pulls her lover from the lake's hole, sobs (for the first time) over his inert body, and then (also for the first time) falls dramatically to the ground. The heavens respond with a purgative downpour of their own, the lake is refilled, the witch drowned in her vault, the prince revived, and the couple, of course, married. And in the process, the light princess—born of such contrary and incompatible parents, and under a curse of selfishness and triviality— has learned that love, as MacDonald writes, is "a beehive of honey and stings." Like Lewis Carroll's *Alice's Adventures Underground* (also written in 1862), MacDonald's story is a commentary on growth and on arrested growth. But as the comparison should further serve to illustrate, MacDonald, in this—his first fairy story for children—was able to retain the essential ethos of that genre, to infuse it with his own interests and artistry, and so to modernize the fairy tale rather than leave it behind in the creation of an entirely new world of fantasy. . . .

I do not wish to imply that the adaptation of traditional folk tale patterns and motifs as a vehicle for an individualized ideology is original with George MacDonald. In fact, the history of the literary tale from its appearance in seventeenth-century French salons onward is a clear example of what Northrop Frye would call the "kidnapping" of a genre, or the appropriation of a traditional literary formula for new purposes. One regular feature of the written tales that clearly distinguishes them from their oral predecessors is the "conscious artistry" of the teller, a feature noticeable in the stylistic embellishments of such early figures as Giambattista Basile and Jacob Grimm. Invariably, the display of such artistry has an influence on the ideology of the tale. Another standard feature of the modernized tale is what Jack Zipes calls the "purposeful appropriation" by educated writers of material from oral tales and the conversion of this material into "a type of literary discourse about morals, manners, and values." In the process of this appropriation, the function of the tales shifts from the entertainment of the folk to the socialization of children. This didactic component in literary fairy tales is a radical departure from what Lüthi calls the "depthlessness" of traditional folk tales. In a sense, then, all written tales are ideologically committed.

What distinguishes the original fairy tales of writers such as d'Aulnoy, Ruskin, and Andersen is that in the pursuit of their own fictive ideas, they continue to embrace the primary generic ethos so enthusiastically. But no one, I would argue, employs as fully or as effectively as MacDonald the fundamental elements of this very ancient genre: its one-dimensional, stock characters; its conventional locales of wood, castle, cave, and cottage; its paratactic narrative line; and above all, its evocative sense of the fantastic, but the fantastic set within the everyday. Nor does any other modern writer of fairy tales outdo MacDonald in the rendering of that primary fairy tale formula, a formula that pits our deepest fears, our goblins, against our greatest desires, whether these be handsome princes, lost parents, or celestial rainbows. What I have been trying to suggest is that an inspired storyteller like MacDonald can incorporate and transform the conventions of a genre and invigorate them with new life in the process. As such, his tales both maintain and advance the essential dynamic of their genre and so stake out a significant place for themselves in the modern evolution of a very special literary form.

Amy Sonheim

SOURCE: "MacDonald and Hughes: The Ideal Mismatch," in *Bookbird,* Vol. 35, No. 1, Spring, 1997, pp. 29-31.

An early feminist, MacDonald verbally portrays his women with vigorous strength; while Hughes, heavily influenced by the chivalrous Pre-Raphaelite circle, portrays the same women with languid loveliness. In a metaphorical joust over how an ideal woman should look and act, MacDonald, a whimsical Quixote, with pen couched, charges against the typical Victorian notions of women as feeble-minded, passive ornaments. He "writes" the wrong by characterizing his fairy-tale heroines as intellectual, assertive individuals who pull their own weight in a romance. [Jack] Zipes explains that MacDonald's artistic vision "rebelled against the strict Victorian code of puritan upbringing by questioning traditional sex roles and creating young protagonists who share their dreams in pursuit of compassionate love and equal partnership." Indeed, in politics, MacDonald and his wife both supported the suffragists. Their eldest son, Greville, remembers his parents being close friends with "protagonists of the feminist movement," namely, Butler, Bodichon, and Reid—whose intimidating female presence made young Greville feel himself quite the worm.

TITLE COMMENTARY

PHANTASIES: A FAERIE ROMANCE (1855)

C. S. Lewis

SOURCE: A letter to Arthur Greeves in *They Stand Together: The Letters of C. S. Lewis to Arthur Greeves* (1914-1963), edited by Walter Hooper, Collins, 1979, pp. 92-4.

I have had a great literary experience this week. I have discovered yet another author to add to our circle—our very own set: never since I first read 'The well at the world's end' have I enjoyed a book so much—and indeed I think my new 'find' is quite as good as Malory or Morris himself. The book, to get to the point, is George Macdonald's 'Faerie Romance', *Phantastes*, which I picked up by hazard in a rather tired Everyman copy—by the way isn't it funny, they cost I/Id. now—on our station bookstall last Saturday. Have you read it? I suppose not, as if you had, you could not have helped telling me about it. At any rate, whatever the book you are reading now, you simply MUST GET THIS AT ONCE: AND IT IS QUITE WORTH GETTING IN A SUPERIOR EVERYMAN BINDING TOO.

Of course it is hopeless for me to try and describe it, but when you have followed the hero Anodos along that little stream to the faery wood, have heard about the terrible ash tree and how the shadow of his gnarled, knotted hand falls upon the book the hero is reading, when you have read about the faery palace—just like that picture in the Dulac book—and

heard the episode of Cosmo, I know that you will quite agree with me. You must not be disappointed at the first chapter which is rather conventional faery tale style, and after it you won't be able to stop until you have finished. There are one or two poems in the tale—as in the Morris tales you know—which, with one or two exceptions are shockingly bad, so don't TRY to appreciate them: it is just a sign, isn't it, of how some geniuses can't work in metrical forms—another example being the Brontes.

DEALINGS WITH THE FAIRIES (INCLUDES *THE LIGHT PRINCESS* AND *THE GOLDEN KEY*, 1867)

The Nation

SOURCE: A review of *Dealings with the Fairies*, in *The Nation*, New York, Vol. V, No. 121, October 24, 1867, pp. 329-30.

Mr. Macdonald's dealings with the fairies are in five longish stories, with cleverly designed but badly-cut wood-engravings by Arthur Hughes. Every one of these stories—or perhaps one might except **"The Giant's Heart"**—are well worth reading. There is a strange kind of fancy about them, and a peculiarly genial kind of thought. We have not known of children who had read them, but it is probable that they would be read with pleasure by five-year-olds, and read over again a little later in life with renewed enjoyment and some suspicion of the moral. **"Cross Purposes"** is the jolliest and liveliest of all; and in that one we think that any six-years boy would see the beauty of resolution and pluck very plainly and very neatly shown. In the others the story would be apt to amuse children who would see nothing but the story—but the incidents are not senseless nor childish in a bad sense. The best story of all is, we think, **"The Shadows,"** but not for such young children. The bright ten-year boys and girls will enjoy that, and it will do them good; those of them, that is, who have the patience and have been taught the good habit to read without wholly reckless skipping and skimming. On the whole, this little book of three hundred small square pages is a very good child's book indeed, and should not be lightly destroyed.

The Bookman

SOURCE: A review of *The Light Princess*, in *The Bookman*, Vol. V, No. 28, January, 1894, pp. 127-28.

As for the fairy stories, Dr. Macdonald says his are for the childlike, even if they be seventy five, but seven and five need not be afraid they are dull for that reason. They are singularly beautiful and poetical, and children in their quieter moods will find them altogether sympathetic. There is such fine, good work in them, that they should be counted with Dr. Macdonald's best.

Saturday Review

SOURCE: A review of *The Light Princess*, in *Saturday Review*, Vol. 45, No. 45, November 10, 1962, p. 37.

One day about a century ago George MacDonald, a Scottish minister, read a fairy story he had written to his class of adult students. It was an amusing tale about a princess who had no gravity and who disconcerted everyone by her inability to keep her feet on the ground. She was also unable to take anything seriously. The students approved it thoroughly; and today it has added meaning for children who are well acquainted with the state of weightlessness.

In this book the story has been "cut for reading aloud," and this will probably introduce many more children to it. The new version makes good reading, emphasizing the fun of the story, but it loses something in the development of the character of the princess, which explained her absolutely heartless treatment of her prince—until she regained her gravity. And although the pictures are amusing, they lack heart—like the Princess. As for the Princess herself, she looks amazingly modern.

Ruth Hill Viguers

SOURCE: A review of *The Light Princess*, in *The Horn Book Magazine*, Vol. XXXVIII, No. 6, December, 1962, p. 605.

Adults who have long loved the story of the princess who, at her christening, was deprived of her "gravity" by a wicked fairy, may feel that the story's pictures are intrinsic, that it needs no special interpretation. However, here it is, with slightly edited text, in a form that should entice many a new reader. The interpretation is definitely [illustrator William Pène] du Bois' own; yet, modern in spirit though it is, the pictures and story are so congruent that they might have been invented together. The illustrations, many in lovely, harmonious color, underline the humor and philosophy of the story and are also as romantically appealing as the most avid reader of fairy tales could wish. A most attractive book.

Ruth Hill Viguers

SOURCE: A review of *The Golden Key*, in *The Horn Book Magazine*, Vol. XLIII, No. 4, August, 1967, p. 464.

A new edition illustrated [by Maurice Sendak] with remarkable sensitivity makes available once more one of the most beautiful of allegorical fairy tales. W. H. Auden's afterword, written for this edition, was published in the April *Horn Book*. The story tells of the girl and boy, Tangle and Mossy, who meet and travel together to a mysterious land. For a while their paths separate as Tangle encounters, one after another, the three Old Men—of the Sea, of the Earth, and of the Fire—and she grows wiser and more beautiful with each stage of her journey. Tangle is reunited at last with Mossy, who carries the golden key, and they reach the rainbow, climbing along it toward the "country whence the shadows fall." The story, full of dreamlike events and exquisite images, is itself a key that will open to many children a door on their own imaginative experiences and the pleasure and mystery of allegorical speculation.

Aileen Murphy

SOURCE: A review of *The Golden Key*, in *School Library Journal*, Vol. 92, No. 16, September 15, 1967, p. 3187.

Sendak's delicate black-and-white drawings are charmingly appropriate and, as always, bring the gift of an extra dimension to this allegorical fairy-tale-cum-mystery. A near classic, this has many prominent adult enthusiasts, including W. H. Auden, who supplied this new edition with an Afterword. The story, which is also available in **The Complete Fairy Tales of George Macdonald** is built around the arduous journey of a boy and girl seeking the door to a mystical land, a door that can be opened with the golden key discovered by the boy. The old-fashioned format with its carefully designed pages and gold-stamped binding, together with Sendak's artistry all support the dream quality of the story and combine to make a distinctive small book.

Helen Gregory

SOURCE: A review of *The Light Princess*, in *School Library Journal*, Vol. 34, No. 11, August, 1988, p. 83.

The long-awaited princess, a newborn only child, is cursed at her christening by an uninvited disgruntled outrageous guest. The curse: lightness of body and spirit. The princess is given to uncontrollable floating and merriment. The cure is love, which makes her cry and brings her down to earth. [Robin] McKinley has cut approximately two thirds of MacDonald's 19th-Century fairy tale, keeping the spirit, grace, and wit of the original. She also keeps the king's inane Chinese philosophers, Hum-Drum and Kopy-Keck, MacDonald's tasteless but harmless creations whose worst fault is that theirs is the section of the story that children skip over and forget—they are truly, deeply boring. Mercifully, here they are cut to a minimum. Treherne's buoyant, stylized, full-page, full-color watercolors are reminiscent of Errol LeCain's. Intricate borders pick up a minor pattern in each picture and frame it with stunning effect. Nothing much has been done with this classic since Maurice Sendak illustrated it with wonderful tongue-in-cheek formality. This new edition brings a younger generation a charming combination of talent.

RANALD BANNERMAN'S BOYHOOD (1871)

The Nation

SOURCE: A review of *Ranald Bannerman's Boyhood,* in *The Nation,* New York, Vol. XI, No. 283, December 1, 1870, p. 373.

Ranald Bannerman's Boyhood is likely to prove interesting to both boys and girls not under twelve, in spite of its formal language, and its tolerably frequent wanderings into the realms of sentimental reminiscence, so dear to old people and so worthless to children. The interest is in the episodes of the story, which read like real occurrences, and are very lively and entertaining. We are at a loss to understand why Mr. MacDonald feels it necessary to keep to such strict English, and apologize so overmuch for the few passages of Scotch dialect that he must introduce. To put the elegant language, with due care for the subjunctive, into the mouths of his Scotch peasants, makes them absurd. There may be somewhat too much of Scotch in the dialogue of a story, as every one knows who has had to seek a glossary to make the sense; but a modified Scotch is not only pleasant to read, but desirable for a boy to understand who has Scott's novels before him. However, we had no intention of going into any artistic considerations in noticing this little story, for its merits end with its morality and its readable anecdotes.

THE PRINCESS AND THE GOBLIN (1872)

The Nation

SOURCE: A review of *The Princess and the Goblin,* in *The Nation,* New York, Vol. XIV, No. 349, March 7, 1872, p. 159.

In this child's story, Mr. Macdonald has simply followed his ingenious fancy, he has forborne all introduction of misplaced preaching, and the result is a charming little tale, pretty but not "goody-goody," and fantastical enough to please any but the most boisterous boys, although we imagine it will rather be the favorite of little girls, therein resembling the fate of his more ambitious works with grown people. It is the story of a little girl, a princess, who lives in a castle on a mountain, and is exposed to great dangers from the kobolds who dwell in the subterranean depths. The story itself we will not abridge; it is very slight, and almost the whole of the charm lies in the telling of it. The invention it shows is so innocent and poetical, the fancy is so ingenious without being artificial, that we would set it above even some of the most highly praised children's books of the day. In comparison with it, in regard to facility of fancy, even *Alice's Adventures* are cold and mechanical, though we dislike to say a word against a book which has that little girl in it. One would never laugh over **The Princess and the Goblin,** but we think it might well become the favorite book of a rather serious child. Even if children should not care for it, their parents might find less entertaining books for an evening's reading. To our mind, it is in this story that Mr. Macdonald is at his best.

The Spectator

SOURCE: A review of *The Princess and the Goblin,* in *The Spectator,* No. 2280, March 9, 1872, p. 316.

Mr. George MacDonald's fairy tales would be the most charming of their kind if—we must be pardoned for the Hibernicism—they *were* fairy tales. The fact is that they are, at least we can never help feeling that they are, allegories. Now, a good fairy tale is simply delightful; an allegory, beautiful as it may be, is somewhat tormenting,—a long riddle which it troubles one to guess at, and which one does not like to leave alone. A fairy tale has no *arrière pensée* of a moral; there is a general impression, indeed, that it is a good thing to be generous and noble and dutiful, but obviously the best thing is to be a third son, or to have a fairy godmother. In the allegory the sense of the moral becomes oppressive. We may be doing Mr. Macdonald an injustice, but we cannot help feeling that the old lady and the king and the little princess and the goblin all mean something, and that we ought to know what this something is, and be edified by it. We wish we had not to know it, and might be simply amused. Mr. Macdonald's delicate humour and fine fancy would really do us all the good we want. Might we hazard a question? Is it not possible that *some* children—weak creatures, we acknowledge, and unworthy of this enlightened age, but still to be consulted, like other weak brethren—might be a little frightened by the very grotesquely-hideous figures with which the volume is embellished? A child ought to know, of course, that these creatures do not and could not belong to the fauna of this present world; but all children are not so well informed as they should be. We are quite certain, from what we remember of our own childhood, that these pictures would have given us hideous dreams for a week. The present writer can still see the horrid forms which were thus made to haunt his sleep.

📖 *THE WISE WOMAN: A PARABLE (1875; ALSO PUBLISHED AS THE LOST PRINCESS; OR THE WISE WOMAN 1895; AND THE LOST PRINCESS: A DOUBLE STORY, 1965)*

New Statesman

SOURCE: A review of *The Lost Princess*, in *The New Statesman*, Vol. LXX, No. 1809, November 12, 1965, p. 749.

Victorian admonitory note of MacDonald's ***The Lost Princess***—a prettily illustrated reprint of a rarity. The book, indeed, has a strange history. It began as a serial in 1875, thereafter appeared in editions on both sides of the Atlantic; then, for about half a century, it vanished, even from lists of the author's works. It is possible to see why. The author is at his most didactic and also at his most 'literary,' while the long and austere sojourns that the arrogant princess and the spoilt little peasant girl deservedly undergo in the Wise Woman's moorland cottage have some very strange undertones. (The whole thing was much admired by Dr. C. S. Lewis.) Yet the story compels even now, for its detail, for the hypnotising effect of the seer-like finger upraised, for the charm of its highly professional narrative. A touch of genius (see Kipling or Kingsley) can carry off the most disconcerting utterances.

Ruth Hill Viguers

SOURCE: A review of *The Lost Princess: A Double Story*, in *The Horn Book Magazine*, Vol. XLII, No. 3, June, 1966, p. 306.

Here are the adventures of tempestuous, unhappy Princess Rosamond, from the time the wise woman took her away from the court and gave her the opportunity to see the kind of Somebody she was until the time when she began to become "a princess over herself." Strong purpose is behind the words of a story so magical that it is immediately engrossing. Only George Macdonald, the master of the allegorical fairy tale, could have given such a story the power to live: it is as important today as it was in the nineteenth century. Children of every period should have available books that can give such imaginative and philosophical experiences as this one can. And in our time, when children's reading is too often limited to staccato sentences and style without nuances, it is very good to give them a book with the beauty and strength of style that demand attention. Elizabeth Yates' introduction gives the history as well as an appreciation of the story, which, out of print since early in the twentieth century, deserves to take its place beside Macdonald's other great fairy tales.

📖 *SIR GIBBIE (1879)*

The Nation

SOURCE: A review of *Sir Gibbie*, in *The Nation*, New York, Vol. XXVIII, No. 721, April 24, 1879, p. 290.

Dr. MacDonald's new story is, to use a Scotch word, full of eerieness; nor, by this, do we mean to put ourselves among those who, the author says with some contempt, will declare his tale unnatural, for it is within nature, but nature at that point of extreme tenuity where it vanishes into the supernatural. In saying this we have in mind only Sir Gibbie himself, for the other characters are framed of the crudest Scotch earth. Sir Gibbie is a dumb child of a drunken father, bred in the streets, neglected, but with an irresistible instinct to be serviceable to every one; at first, he guides his father home at night by gyrating round him so that he cannot fall, and pushing him so that he must go on. After his father's death he watches the streets to do the accustomed service for any who may be in need of it, until the murder of a negro sailor before his eyes drives him from the city to the country, where he finds the most extraordinary opportunities for his gifts; is believed to be at first a "brownie," then a "beast-boy"; lives on a mountain with an old couple whose sheep he tends; performs the most difficult feats in saving the lives of animals, children, and men, during a great flood, which is described with great force and distinctness, until finally he becomes heir to a fortune and is married. Dr. Mac-Donald uses this child-creation, for he does not seem a day older at twenty-one than at six, as an example of instinctive love for all living creatures which finds joy only in service and looks for no return. This is the inevitable moral element in the novel, but for all that the treatment of the incidents and of nature is imaginative often in a high degree; and if one tires of the garrulity of some of the characters, and at times of the preacher's discourse itself, there is much more than enough in the tale to make it interesting to those who look only for pleasure, while the moralizing public could not have more wholesome food.

The Spectator

SOURCE: A review of *Sir Gibbie*, in *The Spectator*, Vol. 52, No. 2680, November 8, 1879, pp. 1415-16.

It is now about a quarter of a century ago since Mr. Macdonald, by the publication of the dramatic poem **Within and Without**, first secured for himself the appreciative sympathy of a limited, perhaps, but, at the same time, thoughtful and cultivated circle of readers. In the interval he has not been idle, and poems, sermons, and novels, especially the last kind of literary work, have given him an honoured name wherever the English language is spoken. But, with the exception of **Within and Without** and the first volume of **David Elginbrod,** we are of opinion that **Sir Gibbie,** take it for all in all, is the finest production of his pen, and, so far from the author having "written himself *out*," as the phrase goes, we would venture to say that the present story only indicates that he has acquired the art of more thoroughly writing himself *in*. But we almost owe an apology to Mr. Macdonald in thus speaking, for of all contemporary novelists, he is the one in whose pages one least discovers any tokens of such effort as is implied in all finished "art." Artlessness, rather than art, is the term which first occurs to us, after perusing any of his writings; and a Celt himself, it seems as if he were in true Celtic fashion, always borne onward on the tide of his inspirations, rather than creating the channel along which they are to flow. As most of our readers need scarcely be reminded, many of his stories wander at their own sweet will, giving one the feeling

that, but for the condition of "three volumes," they might go on for ever; and certainly in **Sir Gibbie** the artlessness in as conspicuous as in any of the writer's previous tales. But in this instance, it has flowed into a coherent unity. Of course, a book like this would not, as Goethe says, come to the author in his sleep; and written, as it has been, for a great and serious purpose—it is, in fact, a special study of psychological evolution—much thought and labour must have gone to the construction of it. But all the same, the story has the freshness and charm of an *improvisation* from beginning to end, but an improvisation shaped, coloured, and directed to the ideal end which first "crept into the study of the imagination" of the author. Mr. Macdonald never attempts fine-writing, and we do not say that any of his more distinguished fellow-labourers in the field of fiction are guilty of this weakness. At the same time, it seems to us that his presentations of nature differ very obviously from those, say, of George Eliot, R. D. Blackmore, and William Black. These three are consummate word-painters—the last especially—of scenery. But we should never dream of including our present author in this category, any more than we should assign to it the greater names of Tennyson and Wordsworth. Nature is simply reflected, not described, in our author's best passages, and our readers will find abundant proof of our assertion in noting the flight of "wee Gibbie" "up Daurside," until the little pilgrim reaches the summit of Glashgar, and stands there in an ecstasy, amid the silence and solitude of the everlasting hills. The description of the thunderstorm is even grand, and not less striking is the narrative of a great flood, which rose and raged and roared, and threatened to bear away in its fierce and resistless sweep all traces of man, of his dwellings or possessions, in the mountainous district in which Sir Gibbie had at first a temporary home, with schooling of the divinest, because most human kind, and ultimately, a permanent haven of rest, after the storms of his early experience.

But it is in a certain city which looks out on the German Ocean—Old Aberdeen, we presume, with its large and stately college, and "the Brig of Don," which Lord Byron has made world-famous—that the opening scenes of the story are laid, and in this provincial town of the "unco' guid" there are to be found as dismal haunts of disease, and drunkenness, and vice manifold, as in London itself. In a miserable shed abutting on a "big hoose," the house of the Galbraiths, a cobbler is at work, but one who is only capable of the very humblest ministrations to pedestrians. This cobbler is a baronet,—Sir George Galbraith; he has had a fair education, but whiskey had been the crave and the curse of the Galbraiths. His grandfather had drunk almost the whole of the Galbraith property, until there was scarcely left a free acre to come to his son. This son was only too easily initiated in "the drink," and having received "nae schuillin'" at all, it was small wonder if he disencumbered himself of "all that was left," and bequeathed to his heir only a legacy of impecuniosity.

Sir George the Cobbler had a curious Sunday conscience. Mrs. Croale's "public," which was Sir George's nightly rendezvous for his toddy and the society of one or two "drouthie neebors," was devoutly closed on the Sabbath Day, as the Scotch persist in calling the first day of the week. But the baronet laid in his liquid commissariat for Sabbath consumption the previous day. The liquor, however, was never tasted until sunset, and one of the most touching, almost grimly touching, passages we have ever read is that in which the muddled cobbler Baronet is revealed to us endeavouring to instruct his son as to the one great aim which should dominate our lives, and which appears in the *Shorter Catechism,* under its first question,—*What is the chief end of man?* but which the unhappy man could not distinctly remember. He could only maunder to Gibbie about the *"chieff en' o' man,"* in a reiteration which made the motherless child dimly imagine that the father whom he guided home night after night, when wholly unfit to direct himself, was laying some new duty upon him, which, perhaps, he would come to understand some day. There was, however, a lesson which Gibbie understood and took to his heart for all his life, and that was the oft-repeated counsel of the victim of whiskey never to touch the accursed thing. Sir George drinks when the sunset of the Sabbath has come; he drinks, he prays—and his prayer is a wonderful unveiling of the struggles of the human soul—and he dies. "He was gone," says the author, reverently, "to learn what God could do for him *there,* for whom nothing more could be done *here.*" In thus representing to us the depths of degradation to which "Scotland's skaith," to use the words of Hector Macniel, can reduce a gentleman born, Mr. Macdonald has well served his age. It is true, that in these days, when the Scotch Judges and lawyers go out "on circuit," there is no longer the necessary presence, as in Lord Cockburn's early experience, of the "lad that louses the neck-cloths" of the gentlemen who have fallen under the table; but we have only too good grounds for believing that both in the North and the South there is a vast amount of, more or less, *private drinking.* The "City" nips of sherry are proverbial, and in this age, when gentlemen come into the drawing-room, like gentlemen, after dinner, what stories could not physicians, the clergy, and editors also tell? Mr. Macdonald is rather merciful, though at the same time very wroth, with drunkards; but if he knew what many know too well, we suspect that he would almost thank God for the respectable Pharisee, who is always sober, who at least provides for his own, who is always capable of managing his own affairs, who scrupulously keeps his appointments, and so far as "this world" is concerned, leaves no entanglements behind him for others to unravel when he has passed away. But Mr. Macdonald is neither pessimist nor fatalist. With him, neither "heredity," nor "drink," nor "love" is inevitably supreme. We inherit proclivities, but in every man is the supernatural power of freewill. The drinking Sir George dies in agony, protesting against his enemy, and loathing to think that he should be called a drunkard; Mistress Croale, the publican, falls, but rises again, again falls under the fierce thirst, but at last comes off victorious; and Sir Gibbie, with all the ravaging heredity in him, is one of the sweetest, purest, most self-denying, and generously helpful of human beings.

The story of his life is admirably developed. Mr. Macdonald means to represent him as one of the elect of God, who are specially trained in sympathy with their brethren, and in whom there burns a passionate readiness to minister to their comfort or well-being. It is a story which will be profitable in various ways, but, in our opinion, it would have been still more profitable if the author had used the pruning-knife before giving it to the world. There is no need, for instance, to introduce the power of "laughing," in consciousness of the immediate presence of the Almighty, as a special token of advanced spiritual life. Donald Grant, the peasant-poet, might have been clothed upon with less grotesque garments, and might have been a little more courteous on a certain occasion to his master's son, the Rev. Fergus Duff. Again, on what physiological data does the author build, when he represents **Sir Gibbie** as a *mute,* who yet had his hearing quite perfect? We must also ask Mr. Macdonald where exactly, in strange contradiction to his general teaching, are we to find the longitude and latitude of the "forsaken region," in which the damned dwell? Is it quite in good-taste, when Sir Gibbie places his hand on Mrs. Sclater's knee, beside that of the lady herself? Does not the reader cry out for a little soap and water? But, more seriously, is it not to undergo the censure of Horace, at least, to describe in such a ghastly fashion the appearance of "Sambo" after his murder? Also, we are of opinion that Mrs. Croale was for a time promoted to too great honour, as she proved, by nearly setting the whole house in which she was established as prima donna on fire. But the author, nevertheless, could very well afford to repeat the legend on the gateway of one of the Aberdeen Colleges, "They say; what do they say? let them say;" since he has written a thoroughly Scotch story, charged with humour, poetry, and piety, and one from the careful perusal of which no one, as we believe, can rise without having a deeper sense of the awful perils, and the not less awful possibilities, of human life.

📖 THE FAIRY FLEET (1936)

Pauline A. O'Melia

SOURCE: A review of *The Fairy Fleet*, in *Library Journal*, Vol. 61, October 1, 1936, p. 733.

The Fairy Fleet is a charming fairy tale by George MacDonald, long out of print, that has been taken out of retirement by Holiday House. The new printing is a fine slim, striped cloth book with distinctive illustrations in the spirit of the tale by Stuyvesant Van Veen. Colin, the little boy in the story, the son of a shepherd, stays at home to keep house all day. His chief delight is a tiny brook that flows into the cottage yard where, because of the dirty pig and untidy cow, it becomes muddy and unpleasant. Colin cuts a new channel for the stream right through the middle of the cottage. Then at night from his bed, he watches the fairy folk glide down stream in their silvery sailboats. Among them is a changeling child, a baby girl, whom Colin, after many trials, saves from the fairy queen, for Scottish fairies are not always well-intentioned. It is a poetically beautiful tale, and a nice book for a special collection.

📖 LITTLE DAYLIGHT (1987)

Publishers Weekly

SOURCE: A review of *Little Daylight,* in *Publishers Weekly,* Vol. 232, No. 18, October 30, 1987, p. 66.

Decked out in gowns of flowing brilliance, a host of good fairies offers gifts to a royal couple's first born, fortuitously named Little Daylight. But an uninvited fairy arrives and casts a spell: the child will sleep through the day and wake at night, waxing and waning with the moon. Duntze's luminous paintings show how the years change Daylight from a playful toddler to a winsome lady whose nocturnal romps attract the notice of a handsome passerby deep within the forest. The illustrations imbue this classic with a true sense of magic, with such inventive details as the bad fairy's conjuring: she uses a configuration of old bones, a fox's tail and raven feathers.

Publishers Weekly

SOURCE: A review of *Little Daylight,* in *Publishers Weekly,* Vol. 34, No. 5, July 29, 1988, p. 229.

Like Sleeping Beauty, the princess in MacDonald's tale is cursed at her christening by a jealous fairy. Little Daylight can awaken only at night, and her beauty must wax and wane with the moon until "a prince comes who shall kiss her without knowing it." A young prince glimpses the beribboned princess dancing in the moonlight and falls in love, but when he next finds her, there is no moon and the princess looks as "wrinkled and drawn" as a withered old woman. The prince, thinking the woman is dying, kisses her and the spell is broken: Little Daylight's face shines "as bright as the never-aging dawn." [Erick] Ingraham's paintings are meticulously rendered. He combines the luminosity of Renaissance portraits with an almost photographic detail, creating a fairy tale world of moonlit beauty.

Janet D. French

SOURCE: A review of *Little Daylight,* in *School Library Journal,* Vol. 35, No. 3, November, 1988, p. 92.

Little Daylight is *Sleeping Beauty* in Victorian guise, with the old story expanded with newly invented detail and the archetypical characters given a measure of individuality. MacDonald's principal change, however, is in the nature of the curse: instead of sleeping 100 years, Little Daylight must sleep when the sun is in the sky. Worse yet, she is ruled by the phases of the moon; young and beautiful when it is full, she ages with its waning. While this embroidered version sacrifices some of the dramatic tension of the original, there is compensation in the haunting nature of the curse and the formidable barrier it presents to a prince's required kiss. There are barriers, too, to an easy assignment of age or interest level for the book. Although adapted, the text retains much of MacDonald's rich style, putting it somewhat at odds with the picture book format in which it is set. Like the text, the full-color acrylic paintings on every page also depart from tradition. In place of generic prin-cesses and fairies, Ingraham's characters reflect the crisp individuality of photographs, although they move in enchanted settings. This will be best used as a read-aloud to primary grade children, who will be moved by the "Lost Horizon" poignancy of the tale whether or not they understand every word.

Additional coverage of MacDonald's life and career is contained in the following sources published by the Gale Group: *Contemporary Authors,* Vols. 106, 137; *Dictionary of Literary Biography,* Vols. 18, 163, 178; *Major Authors and Illustrators for Children and Young Adults; Something about the Author,* Vols. 33, 100; and *Twentieth-Century Literary Criticism,* Vol. 9.

Carl Sandburg
1878-1967

(Full name Charles August Sandburg; also wrote under the pseudonyms Militant and Jack Phillips) American poet, historian, and author of original fairy tales for children.

Major works about the author include: *Carl Sandburg* (Harry Golden, 1961), *Carl Sandburg, Poet and Patriot* (Gladys Zehnpfennig, 1963), *Carl Sandburg* (Richard Crowder, 1964), *America of Carl Sandburg* (Hazel Durnell, 1965), *The Other Carl Sandburg* (Philip Yannella, 1996).

INTRODUCTION

In the preface to his *Complete Poems* (1950), Carl Sandburg, then 72 years old, wrote of himself, "[T]here was a puzzlement as to whether I was a poet, a biographer, a wandering troubadour with a guitar, a Midwest Hans Christian Andersen, or a historian of current events." In fact, Sandburg was all that and more. Honored and recognized for his many achievements in his own lifetime, he is best remembered today for his six-volume biography of Abraham Lincoln, part of which won him a Pulitzer Prize; for his intense, loosely structured poetry about ordinary, hardworking Americans; and for the Midwestern fairy tales he concocted for his three daughters and published for the delight of children all over America.

A revered figure in American literature, Sandburg sought to express the dignity of the common people, in whom he found the spirit and values of American democracy. Distinguished critic and anthologist Louis Untermeyer called Sandburg the "Laureate of Industrial America." Harriet Monroe, founder and first editor of *Poetry: A Magazine of Verse*, described Sandburg as "seeing our national life in the large—its beauty and glory, its baseness and shame." In his poetry, Sandburg realistically evoked the immense diversity of the American people and landscape, but his verse was prosaic and oddly structured, and critics often did not know how to respond to it. Sandburg, who came of age during the social turbulence at the end of the nineteenth century, thought of himself as a "Man's poet," a Socialist, championing the strength, sweat, and labor of the ordinary American and criti-

cizing the society that abused and undervalued him. Sandburg originated the sobriquet "City of the Big Shoulders" for Chicago, and his poetic voice was considered reflective of the experiences and feelings of the common American worker. In her introduction to *Selected Poems* (1926), Rebecca West called Sandburg, "[a] national poet [who] expresses the whole of life of the Middle West of today."

BIOGRAPHICAL INFORMATION

The son of Swedish immigrants, Sandburg was born in Galesburg, Illinois in 1878. His parents worked hard, and at the age of eleven Carl also began working, before and after school. He grew up speaking Swedish and English, and wanted so much to become assimilated into America that for most of his young adulthood he Americanized his first name to Charles. He left school at thirteen to help support his family, and at eighteen he took his first trip to Chicago. For three or four months in 1897 he became one of the army of hoboes traveling free on the railroads, working at menial jobs wherever he could and listening to the speech of his fellow travelers. He volunteered to fight in the Spanish-American War and served in Puerto Rico for two months, enough to earn him free tuition for a year at Lombard College. It was there that he met Professor Philip Green Wright, one of the most important influences of his life, who encouraged his writing and published his first small books, few copies of which have survived.

Sandburg's primary means of living was as a salesman for Underwood, producer of stereopticon equipment and pictures, also known as the magic lantern. He occasionally lectured, worked for various periodicals, and published poetry. When he met Lilian Steichen, sister of photographer Edward Steichen, his life became more focused. Lilian, whom he called Paula, was a bright and independent woman and an active Socialist. She urged him to return to his given name of Carl and to concentrate on his poetry. His wife for fifty-nine years, she was a primary influence in his life and his unfailing support while he was finding his poetic voice and a serious audience for his writing. A Socialist himself, Sandburg became active in local politics and was appointed secretary to Milwaukee's first Socialist mayor, Emil Seidel. He left that post to write for the *Social Democratic Herald* in Milwaukee, then moved his family to Chicago, where he joined the staff of the Socialist *Chicago Evening World,* subsequently working as a reporter and columnist for various magazine and newspapers.

In 1914, Harriet Monroe published six of Sandburg's poems in her poetry journal *Poetry: A Magazine of Verse* and brought him to the attention of such luminaries as Edgar Lee Masters, Theodore Dreiser, Vachel Lindsey, and Ezra Pound. Masters and Dreiser were especially encouraging, and Alice Corbin Henderson, assistant editor of *Poetry,* brought his work to the attention of Alfred Harcourt, at the time a young editor at Henry Holt and Company. Harcourt risked his own job to get *Chicago Poems* published in 1916. While reviews were mixed, there was no question that the book had made a strong impression on the literary world. Amy Lowell, who was otherwise enthusiastically supportive, suggested that there was too much political propaganda in his work, a criticism Sandburg took to heart. Social politics of the time were harsh, with labor strikes, mob violence, and racial conflicts adding to the chaos of World War I, and Sandburg was becoming disillusioned; but he believed that as a poet of democracy, he had a public responsibility to speak about the his-

tory being made around him. Lowell later reviewed *Smoke and Steel* (1920) as giving her "patriotic emotion," much to Sandburg's delight.

In 1921, at the age of 43, Sandburg was comfortably established. He had published three books of poetry which had garnered both a reputation and awards, was comfortably employed by the *Chicago Daily News*, and had a happy marriage and family of three daughters in whom he took great delight. He published the stories he invented for them as *Rootabaga Stories* (1922), the first of three volumes, which soon became known as America's own fairy tales. He traveled frequently on the college lecture circuit, reading his poetry and singing folk songs to his own guitar accompaniment. His interest in collecting traditional American folk songs led to publication of his collection in *Songs of America* (1926) and *The American Songbag* (1927), a testament to his versatility.

When the first two volumes of his Lincoln biography appeared in 1926, they brought him wild acclaim and a new level of financial stability. During the Depression, he devoted his talent to writing his epic prose-poem *The People, Yes* (1936) to lift the hopes and bring consolation to the "seekers and strugglers," the people who created and supported America: in his view, the American heroes. Sandburg called this work the "best memorandum I could file for the present stress." It was his last major poetic work. During the 1940s he lectured, worked as a columnist, and lent himself to the war effort. Both he and his good friend Archibald MacLeish thought that artists should participate fully in World War II. He said, "A writer's silence on living issues can in iteself constitute a propaganda of conduct leading toward the deterioration or death of freedom."

In 1940, he won his first Pulitzer Prize, in history, for *Abraham Lincoln: The War Years* (1939). At sixty-five, on a request from MGM for an historical novel on which to base a film, Sandburg wrote his only novel, *Remembrance Rock*, but it was never made into a film. In 1951, he won his second Pulitzer Prize, in poetry, for *Complete Poems* (1950). In 1953, he wrote the autobiography of his first twenty years, *Always the Young Stranger,* that was condensed and published for children in 1955 as *Prairie-Town Boy.* During the 1950s he lived the life of a celebrity, traveling as far as the Soviet Union with his brother-in-law Edward Steichen, and later to Hollywood for a six-month stint. He was photographed endlessly; he appeared on the new medium of television; he entertained audiences as long as he was able. In 1963, at the celebration of his eighty-fifth birthday he said, "Being a poet is a damn dangerous business."

Sandburg died in Flat Rock, North Carolina at the age of 89. Following his death, a public ceremony to honor him was held at the Lincoln Memorial in Washington, D.C.

MAJOR WORKS

According to Sandburg, he wrote the *Rootabaga Stories* for "people from 5 to 105. I knew that the American children would respond, so I wrote some nonsense tales with American foolin' in them," and the children responded enthusiastically. They wrote him letters telling him that his stories were the funniest stories they had ever heard. He was told of one boy who had tried to read "The Wedding Procession of the Rag Doll and the Broom Handle and Who Was in It" to his class, but was so overcome by laughter that he could barely begin. *Rootabaga Stories,* more about the sounds of words than about things that happen, are the product of Sandburg's child imagination run wild. They are aggressively Midwestern in tone and contain a sort of sense within nonsense: Gimme the Ax and his children Please Gimme and Ax Me No Questions (who named themselves), travel into the flat and endless prairies; the Village of Cream Puffs is often swept away by the prairie winds; the skyscraper's child, who must be free, is a railroad train. The Potato Face Blind Man plays his accordion and spouts poetic philosophy, and Blixie Bimber, Jason Squiff, Bimbo the Snip, and the like live magical lives in rollicking spontaneity. Verlyn Klinkenborg of the *New York Times Book Review* said that when Sandburg wrote for children, he wrote "for the child in himself, for the eternal child, who, when he or she hears language spoken, hears rhythm, not sense." In 1923 Sandburg published a second book of Rootabaga tales, titled *Rootabaga Pigeons,* and a third, *Potato Face,* in 1930.

In his acclaimed multivolume biography of Lincoln, Sandburg relates incidents from Lincoln's life in the manner of a story rather than as a series of historical facts. Although some critics expressed their uneasiness with Sandburg's artistic license and narrative style, most praised his vivid, "folksy" presentation and appreciated the exhaustive and detailed factual research he had accomplished. In the first two volumes, *Abraham Lincoln: The Prairie Years* (1926), Sandburg explores Lincoln's youth and adult life before he was elected President. The remaining four volumes, *Abraham Lincoln: The War Years* (1939), for which he won the Pulitzer Prize, begin with Lincoln's departure from Springfield, Illinois to Washington, D.C and ends with Lincoln's funeral train

bringing him back to Springfield for burial. It includes a panoramic view of the Civil War and a large cast of well-developed historical figures, among them government officials, soldiers, and citizens. Henry Steele Commager praised Sandburg's approach stating, "[Sandburg] has realized that Lincoln belongs to the people, not to the historians, and he has given us a portrait from which a whole generation may draw understanding from the past and inspiration for the future." In 1928 he wrote a biography of Lincoln especially for children titled *Abe Lincoln Grows Up.*

CRITICAL RECEPTION

Critical reception to Sandburg's poetry varied markedly, and critics still debate its importance, although his poems continue to be anthologized. Many contend that his poems are often overly sentimental and resemble randomly arranged prose pieces. Others have noted the power and tenderness of his verses and praised his use of the common language of the American people. Several critics claim that his experiments in free verse presented a substantial challenge to traditional forms of poetry. Some critics, such as William Carlos Williams in his review of *Collected Poems* (1950), seem confused about his work. Williams called the poem "Chicago" brilliant and said the rest were formless and insignificant, yet *Collected Poems* won the Pulitzer Prize. Critics' responses to his biography of Lincoln were similar. Some thought the narrative style was a disservice to history; others saw it as innovative and refreshing; all were astonished at his meticulously detailed research.

AWARDS

Sandburg's artistry was abundantly recognized in his lifetime. He received a large number of awards, among them the Pulitzer Prize in history in 1940 for *Abraham Lincoln: The War Years* and the Pulitzer Prize in 1951 *Complete Poems.* Some of his other awards included the Poetry Society of America Award in 1919 and 1921, the American Academy of Arts and Letters gold medal for history in 1952 and 1953, the Poetry Society of America gold medal for poetry in 1953, the Boston Arts Festival Poetry Prize in 1955, the Albert Einstein Award from Yeshiva College in 1956, and the International Poet's Award in 1963. He received the Friends of Literature Award in 1934 for *Lincoln: The Prairie Years*, the Taminent Institution Award in 1953 for *Always the Young Strangers,* and the Roanoke-Chowan Poetry Cup in

1960 for *Harvest Poems 1910-1960* and in 1961 for *Wind Song.* He was named Phi Beta Kappa Poet for Harvard University in 1928, and in 1965 received the NAACP award for his role as "a major prophet of civil rights in our time." He was also awarded honorary degrees from many colleges and universities.

AUTHOR COMMENTARY

Carl Sandburg

SOURCE: A letter to Alfred Harcourt on July 29, 1922, in *The Letters of Carl Sandburg,* edited by Herbert Mitgang, Harcourt, Brace & World, Inc., 1968, pp. 211-12.

[Chicago]

29 July, 1922.

Dear Alfred: . . .

If we can get stores like Brentano's and McClurg's to fill a show window with rutabagas and cream puffs for a display of *Rootabaga Stories,* I don't know whether it would be worth while. If a half dozen big rutabagas and a dozen cream puffs surmount displays at Xmas shopping time, I don't know whether it will help people to peep into the book or whether the peeping would make 'em want the book. But sometimes I think the projection of the physical or pictured rutabaga and cream puff (nix on liver or onions) might connect people with what is simple and real in the book.

Would a 3-compartment cardboard display rack be any good—each compartment filled with copies of *Rootabaga Stories*—No. 1 marked, "For People Five to Ten Years of Age"—No. 2, "For People Ten to Twenty Years of Age"—No. 3, "For People Twenty to 105 Years of Age"—and would the impress of the point occasionally that the book is "For People from 5 to 105 Years of Age" help cinch the idea that the book is for all ages?

Do we want some reviewer to say, "This book is better than goat glands?" I am going to read the stories at book stores in Chicago and sometimes in other towns. I'm going to talk cold turkey with booksellers about the hot gravy in the stories. I may even say, "Do you realize that Mr. Harcourt is seriously considering at a later period publishing pocket editions of these stories, to be placed in selling cases in drug

stores with guarantees and testimonials that the book is better than nuxated iron and its tonic and healing properties are assured by the editor of the *Journal of the American Medical Association,* who has tried them on himself and his children?" . . .

Carl

Carl Sandburg

SOURCE: A letter to Anne Carroll Moore on November 20, 1922, in *The Letters of Carl Sandburg,* edited by Herbert Mitgang, Harcourt, Brace & World, Inc., 1968, p. 220.

Chicago

20 November, 1922.

Dear Miss Moore:

Sometime we should have a good long talk as I am sure each of us has worth while questions to put. I am enclosing a clipping from the *Metropolitan* magazine which has to do with any answer I would make to the query you put to me before the audience at the Library. Some of the **Rootabaga Stories** were not written at all with the idea of reading to children or telling. They were attempts to catch fantasy, accents, pulses, eye flashes, inconceivably rapid and perfect gestures, sudden pantomimic moments, drawls and drolleries, gazings and musings—authoritative poetic instants—knowing that if the whirr of them were caught quickly and simply enough in words the result would be a child lore interesting to child and grownup. Something like that. . . . Sometime we'll have coffee and go farther on this.

Faithfully yours,

Carl Sandburg

Carl Sandburg

SOURCE: A letter to Helen Keller on October 10, 1929, in *The Letters of Carl Sandburg,* edited by Herbert Mitgang, Harcourt, Brace & World, Inc., 1968, pp. 269-70.

[Harbert, Michigan]

October 10, 1929.

Dear Miss Keller: . . .

I tried to read your letter out loud to my family and some friends at dinner one evening in my home. As I got into the last three paragraphs of your letter I knew all of a sudden that if I went on reading it I would be crying, and knowing this, I stopped reading and said, "I won't read the rest of the letter. You can read it for yourselves if you want to. All she says is that we are good friends because both of us are a little dumb and understand all living things that are dumb."

I have an impression that you are not acquainted with my Potato Face Blind Man. He is the leading character in two books, *Rootabaga Stories* and *Rootabaga Pigeons,* which I wrote for young people, meaning by young people those who are children and those grownups who keep something of the child heart. If you do not have these books I should love to send them to you, for there are pages which travel somewhat as my heart and mind would have if I had gone blind, which twice in my life came near happening. On some trip to New York I shall phone and ask whether I can come out and bring my guitar and songs. I am a vaudevillian too. Perhaps you know my panoramic, tumultuous, transcontinental *The American Songbag.*

May luck stars be over you.

Faithfully yours,

Carl Sandburg

Carl Sandburg

SOURCE: A letter to Anne Carroll Moore on December 7, 1929, in *The Letters of Carl Sandburg,* edited by Herbert Mitgang, Harcourt, Brace & World, Inc., 1968, pp. 271-72.

[Harbert, Michigan]

December 7, 1929.

Dear Miss Moore:

Someone sent me your comment on the *Rootabaga Country* of October 13. You have always been a shrewd and kindly commentator. If my next book, *Potato Face*, is not a little better than the earlier one it is not your fault. Harcourt plans on publishing the book next year. It will have no illustrations. I had decided some time ago that there should before long be a reissue of *Rootabaga* stories, all of them, in a book without pictures. Some day when in New York we will talk over this whole matter of illustrations. More often than not it is a vicious, stultifying business. The mind of a child is creatively occupied with mak-

ing its own country, shaping something for itself in its own independent world; then it turns a page and sees something by Maxfield Parrish which topples the child's imaginative creation as blasphemously as a big ignorant foot kicking over a playhouse which a child had designed out of its own mind. This is an extreme view given to you offhand. I don't want to start a fight about it; I am a Quaker in this regard and don't see where fighting would do any good. However, I know you would reimpart—and some day we will talk it over in various phases.

God love you.

Carl Sandburg

Carl Sandburg

SOURCE: A letter to Frank Lloyd Wright on June 28, 1947, in *The Letters of Carl Sandburg,* edited by Herbert Mitgang, Harcourt, Brace & World, Inc., 1968, pp. 446-47.

[Flat Rock, North Carolina]

[June 28, 1947]

Dear Frank:

Your letter of years ago (Nov 25, 1935) about the *Rootabaga Stories* came to my hands today for a slow reading once and then again. I was pleased when it first came but today it left me with a film over the eyes. I remembered many things, the gay first visit to Taliesin with Lloyd Lewis, the second visit when you went down with pneumonia but there had been time for you to take me thru that little theatre where your students had put on plays from the *Rootabaga Stories,* then that winter night at the [Ken] Holdens when you dropped in to hear a reading of *The People, Yes* in manuscript . . . Anyhow we are standing this *Rootabaga* letter of yours on a mantel for a while and making copies of it so that text can't be lost. It is more than an Award of Merit. You termed it a little posy for my hat-band which it was for that hour though now it is more like a small bronze luckpiece to be kept hidden and taken out when the heart is heavy and dark for a lightsheen it carries. I hope— and have a premonition that way—our ways will cross sometime this coming year. Lloyd Lewis and I in his house last winter, in a long talk about you, agreed it wouldn't quite do for your epitaph but it had something, what the fellow on your place said to the inquiring truck driver: HE'S THE BIGGEST GODDAM ARCHITECK OF 'EM ALL. I suppose I'm extra sentimental about this old letter of yours because of the loveliness and rare lights of a grandson (5) and a granddaughter (4) who shake the house with their promises. . . . Prayers for your health and luck stars be over you and Olga and yours.

As always,

Carl

GENERAL COMMENTARY

Harry Hansen

SOURCE: "Carl Sandburg, Poet of the Streets and of the Prairie," in *Midwest Portraits: A Book of Memories and Friendships,* Harcourt, Brace and Company, 1923, pp. 71-92.

Carl Sandburg seemed to grow perceptibly in stature on the day that he first appeared before us as a teller of tales. Up to that moment he had been a strolling player, a minstrel twanging his lyre to songs of his own invention; now he came to weave together beautiful prose tales that meant romance and adventure to grown men and little children. The moment when he first revealed himself in this new mood comes back most vividly now that a copy of *Rootabaga Stories* lies upon my desk. It was at Schlogl's—Henry Blackman Sell was there, and Jerome Frank, Carlton Washburne, and Keith Preston, and many more, when Carl Sandburg strolled in and nonchalantly called for his coffee and ham on rye. None of the more palatable dishes for Carl—no pickled eel, or baby turkey, or champignons—Carl has never conceded that dining is more than partaking of plain food; and more often than not he prefers to hunt up some hole in the wall where he can "grab off a bite to eat." Nor does he take part in the animated discussion that goes with dining *en masse*—in the criss-cross of words and banter—he is at his best when he has one auditor and can speak at length on his favorite topics. So our prattle did not engage his interest, but there came a lull in the talk, and then Carl fished a manuscript from his pocket. "I've been writing some stories for the kids at home," he said, "reading to them at night and this is as far as I've got. I'll read it to you." It proved to be a fairy tale—the tale of a little lad whose mother had called him Petie-Patta-Tatta, because that is the sound the raindrops made on the roof the day he was born—pat-ta-tat-ta pat-ta tat-ta—a little boy who lived in a town destined to become a familiar

mark on the chart of all childhood; the Village of Liver and Onions. A fairy tale—and yet an entirely new sort of fairy tale, one that wove romance around familiar objects and unromantic scenes. Carl Sandburg, like Hans Christian Andersen before him, had tapped the source of our inspirations—he too had found, as Francis Hackett wrote of Andersen, that fairy tales are our dream and intuition, the hem of our garment of immortality. A new and wonderful vision of Carl as the spinner of tales, sitting among the little folk with his fine, graying head bent down toward them and a wistful earnestness in his eyes, grew up before us. "I've got another one," said Carl, when he had finished reading, "about the Village of Cream Puffs and how they wind it up every night on a spool when the wind blows it away." "Are you going to publish them?" some one asked. "I hadn't thought of that," said Carl, "I've just been writing them for the children."

To tell something of *Rootabaga Stories* we must make a pilgrimage to the home of the Sandburgs, out of Chicago on the St. Charles road. A long pilgrimage it is, for Elmhurst is one of those wooded villages that has slipped out from under the pall of smoke and fumes that hovers over Chicago. The Sandburg house—"it's that little white place with a wooden fence around it," is the way it was described—was once a farmhouse that stood in the center of a sizable plot, but time nibbled down its acreage until it became a city lot and now a well-paved asphalt roadway under the guise of York street runs by where once the cows went lazily to their barns. "Part of this house is over seventy years old," said Carl, and to us of the west that is the equivalent of the New Englander's boast that his home was raised two hundred years ago. A quaint, rambling place it is, a homey place, with many little rooms, cozy and comfortable and without pretense; part of the house was once a little old-fashioned school-house and there is evidence that bits have been added now and then. Mrs. Sandburg is the kindly spirit that hovers over the roof-tree with genial informality, and if you remain long enough three lively youngsters will come romping in, tossing their hats in childish abandon, radiating health and good cheer—Margaret, Janet and the little curly-headed Helga—you will meet them all in the dedications of several of Carl's books, and again in the poems. They are, as Carl will tell you, with a twinkle, "the heirs to the Sandburg millions—millions of clippings."

And that brings us to *Rootabaga Stories.* For if it had not been for these three romping, rollicking youngsters, and their appetite for stories, it is doubtful whether their father would have turned from his rugged lyrics to fashion strange, whimsical stories in limpid prose. What an audience they made—generous, whole-hearted, insatiable. One day Carl was telling how the stories sprang into life and thus he put it in his own way:

"The fox drank cream in the kitchen, measuring himself between drinks, till he had just enough to let himself through the window and out again. The story was told to Janet. Now Janet comes saying, 'Tell me a fox, tell me a fox.' And we are trying to think of more foxes to tell.

"The wolf drank too much cream. He couldn't scrape his full belly through the kitchen window and escape. 'They killed him with an ax.' So the story was told to Janet and Helga, five and three years old. Now each blossom of a child goes saying to father, mother, rag doll Tessie, china doll Betty, and to the invisible spirits of bedtime, 'I kill you with an ax.' With laughing chuckles they keep saying with twinkling eyes that shine straight and merry into your own face, 'I kill you with an ax.'

"There is a blue fox lives under the front porch. The father and mother have told Janet and Helga it is so. And Janet and Helga have repeated it to each other. It has been spoken of so many ways, in relation to so many concrete and particular events, that we all know a blue fox is there under the front porch, alive, with shining eyes, shining white teeth, shining blue hair. 'Tell us a story,' we say to Janet. She will, she won't, she will, she won't. 'Tell us a story,' we beg. 'Blue fox under front porch. Man come. Fox say, "Go away." Man go away.' And that is the story. No adjectives, brief action—a ghost of a blue fox puts its footsteps on a child sky."

So we begin with Margaret, Janet, and Helga. You can see them home from their play, sitting at the feet of this tall, gaunt man, who bends forward to pull dreams out of the clouds for them. Gone are his searchings for powerful speech, for hard-hitting prose, gone are his preoccupations with men of heavy hearts and strange oppressions; he has stepped down among the children and his voice is attuned to childhood's ear. Here we find his strength giving way to gentleness, his love for clarity being superseded by a trick of using words not to be found in any vernacular, and yet words that delight the child mind, his character as a poet of the social order standing aside while he dons the cap and bells. It is an intimate, real, and lovable Sandburg.

The children have been often in Carl's thoughts. In his first book, *Chicago Poems,* he writes of Margaret:

In your blue eyes, O reckless child,
I saw to-day many little wild wishes
Eager as the great morning.

In *Cornhuskers* also there are poems about the children. The dedication of *Cornhuskers* reads: "To Janet and Margaret"; for there was no Helga then, but *Slabs of the Sunburnt West* is dedicated to Helga. What better beginning can any book of fairy tales have than that it was conceived solely to enrich the hours of little folk? Carl was telling these tales at home long before he thought of printing them. He tried one or two on his audiences and found that human beings are always children at heart—for the grown-ups loved them, too. Gradually the stories grew and he found himself in possession of a whimsical imagery that he had not known before. To sit down in the quiet of an evening and write another adventure of the curiously human folk in Rootabaga land became a strong man's play. Only long after did the idea come to him that they might provide joy to other children than his own and to grown-ups were they placed in book form.

Out of a strong man's playtime came these stories of Rootabaga land. Out of a man's realization that, for some of us at least, the play spirit never dies out of life; that we reach out into the unknowable and bring back gifts that enchant us, even though we cannot always justify them by the laws of logic and coherence. There came a time when the opportunity to sit down and meditate on the doings of Rootabaga folk and eventually to write them down on his typewriter was to Carl a hallowed moment of rest and exultation. They expressed the play spirit within him and soon he began to measure his fellows by their response to these fanciful creations. "The stories," Carl would say, "are pure unmuddled joy. They are only for people who understand—who haven't dried up. I've worked harder on them than on anything I have ever done. If the people who read books don't like these stories there is no joy left in the world." It was a happy moment when he found the book tightly clasped in the arms of half the world.

The most outstanding characteristic of *Rootabaga Stories* is that although they are properly fairy tales, none of the lay figures of the fairy story live in them. The objects one encounters have a familiar sound—cornfields, skyscrapers, furnace shovel, coffee pot, potato bugs, blue rats, popcorn hats, policeman's whistles—but truly none belongs to the fairy tale of tradition. And that is because Carl knows that fairy tales, after all, are but an inverted expression of the folk lore of a people, and that when the stories out of foreign lands tell us of princes, knights, giants, ogres, chivalrous knights rescuing beautiful maidens, kings in coat of mail charging across a drawbridge, we are dealing with an historical tradition that is not ours, as a race, save only by indirection. To the people who tell them these castles were as familiar as our skyscrapers, and the giants and ogres were originally the feudal oppressors of the poor. But America has no knights clad in armor, no kings in coats of mail charging across a drawbridge, and left to itself an American child would build the life of its imagination not with these objects but with the actualities of its own environment. That is why the fairies were helping Carl weave these stories just as truly as they worked at the elbows of the brothers Grimm, for just as those men set down the folklore of the people, so Carl crystallized the whimsey, the fantasy, the quaint musings of the child heart of a nation that has skyscrapers for its castles, policemen for captains, railroads for knightly cavalcades, prairies of waving corn, silver blue lakes like blue porcelain breakfast plates— the magic that you can conjure up any day from your bedroom window.

These men are the sprites of a strong man's playtime. They vary in mood, in significance, in treatment, as vary the moods of a thousand readers. The quaint embroidery of familiar objects in childhood lives in such fancies as the potato-face blind man and the man with a popcorn hat, popcorn mittens, and popcorn shoes; the more familiar tale that depends for its movement on a piling up of incidents and the repetition of names and speeches lives in **"How Bimbo the Snip's Thumb Stuck to His Nose When the Wind Changed"** and the tale of **"Three Boys with Kegs of Molasses and Secret Ambitions"**; there is humor that calls for clear, ringing laughter in the story of **"Gimme the Ax"** and his two children, who named themselves Please Gimme and Ax Me No Questions; there is whimsicality and poetry and magical music in the stories of the sand flat shadows and in **"How to Tell Corn Fairies if You See Them."** There are tales out of the warp and woof of our daily life, as in the story of the two skyscrapers that decided to have a child . . . "a free child, not a child standing still all its life on a street corner. . . ." When it came it was an overland passenger train, the **"Golden Spike Limited,"** and the ensuing tragedy is as heart-breaking as any in all fairy lore.

So much for subject matter. If the themes vary, so too does the treatment; there are tales that reveal plain, matter-of-fact story telling, there are others that seek for nuances and overtones. Most interesting is his understanding of the child mind. "Isn't it odd," said Little Ruth to her mother, "that only the fire-born understand blue?" "I don't know what you are talking about," replied the mother. "But it's true," said the child, "for it says so in my story." The child mind grasps readily facts that a grown-up needs to have explained, for the child is building fancies as it reads and has one ready for every image that comes. The more sophisticated oldster, measuring everything by past experience, leaves no play to the imagination. So, too, the odd words that Carl has put into his stories immediately call forth a burst of laughter and approval from little folks, who are ready with an image to fit the case. "I will give you a new ticket," says the ticket agent to Gimme the Ax, when he breaks away with his family to go to the Rootabaga country. "It is a long slick yellow leather slab ticket with a blue spanch across it." Spanch? The children laugh with glee . . . it is a new word, expressive, ready to fill a niche in their imaginations. In a lecture before the students at Northwestern University Carl told this story, using the term "spanch." "Many of you will want to know what sort of word that is," he explained, "but I have not time to stop and tell you about it. If you want to know what it is you will have to look it up." Several of the students took him literally. They wrote him letters beginning: "Dear Mr. Sandburg: We have been unable to find the word spanch. What does it mean? . . . "

The writing of *Rootabaga Stories* was for Carl an invigorating exercise. He could not drop it; it was a tonic to his nerves; it had to go on. And now, after long intervals a story comes from his typewriter, to be brooded over, read to children, and revised again. In time there will be another of *Rootabaga Stories,*— perhaps two, or three. Already the second volume is close to his heart; *Rootabaga Pigeons* it will be called. "It will have more real poetry in it than the first Rootabaga book," said Carl, "but the kids will get it." Sometimes he likes his *Rootabaga Stories* even better than his poems. When he learns that they have pleased others besides himself he chuckles with glee like a small boy. People write him about them; he learns that they have been read in hospitals, in jails, in the rush hours on trains. And although his reputation rests on his poetry this one volume has been much more widely distributed than any of his poems.

Carl himself regards them as the equivalent of simple folklore told in droll stories without the surplusage of most fairy stories. "The child's mind reels with the impact of lonely princesses and castles," he says. "There is nothing marvelous in these tales, they are folklore material in a modern mood, and for that there is no such word as marvelous. Even the pigs with bibs on—it is logical that the checker pigs should have checker bibs on and the polka dot pigs have polka dot bibs on. That may be strange, but hardly marvelous."

"They kept me alive," said Carl; "they have my heart's blood."

No man has a keener sense for the significant phrase in homely surroundings than Carl Sandburg. He is always pulling something out of the air almost—something you want to remember, to reflect on, and then telling you that it came from the clerk at your elbow, the elevator man, the woman with the dust-mop. He has a faculty for alighting upon stray, nomadic items in newspapers and magazines that hold his attention. His pockets are always full of press clippings; invariably, at the end of a conversation he will pull a bunch from his pocket, extract one well-thumbed and curling bit of newspaper print and leave it with you with the remark: "Read that and tell me what you think of it. That fellow says something. I've had my eye on him. Give it back to me when I see you again." Then with a smile he departs. . . . Sometimes in an unwonted place in my desk I find a clipping which reminds me of a remissness in returning irrelevant gifts.

But out of the welter of words men use, out of the well-worn imagery, the stereotyped expressions of commonplace thoughts, Carl gathers a rich haul. Many of his poems have been inspired by a look, a spoken word, an inadvertent remark. He sees poetry in the commonplace—poetry before it is so labeled.

"Our lives are rich with poetry," Carl remarked one day over the coffee cups. "Did you ever hear the court bailiffs administer the oath? Some of them have a sense for rhythm." Carl reproduced their manner in a slow, impressive monotone: "'I solemnly swear to tell the truth, the whole truth, and nothing but the truth, so help me, God!' Others just rattle it off without any sense or feeling for rhythm."

He paused and reflected. "Then take this: there was a woman I ran across in Milwaukee, her husband was the janitor of a building and they lived in the basement. They had had eleven children and buried six, from tuberculosis, and they still lived in the basement. She said to me: 'We work and we work and all that we earn goes into the grave.'" Carl's eyes took on a look of triumph. "That line has a rhythm and a power to it that makes Thomas Hood's 'song of a Shirt' fade out of the picture," he concluded emphatically.

"And then you run across this plain homely philosophy, this summing up. I was talking with a man on the smoker going out to Elmhurst and we were hold-

ing forth on the mixup in local politics—the state's attorney's office or something. He leaned back and said: 'There always was politics; there was politics one thousand years ago; there is politics to-day; there will be politics one thousand years from now; when there ain't no more politics there won't be any human race.'" . . .

In less than ten years Carl Sandburg has become a figure of national significance. To-day he is invariably named as one of the four or five outstanding poets of America, and his influence toward a liberation from classical bondage and the development of wholesome American themes is felt among a host of followers. He has helped direct our thinking back to the primitive forces of our land; to the soil, human labor, the great industries, the masses of men. No matter what he writes in the future the cumulative effect of his poems will survive and be of great influence in our land.

There are those of us who feel that although he may grow in wisdom, round out his philosophy of life, and perhaps even smooth out his lines, his big contribution to American literature in the future will not be in the field of poetry but in prose. He has a flair for interpretative biography, and a keen interest in the humanness of great historical characters. He sees men with their faults and their virtues; he sees them whole. The years that lie between us and a historical character do not blunt the edges of these figures for him; he thinks of them as men who walked this earth, and not as demigods. He has nothing in common with the tendency of most nations to deify leaders of an older generation, and although he is very partial to friendships, and his judgment is often blurred by sympathy with those close to him, he is able to take a fine disinterested and objective view of leaders dead and gone. His kinship toward politicians, labor leaders, teamsters, to the lowly ones who toil, is based upon the very qualities that will make him an able interpreter of men and their aims. In delineating other times, in bringing back to us a "homeliness" that has been lost under a veneer of alien culture, in picturing this age as the logical successor of the past, Carl Sandburg has before him a task that calls for all of his powers, and one that he is well equipped to perform.

Charles H. Compton

SOURCE: "Who Reads Carl Sandburg?" in *The South Atlantic Quarterly,* Vol. XXVIII, No. 2, April, 1929, pp. 190-200.

Ten years ago the critics had their fling at Sandburg. Today he is accepted. Anthologies of modern verse include him—some with due praise, others without enthusiasm. What about the general reader, the gentle reader, the man in the street, the flapper, flaming youth? Are they reading him? Where will you find them, that we may ask them? They are all represented among the users of the modern public library, today the most democratic, and as yet the freest and least restrained agency in placing the fruits of knowledge, (the good and the evil, shall we say) before the people. It is for them to choose—the detective story for the tired business man, the good sweet story for the good sweet woman, but Sandburg for others.

An examination of the records in the public library of a large American city disclosed the identity of about one hundred recent readers of Sandburg's poetry. They in most part have the same street addresses as the characters of Sandburg's own creation. Today everything is measured from the electron to the universe, but who has attempted to measure that elusive and yet certain influence of one personality upon another? We have not even begun to think about the possibility of the measurement of the effect of an author upon his reader. Yet nothing is more certain than that an author read and appropriated with enthusiasm may change the very fabric of the soul of the reader.

The impact of a Sandburg upon the thoughts, the emotions, the feelings, cannot as yet be measured, but it can be taken account of in one's imagination—it can at least be shot at in the dark. As we bring forward some of these hundred readers from the common walks of life, but with something from the neck up worth possessing, perhaps we can sense the effect of a Sandburg upon the stenographer, the typist, the police clerk and the reporter by lines from his writings, taken at random, which seem to speak directly to them.

To the stenographer: "By day the skyscraper looms in the sun and has a soul. . . . It is the men and women, boys and girls, so poured in and out all day, that give the building a soul of dreams and thoughts and memories."

To the typist: "Smiles and tears of each office girl go into the soul of the building, just the same as the master-men who rule the building."

To the Negro reader: "I am the nigger. Singer of songs, Dancer. . . . Softer than fluff of cotton . . . Harder than dark earth Roads beaten in the sun By the bare feet of slaves."

To the minister: "Lay me on an anvil, O God. Beat me and hammer me into a crowbar. Let me pry loose old walls. Let me lift and loosen old foundations."

To the newspaper reporter: "Speak softly—the sacred cows may hear. Speak easy—the sacred cows must be fed."

To the police clerk: "Out of the whirling womb of time come millions of men and their feet crowd the earth and they cut one another's throats for room to stand and among them all are not two thumbs alike."

To the musician: "A man saw the whole world as a grinning skull and cross bones. . . . Then he went to a Mischa Elman concert. . . . Music washed something or other inside of him. Music broke down and rebuilt something or other in his head and heart. . . . He was the same man in the same world as before. Only there was a singing fire and a climb of roses everlastingly over the world he looked on."

To the waitress: "Shake back your hair, O red-headed girl. Let go your laughter and keep your two proud freckles on your chin."

To the manager of a beauty parlor: "The woman named Tomorrow sits with a hairpin in her teeth and takes her time and does her hair in the way she wants it and fastens at last the last braid and coil and puts the hairpin where it belongs and turns and drawls: Well, what of it? My grandmother, Yesterday, is gone. What of it? Let the dead be dead."

To the book agent: "This is a good book? Yes? Throw it at the moon—Let her go—Spang—This book for the moon. . . . Yes? And then—other books, good books, even the best books—shoot 'em with a long twist at the moon—Yes?"

To the man who puts himself down a laborer: "Men who sunk the pilings and mixed the mortar are laid in graves where the wind whistles a wild song without words."

Among others of the hundred readers to whom he does not speak so directly, are many high school and college students, a few grade school children, a good representation of teachers, a department store saleswoman, two advertising men, a mechanic, a printer, a shoe salesman, a physician and the wife of another physician, several who designate themselves as clerks, and the wives of men engaged in similar occupations. The list is as significant in the vocations which are found unrepresented. There is not a lawyer on the list. "Why does a hearse horse snicker, hauling a lawyer away?" There is only one physician and two ministers. There is only one business man and I happen to know that he calls his vocation merely a meal ticket—his avocation being that of a playwright.

It is interesting to observe that a similar recent study of readers of William James indicated that much the same classes of people were reading him as read Sandburg. Perhaps I cannot prove the fact, but I would be willing to wager that on the list of Sandburg readers there are not many "go-getters"—100 per cent. Americans and 20th century "he-men," which words in themselves are sufficient to make most of us swell with over-weaning pride.

In order to find out what these readers thought of Sandburg's poetry, I wrote to some of them, asking them to tell me how they happened to become interested in his poetry; whether they liked or disliked it; did they consider it poetry, and would it live, and what poems did they especially like or dislike? Most of the answers, which in some cases were very full, showed an understanding of Sandburg which in their estimate of his place in present day American literature corresponds rather closely with the varying estimate of the literary critics who have written about him. Here are some extracts from these letters:

A minister writes:

> First of all I should like to say that I found the Chicago poems very interesting and powerful. The latter attribute is the most commendable in any of the works of Sandburg I believe. You ask me if I consider his works poetry and I say without hesitation and very dogmatically 'no.' The most fitting definition of poetry in my estimation is one that I found in a book on German literature which translated would be, 'Poetry is beautiful thought in beautiful form.' Some of his things when weighed in the balance are woefully lacking in beautiful thought or form and all of them lack one or the other. His works may live as a sample of the product of this age but never for their literary value, is my belief.
>
> 'I have seen your painted women standing under the lamp-posts luring the innocent country boys,' he gives us a cross section of life written in powerful prose. That is all we can claim for him.

A janitor in a store drops a word of disparagement as to Sandburg, but calls attention to his own poetry, samples of which he sent me. He says:

> i am quite a greate reader But have not read Sandburgs poems very much for i did not cair much for them so i can not say much about them.
>
> i am a poet myself or think i am aneyhow. i commenced writing Poetry when i was eight years old. i am almost 65 now. Will send you a few samples of my Poor work on that line and you may Be able to do something for me and if you

cant their is no harm done. i can write poor poetry, But make my living by hard work.

A teacher in the public schools of St. Louis expresses her appreciation as follows:

> I became interested in Sandburg's poetry thru a literature course which a roommate at University of Chicago took; and the subsequent reading and discussions of Sandburg's poetry. We often read his Chicago Poems aloud to each other.
>
> Yes, I like his poems, because of his understanding and feeling for life—the expression of thoughts which I have had but could not adequately express. His feelings for the poorer classes of Chicago masses, etc., etc.
>
> In recalling his poems I find that I remember his vivid word pictures, so that his poems are called to mind by the mental visual image the poem made. The uniqueness of form and style are also attractive.
>
> Is it poetry? Yes—and no. Poetry when we consider the beauty of idea and ease of expression, but not poetry if we shall limit ourselves to narrow meter forms, rhyming, etc.
>
> If any of the modern poetry lives (which I think it will), Sandburg's and Teasdale's will always be much read and appreciated.
>
> I am especially fond of **"Lines to a contemporary Bunk-Shooter."** The first time I read it I hated it, but later grew to appreciate it for its frankness, vividness, and life.

The following comes from the pen of a fourteen-year-old high school student:

> Am answering your unusual request because I, like all poor mortals, love to give an opinion, and because I love to write—anything.
>
> I became interested in Sandburg's poetry only after having been obliged by duty to read some modern poet's works. I chose Sandburg's because I had never before read any of them, though I had heard something of the promising author. You may be interested to know that out of a third term English class of forty students, only one chose to read Sandburg.
>
> I am very fond of Carl Sandburg's works at times, though at other times they seem exceedingly hard to become interested in. I believe, though, that one never enjoys the same thing always, so, on the whole,—I do love his poetry,—very much. The reasons for my liking it, are, for the most part unknown to me, though I suppose its main

appeal to me is in that it is so very—different. Then, too, I, with Sandburg, love, admire, and am inspired by the wheat fields of Illinois. Sandburg's is the best description of them I have ever read. Also, my dream city is Chicago. Oh, Sandburg seems to get at the heart of his themes with an astonishing agility.

Most certainly I consider it poetry for it is indeed 'the best words in the best way.' What else could it be but poetry, for it seems to sing, and makes something respond and sing within the reader, too.

As I am not a prophetess at all, I can scarcely say whether or not his poetry will live. Or perhaps I should say, it shall live—in me, though I doubt if it will live in the hearts of the people, as did the works of Longfellow and the other more conservative poets. On the other hand, Poe was not at all conservative, and his poetry is immortal (especially the beautiful Annabel Lee). My poor opinions are as nothing. I cannot say.

It has been such a very long time since I read *Corn Huskers* that I cannot remember any titles. I am sure that the poems dealing with the 'sun on the wheat fields' were my especial favorites. However (you have aroused my interest in Carl Sandburg again, you see!) I intend to read *Corn Huskers* once more and procure from the Public Library others of his works, and then, if you wish, I shall mail you the names of my favorites, and the ones I care least for.

P.S. These are only the opinions of a fourteen-year-old girl, so do not be annoyed at my style of writing and expression of my opinions. My name is at your service, if you wish.

Another teacher writes in part:

Just by way of wanting to know something about Modern American Poets, I took, several years ago, an evening course at Washington University from Professor Jones. I found the course extremely interesting and found that my professor was particularly interested in Carl Sandburg's poetry. It is perhaps because of Professor Jones's interest that I found myself very fond of Carl Sandburg's verse.

I wish that I were home at present and could get at some of my notes. At present I am attending Columbia University, and am quite busy with mid-term exams. If such were not the case, I should enjoy reading over many of Sandburg's poems and should enjoy giving you my impressions.

Not being a poetic scholar, I can not express myself in the language of poets. I believe that his is poetry; of course, his style is very free but that

does not make his product any the less poetry. I love the feeling, the sound, the music that comes to me as I read his **'Cool Tombs'** and **'Grass.'** Those are the two poems that come to my mind as I write.

An advertising man for a manufacturing concern writes at length of himself and his unflattering views of Sandburg, which are quoted here in part:

I am an amateur scribbler with a keen realization of my own limitations but an equally keen enjoyment of an occasional spree in the realm of literary self expression. Like most amateurs of whatever degree of promise. I am afflicted with friends and relatives who persist in regarding me as a potential second Shakespeare. It was in an effort to convince them—a successful effort, by the way—that I was not destined to cast any light on the literary heavens, that led up to my acquaintance with the redoutable Mr. Sandburg.

I cannot say that I either liked or disliked the works of this strange writer. I will confess to an occasional flash of admiration as he created some extremely vivid image, but on the whole, I read his poems with a feeling of tolerant amusement.

I do not consider myself an absolute reactionary, by any means. I read the works of Masefield, Noyes and Lindsay with the utmost enjoyment. Most of Amy Lowell's work—even her free verse, I found enjoyable. Sandburg, however, I found merely grotesque, for the most part.

I may be wrong,—I probably am—but it seems to me that the reason Whitman's work will continue to live is that he plunged deep down into the crucible of life and brought up the pure molten metal. Sandburg, on the contrary, seems to me to have skimmed off the slag.

If you have ever been near a huge steel mill, you will appreciate the above figure of speech. When the slag is dumped, there is a tremendous splash and flying of sparks, but when it has cooled, there is only an ugly shapeless mass. Pure metal, however, runs to the rolling mill and is worked into enduring articles of commerce and enjoys (if one may use that term) a certain sort of immortality analogous to that enjoyed by the works of a true literary genius.

It has been some time since I read any of Mr. Sandburg's works and I cannot recall a single one of them, which made a sufficiently deep impression on me, so that I could say that I either liked or disliked any single bit of his work. My whole feeling toward this man's writings may be caused by conflicting temperament; it probably is. So far as that is concerned, however, if others who comply with your request would be equally frank, you would probably find that they would have to make the same confession, if, by any chance, they had the slightest understanding of the reason for whatever reactions they may have.

I think that one reason why critics are usually treated in such a contemptuous manner, is the fact that so much criticism is based on personal feeling or on a little understood reaction of temperament. After all, what standards have we to guide us in criticising the works of such men as Sandburg?

They are pioneers. Recognizing the fact that poetry, the last thing in the world which ought to be standardized was rapidly declining into a state where poetry, so-called, would be produced after the same fashion as Ford cars, they went to the extreme limit of revolt.

Not all of them went so far as Mr. Sandburg, Lowell and the freak followers of our friend Harriet Monroe in Chicago. Many reached the truly sublime heights. I think that future generations will so regard Masefield, Noyes and to some extent, Frost, Lindsay and Robinson.

As for the utter extremists,—and I regard Sandburg as falling in that category,—it is my opinion—merely an opinion—they will be lumped together in the consideration of future critics as being collectively responsible for the new literary movement, that their names may live in that connection, but that very little of what they have produced will survive any other way than as literary curiosities produced in an era of transition.

The wife of a man, who in the city directory is classified as a clerk, writes appreciatively of Sandburg:

I first became interested in modern poetry when I took a course in 'contemporary poetry' at Washington University. Here I read a few of Sandburg's Poems for the first time. I liked some of them so well I have since read all his works.

I cannot say I like all his poetry but I like some of it. It seems to me that some of it is rather crude and lacks the finish associated with any art. I do not like the strident element in his poetry. Sandburg's object is to give us his impression of life and since some life is crude and strident Sandburg accomplishes what he wishes to do. I admire the technique he employs but do not like what he produces. It seems to me that at times he shows a lack of judgment in his selection of subject matter.

But in many of his poems we have expressions of great beauty and perfect construction and unity. Most of his figures of speech are unique and striking, and if not too prosaic, are pleasing. The most pronounced note in his better poems is his tender

sympathy and understanding of all kinds of life and his resignation to a hopeless death as portrayed in his philosophy of living.

It depends on one's standard for poetry whether or not one can say Sandburg does or does not write it. According to my standard of poetry Sandburg writes poetry. He also writes many poems that are not poetry.

I think Sandburg's most beautiful poems will live because of the merit they have. But we are living in a transitional period of poetry and Sandburg, I believe, is the greatest of this period. For that reason, if not for the merit of his poetry, the best of his work will be preserved.

I like the '**Undertow**,' '**In the Cool Tombs**,' '**The Harbor**,' '**Lost**,' '**The Nurse-Mother**,' '**Joy**,' and his other poems of like nature. I cannot say I really dislike any of his poems but I do not care for '**Chicago**.' No doubt Sandburg in this poem does exactly what he attempts to do but I do not care for that type of poetry. '**Cornhuskers**' and '**Smoke and Steel**' are better, but I do not care for them as I do for his shorter, tenderer poems. Sandburg can be infinitely tender and understanding and his poems in this mood are his best. It seems to me that these are the poems that cause him to rank very high as a poet today.

The wife of the manager of a motor company says she first had her attention called to Sandburg when her pastor quoted from the *Fish Monger*. She writes:

There is, of course, truth in what he says, and from what little I know of his poems, it is well put. You ask if I consider it poetry. In Webster's Dictionary the definition of Poetry is: 'The embodiment in appropriate rhythmical language, usually metrical, of beautiful or high thoughts, imagination, or emotion.' Many of his things surely are not that but they do stir one to better conditions, just as Dickens's descriptions do, and they do paint portions of Chicago in vivid raw colors.

The only letter completely condemning Sandburg came anonymously and reads as follows:

I dislike the poetry of Sandburg because its effects are not aesthetic in any degree.

I do not consider it poetry. It lacks the beauty of expression and thought that characterizes real poetry.

It is doubtful that Sandburg's poetry will live, for it is not sufficiently distinctive; it is merely a part of the mass of so-called modern verse.

I consider Sandburg's poetry vulgar, at times; coarse, brutal, materialistic and sordid. To one who has been held breathless by the musical cadence, the magic imagery, the wealth of word and thought of Shelley and Keats, or any of the real poets, the so-called poetry of Sandburg is as a transition from the sublime to the ridiculous. Slang will never be the medium of poetic expression. The golden chain of poetic thought is roughly torn asunder when a slang or exceedingly common-place phrase is introduced. No, Sandburg may have been a good newspaper man; he could, perhaps, have written essays; but he was no poet. To call his work poetry is a sacrilege to the muse, a desecration of the name of poesy.

Two letters deal especially with Sandburg's *Abraham Lincoln: The Prairie Years*. One is from a teacher of evident literary appreciation. She says in part:

> I have read Carl Sandburg's *Abraham Lincoln*; his poems, one or two volumes, some of the *Rootabaga Stories*; have heard him speak, read his verse and thump his banjo. I like him, the funny stories, the shorter poems and the Lincoln. I was charmed, too, with the man himself.
>
> I first liked Lincoln better after I saw Drinkwater's play; then after I read Sandburg, liked the human touch—I mean one's feeling that he was so humanly humorous or is it the reverse, so humorously human. It has been a long time since I read the book and many things are between then and now. I remember I liked it and stayed up because interested, as well as to do up a two volume set to get it back to the library. My aunt, too, read it and although a very Southern person with traditional prejudices, liked Lincoln better and enjoyed the book.
>
> A man I was talking with the other day who reads considerably, travels (in Europe twice), is a college man of years ago, however, not literary especially, had not heard of Sandburg.
>
> I introduced Sandburg into a literary class last year in a State Teachers College. Except one or two, they had not read any of him; most of them did not know he existed. Kipling and Neihardt were about the only modern poets they knew. They liked Sandburg, especially the men.

The other is from a police clerk:

> In reply to your letter asking for my opinion of Carl Sandburg's *Abraham Lincoln: the Prairie Years*, wish to say that it is one of many books that I shall always be glad that I have had the pleasure to read and enjoy.
>
> I ran across some of Mr. Carl Sandburg's poetry some years ago. I enjoyed it so much that I read everything of Sandburg's that I could find. Later I heard of his new monumental work, *Abraham Lincoln*. I procured it quickly and enjoyed reading every line of it. Ordinarily I find the reading of biographies dull, they are usually smoothed over, white washed here and there, done so I guess because the truth is never fit for publication, but here is one in a different style and purpose, done neatly, clearly and poetically. There are whole pages in it that read like poetry. The description of Lincoln plodding through mud and muck of Illinois country roads is a treat and as real to me as the day I myself plowed through it.
>
> I like reading it because I found it instructive, entertaining and not a page to be dull. I believe Sandburg has painted Lincoln as he really was—a great big giant, come up out of the wilderness and the hinderland with great big broad shoulders and bared chest to strike a new note in the history of his country.
>
> To my mind Sandburg's Lincoln will ring round the world as a work of greatness, for whosoever reads it will come to know Lincoln as no other man has written of him.

I wonder whether the fourteen-year-old girl has not answered the question as to whether Sandburg's poetry will live when she says, "It will live in me," and again the question as to whether it is poetry when she says, "What else could it be but poetry, for it seems to sing and make something sing in the reader, too." I have asked myself the same questions that I put to those whose letters appear here and the answers I give are like theirs, uncontaminated by any knowledge of the technique of poetry. To be sure I have read books on poetry and have enjoyed them, especially Max Eastman's *Enjoyment of Poetry,* but I know not a whit more about how poetry is made on that account, although they have added to my appreciation of poetry. But there is one thing I do know, and that is the effect poetry has on me. If I were to attempt to define poetry, I would say that it was that form of literary expression which in the fewest words can affect man most profoundly. That satisfies me, for it allows me to consider both Keats and Sandburg as poets.

Sandburg's poetry is not like that of Shelley or Keats, yet it stirs my emotions, not the same emotions as does Shelley's *Ode to the Skylark* or Keats's *Autumn,* but just as deeply—perhaps more deeply. More deeply, because Sandburg's poetry goes down deep into the life of this twentieth century of which he is a part—of which I am a part. It is a life I understand. At those ugly things in life at which he rebels—at those things I rebel. Of all the poets I know, not excepting Walt Whitman, Sandburg is not excelled in his sympathy with the common and even the lowest of humanity, with the great unwashed, with the boobs and the flappers, with the seventy-five per cent of our population whom the intelligence testers set down as morons. Sandburg understands them all. He interprets them and draws from them the beauty hidden away in the dark recesses of their outwardly unlovely exteriors.

Will Sandburg's poetry live? I am willing to abide by the answer of the fourteen-year-old girl. It will live in me and from the letters which I have quoted I know that there are other "me's" beside my own, in whom Sandburg's poetry is now living, and I believe that in the years to come there will be still other "me's" yet unborn in whom Carl Sandburg will live and will stir still pools in the hidden places of their souls.

Harry Golden

SOURCE: "In Prose You Say What You Mean," in *Carl Sandburg,* The World Publishing Company, 1961, pp. 221-38.

"The children asked questions, and I answered them," says Carl Sandburg, describing how he wrote the *Rootabaga Stories,* published at the end of 1922 by Harcourt, Brace, illustrated by Maude and Miska Petersham, and advertised as "Fanciful Stories for Children."

Ease of arrangement, spirit of play, simplicity—this is what Sandburg has undertaken in the *Rootabaga Stories.*

Children find great amusement in listening to someone toy with the alphabet; the people who live in Rootabaga Country are all essentially alphabetic curiosities. There is Blixie Bimber who finds a gold buckskin whincher (a good luck charm) and promptly falls in love with a series of "X's"—Silas Baxby, Fritz Axenbax, and James Sixbixdix.

Henry Hagglyhoagly wins Susan Slackentwist by serenading her on a bitterly cold winter night accompanying himself on the guitar with his mittens on. Eeta Peeca Pie, Googler and Gaggler, Dippy the Wisp, and Meeney Miney are all residents of Rootabaga Country. They are different forms of alliteration, sound, and euphony.

While each of the adventures in *Rootabaga Stories* is short, Sandburg relates each with infinite patience. The book has no elliptical sentences. Every word is included and often repeated: "The ticket agent was sitting at the window selling railroad tickets the same as always," is redundant, but it is also unsophisticated.

I do not mean to imply the book is composed solely of nonsense syllables. To the contrary, Mrs. Spider in "Molasses and Secret Ambitions" washes clothes wearing a frying pan on her head.

> "Why do you wear that frying pan on your head?" they asked her.
>
> "In this country all ladies wear the frying pan on their head when they want a new hat."
>
> "But what if you want a hat when you are frying with the frying pan?" asked Eeta Peeca Pie.
>
> "That never happens to any respectable lady in this country."
>
> "Don't you never have no new style hat?" asked Meeney Miney.
>
> "No, but we always have new style frying pans every spring and fall."

Throughout these stories Sandburg employs an artless poetry (I believe it is some of his best): "Sometimes on that kind of a January night the stars look like numbers, look like the arithmetic writing of a girl going to school and just beginning arithmetic." All of the poetry, moreover, uses for its materials what can be included in a child's experience.

Rootabaga Country is an American country. It has a railroad, ragpickers, policemen, ball teams, tall grass. It is mapped out. If it existed, you could get to it and find your way around. Geographic reality is what makes the *Rootabaga Stories* the first genuinely American fairy tales.

The stories are fairy tales because the population of Rootabaga Country does not know about social distinction (although they differ one from the other); and because they do not have money (although the Potato Bug Millionaire collects fleems). The stories are American in diction, in foolishness, in fancy, and American in *place.*

Thus, Rootabaga Country is also more than a fairy tale. Rootabaga Country is Carl Sandburg's Main Street, his Yoknapatawpha County, his Gibbsville, Pennsylvania.

American writers have the compulsion to create their own city or place, house by house, street by street, year by year, word by word. The truths they find differ from author to author and from area to area. But calling Rootabaga Country Sandburg's Main Street is more than a historical or literary convenience.

Rootabaga Country (like Galesburg, Illinois, itself) is a good place to live because of the people who inhabit it. Sandburg never fell for the temptation to seize upon this aspect—life in the small town—and use it for ridicule, and do with it what so many other of our writers have done to point out the dullness and the narrowness of the lives and interests of the people. Sinclair Lewis set the fashion with *Main Street,* Sherwood Anderson in *Winesburg, Ohio,* Phil Stong in *Village Tale,* and James Gould Cozzens in *The Last Adam.* All have dealt with the sinister side of small-town life, the dirty stories around the stove of the general store, the love affairs in haystacks, the sadism, and the abnormalities.

Sandburg understood in the strict sense none of this is true. There are such phases of life, of course, even in Galesburg, Illinois, but they are phases. To dwell on them distorts the picture.

Sinclair Lewis's Main Street and Carl Sandburg's Rootabaga Country are more or less contemporary places. *Main Street* was published in 1920, the ***Rootabaga Stories*** in 1922. (***Rootabaga Pigeons*** was published a year later.)

Main Street by Carl's friend, Sinclair Lewis, was a clinical study of the dismal mediocrity in a small northwestern Minnesota town. What made the book important was not so much Lewis's castigation of the American small-town businessman, his lack of manners and his shameful rejection of culture—all of which were true—but rather that Lewis constructed Gopher Prairie. The town was geographically and poetically real—Lewis saw the buttercups bloom in the wagon ruts, and the pools of mud turn to slippery, black lozenges in the winter. Gopher Prairie became more than a town and more than a symptomatic idea—it became a condition of life, a condition of life at a precise time in American history.

Sandburg did not seek the same truths in his Rootabaga Country. He is not clinical, not trying to recreate mediocrity but creating joyousness. All the same Rootabaga Country is a condition prompted by the same causes that led to Main Street.

Rootabaga Country and Main Street are places in an America caught abandoning the old agrarian values with no substitutes for the responsibilities of a new, emerging urban way of life. As a consequence, much of life is irresolved. The citizens of Gopher Prairie

"had lost the power of play as well as the power of impersonal thought." One of Lewis's more sympathetic residents speculates: "I wonder if the small town isn't, with some lovely exceptions, a social appendix? Some day these dull market towns may be as obsolete as monasteries."

It is exactly the power of play and the power of impersonal thought that the citizens of Rootabaga Country will not give up. They had lived in a house, perhaps in Gopher Prairie, "where everything is the same as it always was," and they have begun to ask each other "Who's who? How much? and What's the answer?" Rootabaga Country is an escape from a condition.

It would be foolish to attempt further correlation between these two books. Perhaps I have already tried too hard to force the same reflections out of diverse books with diverse effects written out of diverse reactions. But the process of literature and history does have multiple reflections. Sandburg and Lewis are mirroring the same image at different angles. It is the image of a changing America lacking a plan for the future.

Because the change has been accomplished, because the market town and the farming community are vanishing, the ***Rootabaga Stories*** have all the attributes of a fairy tale. They are about a place the old folks do not remember, and only children can guess at, about a country without money in which children name themselves.

Hazel Durnell

SOURCE: "Other Forms of Literary Achievement," in *The America of Carl Sandburg,* The University Press of Washington, 1965, pp. 28-30.

Like other famous men Sandburg has many sides. The range of his writing widened considerably after his return from Stockholm, for the range of his experience and of his sympathies broadened; to his writings several new vehicles of literary expression were added, and came to fruition about the same time. Upon his return to Chicago he found his three little girls, Margaret, Janet and Helga, rapidly growing up and asking for stories; and he answered by inventing fairy tales—not of kings and queens and princes and castles—but of people and things set against an American background—fairy tales of the Village of Cream Puffs, the Village of Liver and Onions, of the Wedding of the Rag Doll and the Broom Handle, of Potato Face, of Corn Fairies, of Pigs with Bibs on.

His children so enjoyed these improvisations that before long he was prevailed upon to write down the stories and to publish them in book form for the delight of other children. One volume was published in 1922 under the title of **Rootabaga Stories**, in 1923 came the second volume entitled **Rootabaga Pigeons**. The charm of these children's stories has been well expressed by Frank Lloyd Wright, the nationally known architect who included in his autobiography a letter to Carl Sandburg concerning the **Rootabaga Stories**. One paragraph of the letter reads:

> "All of the children that will be born into the Middle West during the next hundred years are peeping at you now, Carl—between little pink fingers, smiling, knowing in their hearts they have found a friend."

To achieve success in fantasy for the young is very difficult; but Sandburg has done so, not only because of his love for children but also because he himself was young at heart. There are morals to be drawn from his fairy tales, such as the vanity of striving for wealth rather than for character building, as found by Slipfoot in **Rootabaga Pigeons**; or of the value of ideals and dreams such as those of the White Horse Girl and the Blue Wind Boy who could look beyond high hills and tough rocks across "blue water as far as the eye could see. And far off the blue waters met the blue sky." For Carl Sandburg is one of the "fireborn" (a phrase from Swedish folk lore) who understands the path of struggle but also the "blue" of happy imagination.

Herbert Mitgang

SOURCE: An introduction to *The Letters of Carl Sandburg,* edited by Herbert Mitgang, Harcourt, Brace & World, Inc., 1968, pp. v-vii.

Across the first six decades of the twentieth century, Carl Sandburg wrote the story of his life and aspects of his times in more than a score of books and thousands of poems, essays, pronunciamentos in the press, and lecturerecitals on the platform.

Only one of his books, **Always the Young Strangers,** was formal autobiography. It took him through his soldiering days in the Sixth Infantry, Illinois Volunteers, during the Spanish-American War. The persona within his creative years can best be discovered by reading his works especially **Chicago Poems, The People, Yes, Home Front Memo**, and the full six-volume Lincoln drama because the special Sandburg vision informed his poetry, reportage, and even a self-revealing biography of a man from Illinois who became President.

The early years and those that followed when he became known up and down the land as a multifaceted writer and performer would have been lost except to the scholar searching for nuggets of life in his books were it not for the letters Carl Sandburg wrote. These letters help to unfold the life story in his own words: the dreams and achievements as a writer, the knowledge he gained by crisscrossing the country and getting to know the American people and landscape, his journalistic and political expression and identity, the friendships and adventures of a literary lifetime.

This selection of his letters [**The Letters of Carl Sandburg,** edited by Herbert Mitgang] is arranged to form its own biographical pattern. (A detailed chronology appears before the letters to pinpoint specific highlights and publications by year.) Notes have been added after many of the letters as background and explanation of correspondents and circumstances at the time of writing. In the choice of letters from several thousand that are available. I have followed these criteria: progression of Sandburg's life and career; significant literary history and friendships; poetic language and thoughts that make letters interesting in themselves.

Stylistically, the aim has been to preserve the integrity of the original letters. Letters are printed in full. For the sake of consistency and clarity, however, these editorial principles have been applied: places and dates all appear at the top of the letters with a locale or date added in brackets when they were not part of the original letter; first or second names and some abbreviations have been added or spelled out within brackets.

Sandburg's special phraseology and word-plays have been retained even where apparently inconsistent. He frequently used a personal shorthand (most often dropping vowels); where clear, words have not been spelled out or explained. Some slips of the typewriter in spelling have been corrected where of no editorial significance to avoid what may otherwise seem to be typographical errors. But, for the most part, personal punctuation, capitalization, and abbreviations appear as he wrote them. In my view, a little mystery is more in keeping with a writer's letters than a lot of *sics.* As a poet, Sandburg employed language in his own way even in letters.

It is fortunate that, while pursuing one of the most productive writing careers, he still managed to keep up his personal correspondence, for the letters explain a great deal about his life and work. I have deliberately included letters of a nonliterary nature, which may seem less than worldshaking, in order to show Sandburg in the round. A democracy of spirit can be revealed in a letter to a secretary as well as to a President.

I began to bank Sandburg reminiscences, useful for these notes, in the course of talks with him in New Salem, Galesburg, Springfield, Chicago, Gettysburg, and Flat Rock during the last ten years. The labors and memories of all the Sandburgs at Connemara Farm made this book inevitable. Recollections by Carl and Paula Sandburg in the course of various conversations, often in the cheerful presence of Janet Sandburg, unearthed details only they knew and accumulated in formidable files and records. Helga Sandburg provided several early letters. Margaret Sandburg is the main authority on the life and works of her father. Her initial research gave this book its impetus and, thereafter, we were fellow detectives tracking down clues for and about letters all over this country and abroad.

Scores of individuals and holding institutions contributed personal letters, whereabouts of other letters, missing dates, facts about events long forgotten. (Their names are listed in the acknowledgments, together with those who gave other assistance.) Less than a handful of persons could not bear to part with their Sandburg letters; some of these turned up in carbons or from other sources. Since this is a selection of letters, not all friends and associates are represented in detail. Undoubtedly the thousands of Sandburg letters will in the future be assembled in "complete letters" spread across several thick volumes. The major letters and the main turns and interests of Sandburg's life are represented here.

"The delay in replying to you was partly that I seem to delay all letters," he writes here to critic Malcolm Cowley, "and the longer I live the more difficulty I find about answering letters, partly on account of time and partly because writing letters too is writing."

Writing letters too is writing.

That is the theme of [*The Letters of Carl Sandburg*]. At the core of this selection of letters is his writing; within the core, Carl Sandburg himself.

Phoebe Pettingell

SOURCE: "The People's Poet," in *The New Leader,* Vol. LXI, No. 5, February 27, 1978, pp. 19-20.

Born 100 years ago, Carl Sandburg was at his death in 1967 one of America's most celebrated and honored authors. The pundits of the poetry world, however, had snubbed him for decades. For the breezy optimism of *Chicago Poems* had preceded *Prufrock and Other Observations* by only one year, and it seemed somewhat out of place in the 20th century. "Ethics and Art cannot be married," cried Conrad Aiken. Robert Frost gleefully reported as someone else's witticism that Sandburg "was the kind of writer who had everything to gain and nothing to lose by being translated into another language." Writing to Sandburg, Ezra Pound agreed that nothing like "jazz rhythms" had ever been seen before in poetry, but politely hinted that it wouldn't hurt to pay a little more attention to tradition: "What I am getting at, is that sometimes your dialect or your argot seems to me not the best way, not the most controlled way but simply the easiest way. . . . If you had the patience to listen to an old maid like myself . . . it would put more weight in your hammer."

Sandburg did not have the patience. "I'm off the literary, even the poetry crowd lately," he announced scornfully to his editor at *Poetry* magazine. "I like my politics straight and prefer the frank politics of the political world to the politics of the literary world." Over the years, as modern criticism discovered from Eliot, and later from Robert Lowell, that Hell is an enervated city much like Boston, Sandburg continued to exhort generations of schoolchildren to believe that the spirit of poetry was incarnate in Chicago—"Laughing the stormy, husky, brawling laughter of Youth, half-naked, sweating, proud to be Hog Butcher, Tool Marker, Stacker of Wheat, Player with Railroad and Freight Handler to the Nation." . . .

His break came in 1914, when Harriet Monroe headlined **"Chicago"** in her experimental magazine, *Poetry.* The opening line ("Hog Butcher for the World"), the journalistic language and the exuberantly brutal depiction of urban low-life grabbed the reader's attention—the poem was unforgettable.

From then on, Sandburg's reputation was assured. Critical disapproval, which has embittered and destroyed many poets, did not ruffle him, because he was always able to hold a popular audience. Over the next 20 years, his volumes—including *Cornhuskers*; *Smoke and Steel*; *Slabs of the Sunburnt West*; *Good Morning, America*; and *The People, Yes*—celebrated the ordinary lives and aspirations of Americans. . . .

Sandburg's strength lay in the vernacular; his "poetic" language could be disastrously bathetic—and often was. "Nearer than any mother's heart wishes / now is heartbreak time," he wrote of the threat of war in 1938. Worse, "The lips of you are with me tonight. / And the arms of you are a circle of white" rivals any entry in a school literary journal for cliché, triteness and awkward syntax. Sandburg remained devoted to a dated imagism, to imitation haiku and to whimsy ("I am an ashcan. I am a sensitive instrument"). Moreover, a Whitmanesque expansionism impelled him to overstate, over-enumerate, over-explain, indeed, to overeverything.

What Sandburg's poetry does not overdo is its deep belief in human dignity. When used for this purpose, his loose forms and plain speech carry the message loud and clear. In **"Breathing Tokens"** he writes: "You must expect to be in several lost causes before you die. / Why blame your father and mother for your being born; how could they help what they were doing?" The poem is an apology for man's unquenchable desire to live, even in adversity, and a plea to experience life as fully as possible:

> *Be sensitized with winter quicksilver below zero.*
> *Be tongs and handles; find breathing tokens.*
> *See where several good dreams are worth dying for.*

Sandburg often proves, in other words, that Ethics and Art *can* be married.

It was, finally, the oversized enthusiasm the poet peddled that kept him out of sympathy with the main poetic influences in an era of pessimism (certain stylistic and philosophical affinities in the work of Allen Ginsburg probably derive less from Sandburg than from the same misreading of their common source— Whitman). But Carl Sandburg may prove to be vindicated. **"Chicago," "Gone," "Jazz Fantazia,"** and parts of that odd socio-poetical study, *The People, Yes,* are doubtless closer to the most readers' idea of modern poetry than anything by Eliot, Stevens, Williams, or Lowell. Who knows when a new populist verse may evolve out of Sandburg's generous and hopeful humanism?

North Callahan

SOURCE: "To the Children and Chickaming," in *Carl Sandburg: His Life and Works,* The Pennsylvania State University Press, 1987, pp. 104-20.

Solidly beneath all the newspaper reporting, writing of advertisements, criticizing of motion pictures, penning of poems, lecturing and music, Sandburg maintained a steadfast interest in Abraham Lincoln. He wrote to Louis Untermeyer: "I aim to write a trilogy about Lincoln one day, to break down all this sentimentalizing about him. It's curious the company Lin-

coln keeps these days. I find his picture on the walls of politicians and big businessmen who do not understand him and probably would not approve of him if they did."

This was to come later, but in the meantime Sandburg in his spare time was putting on paper some of the stories he had told to his children. These materialized in his first book for children, *Rootabaga Stories,* published by Harcourt, Brace in 1922. "I do not know whether Sandburg's *Rootabaga Stories* are well known, and often read by those professionally concerned with children's literature," said Daniel Hoffman. "If they are not well known, they ought to be. For these tales are a minor classic, a successful attempt to make for American children stories conceived in pure delight. Sandburg, who wrote them for his own daughters, made up several dozen tales that are cadenzas upon the child's pleasure in names, in the sounds of words, in the setting loose of fantasy in a village as wide as the sight in a child's eye. . . . Sandburg's fables offer the child a sunny, cheerful world of pure pleasure, with few shadows and no menacing monsters."

These delightful stories demonstrate perhaps more than anything else the originality and remarkable versatility of Carl Sandburg. Here was a man who could change from the heavy rhythms of Walt Whitman and the tragic story of Abraham Lincoln to a whimsical never-never land of children. The *Rootabaga Stories* appear to be simple and easily written, and yet Sandburg himself said they represented the hardest work he ever did. One can describe the stories as beautiful simplicity; but they were carved out of the hard rock of sweat and toil.

Sandburg had read the fairy tales of Hans Christian Andersen but said he could find no equivalent in American literature. "I wanted something more in the American lingo," he explained. "I was tired of princes and princesses and I sought the American equivalent of elves and gnomes. I knew that American children would respond, so I wrote some nonsense tales with American fooling in them." . . .

It seems remarkable that Carl Sandburg could write so many kinds of things, this capacity inspiring the comment that he could write anything. Yet he said that his children's stories were harder to do than anything he ever wrote. "If the people who read books don't like these stories there is no joy left in the world," he rightly said. And this work was a relaxation to him, a joy in his own life that many readers shared. . . .

Evidently there was one young person who was unsure as to what he meant in these stories. From Providence, Rhode Island, came the following letter: "Dear Mr. Sandburg, I am a junior at the Lincoln School and as one of our English assignments we are to write on an American author. Since I have chosen you as my subject I feel that I must ask you the following questions. I have been reading your *Rootabaga Stories* for the first time and to be perfectly frank do not really find their point. I see a good deal of satire and feel that it shows peoples' dissatisfaction with what exists in life. Am I correct in assuming this? If this is true then did you intend the *Rootabaga Stories* for adolescents and adults as well as for children? Sincerely, Ann Adams."

At the bottom of this letter in the Sandburg Collection, he wrote in his own handwriting, "And this smart little snob thinks she's going to get an answer."

On the other hand, there was a more favorable, if adult, impression. Henry Justin Smith, then in 1925 assistant to the president of the University of Chicago, wrote Sandburg that he had had a letter from Ben Hecht in which he said, "Last night I read aloud from the sagas of Master Sandburg—the *Rootabaga Stories*—imitating as well as I could his potent inflections and rabinical pauses. And everything charming that I know of Chicago returned to me. It occurs to me, also, that I must have been strangely preoccupied not to have known how rich the *Rootabaga Stories* were when I first looked at them."

On the eve of publication of *Rootabaga Pigeons*, Sandburg went to New York to discuss his next book with Alfred Harcourt. By this time the writer was proud—and rightly so, for it is a happy time in the author-publisher relationship when the next book becomes an automatic assumption. Harcourt was ready and Sandburg was glad of it. Harcourt well knew that for years Sandburg had been collecting material on Abraham Lincoln—whom some had termed "Father Abraham"—a figure as far removed from children as could be imagined, yet the author had been concentrating on juvenile books.

Perhaps these two entities could be combined, the shrewd Harcourt suggested. Perhaps Sandburg could write a "life of Lincoln for young adults." The idea struck a strong, resonant note in the man who, though he had been portraying youthful characters, doubtless knew that they could "grow up," especially in the person of such an appealing real-life person as "Honest Abe."

Sandburg agreed.

He recalled to Harcourt how in his Galesburg days he had always been fascinated with Lincoln and was reminded of him daily when he passed the Lincoln-Douglas debate plaque on his morning milk route.

And so began the epic struggle with depicting a mighty figure, which was to end in a monumental masterpiece. . . .

One of the most appealing aspects of Sandburg's musical performances was his competent imitation of those represented in his songs. For instance, W. W. Ball, dean of the school of journalism of the University of South Carolina, wrote Sandburg that he had received a letter from a seventy-nine-year-old woman who was born and brought up on a South Carolina plantation. She wrote, "The record of Sandburg's spiritual you sent us is the best imitation of the real Negro voice that I have heard. The Fiske quartet are Negro voices, but trained Negro voices. Robeson's is unusually well trained, but Sandburg's is the natural cornfield Negro voice as I have heard it."

So it was natural that a book would be published containing the songs that Sandburg had collected, especially since he was already an established author. It was *The American Songbag,* published in 1927 by Broadcast Music Inc. of New York, of which Carl Haverlin was president. He was already a friend of Sandburg and had collected all of his books. "I suggested that it be written, and our company published it," Haverlin reminisced. "It has long been recognized that Sandburg is the father of the current interest in American Folk music." Sandburg went to New York to help with the musical volume, and Haverlin recalled to me how Sandburg worked alone in a big room at a long table covered with notes, manuscripts, and photostats. In his mouth he held a stub of an unsmoked cigar, a frequent custom, and an old cap adorned the back of his shaggy head. Now and then he would lean back, close his eyes, and twang a bit on his guitar as he recalled from memory the songs he would try to put down on paper.

TITLE COMMENTARY

📖 *CORNHUSKERS* (1918)

Louis Untermeyer

SOURCE: "Strong Timber," in *The Dial,* Vol. 65, No. 774, October 5, 1918, pp. 263-64.

When Carl Sandburg's *Chicago Poems* appeared two years ago, most of the official votaries and vestrymen in the temple of the Muse raised their hands in pious horror at this open violation of their carefully enshrined sanctities. In the name of their beloved Past, they prepared a bill of particulars that bristled with charges as contradictory as they were varied. They were all united however on one point—Sandburg's brutality. In this they were correct. And without hastening to soften the acknowledgment, I should like to reprint a short passage from J. M. Synge's Poems and Translations to amplify the admission. In a preface to his brief and astringent verses, a preface that might stand as the credo of the new spirit in our literature, Synge wrote:

> In these days poetry is usually a flower of evil or good; but it is the timber that wears most surely, and there is no timber that has not strong roots in the clay and worms. . . . Even if we grant that exalted poetry can be kept successful by itself, the strong things of life are needed in poetry also, to show that what is exalted or tender is not made by feeble blood. It can almost be said that before verse can be human again, it must learn to be brutal.

In England, Masefield was the first of the moderns to fulfill this prophecy and, with half a dozen racy narratives, he took a generation of readers out of the humid atmosphere of libraries and literary hothouses. He took them out into the coarse sunlight and the unchaste air. He brought back to verse that blend of beauty and brutality which is poetry's most human and enduring quality. He rediscovered the rich and almost vulgar vividness that is the lifeblood of Chaucer and Shakespeare, of Burns and Rabelais, of Horace and Heine, of Swift and Villon and all those who were not only great artists but great humanists. He brought a new glamour to poetry; or rather he brought back the oldest glamour, the splendid illusion of a raw and vigorous reality.

And so Sandburg. With a more uncovered directness, he goes straight to his theme. As in *Chicago Poems,* the first poem of his new volume—*Cornhuskers*—brims with an uplifted coarseness, an almost animal exultation that is none the less an exultation.

> I was born on the prairie, and the milk of its
> wheat, the red of its clover, the eyes of its women,
> gave me a song and a slogan.
> Here the water went down, the icebergs slid with
> gravel, the gaps and the valleys hissed, and
> the black loam came.
> Here between the sheds of the Rocky Mountains
> and the Appalachians, here now a morning star fixes
> a fire sign over the timber claims and cow-
> pastures, the corn-belt, the cotton-belt, the cattle
> ranches.

> Here the grey geese go five hundred miles and
> back with a wind under their wings honking the cry
> for a new home.
> Here I know I will hanker after nothing so much
> as one more sunrise or a sky moon of fire
> doubled to a river moon of water.

> The prairie sings to me in the forenoon and I
> know in the night I rest easy in the prairie arms, on
> the prairie heart.

These are the opening lines of Prairie, a wider and more confident rhythm than Sandburg has yet attempted. The gain in power is evident at once and grows with each section of this new collection. The tone in *Cornhuskers* has more depth and dignity; the note is not louder, but it is larger. In *Chicago Poems* there were times when the poet was so determined to worship ruggedness that one could hear his adjectives strain to achieve a physical strength of their own. One occasionally was put in mind of the professional strong man in front of a mirror, of virility basking in the spotlight, of an epithet exhibiting its muscle. Here the accent is less vociferous, more vitalizing; it is a summoning of strong things rather than the mere stereotypes of strength. Observe the unusual athletic beauty of **"Leather Leggings," "Always the Mob," "The Four Brothers,"** and this muscular **"Prayers of Steel"**:

> Lay me on an anvil, O God.
> Beat me and hammer me into a crowbar.
> Let me pry loose old walls.
> Let me lift and loosen old foundations.

> Lay me on an anvil, O God.
> Beat and hammer me into a steel spike.
> Drive me into the girders that hold a skyscraper to-
> gether.
> Take red-hot rivets and fasten me into the central gird-
> ers.
> Let me be the great nail holding a skyscraper through
> blue nights into white stars.

These and a dozen others seem a direct answer to Whitman's hope of a democratic poetry that would express itself in a democratic and even a distinctively American speech. He maintained that before America could have a powerful poetry our poets would have to learn the use of hard and powerful words; the greatest artists, he insisted, were simple and direct, never merely "polite or obscure." "Words are magic . . . limber, lasting, fierce words," he wrote in an unfinished sketch for a projected lecture. "Do you suppose the liberties and the brawn of These States have to do only with delicate lady-words? with gloved gentlemen-words?" Later he said, "American writers will show far more freedom in the use of names. Ten thousand common and idiomatic words are growing, or are today already grown, out of which vast numbers could be used by American writers—words that would be welcomed by the nation, being of the national blood."

No contemporary is so responsive to these limber and idiomatic phrases as Sandburg. His language lives almost as fervidly as the life from which it is taken. And yet his intensity is not always raucous; it would be a great mistake to believe that Sandburg excels only in verse that is heavy-fisted and stentorian. What could be quieter and yet more vigorous than the suggestive Interior, the calm irony in **"Malice to None,"** the solemn simplicity of **"Grass,"** or the strange requiem note in **"Cool Tombs"**?

> When Abraham Lincoln was shoveled into the tombs, he forgot the copperheads and the assassin . . . in the dust, in the cool tombs.
>
> And Ulysses Grant lost all thought of con men and Wall Street, cash and collateral turned ashes . . . in the dust, in the cool tombs.
>
> Pocahontas' body, lovely as a poplar, sweet as a red haw in November or a paw-paw in May, did she wonder? does she remember? . . . in the dust, in the cool tombs?
>
> Take any streetful of people buying clothes and groceries, cheering a hero or throwing confetti and blowing tin horns . . . tell me if the lovers are losers . . . tell me if any get more than the lovers . . . in the dust . . . in the cool tombs

This creative use of proper names and slang (which would so have delighted Whitman), this interlarding of cheapness and nobility is Sandburg's most characteristic idiom as well as his greatest gift. And it is this mingling that enriches his heritage of mingled blood; the rude practical voice of the American speaks through a strain of ruder Swedish symbolism. Beneath the slang, one is aware of the mystic; (*Cornhuskers* shows a cosmic use of penetrating patois; it is Swedenborg in terms of State Street.) This mysticism shines out of **"Caboose Thoughts," "Wilderness," "Southern Pacific," "Old Timers."** And it is always a more extended and musical spirituality than the earlier volume; the new collection may not be more dynamic, but it is more lyric.

The struggles, the social criticism, the concentrated anger, and the protests are here as prominently as in *Chicago Poems,* but they assert themselves with less effort. The war has temporarily harmonized them; they are still rebellious, but somehow resigned. The chants of revolt are seldom out of tune with Sandburg's purely pictorial pieces. Both are the product of a strength that derives its inspiration from the earth; they are made of tough timber; they have "strong roots in the clay and worms."

O. W. Firkins

SOURCE: A review of *Cornhuskers,* in *The Nation,* New York, Vol. CVIII, No. 2792, January 4, 1919, p. 21.

The Vulcan that Mr. Sandburg was, or chose to appear, in *Chicago Poems* is curiously softened in his new book, *Cornhuskers.* The difference between the two volumes is the difference between black smoke and blue. Black smoke is malign; blue smoke is idyllic. Mr. Sandburg is not quite ready for idyls; his "Evangeline" is not yet in type: but give him time, prosperity, and another rosy-cheeked little girl or so, and he will write it. Even *Cornhuskers* is a fairly amiable and happy book, with compunctious reversions to old-time severity. Between hay-mow and swimming-pool, Summer, the baggage, wins us even in a capitalistic world. The grassy bank might tempt another man, but we are revolutionists; and revolutionists, when they see grass, think of nothing but the aristocrat who bade the people eat it.

Mr. Sandburg has that *general* sense of the tremendousness of his own experience which is so stirring to its possessor and so little stirring to anybody else in the absence of confirmative particulars. He is always hurrying to a rendezvous with Apollo. Apollo's eagerness is less conspicuous than Mr. Sandburg's. The god, spoiled in childhood by a diet of Greek hexameters, finds perhaps something not quite palatable in the half-cooked free verse with which Mr. Sandburg garnishes his board. For all that, Mr. Sandburg has his good moments, his lease of inspiration, his dole of phrase. He can say prettily enough, "The sun rises and the sun sets in her eyes," and forcibly enough (of the lower instincts in man), "I am the keeper of the Zoo." But often, very often, he plans effects which he cannot execute; inspiration is unattainable, and he is left in the energetic but mortifying posture of the man who vehemently flags an inattentive train. I will add the fact that for me Mr. Sandburg is a studious, though hardly a skilful, writer; his very cat-calls are premeditated.

I like him best in the upright and generous mood which dictated the following words: "Out of white lips a question: Shall seven million dead ask for their blood a little land for the living wives and children, a little land for the living brothers and sisters?"

📖 *SLABS OF THE SUNBURNT WEST* (1922)

The New York Times Book Review

SOURCE: "Sandburg's Virile Slabs," in *The New York Times Book Review,* June 4, 1922, p. 11.

No estimate of Carl Sandburg's work is possible without immediate mention of his virile note, and this is a regrettable manner, for it denotes an insistence on a certain attitude toward life that becomes an obsession after a time. It is all very well to be virile. Kipling is virile. So is Sir Henry Newbolt, and so is Walt Whitman. But virility is implicit in their nature. Without the virile note they would not be Kipling and Newbolt and Whitman. They would be nothing at all. Carl Sandburg, too, is virile, but he lapses so often into a quiet, careful note that his virility sticks out all the more when we meet it upon the printed page. In other words, his emphasis upon virility becomes too forced, too conscious; the reader is unpleasantly aware of the fact that Carl Sandburg is saying to himself, "I will be virile. I will write in slang. I will show them that I can hack off slabs of the sunburnt West and juggle them in the air."

Slabs of the Sunburnt West is a book of decided merit, but its highest excellence comes not in the virile portions, but in those quieter, more restrained moments, when a poet, rather unkempt, it is true, naturally flows out of Carl Sandburg. He is already in danger of becoming the Professional Chanter of Virility, and this is too bad, for he certainly has an individual utterance to give America that well may be choked in this emphatic attitude. There are three long poems in this latest book. The best of these is **"And So Today,"** a poem written about the parade and ceremonies attendant upon the burial of the Unknown Soldier in Washington. There is a bitter note here that makes itself manifest in spite of a lack of cohesion in the poem as a whole. Such passages as the following, for instance, may be gruesome, but they awaken a terrible seriousness in the reader:

> Down Pennsylvania Avenue today the riders go,
> men and boys riding horses, roses in their teeth,
> stems of roses, rose leaf stalks, rose-dark leaves—
> the line of the green ends in a red rose flash.
>
> Skeleton men and boys riding skeleton horses,
> the rib-bones shine, the rib-bones curve,
> shine with savage, elegant curves—
> a jawbone runs with a long white arch,
> bone triangles click and rattle,
> elbows, ankles, white line slants—

> shining in the sun, past the White House.
> past the Treasury Building, Army and Navy Buildings,
> on to the mystic white Capitol Dome—
> so they go down Pennsylvania Avenue today,
> skeleton men and boys riding skeleton horses,
> stems of roses in their teeth,
> rose-dark leaves at their white jaw-slants—
> and a horse laugh question nickers and whinnies.
> moans with a whistle out of horsehead teeth:
> why? who? where?

The other two long poems, **"The Windy City,"** a chant for Chicago that is hardly sustained throughout but which contains many a fine passage, and **"Slabs of the Sunburnt West,"** a song of the West that exhibits Carl Sandburg experiencing an ethical unrest that grows a little vague at times, are pieces that we could not well do without, but yet they leave the unpleasant impression that Sandburg could have done them so much better if he had approached his subjects with a more coherent and consistent scheme.

The shorter poems, more vivid in their colorful beauty, are nearly always successful. One begins to wonder if Sandburg is not at his best in these short snatches, if there is not something wrong in the way he handles longer poems. Possibly he does not have the gift of sustaining his magic. He is essentially a poet of moods—and moods, of course, are never very long. They are perfect minutes. How excellent is **"Hoof Dusk,"** for instance.

> The dusk of this box wood
> is leather gold, buckskin gold,
> and the hoofs of a dusk goat
> leave their heel marks on it.
>
> The cover of this wooden box
> is a last-of-the-sunset red,
> a red with a sandman sand
> fixed in evening siftings—
> late evening sands are here.
>
> The gold of old clocks,
> forgotten in garrets,
> hidden out between battles
> of long wars and short wars,
> the smoldering ember gold
> of old clocks found again—
> here is the small smoke fadeout
> of their slow loitering.
>
> Feel me with your fingers,
> measure me in fire and wind:
> maybe I am buckskin gold, old clock gold,
> late evening sunset sand—
>   Let go
>   and loiter
>   in the smoke fadeout.

Clement Wood

SOURCE: "A Homer from Hogwallow," in *The Nation*, New York, Vol. CXV, No. 2977, July 26, 1922, pp. 96-7.

Carl Sandburg strays further than any American poet from the accepted poetic vocabulary. In this small volume page after page erupts with "humdinger," "flooey," "phizzogs," "fixers," "frame-up," "four-flushers," "rakeoff," "getaway," "junk," "fliv," "fake," "come clean," "get 'em bumped off," "a 44-gat," "galoot," "gazook," "gabby mouth," "hoosegow," "teameo," "work plug," "lovey," "slew him in," "bull," "jazz," "scab," "stiffs," "hanky-pank," "hokum," "bum," "buddy," "booze," including two pages hashed brown in this fashion:

> You're trying to crab my act.
> You poor fish, you mackerel,
> You haven't got the sense God
> Gave an oyster—it's raining—
> What you want is an umbrella. . . .
>
> Hush baby!
> Shoot it,
> Shoot it all,
> Coo coo, coo coo.

"This," says the poet, "is one song of Chicago." One page later he has reached another song:

> Venice is a dream of soft waters, Vienna and Bagdad recollections of dark spears and wild turbans; . . .
> Berlin sits amid white scrubbed quadrangles and torn arithmetics and testaments; Moscow brandishes a flag and repeats a dance figure of a man who walks like a bear.
> Chicago fished from its depths a text: Independent as a hog on ice.

Any poetling might have called Venice a dream of soft waters, and evoked Bagdad in a clash of spears and a swivet of turbans; many a pen could have done as well with Moscow as Sandburg does; but only a poet of high rank could have caught that amazing flashlight of verity, Berlin sitting beside her steps scrubbed clean, "amid torn arithmetics and testaments." As for Chicago, Sandburg once called her, "Hog Butcher for the World." "As independent as a corpse" is quite an idea; its utility as a metaphor is increased, if we make it the corpse of a hog. It is a cold, clammy metaphor for a city, at that; it might be livelier. Yet what is the Homer of Hogwallow to do but chronicle faithfully his city's battle-cry?

It is easy to read any page of the book to yourself, or aloud, and decide confidently: Not a line of poetry there! It is no harder to read it in an altered, rarer mood, in which the page possesses, suffuses you, and wakes you to the high delight that flowers only when poetry is the bud. This is the paradox of Sandburg: if you are attuned, receptive, you lay him down with the same emotional thrill that comes from reading Robinson or Robert Frost, De La Mare or Elinor Wylie; yet when you inspect his slang-dipped lines, none of the accustomed road-signs to magic and beauty are to be found—only detours pointing to shanty-towns and hog-pens. One quality he has, a taut-lipped, double-fisted fighting quality:

> The strong men keep coming on.
> They go down shot, hanged, sick, broken.
> They live on fighting, singing, lucky as plungers.
> The strong mothers pulling them on . . .
> The strong mothers pulling them from a dark sea,
> a great prairie, a lone mountain.
> Call hallelujah, call amen, call deep thanks.
> The strong men keep coming on.

The sardonic reverse of this is given in **"At the Gate of Tombs"**:

> If any fool, babbler, gabby mouth, stand up
> and say: Let us make a civilization where the
> sacred and beautiful things of toil and genius
> shall last—
>
> If any such noisy gazook stands up and makes
> himself heard—put him out—tie a can on him—
> Lock him up in Leavenworth—shackle him in the
> Atlanta hoosegow—let him eat from the tin dishes
> at Sing Sing—slew him in as a lifer at San Quentin.

The modest publisher's announcement describes these as "lovely lyrics." The book contains three longish poems, **"The Windy City"**; **"And So Today"**, taking its theme from the burial of the Unknown Soldier; and the title poem. The poet's method does not always succeed. This description of a canyon, from the title poem, is an exhibit:

> An arm-chair for a one-eyed giant,
> two pine trees grow in the left arm of the chair;
> a blue-jay comes, sits, goes, comes again;
> a blue-jay shoots and twitters . . . out and across . . .
> tumbled sky-scrapers and wrecked battleships,
> walls of crucifixions and wedding breakfasts;
> ruin, ruin—a brute gnashed, dug, kept on—
> kept on and quit: and this is It.

But there are rare penetrative flashes that reward the searcher: "the fang cry, the rip claw hiss, the slant of the slit eyes waiting"; "the snouts of the hungry hunting storms"; "so many stars and so few hours to dream"; "red rivers to cross"; "the plows sunk their teeth in."

When we seek to unlock the paradox and unriddle the spell, there is perhaps a real kinship with such workers as Mrs. Wylie, Mr. Frost, Mr. Robinson—a kinship in word-selection. These poets slice away all padding, all adiposity, until at times even the skeleton is nicked. Sandburg, despite his apparent verbal freshets, is a word artist with the best. Deeper than that, his themes are well chosen: they are vital, stark, fit to evoke that thrill that comes from poetry. Having chosen such a theme, this poet usually clothes it in a fish-peddler's patches, or a miner's overalls, ore-stained, blood-stained—a motley of brutality and slang. Thus it comes to us: if we judge solely by appearances, it is slang, crudity, a ramp-rat, an eeler. If we hear it with intent ear, the theme behind comes with its thrill—a thrill the more effective because so unexpected. The effect is that of a perverse imp masking poetry behind the face of a gargoyle.

Once I visited an old gentlewoman who was persuaded to exhibit to me her cut-paper masterpieces. Out of a square-yard of wrapping paper she had snipped and snipped hundreds of fragments. Examined closely, it was patternless, meaningless. Two neighbors held it against the wall; it was still a crazy-quilt of little holes. I was told to walk to the wall across, and turn. The paper now revealed the head of Christ. Again, the Big Dipper is only a dipper from our Gopher Prairie in the starry plains; and as the Dipper's stars are in two streams moving past each other, all likeness to a dipper will vanish at last. So with the poetry of Sandburg. Seen rightly, it is a dipper, and not a cubist lollipop; seen from the right distance, with the right eyes, it is no habble-gabble of nothingness; it possesses that kinship to the divine that breathes through all poetry.

Mr. Sandburg's method, including his vocabulary, limits his audience today, and does more to his lovers of tomorrow. For slang is last night's toadstool growth; some of it is trodden underfoot before the page that uses it leaves the presses. A few of its current phrases will enrich the persisting language; most will not. Whitman, by the use of unfamiliar rhythms, delayed his recognition, and has never reached the crowd he sought; Sandburg uses rhythms as unfamiliar, and a vocabulary that tomorrow will speak only to the archaeologist. The college curriculums of 1950 may bracket his work with *Beowulf* and the *Ancren Riwle*, as Old American or Early Hogwallowan. It will take unusual vitality to overcome this handicap. In any case, he is uniquely himself, penetrating, courageous, heartening. Among our peak poets are many who see life as "still a darkening hill to climb." Their outlook bars them from the loftiest flights; he who has lost faith sinks, as Peter sank. And Carl Sandburg is full of faith: of theirs is the kingdom of song.

ROOTABAGA STORIES (1922; REPRINTED IN 1988, 1994)

The New York Times Book Review

SOURCE: A review of *Rootabaga Stories,* in *The New York Times Book Review,* November 19, 1922, p. 10.

In this book, to which may be applied all those moth-eaten terms of quaint, whimsical and unusual, Carl Sandburg has developed a new field in American fairy-tale conception. He has gone to the American prairies, to the Middle West towns and cities, to the great American corn belt, and conceived a series of tales that smack mightily of American soil. Even to the cadences of his prose, so often implicit of poetry, the reader will find an American spirit. Such tales as those of the Potato Faced Blind Man and his friend, Any Ice Today, or that of Gimme the Ax and his two children, Please Gimme and Ax Me No Questions, or (to mention, another) the story of the animals who traveled from Philadelphia to Medicine Hat to get back their tails, could have been conceived in no other locale than the United States. Particularly is this true of the tale of the Sky Scrapers who had a child. Mr. Sandburg's book is a genuine addition to the season's literature.

The Dial

SOURCE: A review of *Rootabaga Stories,* in *The Dial,* Vol. 74, No., February, 1923, p. 210.

Children may be interested, but adult admirers of Mr Sandburg will find with regret that his ***Rootabaga Stories*** lack his customary pith and sting; they do not come off. Apparently they have been provided with the tinder of imagination, which, however, has required much blowing upon before it has taken fire. The plan is apparently to idealize into fairy tales certain items already familiar to household life; there is the Village of Liver-and-Onions, and characters like Gimme-the-Ax, Any Ice Today, the Potato Faced Blind Man, Hot Dog the Tiger, the Rusty Rats, and so on, who turn out, when all is over, not to mean a great deal. It ought to work out well, no doubt, but the result has rather the effect of a sultry blast from some forced draft theory of nursery education, than a book of ingenuous cool tales for children.

📖 *ROOTABAGA PIGEONS* (1923)

The New Republic

SOURCE: "Back to Rootabaga," in *The New Republic,* Vol. 36, No. 467, November 14, 1923, p. 313.

More tales of the Rootabaga country! It is a source of real delight that Mr. Sandburg brings to the children another revelation of that whimsical, altogether delightful land—the heart of their own America.

There is, it is true, the same unevenness of tone and material that was found in the first volume. A few of the stories have a stronger appeal for the child who grew up than for the child who is still in the process of growing. But it would be an unforgivable calamity to miss the best of both volumes.

Some of the faces are familiar. Blixie Blimber reappears and the Potato Face Blind Man tells new stories of true poetic vision—among them how it is that Slipfoot "nearly always never gets what he goes after" and why the lovely Deep Red Roses "decide to wait until tomorrow to decide again what to decide." Here too is the unforgettable Bozo the Button Buster who bursts off buttons every time he draws breath to boast, and who, when he meets the fate of all idle boasters, is found to be nothing but a heap of empty clothes and meaningless buttons.

It is from Hot Balloons and his two daughters Dippy the Wisp and Slip Me Liz we learn how the Shampoo River may be crossed into the Rootabaga Country. But the simplest way of all to reach it is to bury yourself deep within the covers of the books. And the most unhappy fate would be to get a slipfoot before you arrived there.

Anne Carroll Moore

SOURCE: "The Rootabaga Country," in *The Nation,* New York, Vol. CXVII, No. 3048, December 5, 1923, pp. 651-52.

Critics of children's books are notoriously skeptical or gullible concerning second volumes of popular story books. More often than not—without apparent reading of the book—they are able to say of it either that it is distinctly inferior to the author's first book or that he has "done it again," and nothing comparable has appeared since *Alice in Wonderland* or *Hans Andersen's Fairy Tales.* To one or both of these great classics it is the common habit of American reviewers to contrast all new children's books without regard to content, form, or atmosphere. One critic feels that *Rootabaga Pigeons* bears to *Rootabaga Stories* a relation similar to that borne by Lewis Carroll's second volume of *"Sylvie and Bruno"* to the first.

No such parallel exists in the case of Sandburg. The stories in *Rootabaga Pigeons* were, with one or two exceptions, written long before *Rootabaga Stories* was published. Carl Sandburg had been writing these stories for years just as they came into his mind. He had written enough of them to make two books. Whether two books or one should have been made of the stories is an open question. The situation is that we have two books of his stories—one published last year, one this year—which are equally entitled to fresh, full, and fair consideration for all the nonsense, the folk stuff, the poetry, the beauty, and the genuine child psychology they hold.

Carl Sandburg alone could tell us which of the stories was written first. Does it matter? Are we not more deeply concerned with the nature and quality of his performance in both books?

It is true that the lightning of discovery rarely strikes a reader twice in the same place and those who were fortunate enough to read and like **"How They Broke Away to Go to the Rootabaga Country"** first will doubtless look in vain for any story in *Rootabaga Pigeons* to give them quite the same delicious sensation.

That story was wisely placed first in the first book. It either transports you straight into the Rootabaga Country or it leaves you high and dry where "everything is the same as it always was." There's no half-way station to Rootabaga. You go all the way or you don't go at all. If you go, you are delighted to meet bushel baskets going and coming, saying under their breath: "Bushels, bushels, bushels." It's just what one would expect a bushel basket to be saying, only in this day of records no one has ever recorded it before.

Sandburg's nonsense is fresh nonsense. If pressed for a comparison I would say that he has more in common with Edward Lear than with any other writer for children, but he is not an imitator of anybody and I think it would be impossible to imitate him successfully, for there's an essential truth to the life he knows behind all his stories. Many of them have the quality and charm of an artist's first sketch. Some of them were manifestly not written for children. When Carl Sandburg makes the selection from the two books for a definitive volume of American folk and nonsense stories for children he will have the unusual advantage of knowing which of his stories appeal to children.

Do children really like the stories? Some children do, other children do not. Children have as varied tastes in reading as we do. The children on whom they have been "tried out" by parents or teachers who actively dislike the stories are seldom attracted to them, and no wonder.

"Are you reading out of that book?" I asked a little girl of half-past four. She was looking at the picture of the Potato Face Blind Man playing his accordion in front of the post office.

"Yes, I read about the Potato Face Blind Man. He's playing to the flummywisters yodeling their yisters in the elm trees. They do that out in my yard. I love that Potato Face Blind Man. I read about the Zizzies too. They're so funny. The Zizzies make me laugh." And this little New England nonsense lover, who was born "funny inside," laughed as only a child can laugh who is not yet able to read in the accepted sense. Then she said, as she put the book into my hands, "You read it to me."

"I've never read a book anything like it before," said a twelve-year-old New York boy. "I tried to read the Wedding Procession of the Rag Doll and the Broom Handle aloud and I had to stop I laughed so. There's a whole lot of things I never knew about the West in those stories."

There's still more about the West in *Rootabaga Pigeons*—a little too much perhaps in the keenly satirical story of the Sooners and the Boomers. There are paragraphs in that story which might well be eliminated from a children's book.

But I do not propose to offer any idle, captious criticism of a book which contains, as I believe, so much genuine creative art as is to be found in *Rootabaga Pigeons.* I may not like it better than the first book; certainly I found no more beautiful story than the White Horse Girl and the Blue Wind Boy, and I find *Rootabaga Pigeons* containing stories of more universal appeal, mellower, closer to children, happier in title, and positively charged with the best kind of child psychology.

The story of the Christmas twins born out in a tar-paper shack in a cinder yard holds for me something of that same deep experience of American life, its romance, its humor, its tenderness, its pathos, its playing the game, that Mark Twain began to draw upon when he wrote *Tom Sawyer* and *Huckleberry Finn.*

I'm not comparing Sandburg with Mark Twain. I'm only saying he's writing fresh and very beautiful stories of American life for a new generation of Americans—stories which are bound to influence other writers for children because they stir and challenge the creative faculties of their readers.

📖 *ABRAHAM LINCOLN: THE PRAIRIE YEARS* (1927)

Mark Van Doren

SOURCE: A review of *Abraham Lincoln: The Prairie Years,* in *The Nation*, New York, Vol. CXXII, No. 3162, February 10, 1926, p. 149.

The key to *Abraham Lincoln: The Prairie Years,* by Carl Sandburg is a sentence in the preface. "The folklore Lincoln," says Mr. Sandburg, "the maker of stories, the stalking and elusive Lincoln is a challenge for any artist." Or, if it is not that sentence, it is another one quoted later on from Carlyle, who, writing to Emerson concerning the invasion of the West by Yankees "with most occult unsubduable fire in their belly," broke out: "Oh, if we were not a set of Cant-ridden blockheads, there is no myth of Athene of Herakles equal to this fact;—which I suppose will find its real 'Poets' some day or other; when once the Greek, Semitic, and multifarious other cobwebs are swept away a little!" It is Sandburg the artist, the epic poet, who has attacked this largest and most complicated of all American subjects—the subject being, of course, not merely Lincoln himself, though Lincoln was complicated enough, but in addition the whirlpool of cultures out of which he was flung into fame. Nor does Mr. Sandburg seem to believe that he has finished the job. As Standish O'Grady's *History of Ireland* spaded up legends for Yeats and Synge to cultivate, so this epic in the rough will turn the pens of coming poets, it is implied, in fruitful directions. "Perhaps poetry, art, human behavior in this country, which has need to build on its own traditions, would be served by a life of Lincoln stressing the fifty-two years previous to his Presidency."

I should hasten to say that although I find Mr. Sandburg's book amply and profoundly beautiful I find it so in spite of some rather obvious "poetry" stuck in here and there. "Beyond Indiana was something else," we are told—something much more vague, I suspect, than anything in Lincoln's mind ever was. It is annoying to hear from page to page in the first volume of some tender transcendental want that "still lived in him, lived far under in him, in the deeper blue pools of him." There is no harm in a paragraph like that which ends the thirty-sixth chapter:

> If a blizzard stopped blowing and the wind went down, with the white curve of a snow floor over

Salem Hill looking up to a far blue scoop of winter stars blinking white and gold, with loneliness whispering to loneliness, a man might look on it and feel organization and testimony in the movement of the immense, relentless hubs and sprockets on the sky.

But, in view of Mr. Sandburg's general purpose, there is no particular good in it either.

For the poetry Mr. Sandburg was after, I take it, was the poetry immanent in the facts. And on facts—thousands of them—he ultimately rests his excellent case. He seems to have done an immense amount of what for him was the right kind of research. He walked and talked through the many towns of Kentucky, Indiana, and Illinois where people had known Lincoln. He explored, I am sure, all of the Lincoln literature which had something personal to tell. He read bundles of letters and ran his hands over shelves containing mementos. He pushed his mind to the outermost limits of the world which was to influence Lincoln and which he was to influence—the world of European and American politics, industry, travel, science, letters, religion, and art. He familiarized himself with distant contemporaries—Audubon, Melville, Emerson, P. T. Barnum, Walt Whitman. Then he drew his imagination back to make itself at home in the civilization which actually shaped Lincoln, or helped to shape him. Here is God's plenty indeed. Here is the lining of the old Mid-Western mind. Here are the songs all people sang, the poems they recited, the proverbs they spoke, the superstitions they could not discard, the machines they used, the clothes they wore, the facts they learned in the newspapers, the gods they swore by, the dishes they ate, the jests they laughed at. As Mr. Sandburg goes on he becomes drunk with data, and in true Homeric fashion compiles long lists of things. "Orchards were being planted with new kinds of apple trees, Winter Sweets, Red Streaks, Red Russets, Yellow Hearts, Rainbows." "And there were horses, and men riding and driving who loved horses . . . roans, grays, whites, black horses with white stockings, sorrels with a sorrel forelock down a white face, bays with a white star in the forehead. . . . They spoke of one-horse towns, one-horse lawyers, and one-horse doctors—even of one-horse horse doctors."

Of Mr. Sandburg's picture of Lincoln himself—Lincoln inside and out—it is more difficult to speak. I prefer to leave it quite unspoiled. Few men and women are truly mysterious. Lincoln was, and in my opinion Mr. Sandburg has presented the elements of that mystery more subtly and more completely than I have ever seen them presented before. Jasper Conant

recorded that as he began to paint the candidate for President in 1860 "there came over his face the most marvelously complex expression I have ever seen." Mr. Sandburg comes as near as any man could come to telling why.

John Drinkwater

SOURCE: "An American Epic," in *The Saturday Review of Literature,* Vol. 2, No. 35, March 27, 1926, p. 659.

Mr. Sandburg's is a big book: big in a literal sense. And the practised reader of big books finds that he can generally measure the quality of a work after covering the first few pages, or at most a chapter or two. He may have to wait until the end before he knows whether or not he agrees with general conclusions and whether the governing design has been fitly carried out, but early in his perusal he knows, or thinks he knows, whether there is distinction or fumbling. Mr. Sandburg's *Abraham Lincoln* should warn him against any such agreeable securities. In less than twenty pages, two impressions have asserted themselves. This is obviously a book, we feel, created out of long and patient love; that is well, and the impression remains, as we shall see. But also we are from time to time, even in twenty pages, brought up short in our appreciation by such passages as this of Lincoln's mother before he was born: "And the smell of wild crab-apple blossom, and the low crying of all wild things, came keen that summer to the nostrils of Nancy Hanks." Is it possible, we ask ourselves, that the bleak poet of Chicago can really be falling to this romantic frippery? And then as we read on we find ourselves confronted by a very strange problem of style. For page by page, as such notes recur, we find that this is not romantic frippery at all, but a quite sincere, and cumulatively very touching reversion of a mind, closely disciplined in an almost savage candor, to a natural grace and leniency of sentiment. Confronted by epic character or action, we find, this least compromising of realists can stand up and prophesy with revivalist fervor. And the arresting thing, so genuine is the reality behind his voluble moods, is that he can make this rhetoric a natural modulation of his style. At first we suspect that crab-apple blossom and the crying of the wild things; but very soon we are convinced that they are conceived in an utter simplicity of faith, that they are a complement to the concrete, direct contacts that account for the more familiar aspect of Mr. Sandburg's manner, and we remain so convinced to the end. In such passages he uses what is perhaps the most dangerous of all figures in writing, and as one follows another at appointed intervals we are persuaded that he uses it with entire success.

Mr. Sandburg has been at this work for half a lifetime; it runs to nearly a thousand large and closely printed pages. A brief review can do no more than suggest something of the effect produced by a careful reading. The story covers the years from Lincoln's birth in 1809 until the time when he left Springfield for Washington in 1860. It is more than a biography of Lincoln in those years, it is a minutely elaborated study of the environment in which he grew up and matured, of the social, political, and natural forces that went to the shaping of his character, and of the far-reaching and profoundly significant implications of that character itself. It is, in fact, a comprehensive survey of the development, at once romantic and stark, of middle western America, with Illinois as the centre of the action.

Mr. Sandburg's method is a daring one. At first it may seem that his narrative has little or no consecutive design. His way is to present a scene, a social order, the shaping of political conflict of ideals, or the play of individual character, by means of a rapid succession of images and anecdotes. To read a few pages only of his book would inevitably be to feel that while these impressions separately were effective enough, they were not very strictly selected or combined to a fixed purpose. But to read on is to discover, again, that this view is wrong, and that Mr. Sandburg is using his means steadily to the accomplishment of an elaborately conceived work of art. To make a personal confession, I am a very slow reader, and having in my time absorbed some dozens of volumes about Lincoln I never expected to be beguiled by Mr. Sandburg or anyone else into reading another thousand pages on the matter. But I began to read these volumes and found henceforth that there was no escape, and I have gone on to the end with a growing admiration for a work that slowly reveals itself not only as big in compass but as absorbing in conception and achievement. Chapter by chapter— there are a hundred and sixty-eight of them—Mr. Sandburg convinces us of his skill in handling immense masses of detail. Pioneer life, the spread of population and the assembling of races, the progress of agriculture and industry, finance and the railroads, the ramifications of slavery and abolition, the courage, the disasters and the subtleties of personality, the loneliness and the horizons of a new nation, the drama of men and women looking westward into the wilderness and eastward to old civilization, the quarrels of politicians and the visions of statesmen, all these and countless other circumstances Mr. Sandburg marshals with the industry and the intuition of

genius. And always governing this patient and absorbing argument is the figure of Lincoln, realized here as I believe it has never been realized before, the creation of a perfect blending of historical knowledge with imagination. It is not too much to say that Mr. Sandburg's book is an honor no less to the American people than to himself; it is, indeed, not unlikely that he will be found to have given the world the first great American epic.

Henry McBride

SOURCE: "The Lincoln of the Plains," in *The Dial*, Vol. 80, June 1926, pp. 513-16.

Mr Carl Sandburg, in his new Life, shows a tendency to tell everything, to stand for everything. He admits the shady stories, glories in them. Every man in America knows and always has known that Lincoln had a passion for *risqué* stories but it would have been as much as a Memorial-Day orator's life was worth to have so much as hinted at such a thing. Mr Sandburg does more than hint. He helps you to identify the anecdotes. He admits, too, the shambling gait, the shabby clothes, the rustic speech. Heavens, in restoring to us "our Abe" what does he not ask us to accept as Abe's idiom! The "Mr Cheerman," alas, was *véridique*. Also, he said "idee" for "idea," and "r-a-a-ly" for "really." Well; what of it? Are you laughing? With sympathy, I hope. If not, you may clear out of this, Mr Sandburg's story is not for you. In your innocence did you think you and Henry James had outgrown your accents? Of course Abe had his. All Americans have accents and always will have. The fastidious Edward Fitzgerald felt one even in the tales of Poe. He never denied the man genius but said he couldn't stand the rusticity of the English and had to read the tales in French translations.

Mr Sandburg aims, in short, to give you the complete Lincoln. The emasculated version so much in favour with Civil War veterans is now quite as dilapidated as they are, and the new era requires a more lively image. This is it, and may remain it, unless a sharp Stendhalian intellect comes along to put more emphasis upon the Lincoln brain than this writer does. Lincoln had, by the way, one of the requisites Stendhal insisted upon for geniuses, a sturdy memory. He said himself, "My mind is like a piece of steel— very hard to scratch anything on it, and almost impossible after you get it there to rub it out." Mr Sandburg intended to keep himself out of the picture and very nearly does so. He meant, in these two big volumes, to give everything that went to the making of the man; the landscape, the forbears, the pioneer existence, the gradual softening of conditions, the electioneering, the preaching, the seething moral ferment that finally produced the Rebellion; and he succeeds astonishingly well. He succeeds best with the landscape and what may be called the Lincoln "atmosphere," the thousand and one little details of pioneer conditions that had so much to do with forming Lincoln's famous "common sense." He makes long lists, in Walt Whitman's best style, of everything in the early life. There is a considerable passage enumerating all the slang names for the whiskey of the period, advertisements of everything in the country store, and every little rough-and-tumble village fight is gone into enthusiastically. The atmosphere, indeed, is laid in plentifully and at times obviously. At any recurrence of the word "nature," Mr Sandburg stops a moment and puts some in. When the young Abraham Lincoln becomes engaged temporarily to Ann Rutledge, the little chapter closes thus:

> The cry and the answer of one yellowharrier to another, the wing flash of one bluejay on a home flight to another, the drowsy dreaming of grass and grain coming up with its early green over the moist rolling prairie, these were to be felt that spring together, with the whisper, 'always together.'
>
> He was twenty-six, she was twenty-two; the earth was their foot-stool; the sky was a sheaf of blue dreams; the rise of the blood-gold rim of a full moon in the evening was almost too much to live, see, and remember.

This is suspiciously like "fine writing," and there are many such touches, particularly in the first volume, but on the other hand there is such a genuine love for everything in our system that produces Lincolns when called for, and such a relish for the soil on which this particular great one flourished, that I can imagine only the hypercritical chiding. In fact, this first volume might easily pass as a best-seller especially in the mid-western region thus sympathetically held up to public gaze.

The second volume is drier, dealing as it does with legal and political procedures which are not, apparently, Mr Sandburg's meat. Nevertheless, the vast data of the period have been thoroughly and intelligently marshalled and the Lincoln-lover's heart stops beating at critical moments in the approved fashion and there is no place in it where the reader puts the book down. Lincoln still says "jist" and "sich" instead of "just" and "such," but a scholarly individual who heard the Springfield reply to Douglas compared his impassioned manner to that of a Martin Luther; and among thousands of plain people, thinking the

matter over, was born "an instinct, perhaps a hope, that the voice was their voice."

The plain people, Mr Sandburg makes it abundantly clear, were, for once, right.

James A. Woodburn

SOURCE: A review of *Abraham Lincoln: The Prairie Years,* in *The American Political Science Review,* Vol. 20, August, 1926, pp. 674-77.

These two volumes of nearly a thousand pages deal with the life of Lincoln from his ancestry and birth to the time of his inauguration as president.

One may read many biographies of Lincoln, but he will probably never read a more interesting one than this. There is interest on every page. There is in it so much of poetry and imagination, so much of tradition mingled with fact, that some may doubt whether it be biography at all. It is clearly not within the canons of historical writing. There are no footnotes. No sources are indicated, no citations to authorities. Its 168 chapters, some of them only a page or two long, are without titles, one chapter beginning on the page where the other leaves off. There are no spaces at chapter endings for references, and no references are given throughout the volumes, the author indicating in his preface that his sources are "too numerous to mention." The inquiring student will wish for them, at places; but the lay reader may not miss them and may follow the moving drama the more eagerly because of the omission. There is a good index, the volumes are fine specimens of the publisher's art, and they are richly and most interestingly illustrated.

Mr. Sandburg is not an historical specialist, but he has seen life in varied forms and he grew up not far removed in space and time from the life that Lincoln knew. He writes for what he is a story-teller, a realist, an interpreter, an artist. There is the eye of the genius to see, the power of the poet to express. He, therefore, draws vividly and in a masterly way the scenes and the life of the times which he studied. From Sandburg's pages one sees Lincoln as never before, in his homely, rough, pioneer society; and from the poet's pictures one feels that he is seeing the real Lincoln, not in all details, perhaps, but at least in the main features of his life and character. As the reader will not be led far astray from the essential truth, it may be said that the ensemble justifies all the poetic license which the author has employed.

The reader enjoys the poetic prose, whether concerning the black loam of the soil and the growing corn, or the musing, mystic, melancholy soul of Lincoln.

There are vivid pictures of the prairie society of New Salem and Springfield, and of Lincoln as he appeared among his neighbors. We see the pigs roaming the streets of Springfield "sniffling for food," and the hotel bus mired in mud to the hub; we see the loneliness of Lincoln's life, and again his rollicking fun with his oafish ways; we see him as a "walking, stalking library" of never-ending stories; as an office-seeking politician, always defeated; we see him riding the circuit of twelve counties, living in hotels and court houses, staying from home six months of the year—with a hint that such prolonged absences came from henpecking and domestic infelicities.

One picture follows another. We see Lincoln sitting in a company of men with his boots off, "to give his feet a chance to breathe," as he said; or at the table neglecting to use the butter knife, much to the annoyance of Mrs. Lincoln; or, in place of the servant girl, answering the ring of the front door bell in his shirt sleeves. We see him on a neighborly visit in a pair of loose slippers, wearing a faded pair of trousers fastened with one suspender; or, when asked to examine a brief, replying, "Wait till I fix this plug of my gallus and I'll pitch into that like a dog at a root." There are numberless touches such as these, showing how Lincoln had dropped into the life of the people, in close touch "with their homes, kitchens, barns, fields, churches, schools, hotels, saloons, sports, their places for working, worshiping, and loafing."

Amid this life lived the Lincoln of sadness and melancholy; of love, and courtship; of earnest study; of hope, and strange ambition. "It seemed as though he planned pieces of his life to fit together. Then shapes and events stepped out of the unknown and kicked his plans into lines other than he expected. . . . When dreams came in sleep he tried to fathom their shapes and reckon out events in days to come. Beyond the walls and handles of his eyesight he felt other regions out and away in the stuff of stars and dreams."

Amid the author's rich colors and poetic interpretations one need not look for completeness nor exactness in history, for historic proportions or emphasis. Yet we find Lincoln here in his historic setting, essentially true in bold outline. The author brings into play many facts of prime importance. Not only does he search into the social background and reveal it, but he strikes off in swift dramatic language important events and movements—the Mexican War, the compromise of 1850, the repeal of the Missouri restriction, Mrs. Stowe and *Uncle Tom*, the Kansas war, the great debates with Douglas, Dred Scott, John Brown, and the political campaigns. He makes too much of some of these, too little of others. In the account there are errors of detail. He uses unverified tradition; he puts the cost of the Mexican war at one fourth of the proper sum; the Fugitive Slave Law was hardly a "joke in northern Ohio"; he calls Fillmore a Free Soil candidate; he calls Prudence Crandall "Prudence Campbell"; he puts Crawfordsville, Indiana, on the Wabash River; he describes John Quincy Adams as "a sweet, lovable man"—which he was hardly considered as being even by his friends, certainly not by his opponents in congressional debate. And one wonders if Lincoln actually said "Mr. *Cheerman*" as he began his Cooper Union speech. These lapses and other minor ones are not serious defects and may be easily removed in an historical biography; but it would be hypercritical to allow such flaws to mar the effect of the luminous canvas of this poet-biographer.

Lincoln's principles, his love of law, order, and liberty, and his devotion to the Union are here set forth. For these he stood; for these, if need be, he was ready to die. No man stood more stoutly than he for the radical democracy of the Declaration of Independence. He read Horace Greeley and the Whig Almanac. He read Emerson, Thoreau, and Whitman. The death of Lovejoy, the courage of the Abolitionists, the words of Victor Hugo and Josiah Quincy had their influence upon him. He read how exiles from despotically governed countries were giving up their lives and homes for liberty, martyrs for the freedom of the race. "Lincoln saw and heard. Dreams ran deep in him. He had in him a streak of honest glory; he would live beyond his fleeting day. This want lived in him, far under in him, in the deeper blue pools of him, while he mixed with men with his horse sense, his mathematics, and an eye for the comic."

Such is Sandburg's Lincoln. No matter how extensive may be one's reading on Lincoln he should add these volumes to his list. The perennial interest in Lincoln will continue, and thousands of his countrymen will be grateful to Carl Sandburg for the absorbing volumes which he has added to the Lincoln literature.

THE AMERICAN SONGBAG (1927; REPRINTED IN 1970)

Babette Deutsch

SOURCE: "The Voice of the Land," in *New York Herald Tribune Books,* Vol. 4, No. 12, December 4, 1927, p. 3.

Some seventy years ago Emerson was urging his countrymen to busy themselves with that past upon which their future inevitably rested. Being a wise man and a poet he believed that poetry was the proper tool with which to dig about the roots of the national life. How far he was right Carl Sandburg's magnificent collection of American folk songs is here to prove. The book shows, too, how far he was wrong. "Our log rolling," said Emerson, "our stumps and their politics, our fisheries, our Negroes and Indians, our boasts and our repudiations, the wrath of rogues and the pusillanimity of honest men, the Northern trade, the Southern planting, the Western clearing, Oregon and Texas are yet unsung."

That summons has been partially answered by men like Whitman, Frost, Sandburg himself. But the last named poet has recognized that it was not so much in the individual vision as in the racial experience which is the stuff of common balladry that the history of the nation was to be found. He knew, being closer to American life than the sage of Concord could ever get, that the Northern trade, the Southern planting and the Western clearing have been sung, literally sung, by rogues—and some honest men, too—from the Erie Canal to Macon, from the Great Lakes to the Gulf of Mexico, from the Atlantic to the Pacific Coast. He knew that the voice of the land is to be heard in the homely tunes and lyrics of its half-literate people, in bawdy songs and sailor chanteys and sentimental ditties, wherever there are pick and shovel gangs at work, or dances in lonely hill cabins, or gatherings around prairie fires or lusty sailormen at a keg party. He has brought these popular songs together in a book that can not only create an American night's entertainment and wreck the best intentions for a day's work, but that can also teach you in the most casual and insinuating fashion more about this country and its folk than a whole shelf-full of fatuous scholarship.

Sandburg heard these songs from the lips of all sorts and conditions of men and women: from a Scotch-Irish descendant of pre-Revolutionary settlers, living near Hell-fer-Sartain Creek, from a comrade coal shoveler in Omaha, from a Mexican Negro in an old Texas saloon, from "a 'wobbly' who had been switchman, cowboy, jailbird" from a fellow private fighting in the rain and mud of Porto Rico, from a minstrel cook who had worked on the wagons traveling the Chisholm Trail, from an old fiddler turned milkman as they washed delivery cans together, from railroad workers sitting in their boxcar bunk houses, from "darkies" strumming banjos on the carts of traveling medicine men. And he invited factory girls and college girls, tramps and editors, musicians and cowpunchers to help him in his search for verses and melodies.

The notes that accompany the text are something in the nature of footlights, casting a glow over the humblest ballads and bringing out all the vigor and savor of the best of them. Thus, the prefatory lines above "The Little Old Sod Shanty" tell us that a little girl coming home to Western/Nebraska after a trip East observed that "The East is where trees come between you and the sky," and goes on to describe the sod houses on the Great Plains. Again, Sandburg relates that, according to the singer, "Down in the Valley" is "a good song to be singing while writing a love letter—it is full of wishes and dances a little—and hopes a beloved dancing partner will come back." When he writes about the mountaineer's lyrics he pauses to note that a wanderer in Kentucky, asking his way, was told to go on "about two screeches and a holler." The grand swinging Negro spiritual to which the words of "Old Abe Lincoln Came Out of the Wilderness" have been set is prefaced by the statement:

> Torchlight processions of Republicans sang this in the summer and fall months of 1860. The young Wide Awakes burbled it as the kerosene dripped on their blue oilcloth capes. Quartets and octettes jubilated with it in packed, smoky halls where audiences waited for speakers of the evening. In Springfield, Ill., the Tall Man who was a candidate for the Presidency of the nation, heard his two boys, Tad and Willie, sing it at him.

There are brief evocations of the days before the railroads, when men and horses, plodding along the Erie Canal, carrying merchandise westward and meat and grain to the east, "took their jobs as monotonous, mild burdens," and the men sang a song that Sandburg compares, significantly enough, to that of the Volga barge-towers. Further along mention is made of the American Railway Union strike led by Debs in '93 and one of the songs of the blacklisted strikers is set down, together with the remark of the old railroad man who sang lovely Irish lilts "to keep from goin' bugs." He speaks truly of "the power and restraint of art and genius" in the unembellished stanzas of "My Old Hammah":

> My old hammah
> Shina like silvah,
> Shina lik gol'
> Yes, shina like gol',
>
> Dere ain'-no hammah
> Ina this old mountain,
> Shina like mine,
> Yes, shina like mine!
>
> This old hammah
> Kill my pahtnah,

But it can't kill me,
No, it can't kill me!

I ben a-workin'
Ona this hyer railroad,
Fo' long year, boys,
Yes, fo' long year!

O next winter
Be so col',
Be so col',
Yes, be so col'!

And then, to balance the more aching tunes, there is a thick collection of rollicking nonsense, some of the so-called "high-brow" verses being particularly choice, as witness "In the Days of Old Rameses," a mocking refrain sung by members of the Whitechapel Club, an institution that had "Jack the Ripper" for its patron saint and that was composed, according to one of its charter members, George Ade, of "a little group of thirsty intellectuals who were opposed to everything." This particular song was one that Rudyard Kipling wanted to remember, and with reason.

The collector aptly calls this a book of "singable songs." There are 280 of them here, and I have not found one that I would forego. There are many that have never before been published, some of them old favorites, like "Po' Boy," "Way Up on Clinch Mountain" and "Mary Wore Three Links of Chain." There are a few missing that I wish Sandburg had included—"Green Grow the Rushes O," "John Hardy," "Live A-humble," "The Old Man Come Home One Night" and perhaps half a dozen others. I wish, too, that he had added a glossary of hobo lingo. But the collection is so excellent and the editor so humble ("I should like to have taken ten, twenty, thirty years more in the preparation of this volume," he writes in his apologia) that one cannot touch it without respect. It is packed with beauty and information.

The one fault I have to find is with the arrangements. In several cases the melodies have been prettified and spoiled. Songs like "Willy the Weeper," "The Maid From the Gallows," "I Wish I Had Some One to Love Me" need the little mournful grace notes and the minor harmonies that musicianly fingers have erased from these versions. I remember an evening with Sandburg and Padraic Colum over a decanter of my grandmother's blackberry brandy (eheu fugaces!) when far mellower tunes than these flowed from Sandburg's lips and fingers. And I have heard others render some of these songs more simply and effectively. Sandburg says truly that we have here "a book that is unfinished, that has oddments and reminders, that has tatters and remnants, elsewhere and far away

in many ports and valleys." It is because he conveys this sense of wistful incompleteness as finely as he fulfills the promise of the book's title that the work here begun should flourish and richly bear fruit.

Conrad Aiken

SOURCE: "Those Unknown Singers," in *The Dial*, Vol. 84, May, 1928, pp. 425-27.

Mr Sandburg has performed a very useful cultural service in assembling for us, in this hugely diverting volume, a vast array of what might be called American folk-songs and folk-tunes. Almost everything that one can think of is here. If there is a relatively small selection from the negro spirituals, there is, I suppose, sufficient excuse for that in the fact that these are easily obtainable elsewhere, and, on the whole, better known, because more frequently heard. For the rest, Mr Sandburg has erred, if at all, on the side of compendiousness. Some of these songs—in fact, a good many—are pretty "small beer"; with little value either as verse or as tune. One would willingly lose fifty or a hundred of them in exchange for the omitted I've Been Working on the Railroad, or Grasshopper Sittin' on a Railroad Track. But omissions, in a work of this sort, are inevitable. And on the whole one must congratulate Mr Sandburg on his thoroughness: perhaps only finding fault with him for his inclusion of a group of Mexican songs, and a good many English ballads and popular songs (for example, It's the Syme the Whole World Over) merely on the ground that they are popular, in America, and frequently sung. The criterion, here, seems to be a little awry. It would as well justify the inclusion of Annie Laurie or Ach du lieber Augustin. And if mere popularity is to be the criterion, why should one exclude such popular songs as are *not* anonymous—for example, the Sewanee River? These too, in effect, have become folk-songs; and reflect, as well as anything else, the *Zeitgeist*.

Nevertheless, Mr Sandburg's compendium is extraordinarily entertaining. In a sense, it is a social document of brilliant, and perhaps horrifying, force. Here—as Mr Sandburg intimates in his preface—is America. Here are the songs of working-gangs, the songs of hoboes, the songs of jail-birds and dope-fiends, the songs of farmers and cowpunchers and railroad men, the "blues" of negroes. It is an America which Mr Sandburg loves: he makes this sufficiently clear in the somewhat sentimental prefatory notes with which he introduces each item. He dedicates his book, indeed, "To Those Unknown Singers—Who Made Songs—Out Of Love, Fun, Grief." These are the folk-songs and folk-tunes of a great democracy; and if one loves democracy, shouldn't one love the songs it sings? . . .

Perhaps one should; but in the face of the present evidence, to do so would tax one's generosity to the breaking-point. As pure entertainment, there can be no question about the value of this collection. If one is interested in the manners and customs, and the intellectual and emotional level, of the American masses in the period from 1840 to 1920, then one will find plenty of light on that subject in this huge book, and light of a paralysing intensity. Here is indeed a rich folk material, of a sort—and like all folk material it is racily suggestive of its time and place. But—may democracy forgive us—how crude it is! It is folk-poetry—and folk-song—at its lowest level. Its humour is coarse farce or burlesque; its pathos is the dreariest and most threadbare of sentimentalities. Its poverty, whether of language or of idea, is almost terrifying. One finds it difficult to conceive how the Anglo-Saxon, with his extraordinary genius for the ballad, and with a ballad tradition which is unparalleled, could descend to such ludicrous fumblings as these. His gift of phrase, and of succinct emotional utterance, seems here to have abandoned him entirely. One has only to compare this folk literature with that of almost any other civilized nation to feel at once its abysmal spiritual bankruptcy. It is, in fact, a folk literature without genius.

No doubt many excellent reasons could be given for this. One is accustomed to falling back on the time-honoured notion that "there had not yet been time," and that the pioneer life was too hard to permit of any cultural amenities. Whatever the excuse, one must resign oneself to the fact. These songs are delightful, not because of any real excellence as folk art, but simply *because* they are crude. There are, of course, exceptions to this, notably among the burlesques. The tragic ditties of Cocaine Lil and Willie the Weeper, and such semi-burlesque pathetic ballads as those that compose the Frankie and Johnny cycle, are delicious, as long as one does not ask too much of them. And one can, moreover, discover in many of the cowboy songs or working-gang songs a note of genuine enough feeling: genuine, but not successfully expressed.

Eventually, one comes back to the curious circumstance that only in the negro songs has America produced a folk-literature of any real beauty. In these, one does find a definite genius, both for phrase and melody. The fact that the phrase is frequently nonsense makes no difference: the negro showed an instinctive understanding of the *emotional* values of his adopted language which his white rivals in the art of balladry have nowhere matched. And the same thing is true also of the tunes. Only in the negro songs do we find any profundity of feeling. Compared with the average negro spiritual, or even with some of the "blues," the best of these "American" ballads appear superficial, or tawdry, or mawkish, or simply cheap. They can be, and are, occasionally, very funny, with their characteristic laconic exaggerations or droll understatements: but as poetry they are almost nil. The tunes seldom rise above the mediocre, and are usually best when simplest. It is to be regretted that in a good many instances, in this book, these simple airs have been too elaborately "arranged." What is wanted is a good "running" accompaniment of the plainest sort.

GOOD MORNING, AMERICA (1928)

William Carlos Williams

SOURCE: "Good . . . For What?" in *The Dial,* Vol. 86, 1929, pp. 250-51.

When Mayakovsky, the poet of the Soviets was here five years ago, and had taken his foot down from where he had planted it on the table while reading his poem urging Willie, the Havana street cleaner, to join the Third International—he had something to say about Carl Sandburg whom he had met in Chicago, I think, a few days previously. A sort of showman, a stoutish chap wearing a vest red to the right of the buttons and green to the left, translated for us; Mayakovsky didn't think much of Sandburg.

He couldn't get through his head what Sandburg was after. Is he a poet of the people? Then why . . . doesn't he do something about it besides making pretty pictures? Or maybe he's a Christian. Anyhow, the question was posed. What was Sandburg's idea? Mayakovsky didn't know.

And he didn't know that in this country if you write, Hallelujah, I'm a bum—and mean it, you get put up against a wall for one man out of twelve to shoot a blank cartridge at. But that's what Mayakovsky wanted of Sandburg: To everlastingly say what he implies about common people and things, to say it outright and optimistically and take the beating that should be coming to him.

That would be one thing and as a criticism of Sandburg I think it is valid. He sings that little two-legged joker man in a minor key. It is perhaps the typical

United States song, the song of the beaten. It is a sad plaint in spite of eternal repetition endlessly finding something new to say the same thing about.

All this just to say Sandburg is not a revolutionist.

He is, in my opinion, a writer of excellent hokkus.. *Good Morning, America* is full of them. Or if not hokkus at least short poems. **"Dialogue," "Two Women and Their Fathers," "Windflower Leaf."** He sings and that is all.

Sandburg is profuse, but his profuseness is to tell over and over again the delicate, despairing reality of the world, his world, the United States world; a wish to touch and to cast his love over the actual, that is so often the low. His profuseness is not that of the artist in words—if there be any living; it is a surge of pain. All he can do about it is to sing. I imagine this might be his answer to Mayakovsky.

Heaven help me, I don't know what else you're going to say about Sandburg. There's no sense in listing the poems. The title-piece begins sharply with "facts." When, however, he starts talking ecstatically about eggs I may miss the irony but it sounds to me dangerously like "diaphanous blah."

It is in his lyrism that he can be freely and voluminously enjoyed. Many of our young sonneteers might to their advantage study his language and his sense of metric, for here Sandburg is a master—and most subtly so. Here he is actual, local, alive—in the words and the turn of his lines. Technically he is much improved there too, that is, over earlier work. Even the long title-poem is far better than some of the earlier deadly catalogues wherein he seems to copy the very worst of Whitman.

Sandburg should quit the false local of "these states," "the prairie," etc., etc., and be actually local in his finer sense of the words and metric of which I have spoken above.

To me Sandburg remains a large figure. This book is a good one, in spite of gross faults. The songs are its strength. As there can never be too many songs so there can never be too much Sandburg.

Horace Gregory

SOURCE: A review of *Good Morning, America,* in *Poetry,* Vol. 33, No. 4, January, 1929, pp. 214-18.

It is impossible to dissociate America and Carl Sandburg. He is, simply and effectively, America's poet, identified completely with the life of his people, the product of the Middle West, the city of Chicago. Realizing this, there are a million ways to read him, a million ways to reflect his point of view. But his important function coincides with one of the major functions of all great poetry—the business of making articulate the speech of inarticulate masses, the men and women who cannot talk, men and women who are never heard. If this particular function has not already become obvious in his early work, it is definitely proved by the publication of this latest book. Quite as you think of Scotland in terms of Robert Burns, so you will think of Chicago and the Middle West in terms of Sandburg. These two great nationalists have made the speech of their people intelligible to humanity as a whole. They have made the writing of poetry as simple as the casual speech of one man to another, as intimate as the confidences of two lonely men in the early morning.

Consider a few facts about Sandburg. He was born in Galesburg, Illinois. He has earned pay checks by working with his hands. He is now living in Chicago. Chicago has always been the base of his operations. I am not advancing these facts as reasons for the merit in his work. They may be looked at as chief influences, modifying its characteristics. Their principal importance is that Sandburg has carried on his activities well outside of America's literary belt, the region in and around New York City. I am passing out a broad hint that New York as a literary center is grossly overrated. I suspect that sections of the country, particularly Chicago, are becoming afflicted with various kinds of inferiority complexes.

Because of the concentration of publishing houses in New York, the country west of Manhattan has a tendency to overrate the products of literary gangsters surrounding New York publishers and to ignore or belittle the efforts of someone next door, desperately trying to make a living by setting words down on paper. In time, that person either changes his business, secretly feeling misunderstood and frustrated, or moves to New York. Most of the publications attempted outside of New York make an effort to imitate New York productions. This effort, combined with the general feeling that the New York original was and is far better, leads to failure. The literary gangsters, circling round the New York publishers, are becoming more and more self-centered and smug, yet clinging tenaciously to whatever they may possess in the way of reputation—a natural development of existing conditions. The publishers themselves, though honestly on the lookout for new blood, are greatly influenced by local gangs of critics and their points of view. Class and geographical distinctions are being sharply outlined, with the result that New

York is rapidly becoming another Hollywood, ignorant of the actual needs and outlets of the national reading public.

The New York of today (which covers a period of ten years) has developed only two vehicles of literary expression which modify the general conditions, *The New Masses* and *The American Caravan.* Both ventures have their own obvious limitations, yet they maintain an open mind in the direction of extra-New York literary activities. Both are revolting against the more powerful literary alliances. One soon becomes convinced that the potential forces at work in American literary life and American poetry are not to be found in New York City alone. Let us admit that good poets are scarce and that Sandburg belongs to Chicago; and that during the last ten years New York has received its most important stimuli from the contributors to *This Quarter, Broom, transition,* and *Poetry,* all printed and edited some distance from Fifth Avenue, Washington Square and Broadway. The existence of Sandburg, as well as a number of younger men, still generally unrecognized, amply stresses the point.

Sandburg has suffered less from the evils of popular success than any American poet of his age writing today, with the possible exception of Ezra Pound. Sandburg is still Sandburg, doing the important job of writing his poetry from a steadily maturing point of view. He grows slowly, naturally in all directions. It is becoming increasingly difficult to quote a single poem of Sandburg's and say, "Here he is." His broad appeal is not represented in one poem, not even in his most ambitious job, **Good Morning, America,** from which his book takes its title. You need the entire book, for again, like Robert Burns, his real strength lies in the minute commonplaces, expressing many moods, ideas and desires of many people.

POTATO FACE (1930)

Mark Van Doren

SOURCE: A review of *Potato Face,* in *The Nation,* New York, Vol. CXXII, No. 3162, February 10, 1926, p. 149.

"The rootabaga, as all farmers know, is in size perhaps the greatest vegetable that grows," says Carl Sandburg in his latest, **Potato Face.** Whatever significance this horticultural fact may have, rootabagas and Carl Sandburg combined mean but one thing to the initiated—the **Rootabaga Stories,** with the Village of Liver-and-Onions, the yellow leather slab ticket with the blue spanch across it by means of which one may go away and never come back, the pigs with bibs on and the delightful family of which Gimme the Ax is honorable head. Those stories were for children, as all the world knows, or chiefly for children, and Potato Face was in them, with chapters around him and titles before. But Sandburg's old man with the accordion, who sees the whole human procession though not with his eyes, now makes the chapters himself out of new Rootabaga stories, and these are for grown-ups. At least, they are for grown-ups who like his kind of tale. Potato Face, it appears, is extra-special in the sorts of things he sees.

"He seems to love some of the precious things that are cheap," explains his sponsor in a confiding preface, "such as stars, the wind, pleasant words, time to be lazy, and fools having personality and distinction. He knows, it seems, that young people are young, no matter how many years they live; that there are children born old and brought up to be full of fear; that a young heart keeps young by a certain measure of fooling as the years go by; that men and women old in years sometimes keep a fresh heart and, to the last, salute the dawn and the morning with a mixture of reverence and laughter."

Perhaps you will prefer the tale of Yonder the Yinder, sometimes called Yonder the Yinder the Yoo, and will wish for a yodo so that you may look better while you listen and listen better while you look. Or perhaps you will like the small moon spiders who spin cobwebs to catch the moon and put their numbers on each one; or the bell spiders who hang tiny bells on their lacy hammocks under the hollyhocks. Of course there are alphabet rats to choose, also, and red leather rats who take off red hats to show respect, and cuckoo rats who fix cuckoo clocks and afterward climb on top and cuckoo just to show that rats can cuckoo. Or you may be entranced by the big elephant. Oompah, "with whiskers so long that 16 little elephants walk ahead of him carrying the whiskers, and picking the hay and the weeds and the cockleburrs out of the whiskers." Oompah sleeps a year at a time and then gets up and eats his breakfast in January—and there's more to it than that. More to it, perhaps, than it says. At any rate, should you grow sleepy with listening to Potato Face you could yawn, as did the Balloon sisters and, like them, wrap your yawns in your handkerchiefs and look at them the next morning "to see how a yawn looks if you wrap it in a handkerchief."

You may have indeed abundant choice in these matters. You may prefer Fog Wisp with the pony look to her face, and hear about snoox and spiff talk. Then again you may prefer the tale about trading dreams, wondering of course which are dreams and which are the things that happen—white moonlight and buses being somewhat mixed in both. You may even choose to go along the road toward the Village of Cream Puffs and hear the tale of the Rag Doll and the Broom Handle—old Rootabaga friends—concerned with the Honeymoon tree and the Baby Shoe trees, seeing the slipper blossoms and how baby sox grow.

But if you can bring yourself to have a favorite over and beyond the spotted rat Ezekiel and the Blue Fox who buttons on his ears with buttons, and his chin, "careful," and his toes, pulling on his stripes like stockings, getting ready to go to the Blue Fox school—if you can bring yourself to it, we say, in spite of the winningness of Zeke and his sister Hep— you will prefer over and beyond all else, the tale of the Spink Bug and the Huck.

The spink bug, you must know, unwrapped himself and found he was a bug, looked down outside of himself and saw he was covered with splashes and alphabets, and in fact, thought himself quite excellent. Then along came the huck. "And they stood looking at each other, each one bragging how good he was. . . . Never having seen each other before, the way to find out who was who and which was which, was to fight."

But the spink and the huck stopped and thought it over first, holding counsel with each other, saying, "Even if we are different, we are the same." So they began to talk a bit, to find out why they were going to fight. They talked about salimber trees and snow and rain, "about September and October and the green leaves changing to yellow and saffron and gold, and falling, falling in a grand goodbye for that year," and "about the summer sky and the few stars early in the evening." Spins the tale. "The more they talked . . . the more they forgot to find out why they were going to fight." In the end they decided to go home, but as they had not by any means finished talking of the countless things that interested them, each promised sometimes to write the other "his thoughts in the gloaming."

Perhaps you will say this is all nonsense, even though you may concede it delicious, original and sometimes beautiful. Possibly you are right. Again, there may be something to these jolly tales of Potato Face that you can see better while you listen and listen to better while you look even though you may not have the yodo of Yonder the Yinder the Yoo. But of course that depends entirely upon whether or not you are just that sort of person.

The Nation

SOURCE: A review of *Potato Face,* in *The Nation,* New York, Vol. CXXX, No. 3387, June 4, 1930, p. 658.

Sandburg's new Rootabaga volume contains twelve stories told by the Potato Face Blind Man to some of his little friends. They are all about Yonder the Yinder, Pigeon Foot, Long-arms, Quish and Quee, the Hot Ashes Sisters; and about such extraordinary creatures as "flinyons" and "snooxes" and "spiffs" and "spink bugs." These fancies and fooleries seem, for the most part, intended to be quite meaningless, unmarred by ulterior motives. For certain imaginative children, and also for those adults who have been able to retain a childlike love for preposterous make-believe and funny-sounding cacophony, Potato Face's conversation should prove a delight. And if you have enjoyed the other Rootabaga books you will like this one.

EARLY MOON (1930)

Katharine Gilmour Landon

SOURCE: A review of *Early Moon,* in *The Bookman,* November, 1930, pp. 249-50.

Early Moon in its sombre but striking cover, has been ably decorated by James Daugherty and, containing selections from Sandburg's older work together with several new poems, is a satisfactory introduction to this poet. Here are verses from *The Windy City* and *Smoke and Steel*; the fog that "comes on little cat feet"; and the whistle of the boat that

> Calls and cries unendingly,
> Like some lost child
> In tears and trouble
> Hunting the harbor's breast
> And the harbor's eyes.

Some of the subjects are suggested in Mr. Sandburg's remark, "A farm silo, a concrete grain elevator, a steel barge hauling iron ore on the Great Lakes, or a series of tall coal chutes rising as silhouettes on a moonlight night, may any one of them have as complete a beauty as the Greek Parthenon or a Gothic cathedral." The quotation comes from the preface, "A Short Talk on Poetry," an illuminating slant on the subject written by the poet for boys and girls. Children with widening imaginations will find abiding experience in *Early Moon.* Values will remain for them to enjoy as they grow older, for that is a quality of poetry.

📖 *THE PEOPLE, YES* (1936)

Ben Belitt

SOURCE: "The Majestic People," in *The Nation*, New York, Vol. CXLIII, No. 8, August 22, 1936, pp. 215-16.

When Rebecca West made mention of Sandburg's revolutionary passion" in 1926, pausing to remark that poem after poem is ruined by a coarsely intruding line that turns it from poetry into propaganda," it was in the nature of an afterthought. Sandburg was then concerned even more circumstantially than in the present volume with ice-handlers, dock-wallopers, wheat-stackers, and "contemporary bunkshooters"; but his status as a propagandist was incidental to his function as "poet of the Middle West." *The People, Yes,* which is defined for us in a prefatory lyric as a collection of "stories and poems nobody want to laugh at, interspersed with memoranda worth a second look," is a volume to be considered entirely in terms of its "revolutionary" content. Sandburg's tenderness for ethnological detail has not prevented him from marshaling his facts about a thesis here, the tractarian nature of which becomes unmistakable as the theme gathers bulk and momentum.

The People, Yes is from one standpoint a heroic poem without a hero. The intent has been to celebrate the anonymous Genius of the People as a force capable of molding into its own image not only the language and *mores* of a nation, but its history as well. With more prodigality than order Sandburg has set down the American folk-epic as he conceives it, chiefly by the procedure of overturning upon the pages bushel-baskets of regional legends, phrases, anecdotes, tall tales, allusions, and aphorisms interspersed with comment of his own. Occasionally this material is engrafted upon lyrical themes and knit to the general score by links of logic or contextual reference. Most often, however, the items are thrown up in series, arbitrarily, so that the effect becomes one of chanted portfolio notations rather than an orderly development of a theme.

Sandburg's fundamental conception of "The People" as a historical entity is clear both by direct statement and from a steady stream of tropes which furnish an incidental embroidery to the argument as a whole. There occur such metaphors as a child at school writing howlers, writing answers half-wrong, half-right," a "monster turtle," a monolith, a target, a spectrum, a Pandora's box, an avalanche, an anvil, a cosmos, and a phantasmagoria; at its baldest, however, we are

told: "The People is Everyman, everybody. Everybody is you and I and all others." With complete consistency, then, history becomes "a few Big Names plus People," industry "the daily chores of the people":

> The plow and the hammer, the knife and
> the shovel, the planting hoe and the
> reaping sickle, everywhere these are
> the people's possessions by right of use.

Similarly justice becomes a verdict, not of a quorum, but of a culture. Ultimately, the concept is compacted into a trope of the People as History moving blindly through space and time and achieving destiny not so much through conscious exercise of will as by a gradual, tortured, yet invincible exodus from trial and error to revolution.

Whether such a notion takes into account sufficiently the element of will—of conscious rather than blind self-enlightenment—as a catalyst in the hastening of historical effects, and whether it must not also in the last analysis look wholly to faith for the attainment of its ends—faith in the majestic people," in the eventual "dignity of deepening roots"—are problems to be suggested only in passing. More to the point of present-day issues are the poet's direct avowals of sympathy and indignation: Sandburg has known of verdicts purchased through bribes, of violence hired, of murder paid for, of "payday patriots." "The man in the street is fed with lies in peace, gas in war," he writes, is challenged with the "animal dictate" to "do what we tell you or go hungry; listen to us or you don't eat," while "rare and suave swine . . . pay themselves a fat swag of higher salaries." He calls upon Lincoln as the exemplar of the American folk-conscience to point the way "beyond the present wilderness" of exploitation and deceit, much as Wordsworth invoked the spirit of Milton in 1802. "Always the storm of propaganda blows," he concludes; but "the learning and blundering people will live on."

> The living passion of millions can rise
> into a whirlwind: the storm once loose
> who can ride it? you? or you? or you?
>   only history, only tomorrow, knows
>   for every revolution breaks
> as a child of its own convulsive hour
> shooting patterns never told beforehand.

Many matters of popular moment, it is true, are skirted by a quizzical "Yes and no, no and yes"; and the reader is left to determine for himself whether the "United States of the Earth," of which mention is made in Section 87, is to be construed as an allusion to Tennyson, Marx, or Jesus. A query more easy of resolution is that addressed to the Chinese philosopher in an earlier section: "Was he preaching or writing poetry or talking through his hat?" In the present volume, surely, Sandburg has devoted the greatest part of his energies to the first, considerably less to the second, and nothing at all to the last. The result may make negligible poetry and confused preaching, but it proves Sandburg thoroughly alive to the "shock and contact of ideas" today. On this account alone—if not solely—*The People, Yes* should interest a wider audience than any of his other volumes since *Chicago Poems.*

William Rose Benét

SOURCE: "Memoranda on Americans," in *The Saturday Review,* Vol. 14, No. 17, August 22, 1936, p. 6.

Carl Sandburg, still one of our leading poets, is now within two years of sixty, but you'd never know it from the vigor of his verse. Not content with having given us some of the most vital experimentation in poetry of our time, as well as ventures into valuable biography, tales for children, and collections of native American folk-song, he has now cut loose with a long poem about the American people which has everything in it including the kitchen stove.

> Payments on the car, the bungalow, the
>   radio, the electric icebox, accumu-
>   lated interest on loans for past pay-
>   ments, the writhing point of where
>   the money will come from,
> Crime thrown in their eyes from every
>   angle, crimes against property and
>   person, crime in the prints and films,
>   crime as a lurking shadow ready to
>   spring into reality, crime as a method
>   and a technique,
> Comedy as an offset to crime, the
>   laughmakers, the odd numbers in the
>   news and the movies, original clowns
>   and imitators, and in the best you
>   never know what's coming next even
>   when it's hokum.
> And sports, how a muff in the seventh
>   lost yesterday's game and how now
>   they're learning to hit Dazzy's fade-
>   away ball and did you hear how
>   Foozly plowed through that line for
>   a touchdown this afternoon?
> And daily the death toll of the speed
>   wagons; a cripple a minute in fen-
>   ders, wheels, steel and glass splinters;
>   a stammering witness before a coro-
>   ner's jury, "It happened so sudden I
>   don't know what happened."

"The people, yes, the people," it seems to go on indefinitely. But as it goes on it gets deeper. There is a hypnotic cadence to Sandburg's loose-jointed free verse. He likes catalogues of people and things almost as much as Whitman did, but his is a different view. For one thing his tone is not so much exuberant as ominous. He looks at all the crooks and the cheaters and the exploiters and the pursy hypocrites with a flinty eye. He tells 'em—he tells 'em. . . .

He weaves into his verse every old anecdote and adage he has come across—cracker-barrel, horse-swapping, each, any, and every pithy expression. He summarizes well this Alice-in-wonder-land America in which we live.

> "I came to a country,"
> said a wind-bitten vagabond,
> "Where I saw shoemakers barefoot
> saying they had too many shoes.
> I met carpenters living outdoors
> saying they had built too many houses.
> Clothing workers I talked with,
> bushelmen and armhole-basters,
> said their coats were on a ragged edge
> because they had made too many coats.
> And I talked with farmers, yeomanry,
> the backbone of the country,
> so they were told,
> saying they were in debt and near starvation
> because they had gone ahead like always
> And raised too much wheat and corn
> too many hogs, sheep, cattle.
> When I said, 'You live in a strange
> country,'
> they answered slow, like men
> who wouldn't waste anything, not even
> language:
> 'You ain't far wrong there, young feller.
> We're going to do something, we don't
> know what.'"

He says again, with a swell fixed grin in the corner of his mouth:

> The rights of property are guarded
>   by ten thousand laws and fortresses.
> The right of a man to live by his work—
>   what is this right?
>   and why does it clamor?
>   and who can hush it
>   so it will stay hushed?
>   and why does it speak
>   and though put down speak again
>   with strengths out of the earth?

He sees the American people as "wanters" and "hopers." And Heaven knows he sees them as dumb in every sense. Which is entirely true. No people are cheated worse than the American people. None are bigger suckers to stand for what they stand for. . . . Sandburg speaks of the greatest showman on earth and of how the people love to be humbugged. He collects sayings of the people, making shrewd capital of their half-wittedness.

"Which way to the post-office, boy?"
"I don't know." "You don't know
much, do you?" "No, but I ain't lost."

That is an old story, of course, but a characteristically American one. Sandburg has collected hundreds of such stories and sayings. They all add up to America and the American people. Here are the myths of America, such as Paul Bunyan—here are the "drummer's yarns" (of the milder type), here are the characteristically local expressions. Here are old stories out of the daily news. Wisdom, mirth, and myth. Slang—tons of it.

Even,—marvel of marvels!—I find here imbedded my favorite Irish joke of long years' standing:

"Men, will yez fight or will yez run?"
"We will."
"Yez will what?"
"We will not."
"I t'ought yez would."

Yes, that is how the People laugh; and, as Sandburg says, it is also how the people laughed when the radio operator in the North Atlantic on a storm-lashed sinking Scandinavian ship, sent the message:

"This is no night to be out without an umbrella."

But, for all this mélange, the long sprawly poem—and in spite of all the above things in it (which make it somewhat resemble Hungarian goulash!) it *is* a poem on the whole, deepens into some fine sayings toward the end:

The public *has* a mind?
Yes.
And men can follow a method
and a calculated procedure
for drugging and debauching it?
Yes.
And the whirlwind comes later?
Yes.

Is there a time to repeat, "The living passion of millions can rise into a whirlwind: the storm once loose who can ride it? you? or you? or you? only history, only tomorrow knows for every revolution breaks as a child of its own convulsive hour shooting patterns never told before-hand"?

I should say the main criticism of Sandburg's long effort, interesting as parts of it are, is that it has not enough cohesion. It has not enough structure. And, certainly it does not think through, as does the modern radical economist, the situation in which modern civilization finds itself. Sandburg is too interested in the half-tones of humanity, the highlights of humor, the terse queerness. He is interested in "atmosphere." He has in him the wisdom of an ancient race. And *The People, Yes,* is a good book to pick up and read *at*—but an annoying book if you wish it really to *get* anywhere. Where have the People got or where are they getting, he might answer? But today, it seems at least to one reviewer, that they have definitely reached a much clearer idea than ever before of where they are at and how to get that from which they have been disinherited for so long. That new sapience, it seems to me, is what Sandburg fails to show.

The Christian Science Monitor Weekly Magazine Section

SOURCE: "Carl Sandburg's Firecracker," in *The Christian Science Monitor Weekly Magazine,* September 2, 1936, p. 10.

Carl Sandburg has many affinities. He manages to stay largely on the side of the Imagists, with a nod to Vachel Lindsay and with more than a passing bow to Whitman. However, he is too violent to be conveniently pigeonholed with any or all of these. He is more of a realist than the Imagists, more homely than Lindsay, more down-to-earth, if less profound, than Whitman. And if poetry sometimes seems to escape from the violence of his passion, it is because poetry, in its finest essence, is a more subtle experience, a more specialized kind of utterance than this bull-voiced prophet can always master.

It is not enough to have a message, for, poetically, the thing said can be justified only by contriving a better way for communication of the message than has ever been found before. It is here, in one respect, that ***The People, Yes*** comes to disaster. Mr. Sandburg's long poem—286 pages—is a giant red, white and blue firecracker; the fuse sputters at times, but in the end it does not explode.

The poet has attempted to write the great saga of the American People. It is his thesis that though the people are now asleep, they will one day awaken:

Sleep is a suspension midway
and a conundrum of shadows
lost in meadows of the moon.
   The people sleep.
   Ai! Ai! the people sleep.
Yet the sleepers toss in sleep
and an end comes of sleep

and the sleepers wake.
    Ai! Ai! the sleepers wake!

It is obvious that this is the stuff of poetry, but unfortunately there are few such passages in *The People, Yes*. The poet fills page after page with colloquialisms and adages, broken up into short lines.

On no possible artistic basis can four fifths of Mr. Sandburg's present book be considered seriously as poetry. In the one or two pages where Mr. Sandburg becomes articulate, the poet in him does not sing with his old fervor:

> Hope is a tattered flag and a dream out of time.
> Hope is a heartspun word, the rainbow, the shadblow in white,
> The evening star inviolable over the coal mines,
> The shimmer of northern lights across a bitter winter night,
> The blue hills beyond the smoke of the steel works.
> The birds who go on singing to their mates in peace, war, peace,
> The ten-cent crocus bulb blooming in a used-car salesroom,
> The horseshoe over the door, the luckpiece in the pocket.
> The kiss and the comforting laugh and resolve--
> Hope is an echo, hope ties itself yonder, yonder.

Then if we discard *The People, Yes* as poetry, does it stand on some other basis? Is there here some revelation that will solve the problems that beset us? Mr. Sandburg says the people are oppressed, cheated of their political birthright, hungry, homeless and desolate. Has he, then, a message to offer to them? He has no answer except a belief that the people, as a mass, have a certain integrity and that within them dwells the unrecognized power that will see them through. The people, he tells us, will go on enduring for a long while, but one day they will awaken. As to what they will do after the awakening, he is not sure:

> In the darkness with a great bundle of grief the people march.
> In the night, and overhead a shovel of stars for keeps, the people march:
> "Where to? what next?"

Mr. Sandburg has not decided, it seems, whether his part in the drama is that of John the Baptist crying in the wilderness, or of Moses leading the people to the Promised Land. In point of fact, he is neither. He is a great voice whose violence too often tumbles the beautiful temples of poetry that he patiently labors to build.

ALWAYS THE YOUNG STRANGERS (1952)

Gerald W. Johnson

SOURCE: "The Grass Roots of the Artist," in *The New Republic,* Vol. 128, No. 3, January 19, 1953, p. 18.

Considering Carl Sandburg's literary stature, if his autobiography—or the first installment of his autobiography—had been less than a great book, that would have been news. But while its quality is instantly apparent, an analysis of that quality is not too easy. The thing is loaded with paradox, with apparent contradiction, with dissonance so swiftly resolved that one is three lines past it before it registers on the mind. Its surface ingenuousness covers some of the most guileful writing of our time.

Carl August Sandburg was the son of Swedish immigrants who married in America and settled in Galesburg, Illinois, where August Sandburg was a blacksmith in the railroad repair shops of the Chicago, Burlington & Quincy. The boy grew up there to the age of 19, then went on the road as a hobo for a year, returned and joined the army at the outbreak of the Spanish-American war, served briefly in Puerto Rico, was brought home and mustered out, then entered Lombard College. There the book ends.

That summary suggests a narrative that is of the very essence of the unremarkable, a compendium of the dull, a distillation of the insignificant. And so, in fact, it is; yet it held this ordinarily impatient reader through more than four hundred pages and he laid it down dissatisfied because it ended so soon. Certain it is that there is necromancy here; but how it is worked is known only to the sorcerers' guild.

Part of the spell is Sandburg's uncanny ability to make selective use of the time machine. He knows the trick of rolling back the years emotionally without touching them intellectually. In telling this story he becomes in part but not altogether the young Swedish boy again. He doesn't write like a young Swedish boy, but he feels like one; and this fresh, powerful emotion of youth breaks through the language of the master craftsman, breaks it into startling grammatical and syntactical fragments, often uncouth, sometimes semi-literate.

Yet it cannot master the powerful intelligence developed in later years, so the apparent disorder is always controlled by a larger order and the fragmentation is illusory—every jagged shard falls into a design. The outcome is that we have the story of a nineteenth-century American small town felt by the heart of a young Swedish boy, but seen through the eyes of a master literary craftsman, who is also a poet. Thus it is revealed that what at a glance seems to be an utterly drab background is actually a mixture of every color on the palette, and a tremendous palette, too. It is rich, indescribably rich, yet so completely authentic that anyone who has lived in a small American town, whether in Illinois, or in Georgia, or in Maine, or in any other state will recognize passage after passage as a transcript from his own experience.

This touch of universality reveals the poet, Sandburg, who is not otherwise apparent except now and then through a sudden incandescence in the prose—"her face was a blossom in night rain," "they walked hand in hand and life made rainbows for them," of a Negro cripple "when he smiled or broke into a laugh from his black-skin face it was like promises and flowers." But the Swedish boy was not himself a poet, only the foundation on which in later years a poet was built; and we are here dealing with the Swedish boy.

His outstanding characteristic was abounding health, physical, mental and moral. He lived a hard life but, with few standards of comparison, he didn't realize that it was hard; and in point of fact it wasn't hard, except physically. His father was a stern man, but he loved his children and did his duty by them to the limit of his ability; his mother loved them and wasn't stern. So the boy grew up unwarped and the physical hardships of his youth did no more than make him strong. Without doubt this is the basis of the faith in the future of America that made him predict that in crises "always the young strangers" will come from the end of the street to save the situation.

But one can make no worse mistake than to assume that this is in any sense a literary history. It is hard to imagine a book of less value to a new Hippolyte Taine, interested solely in the means by which a poet learns his craft. Perhaps that will come later; all that this volume asserts is that the discharged soldier who entered Lombard College was not Sandburg, the poet. That character had not yet been born.

This very fact, however, gives the book an intense interest to the reader who is irremediably prosaic; for the fact remains that out of what seemed the most intensely prosaic environment this poet emerged. What happened in Galesburg when Sandburg was a boy happened, with only slight modifications of the extraneous circumstances, in any and every American town of the same period; yet when we see it clearly through the eyes of a great artist we begin to understand that far from being utterly commonplace everything was extraordinary. It asserts that life is miraculous; and surely that assertion is the essence of song.

It is natural, therefore, that critics have described the book as one long poem. But it isn't poetry. It bears the relation to poetry that nacre does to pearl—it is, rather, mother-of-poetry. But for that very reason it may be that it is better adapted to the common uses of life than are the gems too precious for everyday wear.

Hayden Carruth

SOURCE: A review of *Always the Young Strangers,* in *The Nation,* New York, Vol. CLXXVI, No. 4, January 24, 1953, p. 82.

I have heard it said by a man who knows about such matters that the century of the Middle West in this country, the hundred years of American history that were shaped and dominated by the prairie and the prairie town, has just come to a close; it lasted from 1850 to 1950. He likes to cite the many men who exemplified the region—Lincoln, Veblen, Dreiser, Altgeld, McCormick, Meade, Dewey, Hemingway, Sullivan, Field, Haywood, Wright, Pulitzer, Twain, Beiderbeck. All these of course and many others contributed fundamentally to the concept of America, whether it is good or bad, that we all share and that we have exported to the rest of the world. Now the locus of native feeling appears to have shifted westward, to California and the neon-lighted desert; but it will be a long time before the new attitudes engendered there produce anything as unmistakably and beautifully—and of course indefinably—"American" as "The Killers," the New Deal, the Monadnock Building, or the gasoline-driven combine. We can hope, I suppose, that it will be equally long before the West produces anything as ugly as the World's Fair or the Chicago *Daily Tribune.*

Perhaps the dilemma—idiotic but inescapable word!—of the contemporary intellectual in America can be put in terms of his embarrassment over these hundred years. Are they rich or poor, a waste land or a treasure house? We Middle Westerners from New England and the South, shall we admit the beauty of that level land with its mighty arc of sky? Or shall we condemn the dust and bitter cold, the primitive twang of the voices? More profoundly, what shall we do with the material of materialism in its greatest social, artistic, and even topographical expression?

Fortunately, a few, a very few of our critics and social scientists are beginning to realize that the interdisciplines of cultural anthropology and the sociologies of art, religion, and politics can be put to good use in the study of recent American civilization, and soon perhaps some theories and attitudes may emerge with which the artist and the ordinary man can pursue these questions. Carl Sandburg's *Always the Young Strangers* will serve as primary evidence for the study.

Already in the newspapers the book has been called a "masterpiece" and a "classic." Such talk is beyond my comprehension. The book is *not* a masterpiece. It creaks with bad grammar, formlessness, and an unfeeling use of language. It contains some appalling juxtapositions, as when Sandburg quotes part of Franklin's address to the Constitutional Convention in favor of ratification, an impressive specimen of eighteenth-century rhetoric, and then says of the book in which he read it, "It was a honey of a book." Furthermore, Sandburg is loquacious; sometimes his stories are tedious and unnecessary.

Always the Young Strangers is not an autobiography. One learns very little of Sandburg himself—the main impression is of his engaging and genuine modesty. Instead, one reads hundreds of remembrances and observations of Galesburg, Illinois, during the '80's and '90's. Sandburg's parents, brothers and sisters, classmates, neighbors, people in the town, even dogs and cats and horses, all are remembered in bountiful detail. He remembers the cigar his father was given each pay day when the family account was settled at the grocery store: "He smoked an inch or two each Sunday and it lasted him till the next pay day, when he got another cigar." He remembers the advice on marriage given by one drunk to another, overheard on the public square one summer night: "You'll never get what you want and if you do it won't last."

The hard ideal of respectability in spite of poverty, an unfailing loyalty to the Republican Party, a severe piety, whether Lutheran or Catholic, a fear of the rich, distrust of anything "impractical," and with it all a curious, naive humor—these are some of the qualities of the Middle West, where everyone was an immigrant, if not from Sweden or Ireland, then from Pennsylvania or Massachusetts. From Sandburg's roundabout and sometimes vexatious memoir these qualities stand forth in full; and it is important to

have them on paper, now that the era of the Middle West has been gone long enough for us to begin to notice its departure.

PRAIRIE TOWN BOY (1955)

Rae Emerson Donlon

SOURCE: A review of *Prairie Town Boy,* in *The Christian Science Monitor,* Vol. 47, No. 111, April 7, 1955, p. 11.

There is staccato freshness in this self-told story of Carl Sandburg's early years. He seems not to be looking backward, but, rather, presenting pictures of his youth in the light of today. This clarity of thought was born of his simple, wholesome and somewhat difficult boyhood; it was nurtured by honest Swedish parents, who, though loving the Old Country, wanted to make "a go of it in the New Country."

In Galesburg, Illinois, the boy, Carl, lived and grew much as do most of our school boys, playing baseball from dawn to dusk, and doing household chores, such as drawing water from the well and bringing in firewood for the stove.

Later when there seemed a need for money in order that Mary, his sister, might graduate and teach school, Carl worked at anything he could find to do. He "poured milk" from a delivery wagon, worked in the ice harvest and was porter in a barber shop "All had their part," writes the author, "in the education I got outside of books and schools."

Always there was within him a sympathetic awareness of people. Of a neighbor and poetess, Mrs. Julia Carney, he said, "She loved children and wrote poems she hoped children would love." Of another who had a lovely garden—she was a woman of rare inner grace who had gathered wisdom from potatoes and hollyhocks.

In '97, being restless, he took "to the road," as he called it, going west. In a poem are lines that bespeak his heart—

> Hope is a heartspun word, the rainbow, the shad-blow
> in white, . . .
> Hope is an echo, hope ties itself yonder, yonder.

The year following found him home and enlisted in the Army for the Cuban War. After that, as a veteran, he drew free tuition at Lombard University. Here while studying Caesar's Commentaries under a professor who could milk a cow, he worked as fireman and lived at the town firehouse.

"Always deep in my heart now I had hope as never before. Struggles lay ahead, but whatever they were, I was sure I would not be afraid of them."

Carl Sandburg gained his higher education and we, the people, have Carl Sandburg.

Kirkus Reviews

SOURCE: A review of *Prairie Town Boy,* in *Kirkus Reviews,* Vol. XXIII, No. 8, April 15, 1955, p. 285.

The series of American biographies published by Harcourt includes several that are abridgements of full length adult biographies, including the story of Lincoln's boyhood taken from *The Prairie Years,* Carl Sandburg's first part of *Abraham Lincoln,* Now Sandburg has extracted from his own *Always the Young Strangers.* those recollections of his own early life, the parts that will interest young people most. Once again the question at issue is—to what extent is it advisable to assume that teenagers need abridgements. We reviewed *Always the Young Strangers* for *Young Adults* a month after reviewing it in full as "A completely recalled record of the daily living in the Sandburg household—one that gives the feeling of America through small town pattern both in the line of individual personality development and in the larger sense—economically, socially, politically. Not his literary biography, but the roots that made Carl Sandburg what he is today."—Some of that particular value is lost in condensation. While many young people may read an autobiography 179 pages in length who would not read the full length book, we hope that the more mature among them will be directed to the more rewarding book—Americana at its best.

Jennie D. Lindquist

SOURCE: A review of *Prairie Town Boy,* in *The Horn Book Magazine,* Vol. XXXI, No. 3, June, 1955, pp. 189-90.

Because *Always the Young Strangers* is one of my favorite books of recent years, I opened this shortened version of it with some apprehension. I had taken both books from the shelf, thinking I would compare them from time to time as I read. But I began with the first chapter of *Prairie-Town Boy* and read straight through to the end, caught by the pic-

ture it, too, gives not only of the adventure of growing up in America but also of that particular phase of it that colors the childhood of any second-generation Swedish American. Even in this shortened version it all comes clear. It would not be much of a compliment to Mr. Sandburg to say that this is as good as the first book, for of course one does not want to lose anything he writes; and to young people who are up to it I would give *Always the Young Strangers.* Many who would never read that, however, will enjoy this genuine biography, often moving, often full of fun, of the alert, sensitive young Sandburg growing up in Galesburg, Illinois, in a day when there were still people there who had known Abraham Lincoln.

HONEY AND SALT (1963)

Mother Mary Anthony

SOURCE: A review of *Honey and Salt,* in *Best Sellers,* Vol. 22, No. 19, January 1, 1963, pp. 401-02.

Published on the author's 85th birthday, the seventy-seven new poems of Carl Sandburg's *Honey and Salt* combine mellow lyricism and the tang of wisdom, the seeming ease and unrelenting mastery of the craftsman who knows and loves his material and whose fire is still burning.

The forms are free but disciplined—"self-structured" might describe them—each built to its own inner specifications. Diction and theme range from "old music for quiet hearts" to a post-World War III projection of "new types of cripples here and there / and indescribable babbling survivors / listening to plain scholars saying, / should a few plain scholars have come through, / 'As after other wars the peace is something else again.'" There are the familiar white horses in the several sea-pieces, and almost always the strong sense of color and movement—see **"First Sonata for Karlen Paula"**:

Make like before, sweet child.
Be you like five new oranges in a wicker basket.
    Step out like
a summer evening fireworks over black waters.
    Be dizzy in a haze of yellow silk bandanas.
Then in a change of costume
    sit silent in a chair of tarnished bronze
Having spoken with a grave mouth:
    "Now I will be
    a clavichord melody
    in October brown.
    You will see me in
    deep-sea contemplation
    on a yellow horse in a white wind.

There are slight poems and wry ones, love poems and memory poems. Perhaps the most notable is the concluding **"Timesweep,"** some fifteen pages of a new and perfectly controlled "Song of Myself" throughout evolutionary phyla from the "morning of the world" to the final affirmation, "they are named All God's Children." The suggestion of Whitman may echo our implicit acceptance of Carl Sandburg as the true people's poet Whitman heralded.

Lillian Morrison

SOURCE: A review of *Honey and Salt,* in *The Horn Book Magazine,* Vol. XXXIX, No. 5, October, 1963, p. 522.

For all of Sandburg's colloquial language, there is a dreamy, whimsical, soft quality about these poems. There are some good bits of Americana (**"Cahokia"** and **"Lackawanna Twilight"**), some delicate love poems, and a lot of wisps, ghosts, shadows, roses, sunshine—more honey than salt. I think many young people will love it. Although romantic, the poems are unpretentiously so, and most teen-agers will not recognize the lack of really deep, dark colors until they have lived a little longer.

📖 *THE WEDDING PROCESSION OF THE RAG DOLL AND THE BROOM HANDLE AND WHO WAS IN IT* **(1967)**

Zena Sutherland

SOURCE: A review of *The Wedding Procession of the Rag Doll and the Broom Handle and Who Was in It,* in *The Bulletin of the Center for Children's Books,* Vol. 20, No. 10, June, 1967, p. 159.

A picture book version of one of the *Rootabaga Stories* is illustrated with drawings that are inventive, lively, grotesque, and humorous. The double-page spreads are alternately in full color and in white, black, and pink. The format shows to good advantage the groups within the procession, as the revolting Spoon Lickers march by, followed by the Tin Pan Bangers, followed by the Chocolate Chins, et cetera.

Priscilla L. Moulton

SOURCE: A review of *The Wedding Procession of the Rag Doll and the Broom Handle and Who Was in It,* in *The Horn Book Magazine,* Vol. XLIII, No. 3, June, 1967, pp. 337-38.

A splendid procession at the rag doll's wedding is led by the nuptial pair, who are followed by limp and lumpy fun babies. Dolled up in birthday-party colors and quaintly modern costumes, they parade in a line—laughing, licking, tickling, wiggling, chuzzling, snozzling, clear to the "last of all," the staggering Sleepyheads. One can plainly see that the rag doll and her broom-handle groom are ideally matched; also perfectly paired are this nursery fantasia from the *Rootabaga Stories* and the hilariously funny illustrations.

The Times Literary Supplement

SOURCE: A review of *The Wedding Procession of the Rag Doll and the Broom Handle and Who Was in It,* in *The Times Literary Supplement,* No. 3458, June 6, 1968, p. 586.

[I]t was a rare pleasure to discover among a batch of thirty or so new picture books, one which has the makings of a classic. *The Wedding Procession of the Rag Doll and the Broom Handle* was first published in 1922 in America, where its author, the poet Carl Sandburg, is well known as a writer for children. Only now has a British edition come out, and for anyone who likes the sound of words used absurdly and onomatopoeically (with specially invented verbs—chuzzling, snozzling, chubbing, slimpsing), this book is not to be missed. The language reads so well that a child, hearing it once or twice, is able to recite whole passages delightedly off by heart.

The story merely lists the eccentric characters who march in the Rag Doll's wedding procession: the Spoon Lickers, the Tin Pan Bangers, the Chocolate Chins, the Musical Soup Eaters and so on—each contingent having a double page to itself. The illustrations, by Harriet Pincus, defy categorization. In chunky line with subdued colour, they remind one a little of Maurice Sendak, a little of the Struwwelpeter drawings and their decorative, idiosyncratic style fits excellently with the texts. But the artist does not always exploit the opportunities provided by the words—her Chubby Chubs scarcely look like "Roly-poly round-faced smackers and snoozers . . . chubby and easy to squeeze."

📖 *THE SANDBURG TREASURY: PROSE AND POETRY FOR YOUNG PEOPLE* **(1970)**

Publishers Weekly

SOURCE: A review of *The Sandburg Treasury: Prose and Poetry for Young People,* in *Publishers Weekly,* Vol. 198, No. 25, November 16, 1970, p. 77.

A story is a story is a story, but a poem is forever. And it follows, as the night the day, that a present of poetry will be cherished long after the Christmas when it was received. The blockbuster of a Christmas present for this season will surely be *The Sandburg Treasury*—it has not only Carl Sandburg's two books of poetry for young people, *Early Moon* and *Wind Song,* but also his *Rootabaga Stories, Abe Lincoln Grows Up* and *Prairie Town Boy.* With its introduction by Paula Sandburg and its line drawings by Paul Bacon, it is galloping straight toward the winner's circle.

Mary M. Burns

SOURCE: A review of *The Sandburg Treasury: Prose and Poetry for Young People,* in *The Horn Book Magazine,* Vol. XLVII, No. 1, February, 1971, pp. 59-60.

Carl Sandburg's work for young people—*Rootabaga Stories, Early Moon, Wind Song, Prairie-Town Boy, Abe Lincoln Grows Up*—into one volume gives readers an opportunity to examine and appreciate the genius of the literary artist as analyst and visionary. Here with its inexhaustible energy and irrepressible, at times irresponsible, laissez-faire attitude is the American character: sometimes heroic, sometimes wistful, sometimes obnoxious, yet never dull. Each of the volumes included in the anthology was received enthusiastically on its first appearance. Time has not yet diminished the appeal of Sandburg's vigorous, vital style. Unfortunately, the illustrations—pen-and-ink line sketches—are not always adequately synchronized with the text and sometimes seem casually decorative rather than an integral part of the whole. Despite these shortcomings, the volume should be an invaluable addition to home, school, and library collections. An index of titles for stories and poems is included.

Zena Sutherland

SOURCE: A review of *The Sandburg Treasury: Prose and Poetry for Young People,* in *The Bulletin of the Center for Children's Books,* Vol. 24, No. 9, May, 1971, p. 143.

This includes five complete volumes by Sandburg: *Abe Lincoln Grows Up, Rootabaga Stories, Prairie-Town Boy,* and two books of poetry: *Early Moon* and *Wind Song.* The combination of poetry, humor, folk style, biography, and autobiography serves as a good introduction for the new reader of Sandburg or as a varied pleasure for those who are already his

fans. The illustrations add little, and some of the pages are solid with print, but the book is useful as a sampling of Sandburg's work, as additional material in a collection which does not have the single editions, and for home libraries.

RAINBOWS ARE MADE: POEMS BY CARL SANGBURG (1982)

Publishers Weekly

SOURCE: A review of *Rainbows Are Made,* in *Publishers Weekly,* Vol. 222, No. 24, December 17, 1982, p. 75.

Eichenberg's strong, handsome woodcuts strengthen as well as reflect the images in 70 poems, chosen carefully by Hopkins from nearly 1000 by the late Pulitzer Prize winner. The editor's sensitive introduction traces Sandburg's universal appeal to his genius at using language as an art to share thoughts about people and what matters to them. The rugged verses express almost countless feelings—about love, hate, nature and human-made things. **"Lines Written for Gene Kelly to Dance To"** is one of the merry lyrics in the book. There are many more that call for shouts of joy and laughter, among the poet's serious questions about the stupidity of war and the fever to acquire material things: "Money buys everything except love, / personality, freedom, immortality, / silence, peace." Hopkins, a well-known anthologist, presents his most impressive collection, an obvious choice for gift-giving to a special person, child or adult.

Zena Sutherland

SOURCE: A review of *Rainbows Are Made,* in *The Bulletin of the Center for Children's Books,* Vol. 36, No. 7, March, 1983, p. 133.

Carefully selected, this assemblage of Sandburg poems includes many that are not often included in collections of his work intended for young readers. The poems have been grouped in six sections: poems about people, about the night, about the sea, about nature, about everyday objects, and about words and language. The quality of the writing is matched by the strong, dramatic wood engravings, one for each section, and is set off by the spacious format. Title and first line indexes are provided.

Linda Wicher

SOURCE: A review of *Rainbows Are Made*, in *School Library Journal*, Vol. 29, No. 7, March, 1983, p. 196.

Rainbows Are Made offers some 70 short poems by Carl Sandburg and groups them by theme: the seasons, the sea, the imaginative mind, etc. Each theme explores different aspects of poetic creativity as envisioned by Sandburg and illustrated by Fritz Eichenberg's wood engravings. Eichenberg has truly captured the power and vigorousness of Sandburg's verse in images somewhat reminiscent of Blake's spiritual incarnations. The poems have been carefully chosen and placed so that each can be discovered and examined as a gem. No dates are appended to the poems; Hopkins' introduction, however, provides adequate biographical information and an overview of the poet's life work. While not as comprehensive as *The Sandburg Treasury, Rainbows Are Made* does not limit itself to poems for children and about childhood as the earlier collection does. Yes, there is an index of first lines and titles. This is above all, a handsome collection and, secondly, a useful one for the elementary or secondary school library.

Mary M. Burns

SOURCE: A review of *Rainbows Are Made*, in *The Horn Book Magazine*, Vol. LIX, No. 2, April, 1983, p. 180.

In a handsome volume seventy of Carl Sandburg's poems are presented in an inviting and aesthetically pleasing format. The introduction indicates that the choices were intended to demonstrate the elements particularly characteristic of Sandburg's work: his interest in people; his vigorous imagery; his ability to see what is wondrous, challenging, or puzzling in the familiar; his gift for capturing a variety of emotions in everyday language arranged, as in **"Cool Tombs,"** to create a haunting refrain. Quintessentially American, Sandburg's voice is that of the pioneer—gruff and plain-spoken yet endowed with a particular vision. His definitions of poetry reflect an effort to marry the transcendent and the mundane and to give concrete form to abstraction. Consequently, the decision to use several of these definitions for divisional headings is an inspired one, for it provides the opportunity to relate the poet's themes and theories to practice. Thus, the statement "Poetry is a search for syllables to shoot at the barriers of the unknown and the unknowable" precedes such poems as **"Is Wisdom a Lot of Language?" "Bird Talk,"** and **"Different Kinds of Good-by."** Included in this section is

"Metamorphosis," which asks, "When ice turns back into water does it / remember it was ice?" For each of the six sections the artist has created full-page wood engravings in which representational images are combined into impressive interpretations of the introductory quotation. Some, like the frontispiece portrait of Sandburg, are relatively conventional; others suggest the surreal landscapes of the imagination.

MORE ROOTABAGAS (1993)

Kirkus Reviews

SOURCE: A review of *More Rootabagas*, in *Kirkus Reviews*, Vol. LXI, No. 20, October 15, 1993, p. 1336.

Three volumes of the "American fairy tales" the poet called *Rootabaga Stories* were published between 1922 and 1930; later, according to an introduction by Sandburg scholar George Hendrick, he wrote dozens more that have never been published. Here, Hendrick selects ten that "most reflect Sandburg's incomparable storytelling magic." Favorite characters and places—"The Potato Face Blind Man," "Ax Me No Questions," "The Village of Liver and Onions"—join characters with names recalling Sandburg's children's nicknames ("Spink," "Skabootch," "Swipes") and some grand new ones (one trio: "Burnt Chestnuts," "The Beans Are Burning," and "Sweeter Than The Bees Humming"). For connoisseurs of Sandburg's uniquely whimsical and melodious use of the American idiom, these tales are a delight; the ruminative, ear-tickling repetitions, visual images, astonishing juxtapositions, airy surreal happenings, and sly metaphorical comments on human foibles are all here in strength. And Zelinsky's accomplishment is equally great. Using colored pencils on plastivellum drafting film, he mirrors and embellishes Sandburg's fantastical creations with enormous delicacy and imagination, providing dozens of delicious variations on the rutabaga theme (one becomes a coiled blue cat with downward-descending tail, others have fey creatures nestled in their greens), limning characters with characteristic energy, artfully manipulating the very text. His art for the last tale, where the poet makes a cameo appearance, is especially lovely and ingenious. Splendid in every way.

Verlyn Klinkenborg

SOURCE: "Silly Tales on Little Cute Feet," in *The New York Times*, November 14, 1993.

In 1992, the year of *The Waste Land* and *Ulysses*, Carl Sandburg published his fourth book of big-shouldered poems, *Slabs of the Sunburnt West.* He was 44 years old. That same year Sandburg also published *Rootabaga Stories,* the first of three volumes of children's tales written for his daughters, whom he nicknamed Spink, Skabootch and Swipes. (*Rootabaga Pigeons* appeared in 1923 and *Potato Face* in 1930; *Rootabaga Stories* itself was reissued in hardcover in 1988, with terrific illustrations by Michael Hague.) The *Rootabaga Stories* are pointedly American tales, told in a pointedly American tongue by a pointedly American poet. How can you tell? The answer is simple. Tales written for English children cause claustrophobia in adults. The *Rootabaga Stories* cause agoraphobia a fear of the open, of the prairie, of the plains. In the Rootabaga Country, you can always hear "the grass listening to the winds."

George Hendrick, a Sandburg scholar and a professor of English at the University of Illinois, Urbana-Champaign has collected 10 of some "many dozens" of unpublished *Rootabaga Stories* in a book called *More Rootabagas.* The pictures are by Paul O. Zelinsky, whose illustrations for *Hansel and Gretel* and *Rumpelstiltskin* were both Caldecott Honor winners, and these have a fluid, sketchy frivolity about them, very different from the composed whimsy of Mr. Hague's illustrations. These tales are about as good as those Sandburg himself chose to publish, which vary widely in quality. In the foreword to *More Rootabagas,* Mr. Hendrick says that Sandburg stopped publishing *Rootabaga Stories* because researching and writing his enormous biography of Abraham Lincoln took too much out of him. This may be true, in a narrowly factual sense. But the real reason, if you hearken to the *Rootabaga Stories,* is probably that Sandburg, like the steam hog, had simply gone "pfisty-pfoost, pfisty-pfoost, pfisty-pfoost." It is a wise poet, after all, who knows when to stop "yodeling his yister."

"Never has the such of this which been put here this way to me by anybody," says Fire the Goat in a story called "Sand Flat Shadows" from the first volume of *Rootabaga Stories.* And that is pretty much how you feel after a bout with these tales from the Village of Liver-and-Onions, tales about characters with names like Wing Tip the Spick, the Potato Face Blind Man, Dippy the Wisp, Susan Slackentwist and John Jack Johannes Hummadummaduffer, a k a Feed Box. Disarming his audience may not have been Sandburg's main task when first writing the *Rootabaga Stories,* for his audience was Spink, Skabootch and Swipes, names that in themselves suggest unconditional surrender. But it can be hard to tell a bedtime story to posterity, which demands certain concessions in return for its attention.

One of those concessions is that a bedtime story, a children's "classic," shall seem timeless. The *Rootabaga Stories, More Rootabagas* among them, are not timeless. They don't require the ruthless political correcting that some dated children's stories seem to do these days. But you can hear the peculiar voice of the American 20's—slang on stilts—in their beat, and it is worth asking whether that beat, which can sound impossibly cloying in the movies and novels and poems of that era, is still poetry, or whether it ever was poetry, or whether it matters one way or the other. To quote the chairman of one Rootabaga story, I think "the motion is carried both ways it is a razzmatazz."

In so many classic children's stories, it is the atmosphere of containment, the daily staidness of the backdrop that makes the silliness work. But in Sandburg's stories, there is always a kind of linguistic hip-hop, full of Z's and X's and repetitions, going on, itself abundantly silly. And that can make it hard to see how beautiful the backdrop of his prose can sometimes be. For behind his extravagant creations, which at times feel a little labored, a little self-consciously artless, there is a landscape far more extravagant than, say, the Village of Liver-and-Onions, because it is natural. "Far back in the long time," out on the prairies of Rootabaga Country, "the razorback hogs came then, eating pignuts, potatoes, pawpaws, pumpkins. The wild horse, the buffalo, came. The moose, with spraggly branches of antlers spreading out over his head, the moose came and the fox, the wolf."

Poets are used to having their fantasies taken pretty seriously, so it's a wonder they ever get around to writing children's stories. But children make such a lovely audience, taking their own fantasies as seriously as can be, that you're apt to forget what tyrannical critics children are worse, by far, than Samuel Johnson at his most petulant. Whether *More Rootabagas* or the original *Rootabaga Stories* will please your own child is a question whose answer can only be determined empirically, by seeing whether the book ends up under the couch, forgotten and unlamented, or is literally rubbed into extinction by nightly readings.

Of course, you can read these tales strictly for your own pleasure, which would not be mistaking their purpose. It seems clear to me that in the *Rootabaga Stories,* Carl Sandburg was writing for the children in himself—not that simpering New Age inner child, so selfish and demanding and, ultimately, tone-deaf—but for the eternal child, who, when he or she hears language spoken, hears rhythm, not sense.

Betsy Hearne

SOURCE: A review of *More Rootabagas,* in *The Bulletin of the Center for Children's Books,* Vol. 47, No. 4, December, 1993, p. 133.

The three volumes of **Rootabaga** stories published during Carl Sandburg's lifetime are all distinguished by bountiful wordplay, though structure varies widely from sequential description (*The Wedding Procession of the Rag Doll and the Broom Handle and Who Was In It*) to plots with a beginning, middle, and end (**"The Huckabuck Family and How They Raised Popcorn in Nebraska and Quit and Came Back"**). Like its predecessors, this collection features wordplay in fabulous proportion to incident, with wildly inventive images and lyrical repetition building a sense of poetic free association: "And these sleepy songs of the birds in the evening made Burnt Chestnuts feel how it is the birds go to sleep high in the sycamores, high in the oaks and cottonwoods, or snuggled alone in hiding places in the tough wire grass. She murmured to herself, 'I believe I know how they wink and blink and shut their eyes and stick their heads under their wings and fall with fine thin feathers into sleep.'" **Rootabaga** fans will recognize the crazily named characters and the ball-to-bat dialogue rocketing through these ten previously unpublished stories, from **"A Girl Named Silver Pitchers Tells a Story About Egypt, Jesse James and Spanish Onions"** at the book's beginning to **"How the Fairies Went Away . . . and Who Took Their Places"** at the end. It is the cumulative rhythm that produces suspense here: language lovers young and old will sit still in wonder, although action addicts will probably wiggle away. Zelinsky's illustrations create a drama of their own, weaving in and out of the text or demarcating sections of it with skillfully controlled exuberance. Contrasting hues appear subtle by virtue of softly blended color-pencil textures, the drawing itself is fluid, and the interchange between verbal and graphic images results in bookmaking with unusual impact. This is vintage Sandburg, knowledgeably edited, dynamically illustrated.

Kenneth Marantz

SOURCE: A review of *More Rootabagas,* in *School Library Journal,* Vol. 39, No. 12, December, 1993, p. 116.

Sandburg's poetic talents invest these 10 stories with sounds and rhythms that will make readers' imaginations dance. Characters with names like "Ax Me No Questions," "Silver Pitchers," and "Hoboken Kitty-Kitty" will tickle children's funny bones. Words like "slimpsing," "huck bug," and "mooches," and phrases like "sleepy songs soft" and "you snoof of a snitch" will make them realize the potential of language to rise above the mundane. Zelinsky complements the stories with colored-pencil drawings that echo their emotional content while maintaining a more naturalistic array of images. The title page of each piece shows a rootabaga with some subtle but intriguing hints of what's to come. Other illustrations depict bits of action or portraits of characters, piquing interest and eliciting sympathy. The designer has woven text and pictures into a seamless sequence of pages that allows Sandburg's witty wisdom and Zelinsky's artistic inspiration to sing in unison.

GRASS ROOTS (1998)

Kirkus Reviews

SOURCE: A review of *Grassroots,* in *Kirkus Reviews,* Vol. LXVI, No. 5, March 1, 1998, p. 344.

Minor's signature watercolors, limpid and bright, make a visual hymn to the Midwest and thereby echo the poems of Carl Sandburg.

These poems, replete with images of fields, frogs, horses, and harvests, are arranged roughly in order of early spring to late winter. The title poem, **"Grassroots,"** "puts fingers into the dark dirt" while a hawk flies over a field just turning golden under an opalescent sky. A two-page diptych called **"Still Life"** shows a steam train as it passes village, horses, and cows. For a snowman, the poem is **"Metamorphosis"**—"When water turns ice does it remember / one time it was water? / When ice turns back into water does it / remember it was ice?" The book closes with the beautiful **"Red and White"** ("O I have loved red roses and O I have loved white snow") with an equally beautiful painting. An ode to a place, and a worthy introduction to Sandburg's poetry.

Susan Scheps

SOURCE: A review of *Grassroots,* in *School Library Journal,* Vol. 44, No. 6, June, 1998, p. 168.

A collection of 16 poems that describe the seasons in America's heartland and the power of the land itself—the prairie, the river, the woods, the fields. The imagery of Sandburg's poetry is mirrored in Minor's fine realistic watercolor landscapes. Panoramic views show fields of ripe wheat and plains of both lush green and dried brown grasses. Close-ups focus on a shaggy-haired buffalo, a lone cricket perched on an ear of ripe corn, a frog half submerged in a stream, an owl staring down from his perch on a leafless tree branch, the nearly bare limbs of a crabapple tree in autumn, and a barn at daybreak. Readers exposed to these lovely complements of aural and visual imagery cannot help but come away with a better understanding of poetry and a deeper appreciation of language.

Additional coverage of Sandburg's life and career is contained in the following sources published by the Gale Group: *Authors and Artists for Young Adults,* Vol. 24; *Concise Dictionary of American Literary Biography, 1865-1917; Contemporary Authors New Revision Series,* Vol. 35; *Contemporary Literary Criticism,* Vols. 1, 4, 10, 15, 35; *Dictionary of Literary Biography,* Vols. 17, 54; *DISCovering Authors; DISCovering Authors: British; DISCovering Authors Modules: Most-studied Authors, Poets; Major Authors and Illustrators for Children and Young Adults; Major 20th-Century Writers; Poetry Criticism,* Vol. 2; *Something about the Author,* Vol. 8; and *World Literature Criticism.*

How to Use This Index

The main reference

Baum, L(yman) Frank
      1856-1919 .... **15**

lists all author entries in this and previous volumes of *Children's Literature Review*.

The cross-references

See also CA 103; 108; DLB 22; JRDA;
MAICYA; MTCW; SATA 18; TCLC 7

list all author entries in the following Gale biographical and literary sources:

AAYA = *Authors & Artists for Young Adults*
AITN = *Authors in the News*
BLC = *Black Literature Criticism*
BLCS = *Black Literature Criticism Supplement*
BW = *Black Writers*
CA = *Contemporary Authors*
CAAS = *Contemporary Authors Autobiography Series*
CABS = *Contemporary Authors Bibliographical Series*
CANR = *Contemporary Authors New Revision Series*
CAP = *Contemporary Authors Permanent Series*
CDALB = *Concise Dictionary of American Literary Biography*
CDBLB = *Concise Dictionary of British Literary Biography*
CLC = *Contemporary Literary Criticism*
CMLC = *Classical and Medieval Literature Criticism*
DA = *DISCovering Authors*
DAB = *DISCovering Authors: British*
DAC = *DISCovering Authors: Canadian*
DAM = *DISCovering Authors: Modules*
      DRAM: Dramatists Module; MST: Most-Studied Authors Module;
      MULT: Multicultural Authors Module; NOV: Novelists Module;
      POET: Poets Module; POP: Popular Fiction and Genre Authors Module
DC = *Drama Criticism*
DLB = *Dictionary of Literary Biography*
DLBD = *Dictionary of Literary Biography Documentary Series*
DLBY = *Dictionary of Literary Biography Yearbook*
HLC = *Hispanic Literature Criticism*
HLCS = *Hispanic Literature Criticism Supplement*
HW = *Hispanic Writers*
JRDA = *Junior DISCovering Authors*
LC = *Literature Criticism from 1400 to 1800*
MAICYA = *Major Authors and Illustrators for Children and Young Adults*
MTCW = *Major 20th-Century Writers*
NCLC = *Nineteenth-Century Literature Criticism*
NNAL = *Native North American Literature*
PC = *Poetry Criticism*
SAAS = *Something about the Author Autobiography Series*
SATA = *Something about the Author*
SSC = *Short Story Criticism*
TCLC = *Twentieth-Century Literary Criticism*
WLC = *World Literature Criticism, 1500 to the Present*
WLCS = *World Literature Criticism Supplement*
YABC = *Yesterday's Authors of Books for Children*

CLR Cumulative Author Index

CLR Cumulative Nationality Index

CLR Cumulative Title Index

Title Index

Title Index

Title Index

Title Index

Title Index

Title Index

Title Index

ISBN 0-7876-4573-7